Palgrave Studies in Sustainable Business
In Association with Future Earth

Series Editors
Paul Shrivastava
Pennsylvania State University
University Park, PA, USA

László Zsolnai
Corvinus University Budapest
Budapest, Hungary

Sustainability in Business is increasingly becoming the forefront issue for researchers, practitioners and companies the world over. Engaging with this immense challenge, Future Earth is a major international research platform from a range of disciplines, with a common goal to support and achieve global sustainability. This series will define a clear space for the work of Future Earth Finance and Economics Knowledge-Action Network. Publishing key research with a holistic and trans-disciplinary approach, it intends to help reinvent business and economic models for the Anthropocene, geared towards engendering sustainability and creating ecologically conscious organizations.

More information about this series at
http://www.palgrave.com/gp/series/15667

Thomas Walker • Cary Krosinsky
Lisa N. Hasan • Stéfanie D. Kibsey
Editors

Sustainable Real Estate

Multidisciplinary Approaches to an Evolving System

palgrave
macmillan

Editors
Thomas Walker
David O'Brien Centre for Sustainable Enterprise
John Molson School of Business
Concordia University
Montreal, QC, Canada

Lisa N. Hasan
David O'Brien Centre for Sustainable Enterprise
John Molson School of Business
Concordia University
Montreal, QC, Canada

Cary Krosinsky
Yale University
New Haven, CT, USA

Brown University
Providence, RI, USA

Stéfanie D. Kibsey
John Molson School of Business
Concordia University
Montreal, QC, Canada

Palgrave Studies in Sustainable Business In Association with Future Earth
ISBN 978-3-030-06877-6 ISBN 978-3-319-94565-1 (eBook)
https://doi.org/10.1007/978-3-319-94565-1

This Palgrave Macmillan imprint is published by the registered company Springer Nature Switzerland AG
The registered company address is: Gewerbestrasse 11, 6330 Cham, Switzerland

Acknowledgments

We acknowledge the financial support provided through the Sam and Diane Scalia Sustainable Real Estate Program, the David O'Brien Centre for Sustainable Enterprise, and the John Molson School of Business at Concordia University. In addition, we greatly appreciate the networking support provided by Future Earth as well as the research and administrative assistance provided by Amr Addas, Katrina-Frances Gattuso, and Tyler Schwartz at Concordia University. Finally, we are grateful for the excellent copy-editing and editorial assistance we received from Naomi and Stephen Miller.

Contents

Notes on Contributors

Muhammad Umar Bello is a lecturer in the department of Estate Management and Valuation of Abubakar Tafawa Balewa University, Bauchi, Nigeria. He obtained his doctor of philosophy in Real Estate and Facilities Management from the Faculty of Technology Management and Business of Universiti Tun Hussein Onn Malaysia (UTHM) in March 2018. He obtained a master's degree in 2015 in Gender, Environment and Development from Usumanu Danfodiyo University, Sokoto, Nigeria. He attended Abubakar Tafawa Balewa University, Bauchi, for his first degree where he graduated from the Department of Estate Management and Valuation in 2009.

Margarita Caycedo is an economist with a Master's degree in Industrial Economics and a Graduate Diploma in Finance and in Business Administration. She has performed research and project evaluation roles and community involvement work in social economy organizations in Montreal related to sustainable finance, sustainable trade, women's entrepreneurship, and human rights education. Caycedo is studying for the Sustainable Investment Professional Certification at John Molson Executive Centre at Concordia University, Canada.

Pernille H. Christensen is the Course Director for the Bachelor of Property Economics program at the University of Technology Sydney and a member of multiple industry sustainable development advisory committees. Using a multi-disciplinary approach, her research focuses on decision-making related to sustainability in property and planning, specifically enhancing community resilience to flooding, heat island effect and terrorism, operational building management, and developing alternative solutions to affordable housing challenges.

Isa Olalekan Elegbede is a PhD candidate in the chair of Environmental Planning at Brandenburg University of Technology, Cottbus-Senftenberg, Germany. He had previously obtained an MSc in Environmental and Resource Management from the same university. His research area is in Voluntary Sustainability Standards (VSS). He is a member of various organizations of high repute.

Jeremy Gabe is Lecturer in Property at the University of Auckland, New Zealand; an award-winning researcher; and an advisor to various Green Building Council technical committees. His multi-disciplinary research explores green building certification markets, operational building management, urban policy, environmental economics, and affordable housing solutions.

Sarah Gomez is a senior at Yale University, double majoring in History and History of Art and studying through the Energy Studies program. On campus, she is involved in Dwight Hall Socially Responsible Investing, the Sustainability Service Corps, and the Yale Student Environmental Coalition.

Sherif Goubran is a Ph.D. student in the Individualized Program (INDI) at Concordia University, Canada. He conducts interdisciplinary research on sustainability assessments in buildings and the built environment. Goubran holds an M.A.Sc. in Building Engineering and a B.S. in Architecture. His research has been published in engineering, design, and architecture journals, and he has been awarded several honors and grants for his academic excellence and research.

Lisa N. Hasan is a practicing architect, who holds a Master's degree in Architecture from McGill and an MBA from Concordia University, Canada. Her work has focused on green buildings and the development and implementation of sustainable practices for both public and private real estate owners, managers, and investors. Her involvement with the National Research Council of Canada, Canada Green Building Council, urbanism committees, and not-for-profit organizations is testament to her long-term commitment to sustainable real estate.

Russell Heller is an Environmental Studies Major at Yale University, USA, concentrating in Sustainable Business, and is also a part of the Energy Studies Certificate Program. He spent two years as the Board Co-Chair of the Dwight Hall Socially Responsible Investment (SRI) Fund, the nation's first undergraduate-managed Socially Responsible Investment Fund, and the first to file a shareholder resolution with a public company.

Ramzi Kawar has over 30 years of international exposure and multi-disciplinary experience in strategic consulting in architecture, affordable housing, physical planning, community planning, land use planning, sustainable development, risk management, community engagement, contract management, team building, strategic corporate leadership, and innovative business development. He is an engaged leader and advocate for innovative sustainable building practices and is the Manager, Building Design at Housing Nova Scotia.

Willem G. Keeris is Professor Emeritus in Real Estate Management, Development included. His first posting was at Eindhoven University of Technology, Faculty of Architecture, Building, and Planning—Department Real Estate Management & Development, Netherlands. He subsequently became Academic Director of the Executive Master of Real Estate course of Tilburg University, TIAS Business School, and served until 2017 as a visiting professor at Delft University of Technology, Faculty of Architecture—Department Management in the Built Environment. Keeris is also Managing Director of Keeris Vastgoed-Consultancy and was a member of the Supervisory Board of Kadans Science Partner Fund N.V. until the end of March 2017.

Stéfanie D. Kibsey coordinates the Sustainable Investment Professional Certification program at the John Molson School of Business, Canada. She has previously worked at the David O'Brien Center for Sustainable Enterprise and La Caisse de dépôt et placement du Québec. She received a Master's degree in Environmental Studies from the University of Waterloo. Kibsey specializes in connecting sustainability principles with policy and business practices.

Cary Krosinsky writes, advises, and teaches at Yale, Brown, and elsewhere. At Brown, his teaching helps support the Brown University Sustainable Investment Fund within the Endowment. His most recent book is *Sustainable Investing: Revolutions in Theory and Practice* and papers include a "Framework for Asset Owner Strategy on Climate Change for Principles for Responsible Investing (PRI)". He is an ongoing advisor to BlueSky Investment Management and the Carbon Tracker Initiative.

Ruben A. R. Langbroek is the Head of Strategic Development of Global Real Estate Sustainability Benchmark (GRESB) in Asia Pacific. GRESB is an investor-led initiative that aims to enhance and protect shareholder value by evaluating and empowering sustainability practices in the real asset sector, including real estate and infrastructure. Langbroek holds Master of Science degrees in Building Engineering and in Real Estate Investments. He is also a professional Member of the Royal Institute of Chartered Surveyors (MRICS) and is accredited as a Leadership in Energy and Environmental Design (LEED) Green Associate.

Bruno Lee is Assistant Professor of Building Engineering at Concordia University, Canada. He specializes in building energy performance simulation and focuses on the employment of different simulation techniques to study the performance of the built environment in an integrated manner. His research areas cover resilient high-performance smart building, integrated building design through co-simulation, stochastic optimization of energy and durability performance, and BIM (Building Information Modeling)-based automated energy performance simulation.

Behzad Malekpourasl is Assistant Professor of Urban and Regional Planning in the Department of Urban Planning and Design, Shahid Beheshti University (SBU), Tehran, Iran. Malekpourasl's main research lies in the area of urban and regional planning theory with special highlight on developing countries, sustainable development, methods and techniques in planning, the role of planning in energy efficiency, and social issues in planning. His current research is about reassertion of space in critical social planning theory.

Tristan Masson is a Bachelors of Art candidate (2019 expected) in Political Science (Honours) and Sustainability Studies at Concordia University, Montreal, Canada. His research fields are International Relations and Public Policy where he studies the national, regional and global dimensions to policy problems relating to media, technology, climate change and sustainability. He worked as a researcher for the David O'Brien Centre for Sustainable Enterprise (DOCSE) in the summer of 2017. His most recent publications include a chapter with Guy Lachapelle, entitled "Political Coalitions in Canada", in Adrian Albala and Josep Maria Reniu's (eds) *Coalition Politics and Federalism* (Springer, 2018), an article with Guy Lachapelle entitled "Adjusting the Sails: Québec-U.S. Commerce Under the Trump Administration" in *Québec Studies* (December 2017), and a chapter, "Political Advertising in Canada", in Christina Holtz-Bacha et Marion R. Just's (eds) *Routledge Handbook of Political Advertising* (2017).

In addition to his academic work, Masson serves in a number of roles for non-profits such as Sustainable Concordia, Concordia's Sustainability Action Fund and Future Earth. He co-hosts a monthly podcast show on cutting-edge research, projects and people working for sustainable development called The Worlds We Want, in partnership with Future Earth and CJLO 1690AM.

Saheed Matemilola is a Ph.D. candidate at the Department of Public Law, Law of Environment and Planning, Brandenburg University of Technology, Cottbus-Senftenberg, Germany. He holds an M.Sc. in Environmental and Resource Management from the same institution. He studied Estate Management at Abubakar Tafawa Balewa University, Bauchi, Nigeria. He is a member of International Association for Impact Assessment (IAIA), Association for Environmental Impact Assessment of Nigeria (AEIAN), the Environmental Impact Assessment Association Germany (UVP), Nigerian Institute of Safety Professionals (NISP), and Nigerian Institute of Management (NIM).

Molly J. McCabe is founder and President of HaydenTanner, a strategic real estate investment advisory firm focused on accelerating impact and sustainability in the built environment. He is the Chair of the Urban Land Institute's (ULI) Responsible Property Investment Council, Center for Sustainability Advisory Board, and Faculty for the Daniel Rose Fellowship Land Use Program. He is the author of *Practical Greening: The Bottom Line on Sustainable Property Development, Investment and Financing*.

Asma Mehan is a visiting Ph.D. student at École polytechnique fédérale de Lausanne (EPFL) in Lausanne, Switzerland; former research fellow at the Alfred Deakin Institute (ADI) in Deakin University, Melbourne, Australia; and Ph.D. candidate in "Architecture- History- Project" Doctoral Program in the Department of Architecture and Design (DAD), Politecnico di Torino, Torino, Italy. Mehan's main research lies in the area of politics of architecture, Middle Eastern studies, and social sustainability. Her current research on Tehran goes beyond the symbolic capacities of architecture and focuses on the politics of space production.

Gordon Noble has a vast experience in the Australian financial sector, having worked in a variety of positions including as a political adviser, trade union official for a major superannuation fund, and for the pension industry's peak body—the Association of Superannuation Funds of Australia. He is the Principal Adviser for the Better Infrastructure Initiative at the John Grill Centre for Project Leadership and the President of the Network of Sustainable Financial Markets.

Amir Rahdari is the founder of Global Sustainability Research Network, Director of Sustainability Research Group at Universal Scientific Education and Research Network (USERN), associate editor of *International Journal of Sustainable Entrepreneurship and Corporate Social Responsibility* (IJSECSR), and a Sustainability and Social Responsibility Certified Associate in the UK. He was selected as one of the TOP25UNDER25 leaders in sustainable business (2 degrees, UK), a Science Sentinel (publons), and he is a member of Green Building Initiative (GBI) (USA), International Society for Development and Sustainability (ISDS) (Japan), and two dozen sustainability organizations. His research concerns the sustainability-business intersection with a major focus on sustainable business, corporate sustainability, rating systems, transparency, sustainability indicators, and performance evaluation systems.

Sara Levana Schoen is a corporate sustainability advocate with a passion for integrating long-termism into business processes to advance organizational and societal prosperity. She has led sustainability for Clarion Partners and First Potomac Realty Trust and managed private-sector partnerships for the US Green Building Council and the US Department of Energy.

Philippe St-Jean is a LEED BD+C accredited professional and a certified Passivhaus consultant and course instructor. With over 15 years in the construction industry, St-Jean has experience both onsite, as a foreman, and offsite, as a project manager, estimator, construction director, course instructor, and sustainable construction consultant.

Diane Strauss is research director of the Yale Initiative for Sustainable Finance at Yale University, USA. Prior to this, she worked as a policy analyst in the think-thank 2 Investing Initiative in Paris and as a research assistant in World Wide Fund (WWF), Brussels, doing research and advocacy to shift financial flows toward climate-friendly investments.

Thomas Walker has written numerous articles and books in the area of risk management, shareholder litigation, and sustainable finance. He previously directed the David O'Brien Centre for Sustainable Enterprise and has served as the chair of the Finance Department and as Associate Dean, Research, at Concordia University, Canada. He frequently consults in the area of sustainable management and shareholder litigation.

List of Figures

List of Pictures

List of Tables

CHAPTER 1

Introduction

Lisa N. Hasan

This phase of rapid product introduction to an increasingly receptive market has provided the real estate sector with a wide range of solutions. In contrast to the industrial and transportation sectors, the majority of the technologies required to meet resource conservation targets set for the real estate sector are already commercially available and cost effective (IEA, 2013, p. 9). However, this flurry of activity has also created a culture of experimentation, where there is little consensus as to basic definitions and best practices, and capacity building often lags behind innovation implementation. The segmented and conflicting nature of current policies, practices and incentives currently impedes the widespread adoption of the technological and procedural innovations required to meet these ambitious goals (IEA, 2013; UNEP, 2016).

Fortunately, the market is showing signs of maturing. The motivation for engaging in sustainable initiatives is shifting from an idealistic desire to "do the right thing" to a recognition of the business opportunities associated with sustainable practices (McGraw-Hill Construction, 2013). As an increasingly wide spectrum of stakeholders become involved in sustainability around the globe, there is a growing recognition of the need for a

L. N. Hasan (✉)
David O'Brien Centre for Sustainable Enterprise,
John Molson School of Business, Concordia University, Montreal, QC, Canada

T. Walker et al. (eds.), *Sustainable Real Estate*, Palgrave Studies in Sustainable Business In Association with Future Earth,
https://doi.org/10.1007/978-3-319-94565-1_1

shared understanding, common benchmarks and a more holistic approach to sustainability in the real estate sector.

Despite this high-level consensus, achieving a truly sustainable global real estate sector is no small task. Staying abreast of all the changes and their implications is a challenge made all the more daunting by the fact that they have occurred in parallel with the evolution of the definition of sustainability itself. Early reports on sustainable development expressed the need to strike a balance between economic growth and resource conservation (United Nations Conference on the Human Environment, 1972; World Commission on Environment and Development, 1987; United Nations, 1987). These general recommendations evolved into the comprehensive 17 global sustainable development goals and associated targets described in the United Nation's 2030 Agenda for Sustainable Development (UN General Assembly, 2015). This latest framework for understanding sustainable development has profound implications for the real estate industry. It pushes the boundaries of sustainability further beyond the building's walls to include responsible resource production and consumption as well as a range of social issues associated with housing and energy affordability, health and well-being, global urbanization and even climate change.

Achieving the sustainable development targets set out by the UN and refined by local governments will require a concerted effort on the part of all stakeholders working together across traditional disciplinary, geographic and political boundaries. The traditional project lifecycle will also need to be redefined in order to involve more stakeholders in preplanning, post-occupancy and even demolition and redevelopment phases. Implementing piecemeal solutions will not be sufficient to reach the targets set by the Paris Agreement[1], nor to overcome many of the obstacles to the global adoption and implementation of sustainability measures. Integrated solutions, greater information transparency and the continued development of globally adopted but locally adapted, standards, benchmarks and best practices will shape the future of sustainable real estate practice.

By collecting the latest insights in a single volume, this book aims to provide readers from all disciplines with a better appreciation of sustainable real estate as a grand system and shed some light on its past, present and future evolutions. We begin by examining the role that real estate can

[1] http://unfccc.int/paris_agreement/items/9485.php.

play in addressing climate change (Chap. 2). Next, we explore real estate's new role in building and supporting sustainable and resilient communities (Chap. 3). This broad, forward-looking context provides a backdrop to the subsequent chapters that discuss current public-sector regulatory trends (Chap. 4) and the European Union's policy framework in particular (Chap. 5).

Market-driven approaches are then discussed, including critical reviews of green building labeling systems (Chap. 6) and global real estate sustainability benchmarking (Chap. 7). These methods for assessing and comparing sustainability levels are followed by more focused discussions on the business case for green buildings for owner-operators (Chap. 8) and the value of sustainability as an organizational effectiveness tool for real estate management companies (Chap. 9).

Chapters 10–12 discuss methods for delivering affordable, reliable and sustainable energy to real estate projects. This topic is approached from both a design standpoint, through a discussion of building energy simulation for sustainable and resilient buildings (Chap. 10), and a finance perspective, exploring the challenges and solutions driving investment in high-performance buildings (Chap. 11). Chapter 12 covers the specific case of financing rooftop solar for single-family rental properties.

The final portion of the book brings us back to the topic of real estate's role in building and supporting sustainable cities and communities. This section provides case studies from around the globe and shows how multiple stakeholders, under various regulatory and market conditions, have come together to address a number of sustainable real estate issues. A case for sustainable affordable housing in the US (Chap. 13) and an overview of affordable Passive House projects in Nova Scotia (Chap. 14) provide insights into the North American housing market. Investing in Community Sporting Facilities (Chap. 15) outlines a new financing model that is being implemented in Australia to fund social communal infrastructures. Chapter 16 discusses the specificities of sustainable real estate in the Middle East and Chap. 17 provides an overview of sustainable community development in Nigeria.

In sum, the continued success of the sustainable real estate industry hinges on, not only continued technological innovation but also greater integration and awareness of agreed upon best practices. This can only be achieved if a broader spectrum of stakeholders is able to work across traditional disciplinary boundaries at all phases of the real estate development's lifecycle. The next wave of innovation in sustainable development will assuredly be less technology driven and more focused on creating structures conducive to the development, implementation and monitoring of sustainable solutions in real estate. We hope that this book will provide a strong base for future research and thought leadership in sustainable real estate, arguably the only type of real estate that will stand the test of time.

References

Devine, A., & Kok, N. (2015). Green Certification and Building Performance: Implications of Tangibles and Intangibles. The Journal of Portfolio Management (Special Real Estate Issue 7th Edition), 1–14. Retrieved July 30, 2017, from http://www.bentallkennedy.com/news-2015-10-06.php

Dodge Data & Analytics. (2016). World Green Building Trends 2016: Developing Markets Accelerate Global Green Growth. (H. M. Bernstein, M. A. Russo, E. Fitch, & D. Laquidara-Carr, Eds.) Bedford, MA, USA. Retrieved July 27, 2017, from http://www.worldgbc.org/sites/default/files/World%20Green%20Building%20Trends%202016%20SmartMarket%20Report%20FINAL-2.pdf

Eichholtz, P., Kok, N., & Quigley, J. (2013). The Economics of Green Building. *Review of Economics and Statistics, 95*(1), 50–63.

Eichholtz, P., Kok, N., & Quigley, J. M. (2010). Doing Well by Doing Good? Green Office Buildings. *American Economic Review, 100*(December 2010), 2494–2511.

Eichholtz, P., Kok, N., & Yonder, E. (2012). Portfolio greenness and the financial performance of REITs. *Journal of International Money and Finance, 31*(7), 1911–1929.

Fuerst, F., & McAllister, P. (2009). An Investigation of the Effect of Eco=Labelling on Office Occupancy Rates. *Journal of Sustainable Real Estate, 1*(1), 49–64.

Gabe, J. (2016). Successful Greenhouse Gas Mitigation in existing Australian Office Buildings. *Building Research & Innovation, 44*(2), 160–174.

IEA. (2013). Transition to Sustainable Buildings: Strategies and Opportunities to 2050. Paris: International Energy Agency (IEA). Retrieved July 24, 2017, from https://www.iea.org/publications/freepublications/publication/Building2013_free.pdf

McGraw-Hill Construction. (2008). Commercial & Institutional Green Building SmartMarket Report. (M. A. Russo, C. O'Shaughnessy, & S. Lewis, Eds.) Bedford, MA, USA. Retrieved July 30, 2017, from http://mts.sustainable-products.com/Capital_Markets_Partnership/BusinessCase/MHC%20Commercial%20&%20Institutional%20Green%20Building%20SMR%20(2008).pdf

McGraw-Hill Construction. (2009). Green Retrofit & Renovation SmartMarket Report. (M. A. Russo, D. Laquidara-Carr, & J. Miltner, Eds.) Bedford, MA, USA. Retrieved July 30, 2017, from http://mts.sustainableproducts.com/Capital_Markets_Partnership/BusinessCase/MHC%20Green%20Building%20Retrofit%20%26%20Renovation%20SMR%20%282009%29.pdf

McGraw-Hill Construction. (2013). World Green Building Trends—Business Benefits Driving New and Retrofit Market Opportunities in Over 60 Countries. (H. M. Bernstein, M. A. Russo, E. Fitch, & D. Laquidara-Carr, Eds.) Bedford, MA, United States: McGraw-Hill Construction. Retrieved June 20, 2017, from http://www.worldgbc.org/files/8613/6295/6420/World_Green_Building_Trends_SmartMarket_Report_2013.pdf

UN General Assembly. (2015). Transforming our World: The 2030 Agenda for Sustainable Development. Retrieved July 29, 2017, from http://www.un.org/ga/search/view_doc.asp?symbol=A/RES/70/1&Lang=E

UNEP. (2016). The Emissions Gap Report 2016. Nairobi: United Nations Environmental Programme. Retrieved June 21, 2017, from wedocs.unep.org/bitstream/handle/20.500.11822/.../emission gap report_2016.pdf

United Nations. (1987). Our Common Future—Brundtland Report. Oxford: Oxford University Press. Retrieved July 20, 2017, from https://sustainabledevelopment.un.org/content/documents/5987our-common-future.pdf

United Nations Conference on the Human Environment. (1972). Declaration of the United Nations Conference on the Human Environment. Stockholm, Sweden. Retrieved July 20, 2017, from http://www.un-documents.net/unchedec.htm

World Commission on Environment and Development. (1987). *Our Common Future*. Oxford: Oxford University Press.

CHAPTER 2

The Relevance of Real Estate in Solving Climate Change

Cary Krosinsky

Buildings can seem boring to many. But within the world's current and future building stock could well lay the most important area of work ahead for ensuring better environmental and social future outcomes.

Sustainable real estate is in fact a critical baseline for establishing better financial outcomes, as not fixing for the track we are headed down regarding climate change would likely be economically disastrous, perhaps in the many tens of trillions of dollars.[1]

If we are to solve for climate change, however, efficiency emerges as the most important area of carbon reduction potential to be achieved. The International Energy Agency argued in its World Energy Outlook in 2014[2] that for a 2-degree world, over US $1 trillion in annual investment

[1] https://www.privatebank.citibank.com/home/fresh-insight/gps-energy-darwinism.html.

[2] https://www.iea.org/publications/freepublications/publication/WEO2014.pdf.

C. Krosinsky (✉)
Yale University, New Haven, CT, USA

Brown University, Providence, RI, USA
e-mail: cary.krosinsky@yale.edu

T. Walker et al. (eds.), *Sustainable Real Estate*, Palgrave Studies in Sustainable Business In Association with Future Earth,
https://doi.org/10.1007/978-3-319-94565-1_2

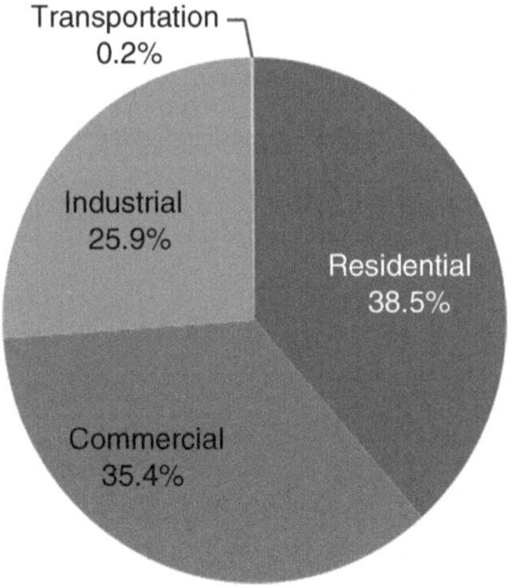

Fig. 2.1 Retail sales of electricity, end use by percent of ultimate customer (https://www.c2es.org/energy/use/residential-commercial)

will be needed on average by 2040, with a majority of this amount falling into the efficiency category.

While efficiency can be a broad term touching all sectors, real estate is a large percentage of the existing global carbon footprint and therefore a large percentage of carbon reduction potential as well. For example, in the US (Fig. 2.1), the largest components of electricity use are residential (38.5%) and commercial (35.4%), and electricity use is the largest component of energy consumption, making building efficiency a very large percentage of what is possible and necessary.

Hence, if necessary reductions in the carbon footprint are expected and necessary from efficiency and finance, and buildings make up the majority of the carbon footprint of consumption, then efficiency in existing buildings stock, both current and new, becomes one of the biggest investment opportunities and this could create a useful paradigm of sorts with increasing and specific focus.

Consider as well the effects of automation, technological innovation, and globalization.[3]

These trends are likely unstoppable and create unrest in previously developed countries where jobs for those less skilled are suddenly disappearing. Add to this what we call the effect of "the entrenched nature of the status quo," largely in the form of people driving existing cars longer

[3] http://www.thejei.com/wp-content/uploads/2015/01/209-713-1-PB.pdf.

and operating existing buildings and power plants past the original length of time expected, and this creates an unsustainable path for ongoing carbon emissions versus reductions required.

In economies which are otherwise economically vibrant, retrofitting at scale and sustainable real estate more generally therefore becomes a means of establishing adequate jobs and necessary efficiency including through creative financing mechanisms so that governments do not take on the entire financial burden.

Many studies show rents are higher and residents happier in more efficient buildings that take into account the environment or otherwise create healthier and happier spaces for both living and working conditions. While often thought of as coming best from new building stock, this could come from revised existing stock as well. The area of retrofit finance is largely untapped but could form a "new deal" of sorts and is arguably essential given this entrenched nature of the status quo previously mentioned. This "new deal" could be politically palatable as well to a disgruntled voting public in countries such as the US and UK where 2016 elections went in unexpected directions. So we see improving existing building stock as a critical and often overlooked component of what might be necessary and possible.

On the new building front, for all the good work occurring on new building standards, there is also growing concern about measurement and net impact, specifically whether standards such as Leadership in Energy and Environmental Design (LEED) and BREEAM (Building Research Establishment Environmental Assessment Method) bring about actual environmental impact reductions, and if so whether they are sufficient. In addition, new building development can often lag behind what might be necessary to create overall levels of necessary building efficiency, given the long time it takes to replace building stock more generally.

At minimum, better standards, methods of analysis, and reporting are needed to ensure that when sustainable real estate projects are chosen through upfront design, there is a specific understanding of what improvement in net impacts are likely and possible, perhaps even from a scenarios perspective, including the better financial outcomes which result from better design choices.

The Rocky Mountain Institute (RMI) has seen all this as well, and is an example of an organization working diligently and thoughtfully to increase efficiency solutions being deployed, including through more efficient cooling and building functionality. RMI, which has long worked in China and increasingly as well in India where climate solutions are being implemented rapidly, sees that 35% of global energy is consumed by buildings, and 60% of consumed energy occurs in buildings, so the potential is clear. They aim to reduce energy consumption in buildings by 390 trillion BTUs (British thermal units) in the US alone, the equivalent of decommissioning 17 coal power plants.[4]

Better standards are also needed on the financing side of building efficiency, with some early examples of energy efficiency financing being achieved by the green banks and infrastructure banks in states such as Connecticut, Rhode Island and New York, and in Europe surrounding groups such as Energy Efficiency Financial Institutions Group (EEFIG) and their new underwriting toolkit,[5] but as per Chap. 5, much more work is needed in Europe on this basis.

Region by region, more and better work is happening, such as Siemens rebuilding Cairo,[6] cities banding together to fight climate change,[7] cities creating benchmarking ordinances[8] and otherwise creating positive environments for new building design and related technological improvement.

Yet we lack a true and robust picture of what is necessary of buildings on a global basis. What would be really helpful is a roadmap of what we need to do and should do in each category of building by region (and by category of owner as well given the significant percentage of family owned building empires doing arguably not enough on this subject in cities such as New York).

We hope that this text starts to provide a roadmap of the many strategies that need to run in parallel to achieve the sustainable real estate sector we now know we can achieve. It can only be achieved through will, intent, design, and successful implementation. We hope to have at least started on this path with this effort.

[4] https://www.rmi.org/our-work/buildings/.

[5] http://www.unepfi.org/wordpress/wp-content/uploads/2017/06/EEFIG_Underwriting_Toolkit_June_2017.pdf.

[6] https://www.siemens.com/eg/en/home/company/topic-areas/egypt-megaproject.html.

[7] http://www.c40.org/.

[8] http://www.phillymag.com/property/2017/07/11/philly-just-misses-the-top-10-for-green-building/.

CHAPTER 3

Evolutions in Sustainability and Sustainable Real Estate

Sherif Goubran, Tristan Masson, and Margarita Caycedo

1 Introduction

In 2015, the United Nations General Assembly (UNGA) pledged to set the world on the path toward sustainability and sustainable development. The resolution adopted at that meeting, entitled *Transforming Our World: The 2030 Agenda for Sustainable Agenda*, has since gained currency in global affairs. Different multilateral institutions, including the G20 (G20, 2017), have espoused the goals outlined in the Agenda and have contrib uted to policy coordination. Sustainable development can be broadly interpreted as development anchored in the principles of and geared toward sustainability. Today, the concept has attained a significant level of popularity and acceptance on a global scale. The role of the real estate sector in attaining sustainability is widely recognized. The complex relationship between the built environment and the pillars of sustainability (i.e. social, environmental and economic) has been explored by many scholars. Moving toward sustainable real estate is crucial considering the alarming effects that traditional buildings have on the environment, society, and local and global economies. The current trends in sustainable real estate

S. Goubran • T. Masson (✉) • M. Caycedo
Concordia University, Montréal, QC, Canada

T. Walker et al. (eds.), *Sustainable Real Estate*, Palgrave Studies in Sustainable Business In Association with Future Earth,
https://doi.org/10.1007/978-3-319-94565-1_3

are creating significant developments in the sector which can lead to the institutionalization of sustainable real estate practices on a global scale.

This chapter begins by reviewing the rise of sustainability as a global concept for governance, from its origins in the early 1970s to the establishment of definitions, approaches, clear goals and objectives. In the second section, the connection between sustainable development goals (SDGs) and real estate is made explicit. The relationship between the real estate sector and the three pillars of sustainability (namely the society, the economy and the environment) is explored. In the third section, the possible means of achieving sustainable real estate are presented. Current trends are critically discussed and possible future trends are identified. In addition, the roles of the many stakeholders involved are highlighted. The concluding section proposes a map for the complex sustainable real estate system that can help contextualize research and approaches to the field.

2 The Rise of Sustainable Development

The United Nations (UN) Conference on the Human Environment, which was held in Stockholm in 1972, marked the beginning of the international community's attempt to attune human activity to the natural environment. The Stockholm Conference placed environmental problems within the context of world affairs. The conference also sought to chart the means toward global solutions. That same year, the influential study *Limits to Growth* was published by the Club of Rome. It sought to describe the complex web of interdependencies made up by technology, environment, economy and population (Meadows, Meadows, Randers, & Behrens III, 1972). The study came to the so-called limits to growth conclusion and became the first robust and popular critique of growth-based development. Several years later, another significant report was published, this time by the International Union for the Conservation of Nature (IUCN). The *World Conservation Strategy: Living Resource Conservation for Sustainable Development* (IUCN, 1980) was unique in that it coined the term "sustainable development" to express the harmonious relationship between human development and the biosphere's integrity. In 1987, the term was used as an integral concept of *Our Common Future*, a report by the World Commission on Environment and Development popularly known as the Brundtland Report (after its principal author, Norway's Prime Minister Gro Harlem Brundtland). In this report, the concept of sustainable development was famously defined as "[…] development that meets the needs of the present without compromising the ability of future generations to meet their own needs".

In 1992, the international community reconvened in Rio de Janeiro (Brazil) at the UN Conference on Environment and Development, which earned the colloquial title of "Rio Earth Summit". From this conference emerged Agenda 21 which put together a comprehensive action plan whereby countries would work together "in global partnership for sustainable development" (UNECD, 1992, chap. 1 subs. 1.1). Agenda 21 was considered the most comprehensive attempt to operationalize sustainable development that had hitherto been developed. It elaborated on the social, economic and environmental dimensions, recognized the importance of multi-stakeholders (beyond governments) and proposed practical means of implementing sustainable development. Two important international arrangements emanated from the Rio Earth Summit: (1) The Convention on Biological Diversity (CBD), which committed the world to the conserve, and (2) the UN Framework Convention on Climate Change (UNFCCC), which challenged the world to stabilize greenhouse gas (GHG) emissions so as to mitigate human disruption of the climate system. A decade after the Rio Earth Summit, Johannesburg (South Africa) hosted the UN World Summit on Sustainable Development (WSSD) where an implementation strategy for Agenda 21 was developed. The strategy incorporated the Millennium Development Goals (MDGs) and paved the way for a holistic understanding of sustainable development that integrated the economic, social and environmental dimensions and recognized them as the mutually reinforcing "pillars" of sustainability (WSSD, 2002, p. 2). A further decade later, the UN Conference on Sustainable Development in Rio de Janeiro (commonly referred to as Rio+20) and the ensuing document *The World We Want* set the scene for the subsequent adoption of the SDGs, which were presented in Agenda 2030 at the UN Sustainable Development Summit (September 2015, New York, USA). The SDGs served as way of mobilizing collective action around a set of common goals.

3 Sustainability and Real Estate

The preamble to Agenda 2030, where the most recent (at the time of writing) iteration of the definition of sustainability is presented, identifies people, the planet, prosperity, peace, and partnerships (the "five Ps") as the key areas of sustainable development (UNGA, 2015, pp. 1–2). It marks a

Table 3.1 How the SDGs relate to sustainable real estate

SDGs	*Description*	*Relevant targets*	*Relevant indicators*
Goal 7	Ensure access to affordable, reliable, sustainable and modern energy for all	7.2. Expand supply of renewable energy	Share of energy from renewables
		7.3. Improve energy efficiency	Rate of primary energy intensity improvement
Goal 11	Make cities and human settlements inclusive, safe, resilient and sustainable	11.1. Affordable housing	Rent burden (% of disposable income)[a]
		11.a. Coordinated urban planning	Share of consumption of food and raw materials within urban areas that are produced and delivered in/from rural areas within the country
Goal 12	Ensure sustainable consumption and production patterns	12.7. Sustainability practices and information in the private-sector	N/A
Goal 13	Take urgent action to combat climate change and its impacts[b]	13.1. Climate adaptation	Presence of urban building codes stipulating the use of either local materials and/or new energy-efficient technologies or with incentives for the same.

Sources: UNGA (2015, p. 14), SDSN (2015, pp. 49–59), Sachs et al. (2017, p. 7)

[a]Applies only to OECD countries

[b]Recognizing that the UNFCCC is the primary international forum for responding to climate change

shift in emphasis from a primarily environmental focus to an integrational approach and it frames sustainable development as a goal-oriented endeavor. The SDGs comprise 17 goals spread across the five Ps (Table 3.1). In keeping with the goal-based agenda, the SDGs are fleshed out into 169 targets and many more indicators. The Sustainable Development Solutions Network (SDSN) has been entrusted with collecting, monitoring and updating the relevant data as the Agenda unfolds over time.

Real estate is both directly and indirectly related to the concept of sustainability and to the SDGs. In effect, real estate has to be understood in the broader context of urban development, since cities lie at the intersection of major challenges such as population growth, urbanization and unsustainability. In other words, although sustainability is global in scope, it requires actions to be scaled to local settings, meaning that the role of real estate in sustainable development, that is, that of providing an "urban opportunity", is crucial (SDSNTGSC, 2015). The Intergovernmental Panel on Climate Change (IPCC)—the research arm of the UNFCCC—dedicated an entire chapter to buildings in its most recent assessment report, which deals with the multifaceted challenge of climate change (Bulkeley, 2012; IPCC, 2014). As the report details, sustainable buildings not only promise emissions reductions through technology and behavioral considerations but also provide benefits from a socioeconomic and health perspective. In the light of this broad view of the role of real estate in sustainable development, SDGs 7, 11, 12 and 13 stand out as being most relevant to real estate, as they cover energy, cities, consumption and production patterns, and climate change.

3.1 Real Estate and the Environment

The unique nature, site and context of each construction project, the large number of stakeholders involved, and the intense financial and time pressures have been identified as key challenges that have mitigated the unsustainable trends in the real estate industry (Teo & Loosemore, 2001). Today, these characteristics are still considered some of the biggest hurdles to the institutionalization, harmonization and broad application of sustainable construction practices. In a paper published in 1992, shortly after the Brundtland report, the effects of construction activities on the environment were organized into the following categories: resource deterioration, physical disruption, chemical pollution, environmental loading, visual impacts and health impacts (Ofori, 1992). These categories have since become the focus of sustainable real estate standards (Brandon & Lombardi, 2010).

Recent studies estimate that buildings consume annually more than 40% of the global energy supply (World Economic Forum, 2016). It is further estimated that 20% of global GHG emissions originate from buildings and that the real estate sector, with more than 8.1Gt of annual emissions, is the single most significant industry in terms of CO_2 contribution (Rashid, Faiz, & Yusoff, 2015; Willmott Dixon, 2010; World Economic Forum, 2016). The building sector is estimated to globally consume about 30% of raw materials and 12% of fresh water, while generating up to 40% of the total landfill waste and 20% of water effluents (World Economic Forum, 2016). The situation is even more alarming in the US, where 40% of the carbon emissions and 88% of the fresh water consumption is attributed to the commercial real estate sector alone (Deloitte, 2014).

Additionally, according to a study published by the Lawrence Livermore National Laboratory on US energy use in 2013, 59% of the total energy produced was rejected and wasted due to inefficient and ineffective use, with the real estate sector and buildings identified as large contributors to this wasted energy (LLNL, 2014). Left unchecked, the effect of real estate on the environment is predicted to worsen. It is projected that, considering the increasingly urban nature of the world's population, the largest 750 cities in the world will require 260 million new homes and 540 million square meters of new office space by 2030 (World Economic Forum, 2016). Furthermore, it is estimated that, by 2030, buildings' CO_2 emissions and proportionate share of global GHG emissions will increase by 56% and 7%, respectively (World Economic Forum, 2016). Since the early 1990s, scholars, activists and policymakers have called for a shift in the real estate sector toward sustainability. Current reports suggest that green buildings, sustainable real estate and development, and environmentally conscious building operations and management have gained significant prominence.

Sustainable building can improve energy and water efficiency and ensure the sustainable use of raw materials (UNEP, 2011). By one estimate, the sustainable construction market could save 23.5 billion kilowatt hours of energy between 2015 and 2018 (The Impact, 2016). The U.S. Green Building Council and Booz Allen Hamilton (2009) report that, in the United States, the energy cost reduction and climate advantages could be lower than financial benefits produced by labor cost-savings and productivity gains for better indoor air quality, natural ventilation, local thermal control, daylighting and rent premium. Increased daylighting and contact with nature also produce benefits in hospitals and schools, improving student performance and patient recovery (Aumann, Heschong, Wright, & Peet, 2004; Ulrich, 1984; UNEP, 2011). It was recently estimated that "green" buildings represent 38% of global building project activities, with the highest proportions being in Singapore, the United Arab Emirates (UAE) and the UK, and that an increasing number of firms are committed to working on "green" projects (Bernstein, Russo, Fitch, & Laquidara-Carr, 2013). These trends are very promising and reflect the active role that sustainable real estate practices may have on the economic and social dimensions.

3.2 *Real Estate and the Economy*

Sustainable economies, as noted by Bukart (2009), are composed of six interconnected sectors: renewable energy, sustainable buildings, sustainable transport, water management, waste management and land management. Real estate will be one of the key sectors in effecting the transition to a low-carbon economy. Sustainable building integrates practices and techniques to reduce the negative effects of its activity on the environment and on human health. Sustainable building can also create job opportunities in design and construction (in developing countries) and in retrofitting (in developed countries) and can serve as a vehicle for social and economic inclusion and housing formalization (UNEP, 2011). Despite the potential benefits of sustainable building, economists recognize that some market failures or specific market and industry structures induce a systematic under-provision of sustainable buildings. The market failures are due to asymmetric information and externalities.

The building process involves mainly negative externalities. For example, construction waste can reduce water and air quality and site selection can affect urban development patterns as well as traffic, air quality and urban visual qualities (Matisoff, Noonan, & Flowers, 2016). The economic and market-based instruments comprise energy performance contracting, cooperative procurement, efficiency certificate schemes and credit schemes. The fiscal instruments comprise tax exemptions and subsidies (grants, subsidized loans and rebates). In the case of capacity support, information and voluntary actions embody voluntary labeling, leadership programs and awareness-raising initiatives. Forces in the private-sector include attractive financial results, changing drivers of asset value and tenant satisfaction, increasing demand and favorable public policy (Morrow, Read-Brown, O'Sullivan, & Garz, 2015). The main opportunity for sustainable building is the lower costs of retrofitting or new construction in terms of emissions-reduction compared with other economic sectors (UNEP, 2011). The net income of responsible investors is increased through lower expenses (as a result of life-cycle assessment and more efficient use of resources) and higher valuations (through lower risk premiums) (Clements-Hunt & Gary, 2007). It is estimated that sustainable real estate practices could reduce emissions from new constructions by almost one-third (29%) by 2020, at near-zero cost, with similarly low investment levels for retrofitting (IPCC, 2007).

3.3 *Real Estate and Society*

The real estate sector plays an important role in addressing social challenges such as affordable housing, inclusive economic development and food security for underserved populations. According to the United Nations Population Fund (2017) and the World Bank (2016), five billion people will live in towns and cities by 2030 (66% of the world population). In many big cities around the world, housing prices have increased beyond inflation over the last ten years, exacerbating the problem of home affordability. Furthermore, the current housing system is not designed to meet future demographic needs. The World Economic Forum (2016) indicates that people over 65 will represent a higher proportion of the global population than people under 50, driving demand for multi-residential and mixed-use developments. Sustainable urban development, wherein real estate plays an important role, is a crucial area of focus and public policy is beginning to recognize this reality. Sustainable urban living, which favors inclusive economic growth and innovation, has the potential to use resources more efficiently, protect the environment, create jobs and provide a nurturing environment for individuals and communities.

Eizenberg and Jabareen (2017) suggested that the physical aspects of human spaces are very important for social sustainability since they may contribute to reducing environmental risks and improving human welfare. UNEP (2011) discussed the benefits of sustainable buildings in terms of worker productivity and well-being, due to reduced indoor air and noise pollution. Additionally, sustainable urban forms can promote a sense of community and safety. Jabareen (2006) and Eizenberg and Jabareen (2017) provide a set of typologies to explain how sustainable urban forms can affect climate-change risk management. Sustainable urban strategies include compactness of cities, integration to public transportation, density, mixed land use, diversity or inclusivity of urban landscapes, optimization of energy production and consumption, bringing nature into the city, renewal and utilization of urban spaces.

Moreover, sustainable building provides employment opportunities and better working conditions for people in developed and developing countries alike. Sustainable real estate, which is expected to grow by 85% by 2030, is impacting the labor market through direct job creation, both in new constructions and in a retrofitting context. These additional jobs are in the areas of power and civil infrastructure (e.g. social housing, hospitals and schools), the production of sustainable materials, appliances and components, and the operation and maintenance of energy-efficiency schemes. Furthermore, there are indirect benefits for employment, through recycling and waste management activities. Various studies have concluded that sustainable buildings generate more employment opportunities than they replace in the traditional energy-supply industry (UNEP, 2011). In developing countries, sustainable real estate could contribute to formalizing or creating decent jobs, to providing better working conditions and to upgrading workers' skills. Decent jobs have been shown to improve quality of life and alleviate poverty (UNEP, 2011).

Given that cities are the intersection between the economy, natural resources management, communities and technology, a major goal should be to make cities and other human settlements more inclusive, safer, more resilient and sustainable. Additionally, since developed countries have better sustainable performance in urban development than emerging economies, it is important to facilitate the international exchange of experiences, knowledge and best practices among countries that are at different stages of urbanization.

4 Toward Sustainable Real Estate

4.1 Current Trends

Sustainability has moved from being a niche in the construction industry to being an approach that is increasingly adopted by firms in the design, construction, operation and even demolition phases of real estate projects (Bernstein et al., 2013). As presented in the previous sections, the environmental, social and economic benefits of sustainable real estate are no longer debated (Deloitte, 2014). Recent studies suggest that the industry is gradually taking a more favorable view of ecological and sustainable buildings due to the decreasing cost of technologies, increasing demand and greater incentives for sustainable development (Arbor, 2005; Bernstein et al., 2013). Additionally, the perception of "sustainable" real estate is shifting: more people are realizing that ecological buildings and sustainable projects are a product of a well-integrated design process and that sustainable projects do not need to be visibly different from traditional buildings (Arbor, 2005). In a report published by Deloitte in 2014 on commercial real estate, which builds on the seminal paper *Doing Well by Doing Good* (Eichholtz, Kok, & Quigley, 2010), it is noted that the implementation of sustainable practices in existing buildings can result in higher internal rates of return than the use of traditional practices (Deloitte, 2014). The report further claims that sustainable investment results in more than just cost-savings and that, for commercial properties, it results in an increase in asset values (Deloitte, 2014). However, some of the reported challenges to the adoption of sustainability principles in buildings include higher initial costs, lack of political support, affordability, lack of market demand and a lack of trained professionals (Bernstein et al., 2013).

It is widely accepted that the current sustainable real estate market is essentially demand driven (Arbor, 2005; Bernstein et al., 2013; DLA Piper, 2014), that is, that the uptake of ecological building activities is mainly driven by commercial factors (such as market transformation and local competition) and that higher building values and lower operating costs are the main influencers of investment decisions (Bernstein et al., 2013; World Economic Forum, 2016). However, it is important to note that the increased internal commitment to sustainability in many firms is also due to a growing recognition of the value of branding opportunities (Bernstein et al., 2013). The McGraw-Hill *World Green Building Trends* report, published in 2013, indicates that for new green buildings, the expected decrease in operation cost is about 15% over five years, the expected increase in asset value is 5%, the expected increase in building value is 7%, and the average payback period for additional costs attributed to "green" features is about eight years (Bernstein et al., 2013). The report also suggests that green products used in buildings are mainly mechanical, electrical, plumbing and waste related and that the most commonly used renewable energy source is solar (Bernstein et al., 2013). This is in alignment with the technical, structured approach to sustainable building that is generally adopted.

Environmental certification and evaluation tools are widely used for making sustainability goals and principles more accessible to industry and a large number of such tools are available (Brandon & Lombardi, 2010). Although some of the building evaluation tools are government-run, they are mostly voluntary third party and privately operated (Ding, 2008). Typically, the selection of the evaluation tools for a project is strongly influenced by the geographic location, while economic and financial aspects may not be considered, which presents a challenge to investors (Ding, 2008; Hens, 2012). Furthermore, although some tools use multi-criteria matrices for evaluation, a large proportion of tools focus solely on one criterion (in many cases, operational site energy) (Ding, 2008).

Practitioners appreciate that these simplifications make the tools easier to adopt in projects (DLA Piper, 2014). However, Morrow et al. (2015) highlight the recent discussion in the real estate industry around the need to take into account not only environmental issues but also occupant productivity, health and well-being. In October 2014, the WELL Building Standard (which is administrated by a Leadership in Energy and Environmental Design [LEED] standard) was launched to promote people's health and well-being. The report foresees that the industry will shift from "green" real estate to a broader perspective of "sustainable" real estate and buildings (Bernstein et al., 2013; Ding, 2008). Thus, while it can be argued that the existing tools serve an important role in improving the sustainability of many projects, by guiding the design, heightening the environmental awareness and structuring the environmental information, many scholars are calling for more comprehensive and advanced approaches to sustainability. Their vision is to be able to assess buildings and real estate projects across a broader range of considerations and to integrate sustainability on the strategic decision-making level (Apanavičiene, Daugeliene, Baltramonaitis, & Maliene, 2015; Cucuzzella, 2009, 2011; Ding, 2008; Fadaei, Iulo, & Yoshida, 2015).

4.2 Criticism of Current Trends

The evolving definition of sustainability, combined with its multifaceted nature, create significant challenges. The field of sustainable building is not without tension (Cucuzzella, 2016). Recent studies suggest that 80% of the industry would prefer a single certification scheme that provides clear guidelines (DLA Piper, 2014). On the other hand, researchers, designers and scholars have heavily criticized the reductionist nature of current evaluation approaches and are developing ever more complex matrices of evaluation (Deshmukh, Herber, & Allison, 2015; Gibberd, 2014; GlobalGiving, 2016; Lynch & Mosbah, 2017; Sustainable Cities Institute, 2013). These scholars argue that current tools, which are usually highly structured and aim for eco-efficiency (Fletcher & Goggin, 2001; Jonas, 1979; Madge, 2008; Naess, 1973), fail to capture the complexity of the topic of sustainability in the built environment (Cucuzzella, 2015b, 2015a; Newsham, Mancini, & Birt, 2009; Sterman, 2015) and are thus presenting designers, owners and investors with significant limitations (Cucuzzella, 2009; Orr, 2006; Papanek, 2000).

In addition, designers are heavily criticizing the excessive dependence on evaluation criteria in defining sustainability in buildings. They argue that the use of these evaluation methods as design tools places the visual character of our cities and buildings at risk and can result in "shallow" green approaches (i.e. buildings being used as demonstrative devices) (Cucuzzella, 2015b, 2015a; Ding, 2008). In other words, with the current focus on the technical aspects of sustainability, architecture and design are marginalized from the debate and a paradigm shift in approach is needed (Chansomsak & Vale, 2008; Fadaei et al., 2015; McLennan, 2004). Others have criticized the universal and rigid criteria of the existing evaluation tools and have called for more regionally adapted, softer methods of assessment (Boyko et al., 2012; Lynch & Mosbah, 2017). A further train of thought aims to reposition tenants, users and occupants at the center of the sustainability debate by actively engaging them in imagining and creating possible sustainable futures (Robinson, Burch, Talwar, O'Shea, & Walsh, 2011; Shaw et al., 2009; Sheppard et al., 2011). Although these critiques, tensions and debates denote the struggle of the industry in embracing sustainability, they also highlight the profound level of understanding that has emerged through the practice of sustainable real estate activities and the remarkable breadth and depth of innovation achieved over the past decade.

4.3 *The Role of Tenants, Investors, Governments and Financial Institutions*

It was argued earlier that the sustainable building sector is mainly market and demand driven. Tenants, especially in the commercial real estate sector, are becoming increasingly aware of the positive financial, health and productivity benefits of green buildings (Deloitte, 2014). Many industry reports suggest that tenants are increasingly willing to share the responsibility of the sustainable operation of buildings and to pay premiums for green properties; furthermore, tenants are increasingly demanding that green features be integrated in their leases (Deloitte, 2014; DLA Piper, 2014; World Economic Forum, 2016). Thus, tenants play an important role in keeping away from "brown" properties (i.e. buildings that are not green, have significantly lower market value and are usually developed in response to high green building activity in the same area). This can help maintain and increase the demand for sustainable urban planning, community development and green building construction and operation (Bernstein et al., 2013; Deloitte, 2014).

Investors, for their part, play an important role in advancing green and sustainable real estate. Although research suggests an increasing rate of sustainable and green building activities in firms across the world, a large proportion of firms and investors are still unsure about the financial and environmental outcomes of their green investments (Bernstein et al., 2013; Deloitte, 2014). Generally, there are three approaches to investment in the sustainable real estate sector: (1) defensive—adhering to written law, (2) responsible—optimizing benefits in line with investment goals and (3) sustainable—a commitment to sustainability in all actions (Apanavičiene et al., 2015). If significant advances in sustainable real estate are to be achieved, investors will have to commit to green and sustainable building practices, to integrate sustainability at all their decision levels and to aim toward sustainable investments.

Considering that defensive investment strategies are still the most prevalent in the market (Apanavičiene et al., 2015), governments are faced with the important responsibility of setting the benchmark and minimum sustainability requirements for developers and owners. A significant number of government bodies, at local, national and multinational levels, have started developing and enforcing regulations, which are usually focused on energy (Deloitte, 2014). Furthermore, a large proportion of firms report that they are required by law to work toward and report sustainability across their activities (World Economic Forum, 2016). However, in general, these minimal and narrow requirements leave considerable scope for improvement. Governments, on the policy and regulation side, must institutionalize green and sustainable building codes, including developing regulatory frameworks for the review, reporting and benchmarking of projects. They also have a key role to play in streamlining the processes for the acquisition of permits for renewable energy sources (Deloitte, 2014; DLA Piper, 2014; World Economic Forum, 2016).

Through collaboration with financial institutions, governments must ensure that the correct incentives are in place to encourage investors and owners to increase their sustainability and environmental focuses. Some of the most popular types of incentives include tax benefits, attractive financing options and lower fees (Deloitte, 2014). Other incentives, such as zoning density bonuses and access to government controlled land, are common in developed and developing countries, respectively. These incentives are important drivers for real estate investors and developers since they create tangible cost reductions and benefits that can significantly improve the internal rate of return of green investments (World Economic Forum, 2016). To generate a broader interest in green building activities, governments have to work with other institutions (such as non-governmental organizations and financial and technical consultants) to align the incentives with the needs of the regional market and investors.

Achieving sustainability in the real estate sector is complex (Putnik, 2009). Investors, governments, owners and tenants readily indicate that the deterrents to green building activities are related to the complexity of the topic. Examples include the multitude of environmental evaluation systems, the large differences in regional regulations and the interconnectedness of sustainability across many levels of the decision-making process (Deloitte, 2014; Ding, 2008; DLA Piper, 2014).

4.4 *Future Directions in Sustainable Real Estate*

Recent initiatives and trends have helped develop and enforcing an interest in sustainability within the real estate industry. However, it is apparent from the criticism presented earlier that moving forward will require some of the current fundamental assumptions and standards to be rethought (Putnik, 2009; Qian, Chan, Visscher, & Lehmann, 2015; Robinson et al., 2011). Approaches that are transdisciplinary—or ideally interdisciplinary—have been advocated as a valid means of tackling sustainability in the real estate and in the built environment (Fisher, 2008; Fry, 2009; McDonough & Braungart, 2002; Walker, 2006). One can argue that approaching sustainability in real estate requires the incorporation of its complexity. Some argue that the key to achieving sustainability in the real estate sector will be to reconceptualize the design profession (Fisher, 2008; Fry, 2009). Others argue that changes in the processes need to be considered (McLennan, 2004), that the way objects are made needs to be rethought completely (McDonough & Braungart, 2002) and that the design profession (Nelson & Stolterman, 2012) can serve as a guiding principal (Walker, 2006) for shaping sustainable real estate.

Although the construction and real estate sector does pose some unique challenges, rethinking the fundamental definition of sustainability in the built environment can serve as an important step in moving forward. Such a definition needs to be embedded in the social, environmental, economic and ethical realms (Ehrenfeld, 2009) and has to consider variations in location, context and scale, both temporal and geographic (Wilbanks, 2007).

The UN's 17 SDGs proposed in 2015 serve as a useful guide for understanding and approaching sustainable real estate from a holistic perspective and highlight the need for continuing to strive toward a balanced approach.

In order to move toward sustainability in the real estate sector, a comprehensive system of sustainability principles needs to be agreed upon (World Economic Forum, 2016). Such a system should include a set of intricate, decision-making frameworks that allow all the elements and their interactions to be optimized and institutionalized (Apanavičiene et al., 2015; Ding, 2008; Putnik, 2009). In addition, the concept of sustainability has to be strongly embedded within all activities throughout the lifecycle of buildings, community development and investment (Deloitte, 2014; Lawrence, 2015). Practically, every project, decision and strategy has to enforce and link that which needs to be developed (individuals, the economy or society), with that which needs to be sustained (nature, life support systems or community) (Robert, Parris, & Leiserowitz, 2005).

5 Conclusion: Mapping the Sustainable Real Estate System

In this chapter, as a backdrop to exploring the ways toward sustainable real estate, different issues and trends related to the topic were presented. The historic overview at the beginning of the chapter highlighted the fact that the concept of sustainability has matured significantly since it was first conceived in the 1970s. The current definition of sustainability, including its three main pillars (social, environmental and economic), is becoming widely accepted and a new reality that interlinks sustainability and real estate is beginning to emerge. In order to expedite this reality, innovative approaches that are embedded in transdisciplinary, holistic methods will be required.

The concept of sustainable development encompasses a number of key dimensions: ethics, policy and governance. The different stakeholders (both private and public, both individuals and communities) have crucial roles to play in moving toward sustainable real estate. The development of goals (such as the SDGs), tools and assessment methods can help guide action. However, these tools must be applicable to all asset types (buildings, infrastructure and common goods), stakeholders (investors, owners and tenants) and processes (design, construction, operation and demolition/end of life). Awareness of the enormous environmental impact of real estate has led to the current situation whereby most tools aim to (1) optimize the performance of buildings (in terms of energy reduction), (2) ensure the efficient use of materials and (3) minimize environmental degradation. In other words, the main focus so far has been on the environmental dimension of sustainability, specifically on operational energy. Future developments in the industry call for holistic approaches that incorporate all three pillars of sustainability and pay greater consideration to the sector's relations to the key natural resources (i.e. materials, energy, food and water).

To conclude this chapter, a map of the sustainable real estate system is proposed (Fig. 3.1). It presents the constituent components and guiding concepts of this complex system and allows the relationship between its elements to be explored systematically. Rooted in the evolving definition of sustainability, which includes a holistic, transdisciplinary approach, a wide variety of topics can emerge by linking the elements of a sustainable real estate system presented.

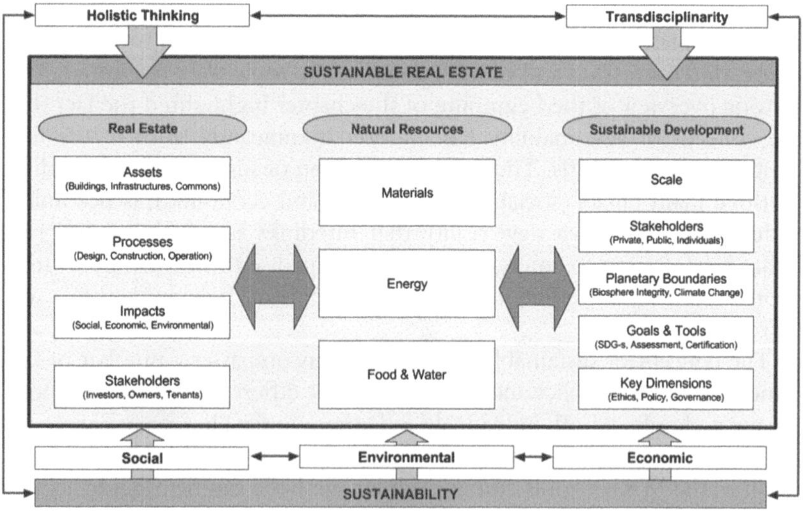

Fig. 3.1 A map of the complex sustainable real estate system

References

Apanavičiene, R., Daugeliene, A., Baltramonaitis, T., & Maliene, V. (2015). Sustainability Aspects of Real Estate Development: Lithuanian Case Study of Sports and Entertainment Arenas. *Sustainability (Switzerland), 7*(6), 6497–6522.

Arbor, A. (2005). *Building Green for the Future: Case Studies of Sustainable Development in Michigan. Handbook—Michigan University*. Michigan

Aumann, D., Heschong, L., Wright, R., & Peet, R. (2004). *Windows and Classrooms: Student Performance and the Indoor Environment*. Proceedings of the 2004 ACEEE Summer Study. 7–1.

Bernstein, H. M., Russo, M. A., Fitch, E., & Laquidara-Carr, D. (Eds.). (2013). *World Green Building Trends—Business Benefits Driving New and Retrofit Market Opportunities in Over 60 Countries*. Bedford, MA: McGraw-Hill Construction Research & Analytics. Retrieved from http://www.worldgbc.org/files/8613/6295/6420/World_Green_Building_Trends_SmartMarket_Report_2013.pdf

Boyko, C. T., Gaterell, M. R., Barber, A. R. G., Brown, J., Bryson, J. R., Butler, D., … Rogers, C. D. F. (2012). Benchmarking Sustainability in Cities: The Role of Indicators and Future Scenarios. *Global Environmental Change, 22*(1), 245–254.

Brandon, P., & Lombardi, P. (2010). *Evaluating Sustainable Development in the Built Environment* (2nd ed.). Chichester, West Sussex: Wiley-Blackwell

Bukart, Karl. (2009). *How Do You Define the 'Green' Economy?. MNN—Mother Nature Network.*

Bulkeley, H. (2012). *Cities and Climate Change*. London: Routledge. https://doi.org/10.4324/9780203077207

Chansomsak, S., & Vale, B. (2008). Can Architecture Really Educate People for Sustainability. In G. Foliente, T. Luetzkendorf, P. Newton, & P. Paevere (Eds.), *2008 World Sustainable Building Conference (SB08)*. Melbourne.

Clements-Hunt, P., & Gary P. (2007). *Responsible Property Investing—What the Leaders Are Doing*, UNEP Finance Initiative.

Cucuzzella, C. (2009). The Limits of Current Evaluation Methods in a Context of Sustainable Design: Prudence as a New Framework. *IJDE International Journal of Design Engineering, 2*(3), 243–261.

Cucuzzella, C. (2011). Why Is Fourth Generation Evaluation Essential for Sustainable Design? *Design Principles and Practices, 5*(1), 239–251. Retrieved from http://www.scopus.com/inward/record.url?eid=2-s2.0-84859534805&partnerID=40&md5=34ccbd8c8800b44e6759adb4546128fd

Cucuzzella, C. (2015a). Is Sustainability Reorienting the Visual Expression of Architecture? *Revue D'art Canadienne/Canadian Art Review (RACAR): Design Studies in Canada (and beyond), 40*, 85–99.

Cucuzzella, C. (2015b). When the Narrative of Environmental Certifications Replaces the Debate on Quality. In Fondation Braillard Architectes (Ed.), *Faire des histoires? Du récit d'urbanisme à l'urbanisme fictionnel: faire la ville à l'heure de la société du spectacle* (pp. 43–47). Geneve: Fondation Braillard Architectes.

Cucuzzella, C. (2016). Creativity, sustainable design and risk management. *Journal of Cleaner Production, 135*, 1548–1558.

Deloitte. (2014). *Breakthrough for Sustainability in Commercial Real Estate.* (S. Sheth & S. Mahajan, Eds.).

Deshmukh, A. P., Herber, D. R., & Allison, J. T. (2015). Bridging the Gap Between Open-Loop and Closed-Loop Control in Co-Design: A Framework for Complete Optimal Plant and Control Architecture Design*. *American Control Conference*, 4916–4922.

Ding, G. K. C. (2008). Sustainable Construction—The Role of Environmental Assessment Tools. *Journal of Environmental Management, 86*(3), 451–464.

DLA Piper. (2014). *Towards a Greener Future—DLA Piper's Market Report on Sustainable Real Estate.*

Ehrenfeld, J. R. (2009). *Sustainability by Design: A Subversive Strategy for Transforming Our Consumer Culture.* New Haven: Yale University Press.

Eichholtz, P., Kok, N., & Quigley, J. (2010). Doing Well by Doing Good? Green Office Buildings. *The American Economic Review, 100*(December), 2494–2511.

Eizenberg, E., & Jabareen, Y. (2017). *Social Sustainability: A New Conceptual Framework. Multidisciplinary Digital Publishing Institute. Sustainability, 2017*(9), 68.

Fadaei, S., Iulo, L. D., & Yoshida, J. (2015). Architecture: A Missing Piece in Real-estate Studies of Sustainable Houses. *Procedia Engineering, 118*, 813–818.

Fisher, T. (2008). *Architectural Design and Ethics: Tools for Survival.* Amsterdam and Boston and London: Elsevier/Architectural Press.

Fletcher, K. T., & Goggin, P. a. (2001). The Dominant Stances on Ecodesign: A Critique. *Design Issues, 17*(3), 15–25.

Fry, T. (2009). *Design Futuring: Sustainability, Ethics, and New Practice.* Oxford, NY: Berg.

G20. (2017). Hamburg Update: Taking Forward the G20 Action Plan on the 2030 Agenda for Sustainable Development. Retrieved July 16, 2017, from https://www.g20.org/Content/DE/_Anlagen/G7_G20/2017-g20-hamburg-upade-en.pdf?__blob=publicationFile&v=4

Gibberd, J. (2014). Measuring Capability for Sustainability: The Built Environment Sustainability Tool (BEST). *Building Research & Information, 3218*(July 2015), 1–13.

GlobalGiving. (2016). Sustainable Development Goals (SDGs). Retrieved December 8, 2016, from https://www.globalgiving.org/sdg/?rf=ggad_15&gclid=CjwKEAiAyanCBRDkiO6M_rDroH0SJAAfZ4KLmsnzfJBGVT_2ZbQtW3P7W9mSSvD4VOChoK-M-kyzyBoCrs3w_wcB

Hens, H. (2012). Passive Houses: What May Happen When Energy Efficiency Becomes the Only Paradigm? *ASHRAE Transactions, 118*(PART 1), 1077–1085.

Intergovernmental Panel on Climate Change (IPCC). (2007). *Climate Change 2007: Impacts, Adaptation and Vulnerability.* Cambridge: Cambridge University Press.

Intergovernmental Panel on Climate Change (IPCC). (2014). *Climate Change 2014: Mitigation of Climate Change. Working Group III Contribution to the Fifth Assessment Report of the Intergovernmental Panel on Climate Change.* https://doi.org/10.1017/CBO9781107415416

International Union for the Conservation for Nature and Natural Resources (IUCN). (1980). *World Conservation Strategy: Living Resource Conservation Through Sustainable Development.* Accessed July 16, 2017, from https://portals.iucn.org/library/efiles/documents/wcs-004.pdf

Jabareen, Y. R. (2006). *Sustainable Urban Forms Their Typologies, Models, and Concepts. J. Plan. Educ. Res., 2006*(26), 38–52.

Jonas, H. (1979). Toward a Philosophy of Technology. *The Hastings Center Report, 9*(1), 34–43.

Lawrence, M. (2015). Reducing the Environmental Impact of Construction by Using Renewable Materials. *Journal of Renewable Materials, 3*(3), 163–174.

LLNL. (2014). Energy Flow Charts. Retrieved December 11, 2015, from https://flowcharts.llnl.gov/

Lynch, A. J., & Mosbah, S. M. (2017). Improving Local Measures of Sustainability: A Study of Built-Environment Indicators in the United States. *Cities, 60*, 301–313.

Madge, P. (2008). Ecological Design. A New Critique. *Design Issues, 13*(2), 44–54. Retrieved from http://books.google.se/books?id=876Vc6CAgRwC

Matisoff, D., Noonan, D., & Flowers, M. (2016). *Policy Monitor—Green Buildings: Economics and Policies. Rev Environ Econ Policy (2016), 10*(2), 329–346.

McDonough, W., & Braungart, M. (2002). *Cradle to Cradle: Remaking the Way We Make Things.* New York: North Point Press.

McLennan, J. F. (2004). *The Philosophy of Sustainable Design: The Future of Architecture.* Kansas City: Ecotone. Retrieved from http://www.google.com/books?id=-Qjadh_0IeMC

Meadows, D. H., Meadows, D. J., Randers, J., & Behrens III, W. W. (1972). *Limits to Growth.* Accessed July 16, 2017, from http://www.donellameadows.org/wp-content/userfiles/Limits-to-Growth-digital-scan-version.pdf

Morrow, D., Read-Brown, A., O'Sullivan, N., & Garz, H. (2015). *Real Estate: Two Steps Forward, One Step Back.* Sector Report. Sustainalytics. Thematic Research. September.

Naess, A. (1973). The Shallow and the Deep, Long-Range Ecology Movement. A Summary*. *Inquiry, 16*(1–4), 95–100.

Nelson, H. G., & Stolterman, E. (2012). *The Design Way: Intentional Change in an Unpredictable World. The Design Way* (Vol. 9, 2nd ed.). Cambridge: The MIT Press.

Newsham, G. R., Mancini, S., & Birt, B. J. (2009). Do LEED-certified Buildings Save Energy? Yes, But.... *Energy and Buildings, 41*(8), 897–905.

Ofori, G. (1992). The Environment: The Fourth Construction Project Objective? *Construction Management and Economics.*

Orr, D. W. (2006). The Nature of Design: Ecology, Culture, and Human Intention. *Design Issues* (Vol. 22).

Papanek, V. (2000). The Tree of Knowledge: Biological Prototypes in Design. In *Design for the Real World: Human Ecology and Social Change* (pp. 186–214). Chicago: Academy Chicago Publishers.

Putnik, G. D. (2009). Complexity Framework for Sustainability: An Analysis of Five Papers. *The Learning Organization, 16*(3), 261–270.

Qian, Q. K., Chan, E. H. W., Visscher, H., & Lehmann, S. (2015). Modeling the Green Building (GB) Investment Decisions of Developers and End-users with Transaction Costs (TCs) Considerations. *Journal of Cleaner Production, 109*(0), 315–325.

Rashid, A., Faiz, A., & Yusoff, S. (2015). A Review of Life Cycle Assessment Method for Building Industry. *Renewable and Sustainable Energy Reviews, 45*, 244–248.

Robert, K. W., Parris, T. M., & Leiserowitz, A. A. (2005). What Is Sustainable Development? Goals, Indicators, Values, and Practice. *Environment: Science and Policy for Sustainable Development, 47*(3), 8–21.

Robinson, J., Burch, S., Talwar, S., O'Shea, M., & Walsh, M. (2011). Envisioning Sustainability: Recent Progress in the Use of Participatory Backcasting Approaches for Sustainability Research. *Technological Forecasting and Social Change, 78*(5), 756–768.

Sachs, J., Schmidt-Traub, G., Kroll, C., Durand-Delacre, D., & Teksoz, K. (2017). *SDG Index and Dashboards Report 2017.* New York: Bertelsmann Stiftung and Sustainable Development Solutions Network (SDSN).

Shaw, A., Sheppard, S., Burch, S., Flanders, D., Wiek, A., Carmichael, J., ... Cohen, S. (2009). Making Local Futures Tangible-Synthesizing, Downscaling, and Visualizing Climate Change Scenarios for Participatory Capacity Building. *Global Environmental Change, 19*(4), 447–463.

Sheppard, S. R. J., Shaw, A., Flanders, D., Burch, S., Wiek, A., Carmichael, J., ... Cohen, S. (2011). Future Visioning of Local Climate Change: A Framework for Community Engagement and Planning with Scenarios and Visualisation. *Futures, 43*(4), 400–412.

Sterman, J. (2015). Stumbling Towards Sustainability. In R. Henderson, R. Gulati, & M. Tushman (Eds.), *Leading Sustainable Change* (pp. 50–80). Oxford: Oxford University Press.

Sustainable Cities Institute. (2013). Topics of Sustainability. Retrieved November 8, 2016, from http://www.sustainablecitiesinstitute.org/topics
Sustainable Development Solutions Network Thematic Group on Sustainable Cities. (2015). The Urban Opportunity: Enabling Transformative and Sustainable Development. Retrieved July 11, 2017, from https://sustainabledevelopment.un.org/content/documents/2579Final-052013-SDSN-TG09-The-Urban-Opportunity.pdf
Teo, M. M. M., & Loosemore, M. (2001). A Theory of Waste Behaviour in the Construction Industry. *Construction Management and Economics, 19*(7), 741–751.
The Impact. (2016). *Real Assets and Impact Investing: A Primer for Families.* May.
U.S. Green Building Council & Booz Allen Hamilton. (2009). *Green Jobs Study.* Washington, DC: U.S. Green Building Council.
Ulrich, R. S. (1984). *View Through a Window May Influence Recovery from Surgery. Science, 224*(4647), 420.
United Nations Conference on Environment & Development (UNCED). (1992). Agenda 21. Retrieved July 16, 2017, from https://sustainabledevelopment.un.org/content/documents/Agenda21.pdf
United Nations Environment Programme (UNEP). (2011). *Buildings: Investing in Energy and Resource Efficiency: Towards a Green Economy.* Retrieved July, 2017, from https://www.unep.org/greeneconomy/resources/green-economy-report
United Nations General Assembly (UNGA). (2015). Transforming Our World: The 2030 Agenda for Sustainable Development. Retrieved July 11, 2017, from http://www.un.org/ga/search/view_doc.asp?symbol=A/RES/70/1&Lang=E
United Nations Population Fund (UNFPA). (2017). *Urbanization Overview.* Retrieved July, 2017, from http://www.unfpa.org/urbanization
Walker, S. (2006). *Sustainable by Design: Exploration in Theory and Practice.* London: Earthscan publications. Retrieved from www.earthscan.co.uk
Wilbanks, T. J. (2007). Scale and Sustainability. *Climate Policy, 7*(4), 278–287.
Willmott Dixon. (2010). *Briefing Note 33: The Impacts of Construction and the Built Environment.*
World Bank. (2016). Poverty Overview. Retrieved July, 2017, from http://www.worldbank.org/en/topic/poverty/overview
World Economic Forum. (2016). *Environmental Sustainability Principles for the Real Estate Industry.* Cologny/Geneva. World Economic Forum (2016). *The World Is About to See an Unprecedented Demographic Shift.* Retrieved July 2017, from https://www.weforum.org/agenda/2016/05/the-world-is-about-to-see-an-unprecendented-demographic-shift?utm_content=buffer8e511&utm_medium=social&utm_source=facebook.com&utm_campaign=buffer
World Summit on Sustainable Development (WSSD). (2002). Plan of Implementation. Retrieved July 17, 2017, from http://www.un.org/esa/sustdev/documents/WSSD_POI_PD/English/WSSD_PlanImpl.pdf

PART I

Regulatory Approaches

CHAPTER 4

Public Regulatory Trends in Sustainable Real Estate

Pernille H. Christensen and Jeremy Gabe

1 Introduction

Over half the global population—more than 3.5 billion people—currently live in cities; by 2030, it is anticipated that proportion will grow to almost 60%. Despite occupying just 2% of the Earth's surface, cities account for 60–80% of the world's energy consumption, 70% of its waste and 75% of its carbon emissions (UN, 2015; Habitat III, 2017). In 2015, the UN General Assembly adopted the *2030 Agenda for Sustainable Development* and its 17 Sustainable Development Goals (SDGs) (UN, 2015). In total, 195 countries adopted the first ever universal, legally binding, global climate deal to limit global warming to well below 2 °C (UN, 2016), and this commitment was further strengthened at Habitat III in October 2016 with the adoption of the *New Urban Agenda* (*NUA*) (Habitat III, 2017). The *NUA* recognizes that "given cities' demographic trends and their

P. H. Christensen (✉)
University of Technology Sydney, Sydney, NSW, Australia
e-mail: Pernille.Christensen@uts.edu.au

J. Gabe
University of Auckland, Auckland, New Zealand
e-mail: j.gabe@auckland.ac.nz

T. Walker et al. (eds.), *Sustainable Real Estate*, Palgrave Studies in Sustainable Business In Association with Future Earth,
https://doi.org/10.1007/978-3-319-94565-1_4

central role in the global economy in the mitigation and adaptation efforts related to climate change and in the use of resources and ecosystems, the way they are planned, financed, developed, built, governed, and managed has a direct impact on sustainability and resilience well beyond the urban boundaries" (Habitat III, 2017, paragraph 63). To assist with the unprecedented challenges of urbanization, the *NUA* presents standards and principles for the planning, development, construction, management and improvement of urban areas in five main application domains: national urban policies, urban legislation and regulations, urban planning and design, local economy and municipal finance, and local implementation. Some of these are discussed in more detail in the following sections.

Each SDG set out in the *2030 Agenda for Sustainable Development* is supported by specific 'targets' to be achieved over the next 15 years, and distinct 'indicators' are associated with each target to ensure that all countries measure progress using comparable metrics. The 17 SDGs (Fig. 4.1), 169 targets and 231 indicators have been used as reference points in subsequent UN documents, as well as supporting policy documents issued by governments around the world, to ensure alignment of goals and metrics among the various strategy documents. Altogether, this system delivers a cross-disciplinary response to the rapidly changing features of our global

Fig. 4.1 The UN Sustainable Development Goals include 17 target areas, many of which directly relate to sustainable development

environment. Although the SDGs are not legally binding, signatory governments have committed to developing strategies to achieve each of the 17 SDGs and to monitor progress toward their implementation. However, the SDGs and targets cannot be achieved at the national level without also bringing regional and local policies and systems for planning and investment into line with national strategies. The inclusion of SDG 11 (*Make cities inclusive, safe, resilient and sustainable*) recognizes that cities will play an integral part in achieving national and global SDGs and targets. This is also recognized in the wording of the *NUA*'s acknowledgment that sustainable development must be a coordinated effort at the "global, regional, national, subnational and local levels, with the participation of all relevant actors" (Habitat III, 2017, paragraph 9). Urban areas (and the plans for them) are expected to deal with all the key global issues represented by the SDGs; thus it is assumed that cities are, and will remain, major contributors to the achievement of SDGs.

In this context, it is important to acknowledge the importance of the built environment in facilitating and planning for the adaptation and mitigation strategies which make up the sustainability and resilience strategies of many global cities. Planning and regulatory intervention are the public means of managing property development to ensure that the built environment is developed with the protection and enhancement of the public interest as a core consideration. The alternative would have been to simply allow market forces and private interests to determine how our cities grow. Planning and policy interventions can be created to accelerate or to inhibit property development. To be effective, planners and policymakers must therefore understand the nuances of the property development process, the risks and rewards that drive property developers and investors, and the impact that planning instruments have on the decision-making process of property developers and investors.

Worldwide, changes have been made at each of the power levels of planning to acknowledge and accommodate the need to create more sustainable urban areas. Depending on the jurisdiction, policymaking and practice implementation may be driven at the national, regional or local level, or at a combination of two or more of these tiers of administrative control.

The *NUA* provides a clear directive as to how its principles can assist public authorities in achieving sustainability outcomes:

> We will anchor the effective implementation of the *New Urban Agenda* in inclusive, implementable, and participatory urban policies, as appropriate, to mainstream sustainable urban and territorial development as part of integrated development strategies and plans, supported, as appropriate, by national, sub-national, and local, institutional and regulatory frameworks, ensuring that they are adequately linked to transparent and accountable finance mechanisms. (Habitat III, 2017, paragraph 83)

In recent decades, national priorities have been established to combat environmental degradation caused by the depletion of natural resources, pollution, global warming and urban sprawl, each of which is associated with population growth. Businesses are increasingly concerned with the social, environmental and economic impacts of these phenomena and, as a result, corporate social responsibility statements are becoming a major factor in the selection of leased space (Christensen, 2012, 2017). With varying degrees of success, the United Kingdom and China have sought to combat sprawl by implementing green belts as a containment strategy (Amati & Yokohari, 2006; Zhao, 2011), although this process has not been without challenges (Amati, 2008). Smart growth, compact cities, new urbanism and liveable communities have also emerged as potential alternative policy solutions to sprawl.

While many cities are grappling with the challenges associated with population growth, other cities are struggling to resolve the opposite problem. Among the impacts of the 2007–2011 global financial crisis (GFC), urban 'shrinkage' has forced some cities to address economic and demographic decline as they struggle to compete for domestic and international capital. Research by Audirac, Fol, and Martinez-Fernandez (2010) discusses the social and economic inefficacy of traditional growth strategies and calls for innovative solutions to address the pressures of depopulation. For some shrinking cities, such solutions have come in the form of increased community engagement and a renewed focus on green buildings and infrastructure (Schilling & Logan, 2008).

Planning strategies to address such urban challenges associated with both under- and overpopulation may take the form of development plans, controls (e.g. form- and performance-based codes) or incentives encouraging sustainable property development (e.g. streamlined approval for 'green' property development). Discussions have begun to emerge about how these strategies contribute to a city's economic viability, level of sustainability and sense of 'place'. It is important to note that 'green', 'environmental' and 'sustainable' are often used interchangeably within planning strategies and instruments.

Within the SDG framework, *Goal 11* includes the following two targets: (1) to 'adopt disaster risk and climate change and adaptation measures' and (2) to 'minimize environmental impact'. Both of these can be specifically addressed, at least in part, through increased green and sustainable property development. This chapter discusses strategic planning, development controls and incentives utilized by planners to encourage increased sustainable property development, and it offers global examples of how some of these strategies have been implemented. However, it should be noted that the relationship between strategic planning, development controls and incentives on the one hand, and sustainable development on the other, is too broad in scope to be examined in detail in a single chapter. Therefore, this chapter focuses on strategies, policies and incentives that have demonstrated an impact on sustainable property development.

2 Strategic Planning, Development Controls and Incentives

Development planning and control functions of a planning system are empowered via legislation (Gurran, 2011). The power structure in a planning system can be assigned by means of a top-down or bottom-up approach. For example, the United Kingdom outlines planning policy at the national level and then assigns responsibility to the local planning authorities for enforcing the planning itself and for developing assessment policies. In contrast, Australia and the United States both limit federal involvement in planning and policy development. Instead, sub-national states are responsible for enacting legislation related to land-use planning and local governments are responsible for the detailed work related to preparing plans and assessing property developments. Interestingly, the actual development application process varies only slightly between these three countries despite variations in the level at which their planning processes are implemented (Christensen & Sayce, 2015), see Fig. 4.2.

The *NUA* and the *International Guidelines on Urban and Territorial Planning*, adopted by the Governing Council of UN-Habitat in April 2015, suggest that a nested hierarchy of state-led, regulation-driven, spatial plans—that include plans at the national, regional and local scales—

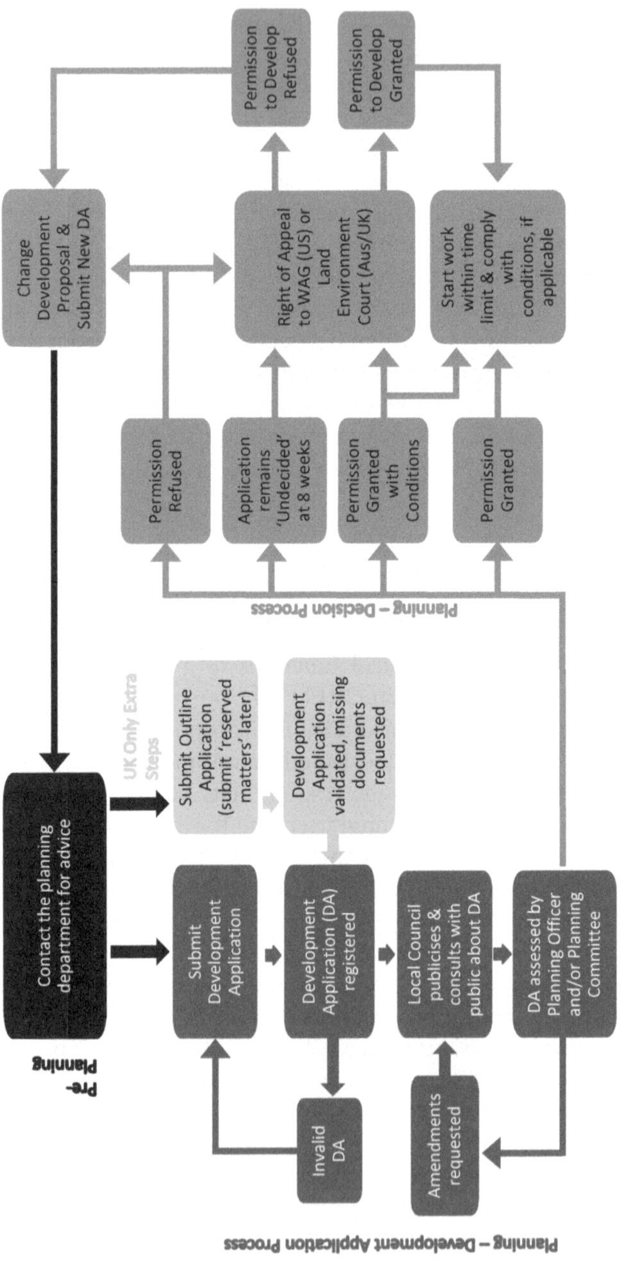

Fig. 4.2 Typical planning process for development applications in the United States, United Kingdom and Australia

should be implemented. Regardless of the power structure, the goal of city and regional planning is to balance the desires of individuals with the best interests of society, not only for the present day but also for future generations. This means that strategic planning and development processes need to control negative externalities (i.e. external costs, management of public/quasi-public goods and distributional injustice) and promote positive externalities (e.g. regenerative development); neither of these is effectively accounted for in inefficient property development markets. The *NUA* suggests that regulatory frameworks should clearly outline and define their expectations for sustainable development:

> We will promote the development of adequate and enforceable regulations in the housing sector, including, as applicable, resilient building codes, standards, development permits, land use by-laws and ordinances, and planning regulations … ensuring sustainability, quality, affordability, health, safety, accessibility, energy and resource efficiency, and resilience. (Habitat III, 2017, paragraph 111)

The very nature of planning means that there will be differences between geographic regions and countries. However, the *NUA* offers direction on the overarching principles, providing common threads among countries. With varying degrees of success, many planning systems have sought to encourage desirable development by offering statute and policy guidance notes to assist local developers in achieving sustainable development outcomes. Three main instruments enable planning authorities to influence the development process are:

1. Forward planning: strategic objectives and policies to achieve them
2. Development control or management: government ordinances, codes and permit requirements that constrain the private use of land and natural resources, so that they conform to public policies
3. Development incentives: an array of benefits designed to encourage sustainable development

Some countries and localities may place greater emphasis on the use of one of these instruments over the use of others. Although strategic planning and development control/management should, in theory, be complementary, in practice there is often a greater emphasis placed on the latter. This may be because many planning authorities have limited resources or expertise to support effective strategic planning and this, in turn, often results in incomplete policy frameworks. The limited attention to strategic planning may also reflect the fact that final decision-making for development applications is often delegated to elected (and therefore politically driven) lay committee members rather than planning professionals who are more likely to be driven by long-term outcomes. In either case, it could be argued that the lack of emphasis on strategic planning is the cause of some of the urban sustainability challenges that many global cities face today.

A planning system is intended to manage land use in such a way as to protect the public interest. It does this by requiring all developments to obtain development approval before a project can proceed. Ideally, decisions on individual applications should be made in the context of mid- to long-term strategic development plans, development controls, written government policy/advice, previous decisions and the development application itself. However, in an effort to streamline the process, developers often engage planning consultants to advise them on negotiation prior to the application being made. As a result, planning is sometimes referred to as a 'negotiated process' in which the process of consultation, often including both community groups and reports from a wide variety of experts, influences the final decision.

Some planning authorities argue that stringent development plans and controls cannot be justified in areas of economic decline (Hall, 2011). However, Hall suggests that planning authorities in such areas should implement policies that incentivize developers to pursue high design standards because such projects are often more profitable. Without strategic planning and development controls, cities would likely see even more extensive urbanization of the rural/urban edge and there would be less land dedicated to community infrastructure, such as open spaces. Furthermore, high-quality developments can add value by promoting regeneration in the community. Thus, Hall notes that "Reluctance on behalf of both parties to pursue higher standards is more in the mind than in the pocket" (Hall, 2011, pp. 90–91). A regulatory strategy that incorporates a directive and guidance for developers is therefore essential for ensuring sustainable development and high design standards as well as for effectively balancing the resultant externalities.

2.1 Forward Planning Strategies

Strategic planning provides the context for development control decisions by detailing mid- and long-term guiding principles, most commonly detailed in a comprehensive plan, and the *NUA* framework offers a critical link between global goals (SDGs) and local action. These principles guide local planning authorities in the development of specific controls for land-use management, spatial planning, environmental and other development issues. For example, local planning authorities may use strategic planning to designate (1) areas targeted for development (e.g. allowing some development uses/scales in a central business district (CBD) but not in a residential one), (2) areas where they would like to encourage development (e.g. by identifying land for specific uses in some areas) and (3) areas where development is discouraged (e.g. by identifying park space).

An integrated, long-term approach to addressing development is not new to city and regional strategic planning practice. A successful, comprehensive plan also incorporates strategies for conserving resources, such as energy (e.g. by offering guidance for efficient transportation planning) and water (e.g. by devising efficient flood and storm water management guidelines). It also considers present and future housing needs and protects health and the environment (e.g. through comprehensive planning of utilities). Furthermore, it does all of this while identifying potential areas for future growth and development. In short, strategic planning helps landowners, developers and investors better understand what type of property development is likely to be accepted.

Saha and Paterson (2008) noted that a small number of American cities had made strong commitments to sustainability by integrating sustainability goals into long-term, comprehensive forward planning documents; however, many more cities had adopted only specific aspects of sustainability (e.g. energy conservation measures, green building programs or affordable housing targets). Furthermore, we note that initiatives related to energy use and conservation are not yet being widely incorporated into zoning ordinances even though many cities identify reduction in carbon emissions as one of their main targets. Although some cities have set minimum energy performance targets for buildings in which they are occupants (to be discussed in the procurement section, below), attempts to address energy issues more broadly by adopting green building technology and renewable energy use by city government are yet to gain ground (Jepson Jr. & Haines, 2014; Saha & Paterson, 2008).

2.1.1 *Comprehensive Planning*

A comprehensive plan can be considered a 'blueprint' for the future. A vision statement should be the foundation of the plan, outlining where the municipality perceives itself to be at present and how it wishes to evolve in the future. This statement should be supported by strategic priorities, objectives, actions and targets, as well as project ideas which translate the vision into reality. It is essential for a city to involve stakeholders (residents, businesses and other government entities) throughout the process to ensure that the comprehensive plan represents the vision of the entire community. Having a system to manage performance data related to various objectives and initiatives to track progress, communicate internally, and maintain alignment between goals, actions and progress is essential for the successful implementation of a strategic plan. The City of Durham, North Carolina, offers an excellent example of how attention to performance measurement and monitoring can help the city align its spending and activities with strategic priorities.[1]

As an example, the *Sustainable Sydney 2030 Plan*[2] outlines the community vision of making Sydney "as green, global and connected as possible by 2030" with the aim of transforming "the way [people] live, work and play". Ten strategic directions were created to provide a framework for action; two of these directions specifically relate to sustainable development practices and the development of 'green' buildings. The first targets sustainable development, renewal and design. The second focuses on becoming a leading environmental performer by striving toward the following six objectives, each of which includes supporting actions, targets and initiatives:

- Increase the capacity for local energy generation and water supply within the boundaries of Sydney.
- Reduce waste generation and stormwater pollutants to the catchment area.
- Improve the environmental performance of existing buildings.
- Demonstrate leadership in environmental performance through City operations and activities.

[1] For more information on the Durham Strategic plan, performance measurement and reporting, see: www.clearpointstrategy.com/wp-content/uploads/2016/04/City-of-Durham.pdf.

[2] For more information about the *Sustainable Sydney 2030 Plan*, see: www.cityofsydney.nsw.gov.au/vision/towards-2030.

- In addition to previous steps focusing on reducing and offsetting City greenhouse gas emissions, the City aims to cut emissions at the source.
- Cut carbon dioxide emissions that come from the City's properties in half.

Further evidence of Sydney's commitment to sustainable development is the establishment of the Greater Sydney Commission (GSC) in 2016. The purpose of the GSC is to coordinate the planning that will shape the future of Greater Sydney. It should be noted that one of the GSC's priorities is to "consider and integrate the 2015 Sustainable Development Goals (SDGs) recently adopted by Australia as a member of the United Nations (UN)".[3]

Berke and Conroy (2000) set out six principles of operational performance for sustainability by which comprehensive plans can be evaluated to determine how well they support sustainable development. These principles comprise harmony with nature, liveable built environments, place-based economy, equity, polluters pay and responsible regionalism. The first four principles address the long-term ability of a community to sustain healthy local social, economic and ecological systems, while the latter two link local to global concerns and reflect each community's broader obligation to others. A balanced comprehensive plan would have each of the six principles equally represented. In their analysis of 30 comprehensive plans across the United States, the authors found a diversity of approaches to advancing sustainability. Jacksonville, Florida's comprehensive plan received the highest score even though the plan does not specifically address the sustainable development principles. Instead, the six principles are advanced on a piecemeal basis, with separate plan elements each focused on achieving one or two principles. In contrast, another high scoring city—Portland, Oregon—balanced multiple principles by weaving policies from all plan elements and using sustainable development principles to create an overarching, integrated strategy. The authors concluded that whether the sustainable development concept was, or was not, explicitly integrated into the plan had limited impact on how well the plan was judged to promote sustainability. It should be noted, however, that this research was conducted in 2000 and that sustainability has become more mainstream over the last

[3] For more information about the Ministerial Statement of Priorities for the Greater Sydney Commission, January 2016, go to: https://gsc-public-1.s3.amazonaws.com/s3fs-public/2016_-_2018_ministerial_statement_of_priorities_for_the_greater_sydney_commission.pdf.

decade. As a consequence, sustainability may have become more integrated into comprehensive planning during this time.

The emergence of the 100 Resilient Cities program, created in 2013 by the Rockefeller Foundation to catalyze an urban resilience movement, represents a further evolution of the sustainable development concept. The program sets out seven qualities that will help cities to withstand, respond to and adapt more readily to shock events and long-term stresses. These qualities are:

1. Being reflective and using past experience to inform future decisions.
2. Being resourceful and recognizing alternative ways to use resources.
3. Being robust and using well-conceived, constructed and managed systems.
4. Maintaining redundancy, with spare capacity purposively created to accommodate disruption.
5. Being flexible, with a willingness and ability to adopt alternative strategies in response to changing circumstances.
6. Adopting an inclusive approach, prioritizing broad consultation to create a sense of shared ownership in decision-making.
7. Adopting an integrated approach, bringing together a range of distinct systems and institutions.

The aim of the program is to "ensure cities around the globe are better able to manage disruptions and plan for the future, so that people are safer, healthier, and have increased livelihood options".[4] 100 Cities around the world are now using this framework to guide their comprehensive planning efforts. In summary, comprehensive plans aimed at sustainable development should create a vision for long-term sustainable growth, prevent future development conflicts and ensure that the social, economic and environmental goals of the city are balanced.

2.2 Development Controls

Control of land use is necessary because individual land owners may wish to develop their land in a manner that does not align with the needs or aspirations of the broader community as outlined in the comprehensive

[4] For more information about the 100 Resilient Cities program and participating cities, visit: http://www.100resilientcities.org/.

plan. Development controls restrict the private use of land and natural resources to conform to public policies. There are several types of land-use regulations including, among others: zoning, building codes, subdivision regulations, curve-cut permit systems, historic preservation laws and tree-cutting laws. Of these, the two primary strategies used to control development are zoning and building codes, which are discussed in more detail below. Controls can be created for (1) multiple locations and scales (e.g. suburb, street or single lot), (2) various types of development (e.g. residential, commercial or industrial), (3) differing purposes of the development (e.g. provision of car parking, stormwater control), (4) diverse building design features (e.g. in terms of scale and appearance) and (5) a range of urban design principles (e.g. setbacks and sidewalks).

Development controls are administrative mechanisms which guide planning authorities in the assessment of development proposals. They can be used by the planning authorities to uphold a development proposal, reject a proposal or allow an exception to the controls if the development offers other tangible or intangible benefits to the community. Landowners, developers and investors may also use local development controls to challenge the strategies and principles of the local development plan in the application of an exception. In some countries, planning agreements can be made to offset the perceived externalities of a development. For example, in the United Kingdom, a community infrastructure levy (a local taxation measure) can be applied to offset a development's perceived negative externalities, such as increased traffic congestion, or to support the creation positive externalities, such as the provision of other community facilities off-site. These agreements can be beneficial to communities with tight public spending budgets because they ensure that the external costs of the development are, at least partly, carried by those who are most likely to benefit financially from the development. In this way, planning authorities can help balance economic gains and the achievement of social goals against the potential environmental costs.

2.2.1 *Prescriptive Zoning*

Zoning ordinances are the most widely used land-use regulation instrument and serve essentially as a means of implementing an authority's forward planning strategies. They commonly include a written description of requirements and standards related to the use of land, as well as a zoning map (a color-coded diagram of the existing zoning classifications: single-family residential, multiunit, mixed-use, agricultural, commercial and industrial). The written portion of the zoning ordinance generally includes the classifications of permitted uses for the different geographic ‘zones’ of land. It will also: describe restrictions, such as lot sizes, setbacks, density and height limitations; set style and design requirements for structures; identify requirements related to the protection of natural resources; outline the procedure for allowing nonconforming uses and for granting variances, amendments and hearing appeals; and explain the penalties for zoning violations.

Traditional zoning regulations in the United States focus on land use and development capacity, primarily with the aim of reducing potential adverse impacts of development to an acceptable level. Critics argue that traditional zoning ordinances contribute to sprawl, increase dependence on automobiles and have a limited impact on the achievement of important objectives, such as sustainable design (Ewing, Bartholomew, Winkelman, Walters, & Chen, 2007; Talen, 2013). Jepson and Haines (Jepson Jr. & Haines, 2014) studied 32 zoning ordinances across the United States and concluded that zoning can be an important tool for promoting sustainable development but also noted a substantial variation in the presence of regulatory measures related to sustainability in their sample. Some alternatives to conventional zoning approaches that aim to increase flexibility for developers and promote sustainable property development include cluster zoning, incentive zoning, inclusionary zoning and overlay zoning.

Cluster zoning is an example of a prescriptive smart growth code. It can be used to preserve open space while increasing density by reducing minimum lot size requirements (Talen, 2013). Also called conservation-oriented development, this mechanism allows the development of homes to be clustered more densely onto one or more individual lots because the density requirements are applied to a large area rather than on a lot-by-lot basis. As long as the overall density requirements for the entire area are met, the developer has greater flexibility when designing the site and locating structures within it. One advantage of allowing concentrated, higher density development is the ability to include smaller, lower-cost housing units and thereby offer a range of housing choices for the diversity of residents that typically comprise a community. The remaining land can then be preserved for public and community uses such as parks, nature/jogging/walking trails, green space, active recreation and community gardens.

Allen, Moorman, Peterson, Hess, and Moore (2012) found that planners perceived that cluster/conservation-oriented development protects natural resources, wildlife habitats and farmland to a greater extent than compact development. Through the use of master planning strategies, such as the clustering of residences and infrastructure on the site to minimize the impact of the development, applying best management practices for rainwater capture and stormwater runoff, and requiring energy-efficient building design, developers in cluster-zoned areas can create development projects that have less of an impact on the environment (Dunham-Jones & Williamson, 2011; Randolph, 2011). Göçmen and LaGro (2016) note that planners and decision-makers, particularly those less familiar with sustainable development, may perceive conservation-oriented development to be more tangible than compact development and other smart growth approaches.

Incentive zoning is a tool that enables developers to develop land in a manner that would not normally be permitted in exchange for providing a public benefit (e.g. a public square, streetscape or park; senior or affordable housing) that the developer would not otherwise have been required to provide. In exchange for the community benefit, developers may receive greater flexibility in relation to required building setbacks, floor heights, floor area ratio, parking requirements or density. Although incentives vary by city, governments commonly calculate the incentive(s) in such a way as to balance the public benefit with the developer's costs and gains.

Local governments have used incentive zoning to accomplish a wide range of goals, including historic preservation, economic development and conservation. Chicago first used incentive zoning in 1957 to stimulate skyscraper construction in its downtown area (Costonis, 1972; Schwieterman & Caspall, 2006). More recently, the City of Seattle offered increased floor area for projects that either (1) include affordable housing or other public amenities (such as a daycare center, open space, green street improvements or on-site amenities) or (2) use a transfer of development rights (TDR) to protect historic structures, create open space or protect regional farms and forests. To receive the incentive, developers must also meet certain minimum requirements. Although these requirements vary by zoning classification, they generally include a green building certification (e.g. Leadership in Energy and Environmental Design (LEED)) and the creation of a Transportation Management Plan.[5] New York City offers height density bonuses (a greater number of floors

[5] More information can be found at: www.seattle.gov/dpd/cs/groups/pan/@pan/documents/web_informational/s048509.pdf.

in a high-rise building) in exchange for the provision of public plazas (privately-owned public spaces), visual or performing arts spaces, subway improvements, theater preservation, FRESH food stores and affordable housing.[6] The American Planning Association notes that communities with a high demand for land and well-established planning regulations that are in need of specific public amenities or types of development are in the best position to benefit from incentive zoning. They warn, however, that communities considering incentive zoning need also to consider the potential hidden costs associated with every project, including long-term costs such as infrastructure challenges and congestion.[7]

Inclusionary zoning is similar to incentive zoning, but this strategy focuses more on generating social benefits, such as creating greater housing options for specified categories of residents within the community. In contrast to incentive zoning, inclusionary zoning *requires* developers to generate the required social benefit, but many cities also offer offsets to balance the generation of the positive externality. Offsets for including a certain percentage of affordable family housing units, senior housing units and/or multiunit housing within a particular development project or land area vary by city, but they may include expedited granting of permits, fee waivers, tax abatements, modified development standards, density bonuses (typically height increases) or reduced parking requirements. As of January 2018, nearly 500 municipalities in the United States have adopted inclusionary zoning regulations, with California and New Jersey accounting for almost two-thirds of the programs.

The requirements of inclusionary zoning programs vary. For example, in Boston, 13% of the units in new buildings must be offered at rents which are affordable to a household earning 70% of the median income in the area.[8] New York City requires 20% of the units to be affordable to families on 80% of the area's median income.[9] Some cities allow developers to pay a comparable fee in lieu of providing subsidized units in their

[6] More information can be found at: https://www1.nyc.gov/site/planning/zoning/glossary.page.

[7] More information can be found at: www.planning.org/divisions/planningandlaw/propertytopics.htm.

[8] The Executive Order by Mayor Martin J. Walsh on December 9, 2015 can be found at: https://www.cityofboston.gov/news/uploads/2868_55_10_12.pdf. Additional explanation can be found at: https://www.cityofboston.gov/news/Default.aspx?id=20463.

[9] More information about the New York City's Inclusionary Housing Program can be found at: http://www.nyc.gov/html/ia/gprb/downloads/pdf/NYC_Planning_InclusionaryZoning.

buildings (Porter & Davison, 2009) with the money used to fund affordable housing projects elsewhere in the city. Lens and Monkkonen (2015) note that inclusionary zoning is more likely to reduce income segregation than strategies that aim to bring higher-income households into lower-income parts of the city. This view is supported by Jacobus (2015) who argues that inclusionary zoning is one of the few proven regulatory strategies resulting in affordable housing being integrated into higher-income neighborhoods—and he notes that it has additional positive benefits such as access to quality schools, public services and better jobs. If the development incentive is offered in the form of extra density, inclusionary zoning can also contribute to creating more sustainable urban development that is compact and walkable. However, critics of inclusionary zoning argue that it imposes costs that are not sufficiently offset and can therefore suppress homebuilding. This in turn has the potential to limit housing choices, inflate home prices, accelerate the displacement of working families, erect walls to opportunity and inclusion, and forestall both density and affordability. Jacobus (2015) offers an excellent discussion of the benefits and challenges of implementing successful inclusionary zoning programs.

Overlay zoning (also known as overlay districts) is applied over one or more previously established zoning districts to establish additional requirements to those currently in place in the district(s). Regulations or incentives are often attached to the overlay district to protect unique features in the community (e.g. historic buildings, wetlands, steep slopes and waterfronts) or to promote stricter standards and criteria for specific types of development project, such as mixed-used developments, waterfront developments, housing along transit corridors or affordable housing. Overlay districts can be very effective, politically viable regulatory tools because they are created specifically for a given district to meet its unique community goals. For example, Cleveland, Ohio, created a Live-Work Overlay District to encourage the re-use of older, underutilized industrial buildings for a combination of living and working space, even in industrial districts that otherwise prohibit residential use. In addition to revitalizing an underused area of town, the overlay district contributes to the City's goal of reducing carbon emissions by encouraging the re-use of existing buildings; this strategy requires less energy and resource usage than new con-

pdf and https://www1.nyc.gov/site/planning/zoning/districts-tools/affordable-housing-production-in-ih.page.

struction.[10] The Town of Empire, Wisconsin, created a Critical Areas Overlay (CAO) District to preserve the unique and valuable geologic and natural resources in the area and to minimize development in other areas that were difficult to develop safely or that were prone to unwanted soil erosion or groundwater contamination.[11]

2.2.2 *Performance-Based Zoning*

As an alternative to the conventional (prescriptive) zoning methods, performance standards regulate development by establishing goals for the *outcome* of the development rather than regulating how those goals are achieved. For example, rather than restricting a property's specific uses, the regulator allows any use, provided the development achieves a defined set of performance requirements. These requirements relate to the same outcomes as traditional zoning ordinances (e.g. environmental protection, neighborhood character, traffic control). The difference is that the developer has greater flexibility in deciding how those goals are to be met and can develop the property in any way that meets the set standard. Cities adopting this strategy argue that it enables them to codify values and goals without restricting *how* those goals are achieved, which can in turn create neighborhoods with a richer and more diverse character. Critics of performance-based zoning argue that its flexibility makes it challenging and expensive to enforce, which could result in substandard design or permit uses that are incompatible with surrounding structures. Although performance-based zoning (and other regulations) can be politically difficult to adopt for this reason, an increasing number of cities in the United States and internationally are integrating this particular type of zoning system into their regulatory processes. They do this because performance-based systems encourage more innovative solutions and enable developers to meet the goals of the city while achieving higher levels of sustainability than conventional zoning would have allowed. Prescriptive and performance-based zoning and other supporting ordinances typically exist simultaneously, allowing designers to choose a preferred compliance pathway. One example is Queensland's

[10] A more in-depth discussion of Cleveland's efforts related to amending their zoning code to promote sustainable development can be found at: http://planning.city.cleveland.oh.us/cwp/sus_oview.php.

[11] The Town of Empire, Wisconsin Zoning Ordinance can be reviewed at: http://www.fdlco.wi.gov/home/showdocument?id=6525.

Sustainable Planning Act 2009,[12] which allows developers to choose between a traditional 'code assessable' track or an alternative 'impact assessable' option. The latter is a potentially more flexible approach requiring more interpretive, performance-based criteria to be met.

An example of how flexibility in performance-based zoning can inspire green building is the collaboration between the Bullitt Center and the City of Seattle. During the pre-construction planning stages, concern arose about whether the owner's building performance goals were feasible. Many of the proposed design and sustainability features had legal or code-related hurdles that needed to be overcome; these included the legality of solar panels that overhang public sidewalks, the consumption of rainwater, graywater infiltration in an urban bioswale, and the use of composting toilets in commercial buildings.[13] The Bullitt Foundation worked with the City of Seattle's Planning Department and other agencies to relax some of the prescriptive standards in exchange for meeting negotiated performance-based standards. Through this collaboration, the Bullitt Center was able to achieve a full Living Building Challenge certification in 2015 and has been regarded as the 'world's greenest commercial' building.[14] This achievement was only possible because the City of Seattle created an alternative compliance pathway, the Living Building and 2030 Challenge pilot programs, which allowed for specific departures from code requirements to encourage the development of more sustainable buildings. The pilot programs have now been fully integrated into Seattle's Design Guidelines, which state that "in contrast to the very specific regulations of the City's Land Use Code (Title 23 Seattle Municipal Code), the Seattle Design Guidelines set the stage for flexibility and dialogue during project review. An applicant may be granted a departure from the Land Use Code by demonstrating that the alternate design solution better meets the intent of the design guidelines" (City of Seattle, 2013, p. iv).

[12] More information can be found at: www.dilgp.qld.gov.au/planning/framework/previous/sustainable-planning-act-2009.html.

[13] An Urban Land Institute (ULI) case study with additional details can be found at: casestudies.uli.org/bullitt-center/#planning.

[14] The Bullitt Center Achieves Full Living Building Challenge Petal Certification! Published June 26, 2015 at: http://www.bullitt.org/2015/06/26/the-bullitt-center-achieves-full-living-building-challenge-petal-certification/.

2.2.3 *Prescriptive Versus Performance-Based Building Codes*

In this chapter, the discussion up until this point has been primarily focused on the task of planning at a neighborhood, city or regional level. This section focuses on the importance of regulations at the level of the building, explaining how these are important to achieving larger scale outcomes.

Building codes, which may refer to prescriptive specification criteria or to performance outcomes required of all new construction or major renovations, traditionally served to regulate structural safety and fire safety. From a planning perspective, building codes also mitigate negative external costs. This is particularly evident with fire safety, as fires commonly spread and thus affect outcomes at larger scales. However, from a more modern perspective, building codes may also contribute to the achievement of social and environmental objectives. The most common example of this in the sustainability context is the use of 'energy codes', which are building codes designed to influence the energy efficiency of a building (Jacobsen & Kotchen, 2013). The *NUA* offers a guiding principle to ensure that public authorities focus on the performance of assets to promote sustainable development in their community:

> We recognize that urban form, infrastructure, and building design are among the greatest drivers of cost and resource efficiencies, through the benefits of economy of scale and agglomeration, and fostering energy efficiency, renewable energy, resilience, productivity, environmental protection, and sustainable growth in the urban economy. (Habitat III, 2017, paragraph 44)

In common with planning instruments such as zoning regulations, building codes take two forms: prescriptive and performance based. Prescriptive codes mandate a design specification. For example, in an energy efficiency-seeking building code, this could be a minimum insulation rating for a floor, wall or ceiling construction. Performance-based building codes attempt to specify the outcome rather than a particular design or technique. In this scenario, an energy efficiency-seeking performance code could require a maximum energy-use intensity for space heating. As noted with zoning ordinances, prescriptive and performance-based building codes typically exist simultaneously and permit designers to choose their preferred compliance pathway.

This choice is ultimately a trade-off between expediency and flexibility. Because they are easy to audit, prescriptive pathways reduce regulatory risk and are preferred by those wishing to build as quickly as possible, such as speculative or residential developers. Performance-based building codes allow designers to bypass the rigidity inherent in a prescriptive solution and are preferred by those engaging in innovative or bespoke designs. But the cost of bypassing the rigidity is additional time and costs associated with proving to an assessor that the design meets the required performance outcome.

Armstrong, Wright, Ashea, and Nielsen (2017) note that although Australia has had compliance choice for 20 years, prescriptive compliance is a more popular choice than performance-based compliance. The authors argue that this preference leads to societal losses through stifled innovation and they criticize industry 'mind-sets' for failing to use performance-based pathways. Furthermore, they explain that energy codes present a uniquely quantifiable outcome, and thus are best suited to performance-based compliance. The increased voluntary use of NABERS[15] energy ratings in the market over the past decade and adoption of recent NABERS disclosure requirements indicates that the industry and government have finally begun to make this shift. Indeed, for nearly half a century, most US states have used energy codes that rely exclusively on performance-based compliance pathways (Jacobsen & Kotchen, 2013).

However, innovation is also needed in the standards themselves. Energy is easily codified because it is easy to measure, but other dimensions of the SDGs such as health and well-being or biodiversity are more difficult to associate with building design choices or measurable performance requirements. Chapter 6 discusses the development of private green building codes such as LEED, BREEAM and Green Star, which are used around the world to label buildings as environmentally efficient. Since many environmental outcomes are not easily measured or simulated pre-occupancy at the building scale, private green building codes often rely on *prescriptive* design requirements for these dimensions. For example, alternative transportation requirements often involve specifying the location and number of bicycle parking facilities, while material sustainability requires specification of listed products. Nevertheless, most private green building codes adopt *performance*-based compliance where possible, such as specifying maximum water or energy consumption intensities.

The California Green Building Standards Code (2016) is one of the world's most progressive statutory building codes regarding sustainability

[15] NABERS (National Australian Built Environment Rating System) is a national rating system that measures the environmental performance of Australian buildings, tenancies, and homes in the areas of energy efficiency, water usage, waste management, and indoor environment quality to rate its impact on the environment.

objectives—and its design is strongly influenced by the private LEED building code. Early attempts at integrating LEED and other private sustainable building codes into statutory building codes simply involved equating the statutory code with a requirement to comply with a particular private label and labeling threshold (e.g. LEED Silver). However, legal experts argued that such practice amounted to an outsourcing of democratic governance to private industry (Schindler, 2010). In response, the State of California wrote the California Green Building Standards Code, which includes mandatory code requirements associated with the traditional scope of LEED (see Chap. 6), except for the energy efficiency category which was already regulated in the existing state energy code. Specifically, the state developed prescriptive code requirements for indoor air quality, stormwater management, alternative transport facilities, light pollution, waste management and commissioning of mechanical services. Interestingly, even in this progressive public green building code, most of the requirements are prescriptive, such as specifying the number and location of bicycle parking facilities. This reflects the argument of Armstrong et al. (2017) that it is challenging to measure most performance outcomes, such as the desired mode share of bicycle transport, particularly before a building is constructed. The California Green Building Standards Code also includes 'voluntary requirements'—these are more stringent prescriptive measures that local governments may opt to mandate within their jurisdiction.

The National Construction Code (NCC) of Australia has been a performance-based code since 1996. Similarly, the Building Code of Australia (BCA) shifted from a prescriptive- to a performance-based code in 1996. However, difficulties in quantifying performance requirements resulted in designers and practitioners lacking confidence in using some of the performance criteria (e.g. energy efficiency) and led to continued heavy reliance on prescriptive solutions (Armstrong et al., 2017). Although the uptake of a performance-based culture has seemed slow, even at times regressing to a prescriptive mind-set, a 2012 report by the Australian Building Codes Board estimated that the shift toward a performance-based approach has resulted a significant benefit to the economy. The report estimated that the economic benefit ranged between US$ 280 million–US$ 1.54 billion annually (giving a mid-point estimate of US$ 770 million) from the implementation of performance-based codes. The report also identified the potential for similar productivity gains through further increases in the use of performance solutions (CIE, 2012). Many local and state governments in Australia have also integrated environmental performance standards into local ordinances to encourage sustainable development in their regions. Rose and Manley note that "recent reforms in environmental standards/benchmarks have helped to encourage the uptake of innovative sustainable products, yet greater emphasis on environmental performance, mandatory sustainability standards, and performance-based regulations, is encouraged" (Rose & Manley, 2011, p. 9).

In addition to these reports and articles suggesting that performance-based regulations enable higher levels of sustainability to be achieved, a compelling argument in their favor is that the prescriptive requirements in existing codes have, to date, failed to deliver the building outcomes required by the UN SDGs. This implies that the innovation and flexibility allowed by performance-based compliance is required. Many local, state and federal governments, such as the City of Seattle (2013), the State of California (2016) and Australia (Armstrong et al., 2017) concur with this view and are seeking to expand the scope of current zoning and building codes to allow increased performance flexibility across the entire code. Jacobsen and Kotchen (2013) compiled empirical evidence that increasing the stringency of performance-based energy codes in Florida, while still allowing developers the flexibility of developing innovative solutions, resulted in homes with a statistically significant reduction in energy consumption. These examples of statutory integration of performance-based sustainable building codes could be forerunners of a future trend. As public and private green building codes grow in popularity and more clearly align themselves with strategic governance objectives, such as the UN SDGs reflected in local planning regulations, property developers will have ample guidance to achieve sustainable development outcomes.

2.3 Development Incentives

Development incentives may be the most effective tools that planning authorities can use to stimulate sustainable property development and investment within their communities. Incentives (such as the reduction in development contributions, tax giveaways, financial subsidies and the streamlining of approval processes) can be used to encourage development in certain areas within a city.

Despite the proven value of incentive schemes, local governments around the world have experienced cutbacks from federal governments and this has limited their ability to use federal aid to incentivize sustainable property development. Cities and councils have therefore had to develop alternative innovative strategies and incentives to attract and support sustainable development projects in their communities. Local incentive schemes are heavily relied upon; these may include tax increment financing, special assessment districts, tax abatements, land swaps, lease/purchase agreements, capital improvements and value-creating trade-offs based on zoning bonuses. There is also increasing use of public-private partnership agreements, where the local government absorbs some of the development risk in exchange for a direct financial stake in the project through participatory leases and/or profit-sharing agreements. Although profit-sharing revenues deliver only modest profits to the local community during the initial years, they can provide other non-financial benefits, such as political protection to city councils vulnerable to charges that they are giving away too much; by creating an agreement to share financial returns the city is signaling to stakeholders that it is acting responsibly and effectively (Christensen & Sayce, 2015).

There are two primary methods by which regulatory and financial incentives can promote sustainable property development: carrots and sticks. 'Carrots' are positive financial incentives to encourage positive externalities by the developer, that is, 'doing the right thing' and may include rebates and grants (e.g. the Photovoltaic Rebate Program and the Greenhouse Gas Abatement Grant, both in Australia), carbon credit trading (allowed by the Kyoto Protocol) or streamlining of the development application process (which generally results in quicker completion time and reduced holding costs) (Christensen & Sayce, 2015). Clark (2003) offers a thorough discussion of the various incentive programs available in Australia.

In contrast, 'sticks' are a means of imposing a penalty or constraint on the developer to prevent negative externalities and thereby promote sustainable property development. These may include local zoning and building codes, taxes and levies (e.g. landfill levies), mandated renewable energy certificates (e.g. the Australian *Renewable Energy Act 2000*) and/or slower processing times for development applications if projects do not include the desired sustainability outcomes.

Denis Hayes, President and CEO of the Bullitt Foundation, noted[16] that one of the primary concerns for property developers is time. Most speculative property developers aim to sell the property upon completion

[16] In a personal phone interview with the author on May 5, 2014.

and therefore do not have the benefit of the holding period to recoup additional costs associated with sustainable development through green lease agreements and capital gains. Furthermore, although market demands drive sustainable property development in some markets, this is not yet the case in all cities (and certainly not in rural areas). Hayes notes that 'time = money' for most developers, and that being able to process the development application more quickly is a significant incentive for many developers in Seattle.[17] He suggests that local planning authorities should focus on incentives that positively, or negatively, impact a developer's bottom line to promote more sustainable development. In addition to working with the City of Seattle to develop the Living Building Pilot program, the Bullitt Foundation also inspired two permit-based incentives to promote green property development:

- *Priority Green Expedited*: Available for all new construction projects, this scheme gives the developer faster building permit review and processing for projects that meet green building standards.
- *Priority Green Facilitated:* A streamlined permitting process for master use permits in exchange for meeting green building standards.[18]

Sayce, Ellison, and Parnell (2007) surveyed institutional investors, valuation surveyors, property developers and property-investing banks in the United Kingdom to gain a better understanding of the drivers of, and barriers to sustainable development, including the potential of financial incentives to stimulate market activity. Exemption from stamp duty land tax was the most popular incentive and was identified as easy to implement and potentially capable of having a significant impact on capital and rental values. Provision of a discount on non-domestic rates for sustainable buildings was also identified as a popular incentive with the potential to affect both capital and rental values; however, it was also seen as the most difficult to implement. Of all the incentive schemes, widening the scope of

[17] For information about other state and local government green building incentives and a discussion on how to determine which incentives best meet the needs of both local governments and property developers, see American Institute of Architects (AIA) and the National Association of Counties (NACo). *Local leaders in sustainability: Green building incentive trends—strengthening communities, building green economies.* The American Institute of Architects, 2012, at: www.aia.org/aiaucmp/groups/aia/documents/pdf/aiab093472.pdf.

[18] For more information go to: www.seattle.gov/dpd/permits/greenbuildingincentives/default.htm.

the capital allowance on energy-efficient plant and machinery was identified as the easiest to implement considered highly likely to be effective at encouraging change within the construction sector. However, its impact on capital and rental values was seen as minimal. Rose and Manley (2011) found that Australian local governments—in their various roles as clients, regulators and funders of education, training and research and development—have played a key role in increasing the adoption of sustainable products. However, the authors also noted that although the combination of regulatory and financial incentives was having a positive effect, there was scope for innovative financial incentives to promote sustainable development even further. Furthermore, additional investment into educational programs for project-based firms and client/end users about the benefits of innovative sustainability solutions could further improve the uptake of sustainable products.

3 Mandatory Disclosure and Integrated Reporting

As climate change has become an increasing concern for governments across the world, multiple studies have investigated how and where investment into carbon emission reduction can be optimized. The building and construction industry has emerged as a key sector which local governments have targeted for significant reductions in emissions. However, progress toward reduction targets using voluntary participation in control schemes has proven too slow in many countries. As a result, an increasing number of governments have developed mandatory certification and reporting schemes, which require either a certificate to be obtained or a standard to be met.

The United Kingdom is a good example of this trend. The United Kingdom has set legislative targets stating that CO_2 emissions from all buildings must be 'close to zero' by 2050. Since 2008, all buildings have been required to have an Energy Performance Certificate (EPC) issued prior to sale. Unfortunately, there has been no mandate as to the level that has to be achieved, as this is initially an awareness-raising exercise; hence, the impact of the EPC scheme has been minimal. However, beginning in 2018, changes in EPC regulation will focus on more stringent minimum energy efficiency standards (MEES) and it will become illegal to let or lease a residential or commercial property with a poor EPC rating. New MEES regulations will require all buildings to achieve an EPC rating of at least E (corresponding to at least 39 points on a scale extending to 100 = maximum energy efficiency) before granting a lease; this extends to both new leases and lease renewals and will apply to all privately rented non-domestic properties. The MEES regulation has the potential to significantly impact landlords who may find that some properties are no longer marketable without upgrading to meet the minimum standards (20–35% of existing properties are estimated to be in the F & G rating brackets and may be negatively impacted by the new regulation). The affected properties are also likely to suffer a reduction in their value. The government has indicated that the 'Green Deal' policy may offer a financial solution to assist with energy efficiency refurbishment and retrofit projects. A recent Colliers International report noted that one of the aims of the new regulation is to help overcome the traditional 'split incentive' barrier which applies to buildings where the landlord foots the bill for energy efficiency improvements that benefit the tenant.[19]

Another strategy that is increasingly being employed by local governments is the process of transforming a voluntary scheme (e.g. LEED or BREEAM) into a mandated requirement and integrating the requirement into the local planning controls. In the United Kingdom and the United States, it is an increasingly common condition of a planning consent that a development achieves some level of green certification. Many UK Councils require a BREEAM 'Very Good' rating as a minimum, and many local planning authorities increase this requirement to 'Excellent' for all new developments of government buildings. Similarly, many local governments in the United States require EnergyStar or LEED ratings for all new developments. As schemes become increasingly mandated and integrated with regulatory codes, it is likely that buildings previously seen as 'sustainable' when compared to other stock will become regarded as the norm.

Sustainability reporting (SR) is another strategy used by public-sector agencies to track and disclose progress toward sustainability targets. Guthrie and Farneti (2008) investigated which aspects of 'sustainability' were disclosed in annual reports and found that public-sector reporting is heavily influenced by the Global Reporting Initiatives (GRI). Although early GRI research (2010) reveals that the uptake of the GRI framework

[19] More information about MEES regulations can be found at: www.colliers.com/-/media/files/emea/uk/research/speciality/15047-a-mees-summary-flyer-v9-web.pdf?la=en-gb.

in the public-sector was slow, more recent examination of its Sustainability Disclosure Database indicates a 218% growth in public-sector reporting using the GRI framework between 2007 and 2011 (GRI, 2013). Farneti and Guthrie (2009) found that most public-sector organizations began reporting using a triple bottom line (TBL) or balanced scorecard (BSC) strategy and only recently transitioned to the GRI framework. However, the application of GRI is often fragmentary, with many organizations selecting only the particular GRI indicators that they wish to disclose. The indicators are often chosen based on the underlying reason the public-sector organization has decided to report. The GRI Sector Supplement for Public Agencies 2 (GRI, 2005, p. 8) states that a public agency may decide to conduct SR in order to:

- Promote transparency and accountability
- Reinforce organizational commitments and demonstrate progress
- Serve as a role model for the private-sector
- Improve internal governance
- Highlight the significance of its role as a consumer and employer in various economies
- Meet disclosure expectations and make information available to facilitate dialogue and effective engagement with stakeholders

There is a supporting body of literature on sustainability benchmarking, balanced scorecards and new public management which stresses the need to manage performance toward the achievement of specified outcomes. This literature reveals that the public-sector's growing interest in the use of performance measures is driven by both internal and external reporting expectations. Adams, Muir, and Hoque (2014) note that the increased emphasis on performance assessment by the public-sector in Australia is reflective of the increased pressure on organizations to continually improve performance across a variety of metrics. However, they note that sustainability, environmental and social responsibility measures were the least used performance measures. The authors conclude that "the comprehensive implementation of sustainability reporting and use of environmental and social performance measures are unlikely to be adopted in the public -sector while they remain voluntary and there is no competitive advantage in the adoption of such measures. Either the reporting needs to be made mandatory or the non-competitive nature of their operations needs to change, even if this is just by tying resources competitively to performance measurement across all sustainability indicators" (ibid., 2014, p. 58).

Beare, Buslovich, and Searcy (2014) found that the federal government in Canada has been happy to allow businesses to lead the way in formulating their SR. They identified a perceived need for the government to provide guidance on linking corporate SR to public policy. Ball, Grubnic, and Birchall (2014) argue that the public-sector has assumed a greater share of the responsibility for sustainability in cities than the for-profit commercial sector, and they highlight the need for a distinct agenda for sustainability disclosure and reporting in the public-sector. Based on examples from the United Kingdom and New Zealand, they note that SR for public-sector organizations should include a sustainability policy and strategy, as well as sustainability programs, outcomes and operational impacts (such as procurement, management of assets and performance efficiencies). Ball et al. (2014) also discuss strategies that can help develop multilevel, multiagency thinking about sustainability—thinking that can in turn transform public-sector sustainability practice. These strategies include disclosures about policy outcomes and inclusiveness in policymaking, carbon accounting, use of quality of life indicators and improved accounting for natural and social capital. With the broad adoption of the *2030 Agenda for Sustainable Development* and the *NUA*, it will be interesting to see how benchmarking, monitoring and reporting of progress toward the SDGs will begin to influence public-sector sustainability disclosure and reporting practices.

4 Public Procurement Standards

As an increasing number of cities set goals of carbon neutrality or significant emissions reduction, many are looking to optimize every stage of delivering a built environment asset, including the procurement stage. Many governments have created frameworks for enabling low-carbon supply chains for infrastructure procurement (e.g. in the United Kingdom [BSI, 2016] and in Australia [Hargroves, 2015]), but research indicates that uptake is slow. This may be partly because tracking carbon flows in local and global supply chains and in emission trading schemes is still an emerging area of research (e.g. Chen, Wiedmann, Wang, & Hadjikakou, 2016; Teh, Wiedmann, Schinabeck, Rowley, & Moore, 2015). All materials used in construction have an environmental signature linked with their manufacture, assembly, transport and service life (e.g. energy, water, emissions, waste, etc.). In addition to the operational carbon emissions over the life of a building, one of the most significant components of built environment performance relates to a building's embodied carbon, which refers to carbon dioxide emitted during the manufacture, transport and construction of building materials, as well as the end of life emissions. However, many governments have avoided the challenging task of calculating and reducing embodied carbon and have instead focused on improving operational efficiency in buildings. Newton, Pears, Whiteman, and Astle (2012) suggest that we are approaching a juncture where the operational energy efficiency of buildings is beginning to equate with embodied energy over the life-cycle of the building.

Testa, Annunziata, Iraldo, and Frey (2016) discuss the critical role of the public-sector, at both global and local levels, in creating and building the 'virtuous cycle'. The authors examine three mutually reinforcing actions necessary for the 'virtuous cycle' to stimulate the green economy: (1) improving the environmental performance of products throughout their life-cycle; (2) promoting and stimulating the demand for better products and production technologies on behalf of the markets; and (3) helping consumers to make better informed choices (p. 1893; referring to European Commission, 2013). The *NUA* addresses the challenges of creating the 'virtuous cycle', as well as the role of regional and local government efforts in supporting initiatives to decrease the impact of economic activity on the environment:

> We will ensure universal access to affordable, reliable and modern energy services by promoting energy efficiency and sustainable renewable energy, and supporting sub-national and local efforts; **to apply them in public buildings, infrastructure and facilities**, as well as in taking advantage of their direct control, where applicable, of local infrastructure and codes, to foster uptake in end-use sectors, such as residential, commercial, and industrial buildings, industry, transport, waste, and sanitation. We also encourage the adoption of building performance codes and standards, renewable portfolio targets, energy efficiency labelling, retrofitting of existing buildings and public procurement policies on energy, among other modalities as appropriate, to achieve energy efficiency targets. We will also prioritize smart grid, district energy systems, and community energy plans to improve synergies between renewable energy and energy efficiency. (Habitat III, 2017, paragraph 121)

In addition to their role in creating guidelines, incentives and regulatory instruments, public organizations can also participate in the green economy as consumers of products through the adoption of green procurement practice (GPP). GPP has been defined as "a process whereby public authorities seek to procure goods, services and works with a reduced environmental impact throughout their life-cycle when compared to goods, services and works with the same primary function that would otherwise be procured" (European Commission, 2008, p. 4). Public authorities are major consumers in Europe, spending an estimated €1.8 trillion annually, representing around 14% of the EU's gross domestic product (GDP). By using that purchasing power to support goods and services which have less of an impact on the environment, they can have a significant impact on sustainable consumption and production (European Commission, 2008). Similarly, from a more global perspective, because the sums spent by national governments are so large,[20] those governments have the greatest potential to influence sustainable procurement. The magnitude of their impact is followed by that of corporate occupiers, local government, public opinion, and developers and architects (Hartwell, 2013; ISEAL, 2013).

Traditional procurement methods are influenced by three interdependent criteria: time, cost and quality. Time relates to the speed of a development and/or the priority placed on completing it by a set date. This is a commonly occurring factor in procurement for major sporting venues such as those for the Olympics and Soccer World Cup. Cost prioritizes cost certainty to help minimize the risk exposure of a project. Quality focuses on performance and functionality. The person commissioning the public tender or contract must decide whether the project's highest priority is time, cost management or quality because each priority supports different procurement choices. Hartwell (2013) notes that whenever one of these criteria is emphasized more heavily, it may be at the expense of another. All too often, cost is the driving criterion at the expense of quality; as a consequence, sustainability performance, which is not even considered in the traditional framework, also suffers (Robichaud & Anantatmula, 2011).

Hartwell (2013) recommends a modification to the conventional procurement framework whereby sustainability considerations are embedded into the assessment of time, cost and quality, and suggests that this will

[20] For example, according to Testa et al. (2016), public procurement accounts for an estimated 17% of Organisation for Economic Co-operation and Development (OECD) countries' gross domestic product (GDP).

enable developers and their teams to more easily balance environmental and social impacts and to reconcile them with economic costs. In public-sector developments, the commissioning agents are able to consider 'big picture' impacts, thus enabling some sustainability criteria to be embedded within the core decision criteria used in the procurement process. However, many key sustainability factors are generally neglected in the public procurement process and it should be noted that there is significant variation in the extent and type of sustainability factors considered by governments (Brammer & Walker, 2011).

The public-sector is generally able to take a long-term view of payback periods and life-cycle costing. This enables them to avoid product specifications for less durable, but often cheaper, materials which can cost more to maintain and operate over time. Because economic costs in the public-sector are considered in terms of 'best value' rather than lowest cost, they are able to thoroughly consider challenging social and environmental issues associated with a development project.

The public-sector and government agencies are the most important developers in many countries. Indeed, after the global financial crises, it was often public-sector-led construction activity that was instrumental in stimulating local economies. Since local authorities are often owners, they tend to maintain a long-term interest in their buildings and typically develop them for occupancy by their own departments, for community use (e.g. housing) or to provide local infrastructure. Furthermore, their limited financial resources, together with their legal status and obligations tend to make them accountable to their communities.

However, although many governments (e.g. European Union, United States, Canada, Australia, Japan and South Africa) have committed themselves to sustainable procurement of services and buildings (through a mix of legislation, operational incentives and education), they have found it challenging to convert their ambitions into practice. Brammer and Walker (2011) suggest four factors that may influence how well Green Public Purchasing (GPP) policies get translated into practice: (1) perceived costs and benefits of GPP policies; (2) familiarity with policies; (3) the availability of sustainably produced services and goods; and (4) organizational incentives and pressures for GPP. The authors note that public procurement staff sometimes lack awareness of GPP techniques and may also lack the necessary technical expertise to fully include environmental criteria in public tenders. Ultimately, this lack of expert knowledge combined with resource constraints and underdeveloped frameworks are the key barriers to the successful implementation of GPP in the public-sector (ISEAL, 2013).

Governments are, in many respects, leading the way, with legislation and minimum quality requirements for buildings in which they procure occupancy and/or commission for new development. For example, in Australia, the government requires that a building achieve a minimum of a four-star NABERS rating in order to lease space in the building. This has driven the owners in some sectors of the commercial market to redevelop and/or retrofit buildings to attract government tenants (considered quality tenants due to lease length and low-risk of payment default). Although such government tenancy requirements are driving change in the market, there is still a perception that it costs significantly more to increase the sustainability performance of buildings than it does. Furthermore, research findings indicate that cost premia are declining (World Green Building Council, 2013), so the challenge now is to change the industry perception of costs associated with creating sustainable buildings.

Governments, the public-sector and policy agencies require both good advice and deep internal knowledge to act as effective drivers of sustainable development, particularly with regard to the procurement process. Although this level of expertise already exists in some localities, governments worldwide are currently investing heavily in knowledge creation to increase the capacity and capability of their staff. While policy and legislation were identified as the primary determinants of the degree to which public-sector organizations engage in GPP, the leadership of senior managers (who may influence whether GPP is incorporated into planning, strategies and goal setting) was also found to be a crucial factor. In summary, clear legislative and regulatory direction should be provided along with sufficient budgetary flexibility to allow the necessary investment in GPP, recognizing that the exercise might only be financially efficient when viewed from a long-term perspective (Brammer & Walker, 2011).

5 Discussion and Recommendations

Looking to the future, what can be learned from our review of the public regulatory trends? And how can sustainability considerations be better integrated into development, reporting and procurement policies? In this concluding section, we discuss three recommendations to improve the power of public policy to increase the uptake of sustainable development practices across both private and public-sectors, and to better integrate design with operation. There is a general theme in these proposals: the need for an explorative and collaborative approach to establishing stakeholder buy-in. Standing in the way of this future is the public-sector's hesitancy to mandate the application of SDGs at all levels of government and the lack of resources for implementation.

5.1 *Application of the UN SDGs to Improve Sustainability Outcomes in Strategic Planning*

Although the SDG goals and targets have been criticized for a wide range of reasons (e.g. the goals are too broad; the targets are too aspirational and pose challenges in relation to measurement and implementation [ICSU, 2015, p. 6]), they do, at least, identify the multifaceted, structural problems which need to be addressed at the global level. We propose that the SDGs offer three benefits which can improve strategic planning for cities.

First, the SDGs provide a common framework and language across government levels and offer public-sector leaders a common stretch agenda[21] to encourage them to think creatively about how to scope policy. Strategies should be based on an integrated and multi-dimensional approach to inclusive and sustainable development. For example, in Valencia, Spain, they have used the SDG framework to promote consistency of policy among the different government departments by adopting a law requiring them to include the SDGs in their development cooperation strategy by adopting a new policy that requires the entire government to get involved. It should be noted that not all 17 SDGs will be equally important or applicable across all jurisdictions; therefore, an important initial step in localizing the global goals is to assess the alignment between local issues and the regional, national and global targets (Global Taskforce of Local and Regional Governments, 2016). Local priorities should be developed, implemented and monitored with the involvement of the major territorial stakeholders in the context of broad participatory governance.

[21] A detailed discussion of the Stretch Agenda concept can be found at: www.interfacecut-thefluff.com/wp-content/uploads/2012/09/The-Stretch-Agenda-Breakthrough-in-the-Boardroom.pdf.

Second, in the context of increasingly scarce resources, the SDGs can offer guidance to help governments more efficiently align their budgets with the priorities identified in local, regional and national strategic planning policies.

Third, the SDGs provide clear measures and a framework for monitoring and review. Having consistency of measurement across government levels may offer greater accountability in relation to spending and it may support increased implementation of sustainable development policies. Research in the private-sector indicates that performance monitoring can improve the connection between actions and outcomes. A clear monitoring and review framework for the public-sector could therefore have a big impact on the alignment of local priorities with the allocation of resources.

Ji and Darnall's (2017) discussion of local governments' strategies for addressing sustainability issues highlights the variations in approach. They note that some local governments take an 'exploitation approach', focusing on fewer sustainability issues with more reliable short-term economic benefits and employing more first-generation policy instruments to address them. Other local governments take an 'exploration approach', tackling a broader array of sustainability issues and using a variety of policy instruments to address them. The authors posit that the latter's more comprehensive focus and use of experimental and innovative policy instruments enables these governments to tackle more complex sustainability issues—and to be more effective in influencing the behavior of individual organizations in relation to those issues. We posit that the SDG structure can assist local governments by providing a framework for applying an explorative strategy to enhance sustainable development in their communities.

5.2 *Increasing the Impact of Mandatory Disclosure and Integrated Reporting Requirements*

To increase the development of 'green' and sustainable building, the public-sector can play a critical role in driving integration of sustainability considerations by requiring mandatory disclosure of energy, waste, water and carbon emissions. The life-cycle for all developments begins when the project is conceived and the desired performance levels are specified. These levels should be specified for all stages of a building's lifecycle from planning, design, construction, operation, including how the building performance is monitored and managed until the building's end of life (this should include consideration of deconstruction, re-use, retrofit, recycle of materials, disposal options). Among industry leaders, carbon footprint is considered one of the most important metrics they monitor, as it represents a proxy for the overall performance of the building. Despite the importance of this metric, policies and practices directed toward minimizing an asset's carbon emissions (as well as its cost) over a building's life-cycle are not yet mainstream nor are the requirements for benchmarking, monitoring, commissioning and disclosing performance. There is a still significant room for improvement in this area and the public-sector has an opportunity to lead the industry toward standardization and transparency through mandatory disclosure and integrated reporting requirements.

5.3 *Incentives that More Accurately Reflect the Value-Add of Sustainable Development*

Sayce et al. (2007) question how far fiscal incentives can drive market transformation. They note that although the private-sector has moved rapidly toward the mainstreaming of sustainability issues in their strategic positioning and reporting approaches, the impact of sustainability policies on private-sector decision-making related to real estate has proved more tenuous. The authors note that fiscal incentives would be welcomed in the private-sector, although they acknowledge that challenges to implementation still need to be resolved. Brain argues that policymakers strive to "… achieve an end with means that are never neutral in themselves. In the context of the urban landscape, every design and planning decision is a value proposition, and a proposition that has to do with social and political relationships" (Brain, 2005, p. 233). His contention is that value propositions and value positions cannot be ignored when considering the relationship between the means (policy instruments) and ends (sustainable property development). If we truly aim to develop property in a more sustainable manner, we must begin to assert these values in the property development process.

Financial and planning incentives (e.g. tax abatement and relaxations in zoning), if they strategically negotiate this value proposition, can encourage positive development outcomes. All property development projects interact with the planning system as soon as the development application is submitted to the local planning authority; the project must proceed within the confines of the applicable planning controls and regulations. Creating planning incentives that have the potential to directly impact a developer's bottom line, such as streamlining the approval process and reducing the review period, are likely to be the most influential in promoting sustainable development.

Current planning practice often rewards non-innovative, code-compliant development, that is, pre-approved solutions that save time and hence save money (since time = money to developers). This approach encourages the use of geared buy-develop-sell strategies by developers because they maximize capital gain. In contrast, development projects that incorporate innovative sustainable solutions commonly invest significant effort into 'proving' to the planning authority that they will generate improved building performance before the developer can obtain approval.

We need a paradigm shift. Planning authorities must base their decisions on the proposition that increased sustainability performance offers value to their communities beyond simply reducing negative externalities—it also has the potential to reduce the long-term planning and regulatory costs associated with those externalities. Rose and Manley (2011) note that many planning authorities lack adequate understanding of the net benefits associated with particular sustainable product innovations. Developing and regulating the use of scientifically validated, government-endorsed instruments (data and tools) that are able to more accurately assess the life-cycle and eco-efficiency impacts of materials and products is the first step toward shifting the paradigm. This must be done at building, precinct and urban levels. In addition, we recommend increasing education and training programs to enable public-sector staff in planning departments to make more informed decisions based on the robust assessment of long-term value, whole life-cycle costs and benefits, and wider environmental benefits. Finally, governments now have the opportunity to positively influence industry practice by (1) systematically and progressively aligning incentives with the SDG principles embedded in a given policy instrument and (2) evaluating both the tangible and intangible benefits of sustainable development using integrated valuation models. In this way, they can promote development that is better aligned with their community vision and sustainability goals.

References

Adams, C. A., Muir, S., & Hoque, Z. (2014). Measurement of Sustainability Performance in the Public Sector. *Sustainability Accounting, Management and Policy Journal, 5*(1), 46–67. https://doi.org/10.1108/SAMPJ-04-2012-0018

Allen, S. C., Moorman, C. E., Peterson, M. N., Hess, G. R., & Moore, S. E. (2012). Overcoming Socio-Economic Barriers to Conservation Subdivisions: A Case-Study of Four Successful Communities. *Landscape and Urban Planning, 106*(1), 244–252.

Amati, M. (Ed.). (2008). *Urban Green Belts in the Twenty-First Century.* New York: Routledge.

Amati, M., & Yokohari, M. (2006). Temporal Changes and Local Variations in the Functions of London's Green Belt. *Landscape and Urban Planning, 75*(1), 125–142.

Armstrong, A., Wright, C., Ashea, B., & Nielsen, H. (2017). Enabling Innovation in Building Sustainability: Australia's National Construction Code. *Procedia Engineering, 180*(1), 320–330.

Audirac, I., Fol, S., & Martinez-Fernandez, C. (2010). Shrinking Cities in a Time of Crisis. *Berkeley Planning Journal, 23*(1), 51–57.

Ball, A., Grubnic, S., & Birchall, F. (2014). Sustainability Accounting and Accountability in the Public Sector. In J. Bebbington, J. Unerman, & B. O'Dwyer (Eds.), *Sustainability Accounting and Accountability* (pp. 176–195). New York: Routledge.

Beare, D., Buslovich, R., & Searcy, C. (2014). Linkages Between Corporate Sustainability Reporting and Public Policy. *Corporate Social Responsibility and Environmental Management, 21*(6), 336–350. https://doi.org/10.1002/csr.1323

Berke, P. R., & Conroy, M. M. (2000). Are We Planning for Sustainable Development? *Journal of the American Planning Association, 66*(1), 21–33. https://doi.org/10.1080/01944360008976081

Brain, D. (2005). From Good Neighbourhoods to Sustainable Cities: Social Science and the Social Agenda of the New Urbanism. *International Regional Science Review, 28*(2), 217–238.

Brammer, S., & Walker, H. (2011). Sustainable Procurement in the Public Sector: An International Comparative Study. *International Journal of Operations & Production Management, 31*(4), 452–476. https://doi.org/10.1108/01443571111119551

British Standards Institute (BSI). (2016). *PAS 2080:2016 Carbon Management in Infrastructure.* London: HM Treasury.

Centre for International Economics. (2012). *Benefits of Building Regulation Reform.* Canberra: Centre for International Economics.

Chen, G., Wiedmann, T., Wang, Y., & Hadjikakou, M. (2016). Transnational City Carbon Ffootprint Networks – Exploring Carbon Links Between Australian and Chinese Cities. *Applied Energy, 184*(1), 1082–1092.

Christensen, P. H. (2012). *Key Strategies of Sustainable Real Estate Decision-Making in the United States: A Delphi Study of the Stakeholders*. Diss. Clemson U, Print.

Christensen, P. H. (2017). A Post-Global Financial Crisis (GFC) Framework for Strategic Planning, Assessment and Management Decision Making for US Sustainable Commercial Real Estate. *Journal of Property Investment and Finance, 35*(6), 1–32.

Christensen, P. H., & Sayce, S. (2015). Planning and Regulatory Issues Impacting Sustainable Property Development. In S. J. Wilkinson, S. L. Sayce, & P. H. Christensen (Eds.), *Developing Property Sustainably*. New York: Routledge.

City of Seattle. (2013). *Seattle Design Guidelines*. Department of Planning and Development. Retrieved August 12, 2017, from www.seattle.gov/dpd/cs/groups/pan/@pan/documents/web_informational/p2083771.pdf.

Clark, D. (2003). *Incentives for Sustainable Buildings in Australia – A Designer's Perspective*. Sinclair Knight Merz Technical Paper. Melbourne: Sinclair Knight Merz. Retrieved September 15, from citeseerx.ist.psu.edu/viewdoc/download?doi=10.1.1.574.8495&rep=rep1&type=pdf.

Costonis, J. (1972). The Chicago Plan: Incentive Zoning and the Preservation of Urban Landmarks. Faculty Scholarship. Paper 63. Retrieved September 17, 2017, from digitalcommons.law.lsu.edu/faculty_scholarship/63.

Dunham-Jones, E., & Williamson, J. (2011). *Retrofitting Suburbia: Urban Design Solutions for Redesigning Suburbs*. Hoboken, NJ: John Wiley and Sons.

European Commission. (2008). *Public Procurement for a Better Environment, COM(2008) 400: Communication from the Commission to the European Parliament, the Council, the European Economic and Social Committee and the Committee of the Regions*. Brussels: European Commission. Retrieved 16 September 2017, from http://eur-lex.europa.eu/legal-content/EN/TXT/?uri=CELEX:52008DC0400

European Commission. (2013). *Communication from the Commission to the European Parliament and the Council. Building the Single Market for Green Products – Facilitating Better Information on the Environmental Performance of Products and Organisations*. Brussels: European Commission. Retrieved 16 September 2017, from http://eur-lex.europa.eu/LexUriServ/LexUriServ.do?uri=COM:2013:0196:FIN:%20EN:PDF

Ewing, R., Bartholomew, K., Winkelman, S., Walters, J., & Chen, D. (2007). *Growing Cooler: The Evidence on Urban Development and Climate Change*. Chicago, IL: Urban Land Institute.

Farneti, F., & Guthrie, J. (2009). Sustainability Reporting by Australian Public Sector Organisations: Why they Report. *Accounting Forum, 33*(2), 89–98. https://doi.org/10.1016/j.accfor.2009.04.002

Global Reporting Initiative. (2005). GRI Sector Supplement for Public Agencies. Retrieved February 23, 2018, from www.globalreporting.org/information/g4/sector-guidance/sector-guidance/pilot-versions/public-agency/Pages/default.aspx.

Global Reporting Initiative. (2013, January 10). GRI Reporting: Public Sector Progress. Retrieved February 23, 2018, from www.globalreporting.org/information/news-and-press-center/Pages/GRI-reporting-Public-sector-progress.aspx.

Global Taskforce of Local and Regional Governments. (2016). *Roadmap for Localizing the SDGs: Implementation and Monitoring at Subnational Level.* Retrieved September 16, 2017, from https://www.uclg.org/sites/default/files/roadmap_for_localizing_the_sdgs_0.pdf

Göçmen, Z. A., & LaGro, J. A., Jr. (2016). Assessing Local Planning Capacity to Promote Environmentally Sustainable Residential Development. *Journal of Environmental Planning and Management, 59*(8), 1513–1535. https://doi.org/10.1080/09640568.2015.1080673

Gurran, N. (2011). *Australian Urban Land Use Planning: Principles, Systems and Practice* (2nd ed.). Sydney: Sydney University Press.

Guthrie, J., & Farneti, F. (2008). GRI Sustainability Reporting by Australian Public Sector Organizations. *Public Money and Management, 28*(6), 361–366.

Hall, T. (2011). Proactive Engagement in Urban Design – The Case of Chelmsford. In S. Tiesdell & D. Adams (Eds.), *Real Estate Issues: Urban Design in the Real Estate Development Process* (pp. 74–91). Hoboken, NJ: Wiley-Blackwell.

Hargroves, K. (2015). *Low Carbon Inclusions in Commonwealth and NSW Government Built Environment Sector Procurement.* Sydney: CRC for Low Carbon Living Ltd.

Hartwell, J. (2013). Sustainable Procurement. In A. Cotgrave & M. Riley (Eds.), *Total Sustainability in the Built Environment.* Hampshire: Palgrave Macmillan.

International Council for Science (ICSU). (2015). *ISSC Review of the Sustainable Development Goals: The Science Perspective.* Paris: International Council for Science.

ISEAL Alliance. 2013. London: ISEAL Alliance. Retrieved September 18, from www.isealalliance.org/sites/default/files/ISEALSPP-Report-Full-Document.pdf.

Jacobsen, G. D., & Kotchen, M. J. (2013). Are Building Codes Effective at Saving Energy? Evidence from Residential Billing Data in Florida. *Review of Economics and Statistics, 95*(1), 34–49.

Jacobus, R. (2015). *Inclusionary Housing Creating and Maintaining Inclusive Communities.* Policy Focus Report. Cambridge, MA: Lincoln Institute of Land Policy.

Jepson, E. J., Jr., & Haines, A. L. (2014). Zoning for Sustainability: A Review and Analysis of the Zoning Ordinances of 32 Cities in the United States. *Journal of the American Planning Association, 80*(3), 239–252. https://doi.org/10.1080/01944363.2014.981200

Ji, H., & Darnall, N. (2017). All Are Not Created Equal: Assessing Local Governments' Strategic Approaches Towards Sustainability. *Public Management Review*, 1–22. https://doi.org/10.1080/14719037.2017.1293147

Lens, M. C., & Monkkonen, P. (2015). Do Strict Land Use Regulations Make Metropolitan Areas More Segregated by Income? *Journal of the American Planning Association, 82*(1), 6–21.

Newton, P., Pears, A., Whiteman, J., & Astle, R. (2012). The Energy and Carbon Footprints of Urban Housing and Transport: Current Trends and Future Prospects. In R. Tomlinson (Ed.), *The Unintended City*. Melbourne: CSIRO Publishing.

Porter, D. R., & Davison, E. B. (2009). Evaluation of In-Lieu Fees and Offsite Construction as Incentives for Affordable Housing Production. *Cityscape: A Journal of Policy Development and Research, 11*(2), 27–60.

Randolph, J. (2011). *Environmental Land Use Planning and Management* (2nd ed.). Washington, DC: Island Press.

Robichaud, L. B., & Anantatmula, V. S. (2011). Greening Project Management Practices for Sustainable Construction. *Journal of Management in Engineering, 27*(1), 48–57.

Rose, T., & Manley, K. (2011). Development of the Sustainable Building and Construction Products Industry in Australia. In J. W. F. Wamelink, R. P. Geraedts, & L. Volker (Eds.), *MISBE2011: Proceedings of the International Conference on Management and Innovation for a Sustainable Built Environment* (pp. 1–9). Amsterdam: Delft University of Technology Accessed September 12, from http://eprints.qut.edu.au/46225/

Saha, D., & Paterson, R. G. (2008). Local Government Efforts to Promote the "Three Es" of Sustainable Development Survey in Medium to Large Cities in the United States. *Journal of Planning Education and Research, 28*(1), 21–37. https://doi.org/10.1177/0739456X08321803

Sayce, S., Ellison, L., & Parnell, P. (2007). Understanding Investment Drivers for UK Sustainable Property. *Building Research & Information, 35*(6), 629–643. https://doi.org/10.1080/09613210701559515

Schilling, J., & Logan, J. (2008). Greening the Rust Belt: A Green Infrastructure Model for Right Sizing America's Shrinking Cities. *Journal of the American Planning Association, 74*(4), 451–466.

Schindler, S. B. (2010). Following Industry's LEED: Municipal Adoption of Private Green Building Standards. *Florida Law Review, 62*(2), 285–350.

Schwieterman, J. P., & Caspall, D. M. (2006). *The Politics of Place: A History of Zoning in Chicago*. Chicago: Lake Claremont Press.

Talen, E. (2013). Zoning For and Against Sprawl: The Case for Form-Based Codes. *Journal of Urban Design, 18*(2), 175–200. https://doi.org/10.1080/13574809.2017.1337495

Teh, S. H., Wiedmann, T., Schinabeck, J., Rowley, H., & Moore, S. (2015). Integrated Carbon Metrics and Assessment for the Built Environment. *Procedia CIRP, 29*(1), 480–485.

Testa, F., Annunziata, E., Iraldo, F., & Frey, M. (2016). Drawbacks and Opportunities of Green Public Procurement: An Effective Tool for Sustainable Production. *Journal of Cleaner Production, 112*(3), 1893–1900.

United Nations. (2015). *Transforming Our World: The 2030 Agenda for Sustainable Development*. Retrieved August 12, from sustainabledevelopment.un.org/post2015/transformingourworld

United Nations. (2016). United Nations Sustainable Development Goals. Retrieved 12 August 2017, from www.un.org/sustainabledevelopment/

United Nations Conference on Housing and Sustainable Urban Development (Habitat III). (2017). A/RES/71/256: New Urban Agenda. ISBN: 978-92-1-132731-1. Retrieved August 12, 2017, from habitat3.org/the-new-urban-agenda

World Green Building Council. (2013). *The Business Case for Green Building: A Review of the Costs and Benefits for Developers, Investors and Occupants*. Retrieved September 15, 2017, from www.worldgbc.org/sites/default/files/Business_Case_For_Green_Building_Report_WEB_2013-04-11-2.pdf.

Zhao, P. (2011). Managing Urban Growth in a Transforming China: Evidence from Beijing. *Land Use Policy, 28*(1), 96–109.

CHAPTER 5

A Policy Framework for Sustainable Real Estate in the European Union

Diane Strauss

1 Introduction

This chapter intends to summarize the existing knowledge on sustainable real estate in Europe. It is designed as a literature and policy review. It provides an overview of where the European Union (EU) and European countries stand regarding the deployment of sustainable real estate. The following section addresses the crucial role of the EU in raising awareness and promoting minimum standards and common practices across Member States. It explores the legislative and financial policies designed by European institutions to boost the transition of national building stocks toward greater sustainability. The third section examines the diversity of European countries, their different approaches and uneven progress toward "smart-readiness". Three major challenges are identified: the difficult financing of building renovation, the necessity to alleviate energy poverty and the current transition toward connected buildings. Key

Maps have been designed with mapchart.net

D. Strauss (✉)
Yale University, New Haven, CT, USA
e-mail: twalker@jmsb.concordia.ca

T. Walker et al. (eds.), *Sustainable Real Estate*, Palgrave Studies in Sustainable Business In Association with Future Earth,
https://doi.org/10.1007/978-3-319-94565-1_5

national policies are sampled to illustrate the diversity of the paths chosen by European countries.

When available, data on non-EU countries of the European continents will be presented along with the EU results. In this chapter, the UK is considered part of the EU, therefore counting 28 Members, although it should be noted that the effect of Brexit on future policies and engagement is impossible to predict.

This chapter builds on information issued from several types of media, including academic and non-academic literature, think-tank research, studies by interest groups and legislative texts. It also provides an overview of projects and best practices in the European countries and will hopefully contribute to an improved international exchange regarding policy avenues to encourage sustainable real estate.

2 The European Union Walks the Talk on Sustainable Real Estate

This section offers a review of the policies conducted by the EU to push the sustainable real estate agenda in 2017. This overarching institution has been a key player in the definition of the debate, by shaping the legal framework and providing crucial incentives.

2.1 A Common Framework of Standards and Practices

Over the last ten years, the issue of the sustainability of the building stock has grown increasingly high on the European agenda. It is now enshrined as one of the priorities of the EU for "smart, sustainable and inclusive growth" and a consistent element of the EU climate and energy policy.

Nevertheless, the definition of "sustainable" real estate remains largely focused on the issue of energy efficiency and energy efficient buildings. The use of materials in recycling and demolishing, and considerations around resilience or waste and water in buildings are barely addressed in the legal and mandatory framework designed by the EU. The focus may evolve with time, as demonstrated by the European Demolition and Construction Waste Protocol published end of 2016 (European Commission, 2016e), but to date, only energy efficiency and grids have yet been thoroughly addressed.

It is important to remember that European Directives must be integrated into National Law (in technical terms, transposed). Member States, that is, countries that are members of the EU, have the possibility to strengthen these requirements in their National Law, but they cannot soften them. The non-transposition of European Law into National Law eventually results in an "infringement procedure" and may lead to financial compensations. The European legal framework therefore works as a common background for the 28 Member States. The framework is designed to offer certain flexibility to Member States, ensuring the possibility to adapt standards to their climatic, political and economic situations. As a result, and as presented throughout this chapter, the same practices take place in Member States but they vary greatly in quality.

The central piece of this legal framework is the Efficiency Performance Building Directive (EPBD, 2010/31/EU; EU, 2010b). The Energy Efficiency Directive (EED), the Ecolabel Directive and the Ecodesign Directive complement this text. Together, they are the cornerstone of the EU's strategy to reach its objective of 30% reduction in primary energy use by 2030.

In November 2016, the European Commission proposed a package of measures updating this legal framework (European Commission, 2016c). The "Clean Energy for All Europeans" package will improve the consistency between the Directives and introduce clarification on a number of technical points. However, it is expected that it will not drastically increase the level of requirements. It should rather attempt to reduce market barriers through non-regulatory policies including capacity building and financial support, as discussed further in Sect. 2.2. The following paragraphs cover the most interesting aspects of the mandatory framework (and its review). It hopefully provides a good understanding of where the 28 Member States stand and how they are expected to develop.

2.1.1 *Member States to Save 1.5% Primary Energy and Renovate 3% of Public Buildings*

The most important aspect of the EED 2012/27/EU (European Union, 2012) is the obligation for energy distributors, or retail energy sales companies, to achieve 1.5% energy savings per year via the implementation of energy efficiency measures. The "Energy Efficiency Obligation" is seen as a key incentive toward the renovation of the building stock and has given birth to a number of innovative national schemes. Examples of such schemes include fiscal incentives, energy and CO_2 tax, or the successful trade of White Certificates against energy efficiency measures in Italy (European Commission, 2016a; Giraudet & Finon, 2014; Kaar, Turner, & Forster, 2017).

Articles 5 and 9 of the EED Directive deal specifically with the building sector. They require an annual renovation of 3% of the buildings owned or occupied by public bodies and free access to consumer data by individual metering. The implementation of the Directive faced a slow uptake, with 26 countries under infringement procedure in 2015 (Crisp, 2015) and two remaining in 2016 (Concerted Action EED, 2016). To date, however, the requirements of the Directive are reflected in the National law of the 28 Member States.

2.1.2 European Standards and Labels for Products

The Ecodesign Directive (2009/125/EC; European Union, 2009) has set common minimum standards for all energy-related products used in the building sector, such as boilers, pumps and ventilators. The Energy Labelling Directive (2010/30/EU; European Union, 2010a) requires the implementation of efficiency labeling schemes (rated A to G) for energy technologies used in buildings.

2.1.3 Set National Requirements that Respect the Principle of Cost Optimality in Construction and Renovation

One of the major movements of the EPBD Directive was to require that Member States set "minimum energy performance requirements" for construction, major renovations and buildings systems (articles 3, 6, 7 and 11). Importantly, these requirements must be designed "in views to achieving cost-optimal levels" (article 3). In other words, Member States are not required to set standards which are not cost-effective over the estimated economic life-cycle of the building. These standards shall be updated every five years.

The Annex of the Directive aims to provide a common methodology for the design of these requirements. It includes (a) a methodology to help calculate cost optimality (the energy performance level which leads to the lowest cost during the estimated economic life-cycle) and (b) it imposes a way to design the requirements based on national reference buildings.

In practice, however, the calculation methods differ widely from one country to another, which renders comparison of standards extremely difficult. For example, Member States have different approaches on how to handle renewable energy sources in their definition of energy performance.

Seventeen Member States include electricity from photovoltaic (PV), while 12 include electricity from local wind turbines and combined heat and power (CHP) and 9 include hydropower (Engelund & Wittchen, 2015). In addition, the number of national reference buildings varies from 4 to 40 among Member States. To harmonize these definitions, and obtain a better understanding of the associated responsibilities, the European-funded agency Concerted Action Europe (CA EPBD) and the European Committee for Standardization are working with Member States to ensure accuracy in the standards and to share best practices (Engelund & Wittchen, 2015).

2.1.4 *Construct Only Nearly Zero-Energy Building by 2021*

As we approach 2021, the national standards for new construction are converging toward the national definition of nZEB (nearly zero-energy buildings). In the EU, all new buildings constructed after the 31 December 2021 shall be nZEB (Article 9 of the EPBD). For buildings owned or occupied by governments, the obligation is valid as of the end of 2018. This is undoubtedly the most ambitious disposition of the EPBD, although the Directive leaves ample space for national definitions. Member States must draw up national plans with targets for the different categories of buildings.

As of 2015, when they handed in their intermediary reports, 15 Member States had set a clear definition of nZEB. They vary in many ways, but 80% of them are calculated in primary energy requirements (between 20 and 117 kWh/m^2/year), 53% include requirements for using renewable energy and 33% set final energy use requirements (Erhorn & Erhorn-Kluttig, 2015). The research institute Building Performance Institute Europe (BPIE), a not-for profit research organization based in Brussels (BPIE, 2015), and the Joint Research Center (D'Agostino, Zangheri, Cuniberti, Paci, & Bertoldi, 2016) have referenced all definitions in comprehensive tables that are reproduced here.

The penetration of nearly nZEB also varies across Europe. In 2014 in France, 100% of the residential and non-residential buildings newly constructed were nZEB. This means that, in France, the current thermal law respects the national definition of nZEB of 50 kW/m^2/year. The same year in Poland, 40% of the new non-residential buildings and 11% of the residential ones were nZEB, while Italy constructed 16% of its residential buildings and 10% of non-residential buildings according to nZEB standards. These three countries are at the forefront of nZEB construction among European countries (Toleikyte et al., 2016).

2.1.5 *Deliver Energy Performance Certificates (EPCs) to Buildings*

Article 11 of the EPBD Directive requires that Member States establish a system of energy performance certification for all types of buildings. The Energy Performance Certificate (EPC) must help the customer to compare its dwelling with the minimum legal requirements. It must also provide recommendations for major and non-major energy renovation in the building. These certificates are to be issued for any building or building-unit constructed, sold or rented to a new tenant everywhere in Europe.

In practice, and as for the other clauses, the quality of EPCs has varied widely across Member States. According to the report of the BPIE (Arcipowska, Anagnostopoulos, Mariottini, & Kunkel, 2014), there are up to 35 different national and regional methodologies to calculate the energy performance of a building. Respondents to the evaluation of the EPBD by Ecofys (Boermans et al., 2015) highlight the poor quality of some EPCs and the lack of monitoring from independent entities. The variety of design and calculation methods is an impediment to a sound analysis of the European building stock and can represent a barrier to cross-boundary investments. To date, however, the proposed package of the European Commission does not pave the way for greater harmonization. The recent text only suggests that Member States set up an EPC database that "shall contain the actual energy consumption data of buildings frequently visited by the public". The data—made anonymous in compliance with the European text on data protection—shall be made available on request for research purposes.

2.1.6 *Ensure Improved Connectivity in New Constructions*

The update of the EPBD 2016 puts a great emphasis on the connectivity of buildings, requiring reinforced automation of buildings control systems as a replacement to physical inspections. The information gathered by automatic control systems will support the design of EPCs as well as verifications of compliance with the minimum requirements. In addition, the text imposes the connection of the building to charging infrastructure for electric vehicles in all non-residential buildings (proposed update of Article 8 of the EPBD, European Commission, 2016f).

To conclude on the legislative framework in the EU, stakeholders agreed that the EPBD has been critical in shaping the debate on sustainable real estate in Europe (Boermans et al., 2015).

The Directive was successful in raising awareness on energy efficiency in buildings across European markets. Increased awareness is visible in market studies and seems to translate in rising interest for environmental, social, and governance (ESG) monitoring and reporting practices. The 2015 edition of the consultancy PricewaterhouseCoopers (PWC) on "emerging trends in real estate in Europe" (PWC, 2015) reflects the mindset of market players. Seventy percent of respondents say that they incorporate sustainability into their business strategies. "It's mandatory and unavoidable", tells one of the interviewee. Markets are rather optimistic with 65% of respondents thinking that sustainable assets will achieve higher rents. In 2016, 390 European real estate companies benchmarked the ESG performance of their assets within the Global Real Estate Sustainability Benchmark (GRESB). However, and despite this encouraging position from market players, only 2% of Europe's building stock is BREEAM-certified. Building Research Establishment Environmental Assessment Method (BREEAM) is the largest European certification scheme and the vast majority of this certification takes place in France, Germany, the Netherlands, Belgium, Norway and the UK. On top, efforts of markets players are mostly focused on reducing energy consumption in new constructions.

If the Directive brought a common strategic vision for Europe and succeeded in driving innovation in the construction sector, it has fallen short in other ways. The EPBD failed to ensure a common playing field across Member States. Within the same legal framework, Member States have developed their own methodologies and calculations that prevent data comparison and aggregation. Standardization is said to be a big challenge for the market (PWC, 2015) and stakeholders lack clear evidence of the transformation of the housing stock.

Finally, while the impact of this text is measurable on new constructions, the EPBD seems to have had little influence on the renovation of existing buildings. The "Clean Energy for All Europeans" package, produced in 2016, partly addresses this concern. Although the European Commission introduces few new legal obligations, it designs new incentives for the renovation of the building stock, including the increase of financial resources (discussed further in Sect. 2.2). The updated EPBD shall require Member States to "set out a roadmap with clear milestones and measures to deliver on the long-term 2050 goal to decarbonize their national building stock, with specific milestones for 2030" (European Commission, 2016f).

The same "Clean Energy for All Europeans Package" proposed other interesting, non-regulatory avenues to move toward a broader definition of smart and sustainable buildings. A "smartness indicator" will be designed to rate the smart-readiness of buildings. It is very likely that this smartness assessment tool will be based on the rating scale designed by

BPIE presented in Sect. 3.1. In addition, the package came along with a voluntary Construction and Demolition Waste Protocol that aims at boosting the recycling rate of materials in these sectors from 50% to 90%.

2.2 The EU Budget to Reduce Market Barriers

The challenge of the sustainable transformation of European real estate has been fully incorporated into the priorities of the EU for "smart, sustainable and inclusive growth". As such, a substantial part of the European financial resource is dedicated to financing the renovation of national building stocks, to de-risk private investments and trigger market innovations. Altogether, the EU will account for more than €20 billion of public investment in energy efficiency projects for the period 2014–2020, most of this in the form of guaranteed debt. In addition, €380 million have been spent in grants between 2014 and 2016 to boost research and innovation and reduce market barriers in the sector (European Commission, 2016d).

2.2.1 De-Risking Private Investments in Renovation

The EU is increasingly employing the European budget as a way to drive, leverage and de-risk private investments toward the renovation of the building stock. The most important vehicles, the "Structural Funds" and the "Strategic Fund", are mandated to invest part of their capital in energy efficiency projects and the low-carbon economy.

The European Investment Bank (EIB)—the European lending institutions whose stakeholders are Member States—is responsible for the management of the Strategic Fund. It also plays a critical role by providing technical assistance to municipalities in the development of their renovation projects. The "Smart Financing for Smart Building" program announced as part of the "Clean Energy for All European" package in 2016 should lead to an increase in European capital dedicated to the renovation of the European building stock. The most relevant funds are described in the following section and Table 5.1 provides a brief summary of their beneficiaries and stakeholders.

Structural Funds

The first vehicle used to finance energy efficiency projects in Europe is the "European Structural and Investment Fund" (ESI Fund), also called "Cohesion Policy Funds". They represent the main share of the EU budget, adopted every seven years in the Multiannual Financial Framework

Table 5.1 European funds driving financial capital toward the transformation of the EU building stock

Name	*Amount for energy efficiency*	*Investors*	*Projects targeted*	*Type of finance*
Cohesion Policy Fund (ERDF+CF)	18bn€ 2014–2020	EU budget Member States + leverage	Projects led by Member States aligned with the EU priorities	Debt and grants
EFSO (Juncker Plan)	2.7bn€ 2020	2014 European Commission EIB + expected leverage	Strategic projects in many sectors including building refurbishment	Guaranteed debt
PF4EE	80m€	EU Commission EIB	Guaranteed loans to national retail financial institutions	Guaranteed debt
European Energy Efficiency Fund	265m€	EU Commission EIB Private Ranks	Large private energy projects	Debt and equity
ELENA	95m€ 2009–2016	EIB	Technical development assistance for municipalities	Grant of 1€ for 15€ invested by the project developer

Source: European Commission (2016b)

(European Union, 2013), and account for €352 billion for the period 2014–2020. These funds are allocated by the EU to Member States to develop and support actions related to the key Union priorities of smart, sustainable and inclusive growth. National co-financing constitutes an integral and obligatory part of these resources. They are not managed by the EIB.

Not all of the €352 billion are invested in sustainable buildings. According to the European Commission, about €19 billion should be invested in energy efficiency, €6 billion in renewable energy (notably in buildings and district heating and cooling) and around €1 billion in smart distribution grids, for the period 2014–2020 (European Commission, 2016d). This should result in the renovation of 850,000 residential buildings and 57,000 industrial buildings, the connection of 3.3 million users to smart grids and savings of 5.5 TWh/year in public buildings (Miladinova, 2015).

Juncker Plan

The second vehicle investing in the smart renovation of the building stock is the "European Fund for Strategic Investment" (EFSI), set up in 2014. The fund, also called the "Juncker investment plan", has been set up by the European Commission (executive arm of the EU) and the EIB to provide financing for economically viable projects, including projects with a higher risk profile than ordinary EIB activities. Emphasis is put on key sectors identified under Article 9 of the EFSI Regulation, including infrastructure, energy, research and education. The fund currently consists of a €16 billion guarantee from the EU budget and €5 billion from the EIB. The expected multiplier effect is 1 to 15 in private investment (€1 from the EU for €15 from the private-sector). The EFSI delivers guaranteed debt to projects, thereby reducing the risk taken by private investors. According to the working paper to the EPBD (European Commission, 2016b), energy efficiency projects accounted for €2.7 billion investment and about 10% of EFSI guarantee usage. This fund is demand driven, which means that funds are allocated to economically viable projects presented by municipalities. This capital can be allocated in addition to the structural funds described previously.

ELENA Fund, Technical Assistance for Municipalities

The European fund European Local Energy Assistance (ELENA) (EIB, 2017) is another important initiative of the EU. Managed by the EIB, ELENA provides project development assistance to municipalities for major energy efficiency projects. This facility has helped develop most of the emerging financing models in the EU, including Renewables and Energy Efficiency Diputación de Barcelona (REDIBA) in Barcelona (Spain), RE:FIT in London (UK), Energy efficiency Milan Covenant of Mayors (EEMCM) in Milan (Italy) and Service Public de l'Efficacité Energétique (SPEE) in Picardie (France) (see Sect. 3.2).

The plans for the "Smart Financing for Smart Buildings" initiative announced an increase in funding dedicated to building renovation in the EFSI and ELENA schemes. The European Commission also announced its increasing involvement in the capacity building of public, national and regional fund managers across Europe.

The EU endorsed the development of a European-wide "De-risking Energy Efficiency Platform", namely a database that discloses the financial and technical performance of at least 5000 European industrial and building energy efficiency projects and designed as an informative track record of projects for investors (the DEEP database is already available online (DEEP Platform, 2017)).

2.2.2 *Financing Innovation to Tackle Market Barriers*

Another avenue to support the development of sustainable real estate is the European commitment to reduce market failure by investing in research and innovation. With a budget of more than €80 billion for the period 2014–2020, Horizon 2020 (H2020) is the largest EU framework for research and innovation. This program aims at fostering innovation for a "smart, sustainable and inclusive economic growth" in Europe. The sustainable buildings sector should gather €2.5 billion of this amount issued from the "Energy Efficiency" and "Energy Efficient Building" funding lines (European Commission, 2016d). Additional research and innovation in waste and materials may be beneficial to the building sector as well. While the funding line termed "Energy Efficient Building" focuses on the development of large private and public technical and engineering solutions, the "Energy Efficiency" line attempts to tackle a diverse range of market barriers. Innovation to overcome these barriers includes data gathering, policy exchange and monitoring techniques or research on behavioral change. Three successful projects are presented in the following section to illustrate this approach.

Setting a European Exchange Platform to Share Best Practices

The *BUILD UP Skills* project (Build Up Skills, 2017) organized training sessions and exchange meetings all around Europe with policymakers and practitioners. With more than 2000 training sessions, the project resulted in the creation of national multi-stakeholder platforms, gathering representatives of the construction sector, policymakers and energy services companies (ESCOs) and so on. This project was highlighted as one of the best practices in construction by the World Economic Forum (Renz & Solas, 2016).

Support the Uptake of Promising Low-Cost Renovation Techniques

Energiesprong is a new and proven concept for the refurbishment of housing into nZEB. This is made possible by the installation of prefabricated facades, efficient heating systems and insulated roofs equipped with solar panels. The installation takes less than a week and the inhabitants do not need to leave their homes (Energiesprong, 2017).

Born in the Netherlands, the concept is expending to France and the UK, as well as New York State (USA). The EU has supported the uptake of Energiesprong projects in Europe by financing the work related to aggregation of demand, the coordination of public and private actors and the demonstration of the viability of the concept.

Provide European-Wide Information on Building Stocks, Renovation and Construction Rates and Policies

A key challenge to monitoring sustainable building policies is the lack of initial data on the building stock. The European Building Stock Observatory is now gathering and displaying European building data on residential and non-residential buildings. The online mapping tool includes information on building characteristics, performance, systems, renovation and construction rates, energy consumption and energy poverty throughout Europe. A sizable share of the data of this observatory comes from the Episcope data hub project financed by H2020 and from the insights of the BPIE.

To conclude this section, it can be said that the EU played a substantial role in the move toward the transformation of European building stock, trying to shepherd the lagers with common standards and objectives as well as tailoring incentives to overcome market barriers.

Member States have also started to address the question of sustainable real estate, albeit some earlier than others. European countries have developed a plurality of approaches, focusing on different but complementary aspects of a smart and sustainable building.

3 Diversity in National Approaches

The European building stock is very diverse across countries. It reflects the history of the countries, the socio-economic patterns and the climate conditions. The levels of ambition of the national governments are also unequal and can evolve fast. However, awareness is rising throughout Europe on the benefits of energy efficient real estate, partly due to the efforts of the EU. The strategies and policies developed are so diverse that it is almost impossible to draw comparisons. Increasing amounts of data are being gathered by European research institutions such as The European Building Observatory, Zebra and the BPIE which provide interesting analyses in this area. This section provides an overview of where European countries stand regarding the smart-readiness of their building stock. A more detailed exploration is also provided regarding the three major challenges to the transformation of the European building stock: the financing of the renovation, the alleviation of energy poverty and the connection of buildings to smart grids. Finally, we offer a snapshot of a number of interesting national policies and initiatives.

3.1 Countries Mapping

The BPIE (De Groote, Volt, & Bean, 2017) recently performed a complete analysis of the "smart-readiness" of European countries; "smart-readiness" meaning the ability of the legal and competitive environment of Member States to welcome the takeoff of sustainable real estate.

The data in this chapter were gathered by BPIE from the EU Building Stock Observatory and Eurostat, the Smart Energy Demand Coalition (SEDC, 2015), the European Commission's Joint Research Centre (Bertoldi, Zancanella, & Boza-kiss, 2016, JCR), the European Commission's DG Energy, the Agency for the Cooperation of Energy Regulators (ACER/CEER, 2015), Germany Trade & Invest (GTAI) (Rothacher, 2016) and the European Automobile Manufacturers Association. The work of BPIE is here complemented by a review of further specialized publications.

The study evaluates this "smart-readiness" based on 12 indicators, from building performance to connectivity and the integration of renewable energy. These 12 indicators give a detailed representation of the strengths and weaknesses of each country. The map (Fig. 5.1) illustrates the overall results of the European countries in terms of smart-readiness.

The spatial representation of the "smart-readiness" of countries offers a rather traditional cut of the territory in European geographic regions. While no country is fully "smart-ready", the Northern countries, such as Denmark, Finland, Sweden and the Netherlands are doing better than their counterparts. Western European countries (Germany, Italy, the UK, France, Austria and Ireland) are "slow movers" or "followers", even though they may excel on one particular aspect of smart-readiness (see Table 5.2, national strengths are further developed in Sect. 3.3). Mediterranean and Eastern European countries are "cautious adopters". Six countries across Europe have been identified as lagers or "slow-starters".

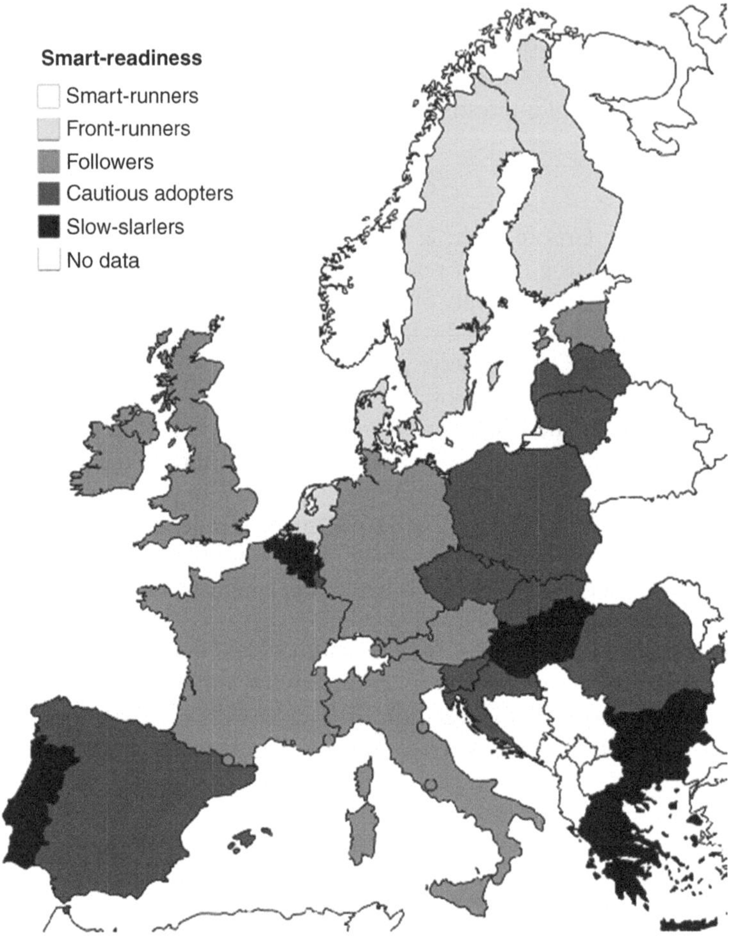

Fig. 5.1 Smart-readiness in Europe. Source: De Groote et al. (2017), BPIE

3.2 *Major Challenges to Sustainable Real Estate*

3.2.1 *Financing the Renovation*

Although a sustainable renovation of European real estate may unlock number of economic and social benefits, countries in the EU—like most countries worldwide—are struggling to finance the refurbishment of their

Table 5.2 National and municipal refurbishment initiatives by type of beneficiaries

Program	*Country*	*Scope*	*Public*	*Commercial*	*Residential*	*Industrial*
REDIBA	Spain	Barcelona province	X			
Berlin Energy Saving Partnership	Germany	Berlin State	X	X		
RE:FIT	UK	Greater London	X			
Vlaams Energiebedrijf	Belgium	Flander region	X			
OSER	France	Rhones-Alpes region	X			
Fedesco	Belgium	Belgium Federal State	X			
Eandis EDLB	Belgium	Flander region	X			
ESCOLimburg 2020	Belgium	Limburg city	X			
Eco'Energies	France	Nice Côte-d'Azur region		X		
Energy Fund Den Haag	The Netherlands	The Hague city	X	X	X	X
Energies POSIT'IF	France	Ile-de-France region			X	
Climate Community Saerbeck	Germany	Saerbeck city	X	X	X	X
Cambridgeshire MLEI	UK	Cambridgeshire county	X	X		
Oxfutures	UK	Oxford county	X	X		X
Rotterdam Green Buildings	The Netherlands	Rotterdam city	X			
Energy efficiency Milan	Italy	Milan province	X			
ENSAMB	Norway	Sør-Østerdal region	X			
Brixton Energy Co-op	UK	Lambeth district			X	
EERFS	Bulgaria	Bulgaria	X	X	X	X
SUNSHINE	Latvia	Latvia	X		X	
Warm up North	UK	North East England	X		X	
SPEE Picardie	France	Picardie region			X	
KredEx	Estonia	Estonia			X	
PadovaFIT!	Italy	Padova city	X	X	X	

Source: Vanstraelen et al. (2015), CITYnvest

building stock. This section provides information on the current state of the building stock in Europe, explores European models to finance its renovation and looks more closely to some recent renovation projects carried at municipal levels.

The socio-economic benefits to sustainable renovation in Europe are high. They include job creation, health improvement and reduced air pollution in addition to energy savings. Studies estimate that a million euros invested in renovation in Europe could create between 13.5 and 17 new jobs (Meijer, Visscher, Nieboer, & Kroese, 2012). Overall, 0.4 million jobs could be maintained or created by 2050 in a "slow and shallow" scenario, while job creation could reach almost two million by 2050 in a "deep renovation scenario" (BPIE, 2011). The health benefits originating from improved indoor climate are not negligible either. They are assessed between €42 and €88 billion per year by the consultancy Copenhagen Economics (Naess-Schmidt, Bo Hansen, & Von utfall Danielsson, 2012).

Unfortunately, the rate of major renovation in Europe remains too low to reach these forecasts. It stalls at an average of 1% of the building stock per year. Countries like Germany, France or Austria lead the way with 1.5% of major renovation per year. Out of these renovations, not all may meet the nearly zero-energy standard, since renovation standards are set by minimum requirements at national level.

Renovation in Europe is all the more critical than more than half of the residential stock was built before the first thermal regulations (i.e. before 1970) when buildings were poorly insulated (European Building Stock Observatory, 2017) (see Fig. 5.2a, b).

The characteristics of the building stock vary widely by country and may impact the renovation strategies. For example, the tenure rate is an important factor. It negatively influences the likelihood of carrying out energy efficient measures due to split incentives, that is, owners have little incentive to invest if the tenant pays the energy bill. While ownership reaches 80% in Eastern European Countries, tenure rates are higher in Western Europe with 30% to 50% of the population renting their homes in Germany, Austria, Denmark, the UK, France and the Netherlands (European Building Stock Observatory, 2014). A thorough review of the European building stock in Europe is offered by the publication "Europe's Buildings Under the Microscope" (BPIE, 2011).

Renovation schemes in Europe have been designed with a creative mix of private finance, public guaranteed debt from the EU (as presented in Sect. 2.2), and the Member State and local regions, sometimes associated

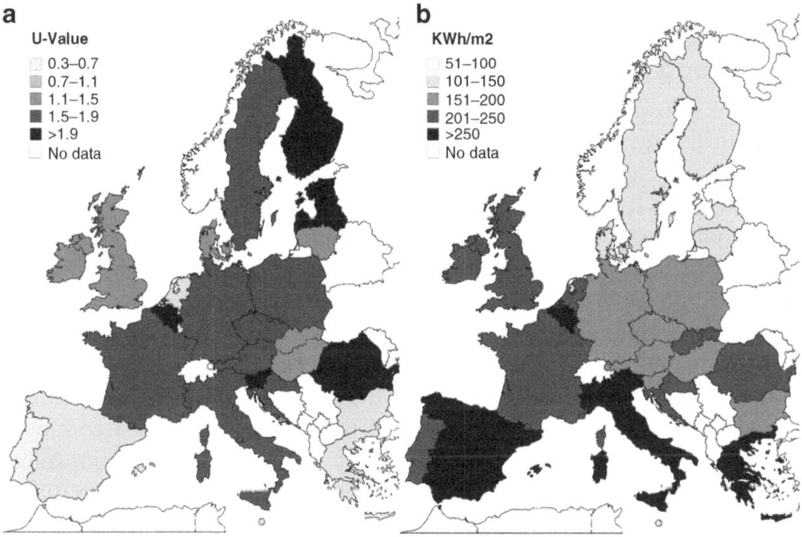

Fig. 5.2 (**a**) Building envelope, U-value of building envelope for residential and non-residential buildings; (**b**) Final energy consumption under normal climate conditions, kWh/m^2 for residential and non-residential buildings. Source: De Groote et al. (2017), BPIE and European Building Stock Observatory

with grants, the objective being to slowly but surely increase the share of private financing. It is difficult to draw out a "European model" of financing. Each country and region has developed its own approach, with various levels of implication and integration for the different stakeholders. However, it is worth mentioning that, to date, the EU is not at the forefront of innovative financing. Unlike the USA, the EU does not allow the issuance of qualified energy conservation bonds. These bonds, authorized by the US Congress and allocated to US States, amount to US $3.2 billion and allow private investors to participate in the financing of local energy efficiency projects (Energy programs consortium, 2013). This approach could be a way forward to increase the share of private finance in deep renovation projects.

In 2006, Germany started a pioneering model for financing the energy efficiency measures in housing renovation. The public development bank *Kreditanstalt für Wiederaufbau* (KfW) distributed soft loans and grants for refurbishment and construction that meet higher standards than the reference building described in the ordinance of the Energy Saving Act. For interested readers, a fact sheet was developed by Concerted Action EED in 2013 and describes the process in a consistent manner (Concerted Action EED, 2013). However, an evaluation of the KfW scheme by the German Energy Agency (Kunde, 2016), demonstrates that this Federal program may have reached a threshold and even lost attractiveness over the past years. In the last three years, the number of constructions benefitting from this scheme leveled off at 80,000 dwellings a year, while the number of renovations constantly decreased from 24,000 in 2009 to 10,000 in 2015. While the reasons remain to be assessed, stakeholders in Germany are calling for a reform in the financing scheme.

In Bulgaria, the central government launched the "Energy Efficiency and Renewable Sources Fund" (EERSF), formerly known as the "Bulgarian Energy Efficiency Fund" (BEEF). It operates as a commercially oriented public-private finance facility and pursues three major roles: it is a lending institution, a credit guarantee facility, and at the same time, a technical assistance provider. Beneficiaries of the technical assistance are Bulgarian enterprises, municipalities and residents who develop energy efficiency and renewable energy source projects. It provides financing or co-financing, or acts as a guarantor toward other financing institutions or commercial lenders (Vanstraelen, Marchand, Casas, Creupelandt, & Steyaert, 2015).

In France, regions have been key stakeholders in promoting climate policies and refurbishment schemes, paving the way for the development of innovative financing schemes. The Law on the Energy Transition (Legifrance, 2015), adopted in August 2015, now requires all regions to set up platforms functioning as a one-stop-shop, gathering all stakeholders, (e.g. architects, NGOs, etc.), and providing free advice to consumers.

Municipalities, more than Member States, have been at the forefront of innovative financing to renovate parts of their housing stock. The research and innovation platform, CITYnvest, specializing in municipal capacity buildings in Europe, provided an in-depth review of 24 municipal initiatives (Vanstraelen et al., 2015). This analysis demonstrated that the majority of municipal projects have focused on public buildings (18 out of 24). This may be due to the EED obligation to renovate 3% of public buildings per year, and also triggered by the fact that public entities can easily manage and renovate their own building stock. The CITYnvest review also offers an interesting framework to analyze the ambition of the refurbishment projects. It illustrates that most renovation projects have not yet fulfilled the long-term objective of deep renovation. Out of 24 initiatives, 16 are part of the perimeter with the lowest level of ambition, which means that the contract durations are less than 15 years, that retrofits are limited to basic climate and electrical engineering installations (renovation rate below 35%) and that costs are less than €50/m^2. Only one initiative is part of the most ambitious perimeter, which aims at carbon neutrality.

Despite the financial support of the EU, the path toward a decarbonized building stock by 2050 is a long one. Three interesting initiatives for the renovation of residential housing are presented in the following section.

Energies POSIT'IF (Ile-de-France, France)

This case is interesting for two reasons. First, it takes place in large multifamily condominiums where the decision power is diluted and the decision process can be lengthy. Second, it deals with a large majority of heavily indebted owners (due to very high price markets) who are not willing to contract additional loans. The project aims at the renovation of one million condominiums with EPCs rated E, F or G (230–450 kWh/m^2/year), with the purpose of reaching an energy performance below 104 kWh/m^2/year. To achieve this, the region Ile-de-France created its own energy company "POSIT'IF (Promote, Organize, Support, Imagine the Energy Transition in Ile-de-France Territory)", as a semi-public company acting under market rules. The role of POSIT'IF is to integrate the different stages of the process: energy audits, discussion with the owner association, contractual agreement, outsourcing of the sub-contractors with performance guarantees, and assistance in the financial structuring (Energies Posit'IF, 2017).

In some cases, POSIT'IF acts as facilitator between the condominium and the bank. It helps the condominium in accessing relevant grants and subsidies. In the other case, POSIT'IF takes the loan on behalf of the condominium and complements this with grants/subsidies and its own budget. The condominium pays monthly or quarterly installments and a service fee to POSIT'IF, which repays the bank (Vanstraelen et al., 2015).

According to Energies (2017), 30 contracts have been signed to date, which amounts to 4500 dwellings to be retrofitted in the coming years and €50 million in investment.

Picardie Pass Renovation (Picardie, France)

Another interesting initiative aims at achieving deep renovation to save between 50% and 75% of final energy costs in detached houses. To do so, Picardie region set up a "one-stop-shop" which offers third-party financing. It lends to owners based on future energy savings, a financing option which is generally not offered by the banks. Out of the energy gains, 85% finance the thermal retrofit and 15% benefit the end user. The average cost of retrofit is €30,000 per house and €15,000 per apartment. The scheme offers the possibility to get grants in addition to pre-financing and loans (Vanstraelen et al., 2015). The objective of SPEE Picardie is "*to renovate 10.000 units per year by mid 2018*" *(SPEE Picardie website, 2017).*

Saerbeck (Germany)

Finally, the Saerbeck project is the most surprising and interesting since it has been originated and partly financed by the local community. The initiative, starting in 2008 was part of a broader objective of the community to be independent of the grid and produce 100% renewable energy by 2030. As a result of this initiative, in 2016, the community has installed over 438 PV installations on the roofs of private houses and schools, it is running its own local electricity grid and it has built a central heating plant. On top of this, it started an educational program and transformed a former ammunition park into a bioenergy park including seven wind turbines, a biogas plant, a bio waste treatment plant with a digestion stage and a PV park. The community already produces about 3.5 times more renewable energy than the local consumption required, and the CO_2 per capita has decreased from 9 tons to 5.5 tons. Part of this project was directly related to sustainable buildings. Participants could get loans from local banks as well as local incentives and technical advice to install solar panels on their roofs and to refurbish their homes. Heating is now provided through a central heating plant fueled by wood pellets and subsidized by the Nordrhein-Westfalen government. The wind turbines, the PV solar park, the biogas plant and the composting plant were financed by a mix of local investors, local banks and public investments (Vanstraelen et al., 2015).

3.2.2 Energy Poverty

Energy poverty is one of the major social issues in Europe; and financing the energy renovation in low-income or highly indebted households constitutes an additional challenge for public authorities.

To date, the definition of energy poverty is not harmonized at a European level, which illustrates the low priority level of this question on the political agenda. Articles from Thomson and Snell (2013), Bouzarovski, Petrova, and Sarlamanov (2012), the BPIE (Atanasiu, Kontonasiou, & Mariottini, 2014) and the EU Joint Research Center (Saheb, Bódis, Szabo, Ossenbrink, & Panev, 2015) have selected samples of Eurostat indicators to produce a comparative European analysis. Table 5.3 presents the results of the three most common indicators as of 2015. On average in 2015, 15% of Europeans lived in dwellings with a leaking roof, damp walls, floors or foundation, or rotten window frames or floors; 9% were

Table 5.3 Fuel poverty in European countries in percentage of the population in 2015

European countries	*Arrears on utility bills*	*Inability to keep house warm*	*Dwellings with leaking roofs and damp walls*	*European countries*	*Arrears on utility bills*	*Inability to keep house warm*	*Dwellings with leaking roofs and damp walls*
Bulgaria	31.4	39.2	12.9	Slovakia	5.7	5.8	6.3
Lithuania	8.4	31.1	17.0	Slovenia	17.5	5.6	26.9
Greece	42.0	29.2	15.1	France	5.9	5.5	12.6
Cyprus	20.1	28.3	26.1	Belgium	5.1	5.2	18.2
Portugal	7.8	23.8	28.1	Czech Republic	3.0	5.0	8.9
Republic of Macedonia	40.1	23.4	12.2	Germany	4.0	4.1	12.6
Italy	12.6	17.0	24.1	Denmark	3.4	3.6	16.1
Serbia	34.8	15.2	23.4	Netherlands	2.7	2.8	15.7
Latvia	16.7	14.5	24.4	Austria	3.5	2.6	11.7
Malta	10.2	13.9	10.2	Estonia	7.9	2.0	13.4
Romania	17.4	13.1	12.2	Finland	7.5	1.7	4.4
Spain	8.8	10.6	15.2	Sweden	2.7	0.9	7.5
Croatia	28.5	10.0	10.9	Luxembourg	2.4	0.9	14.4
Hungary	19.4	9.6	25.4	Switzerland	3.6	0.6	11.9
Ireland	15.1	9.0	13.6	Norway	3.2	0.4	6.8
UK	7.0	7.8	14.8	EU (28 MS)	9.1	9.4	15.2
Poland	9.2	7.5	11.9	Euro area (18 MS)	8.4	9.2	16.0

unable to keep their home adequately warm and 9.1% of Europeans were unable to pay their bills.

Eastern European and Mediterranean countries are the Member States where fuel poverty is the most acute. Bulgaria, Lithuania, Greece, Cyprus, Portugal and Macedonia have more than 20% of their population unable to keep their home adequately warm. In Slovenia and Hungary, more than one-fourth of the dwellings have poor environmental conditions, such as leaking roofs and damp walls. In Greece and Macedonia, more than 40% of the population is in arrears on their utility bill payments. The situation is less critical in Northern countries despite cold temperatures.

There is no clear tendency on how fuel poverty develops in the European region between 2007 and 2015. Fuel poverty seems to be mostly staling, if not increasing in some countries. Arrears on utility bills increased in many countries throughout Europe such as Bulgaria (29–31%), Slovenia (11–17%), Romania (8–17%), Ireland (6–15%), Italy (10–12%) and Spain (4–9%), while the inability to keep homes warm reduced tremendously in Bulgaria (67–40%), Portugal (41–23%), Latvia (20–14%) and Romania (33–13%). The same factor increased in Lithuania (22–31%) and Italy (10–17%). The case of Greece is particularly striking. As a consequence of the debt crisis and increasing energy price, arrears in Greece have skyrocketed from 15.7% in 2007 to 42% in 2015 and the number of people unable to keep their home warm has more than doubled from 13% in 2007 to 29% in 2015.

Not surprisingly, low-income people are more likely to be exposed to fuel poverty. The BPIE study shows a strong correlation between the percentage of people living at risk of poverty and people failing to pay their arrears (0.84) or being able to keep their home warm (0.77) (Atanasiu et al., 2014). Those in fuel poverty are also more exposed to health problems and a higher share of low-income people face excess winter deaths.

The alleviation of fuel poverty goes hand in hand with the definition of large renovation policies that target the poorest. Since 2010, the EU has required Member States to develop long-term solutions that are not only related to the repayment of energy bills, and a limited number of schemes have been launched in the UK, France, Lithuania, Romania and Ireland (Atanasiu et al., 2014). All these programs have been designed to distribute grants for the installation of energy efficiency measures in low-income properties; some may include a mixture of grants and low interest rate loans. All of these show very positive results on the comfort and warmth, as well as the physical and mental health of residents. Generally, energy bills have decreased. In the cases where bills remained the same, the retrofit had actually absorbed the rise in energy prices that would have otherwise translated into increased payments.

The UK has been the front-runner for several years as it has developed four different schemes targeting the retrofit of low-income properties since 2000. The Warm Front Scheme provides a good example of how these programs work. The scheme took place between 2000 and 2012 in the UK and consisted of the subsidized implementation of energy efficiency measures such as the installation of new efficient boilers and the insulation of walls. Grants could amount up to £3500 (or £6000 where an oil heating system or renewable technology was recommended). Overall 1.5 million households benefitted from the scheme from 2005 to 2013. On average two measures were installed per household.

Evaluations of this scheme (Green & Gilbertson, 2008; Ipsos MORI and University College London, 2014) explain that one of the major challenges was the definition of energy poverty. Eligibility criteria were modified and tightened several times and by the end of the program, in 2013, 80% of the eligible participants lived in "hard-to-treat" properties. The latest designates properties with solid walls, which are harder to insulate than cavity walls, or houses that have no connection to the gas network. The scheme had positive impacts on the mental and physical health of the recipients, and the prevalence for anxiety and depression fell by 48%. In 2013, the Warm Front Scheme was replaced by another similar scheme, the Affordable Warmth Grant, with beneficiaries able to test their eligibility for the program directly online.

3.2.3 Smart Grid and Demand Response

The EU is slowly getting on track with enhanced demand-response, that is, the ability for buildings to adapt their energy demand depending on market energy price, thereby avoiding expensive and fuel-intensive peak loads. The proper implementation of demand-response is a challenge and entails several policies and evolutions. It requires the revision of national legislation on energy markets, the rollout of smart meters in all buildings and an evolution of consumer behaviors.

Article 15 of the EED requires from Members States to remove all legal barriers to demand-response. As a matter of fact, only six countries in Europe (France, the UK, Ireland, Belgium, Switzerland and Finland) have yet successfully adapted their legislation to ensure commercially viable solutions for demand-response. Others, such as Sweden, the Netherlands, Austria, Germany, Slovenia, Poland and Denmark have taken preliminary steps (SEDC, 2015).

As for the rollout of smart meters, the EU forecasts that 72% of European households should install a smart meter for electricity in 2020. We are not there yet. To date only a handful of countries including Italy, Sweden, France and Croatia will have completed the rollout of smart electricity meters by 2020. Smart meters are a condition for dynamic pricing, meaning that consumers can adapt their consumption based on signals sent by the meter (e.g. by delaying starting their dishwasher). As illustrated in Fig. 5.3, dynamic pricing for electricity is starting to be available to Europeans while fewer countries have yet tackled the question of smart metering and dynamic pricing for gas.

In the process, a number of national regulators have raised the concern that smart metering may not be cost-efficient. In a study performed by the CEER (2013), they stress that consumers in Europe have demonstrated little interest in dynamic pricing. Part of the reason is probably the limited awareness of the possible financial benefits of dynamic pricing. However, because of the low volatility in European energy prices, consumers may consider that dynamic pricing brings insufficient savings. Regulators also point out an increasing preference of consumers for fixed-price contracts that are not compatible with dynamic pricing and demand-response. In addition to these consumer-related obstacles, Member States who have already deployed smart meters have had difficulties in communicating an adequate price signal to consumers. Market prices and supply prices may differ and evolve in different directions and regulators have struggled to reflect prices in the best interest of the consumer (ACER/CEER, 2015).

Despite all these difficulties, European Member States are moving forward with the deployment of smart meters. The future generation of smart meters should hopefully integrate a number of common features (CEER, 2013), including remote reading, two-way communication, interval metering and access to a web portal. Early movers, for example Sweden and Italy, will need to update their devices to ensure that all these functionalities are available (De Groote et al., 2017).

3.3 Interesting National Initiatives

It would make little sense to present the European diversity of practices without focusing on some innovative policies implemented in European countries. The coming review is not meant to be an exhaustive analysis of the national regulations in place in each country but rather a brief scan of the paths and directions taken by some of them to support market developments toward sustainable real estate.

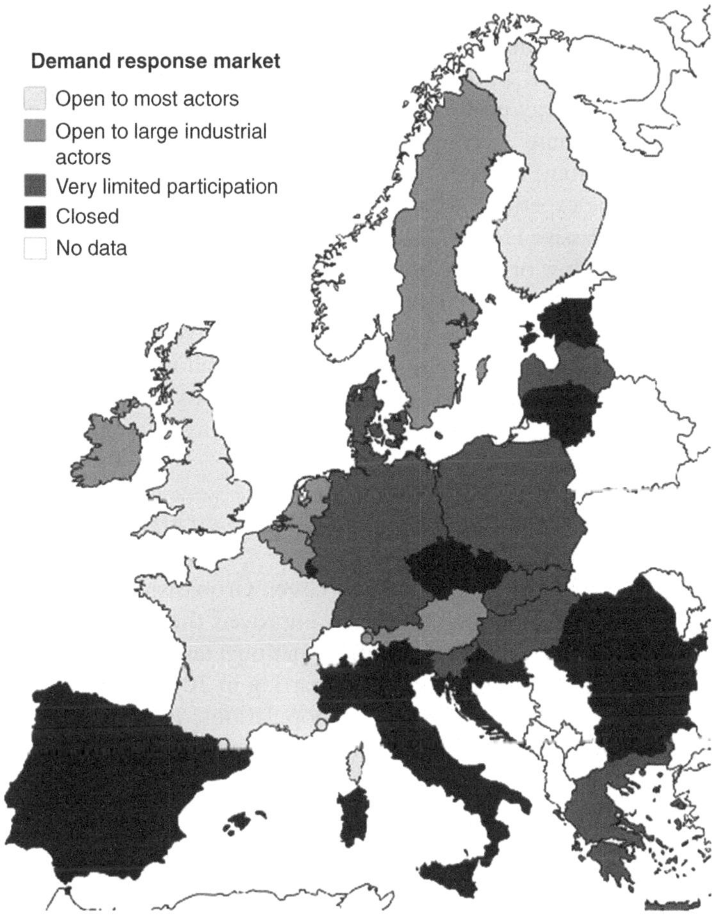

Fig. 5.3 Implicit demand response availability across the EU in 2015. Source: De Groote et al. (2017), BPIE; Bertoldi et al. (2016), JCR; ACER/CEER (2015)

3.3.1 Brussels Region (Belgium) to Define Passive House as the Standard for Construction

Within four years, the Brussels-Capital region moved from lager to front-runner in the construction and renovation of sustainable buildings. In 2007, the government of Brussels-Capital started the Building Exemplary initiative. This public call for project co-financed a handful of projects able to renovate and construct buildings respecting the "Passive House" standard. The program happened to be very successful and six consecutive calls were submitted. In 2014, the project had resulted in 621,000 m^2 with very high energy performance standards, of which 350,000 m^2 met the "Passive House" requirements (Govaert, Knipping, Mortehan, Rouard, & Squilbin, 2014).

Based on the experience accumulated, the Brussels-Capital Region has imposed the "Passive House" standard on new construction in the public-sector, and the "low or even very low energy standard" for all renovations from 2011 onwards. Since 2015, all new buildings constructed must meet the maximum insulation standards, defined as "passive ambition" (Region Bruxelles-Capitale, 2013). While no single study allows to draw conclusions on whether, and how, the market could adapt to these standards, the Brussels-Capital Region stands as the most ambitious region in Europe for construction in this field.

3.3.2 *France to Boost Renovation with a Focus on Larger Environmental Concerns*

The Law on the Energy Transition and Green Growth adopted in August 2015 in France (Legifrance, 2015) has improved the legal environment for sustainable building and set ambitious national targets. The law aims at renovating 500,000 dwellings per year, starting in 2017, of which half are inhabited by modest and low-income populations, thereby planning to reduce fuel poverty by 15% in 2020. To do so, all buildings with primary energy consumption of more than 330 kWh/m^2/year should be renovated (article 5). In practice, the French government did not yet publish any implementation text to clarify how this article should be enforced, but the law includes a number of practical requirements that should contribute to reaching the target. For example, routine renovation work (facade roof, windows) will have to come with improvements in energy efficiency (article 14) and planning rules will get soften to facilitate energy retrofits. The law also includes the set up an online building booklet and the development of a fund to fight energy poverty.

The text goes beyond energy efficiency. A certification on "environmental exemplarity" will integrate criteria related to water, waste, CO_2, energy, rainfall management, vegetation, materials and air quality (articles 7 and 8 as well as the implementation decree). All new public buildings should be certified with energy exemplarity, environmental exemplarity and when possible, be certified energy positive.

3.3.3 *Germany, First on Battery Storage*

Energy storage in households is key to ensuring a reduction of peak load consumption as it can store and release the energy produced by the building independently of the grid. Energy storage should also develop the ability of positive energy buildings to release energy to the grid when needed. Since 2013, the KfW development bank has offered soft loans and grants for batteries combined with grid-connected solar PV systems. At the end of 2015, Germany had more than 35,000 PV battery systems installed (De Groote et al., 2017). The growth potential is estimated by the economic development agency of Germany (GTAI) at around 50,000 new residential batteries per year by 2020 (Rothacher, 2016).

3.3.4 *The Netherlands, Leader in the Management of Energy Performance Certificates*

EPCs are key to inform households of the energy performance of their dwelling, provide advise on energy efficient measures, boost the competitiveness of efficient buildings, and more generally, keep track of the evolution of the building stock at national level. However, many countries have struggled to ensure qualitative certified EPC as well as to record the results in aggregated databases. In the Netherlands, energy performance certification (EPC) is available online for only €25. In 2015, a simplified EPC template was developed in cooperation with all stakeholders. Each building owner receives a free temporary EPC calculated based on the cadaster data by mail. Owners can digitally change or adapt this estimate through an online platform, if they justify changes with invoices or pictures. The EPC process online is only composed of four steps. The existing and new data are verified by a certified expert who will enter a final EPC in the database (European Commission, 2016).

3.3.5 *Denmark and Finland, Leaders in Heat Recovery*

In Denmark, 60% of Danish consumers benefit from district heating. A majority of this heat (55%) originates from non-fossil fuel energy sources such as waste, renewable energy or recovered energy via heat pumps (Danish Energy Agency, 2016). The country has developed its infrastructure accordingly for the past 30 years. The majority of buildings have been equipped with water-based heating systems, radiators or floor heating systems, to convey district heating. The large majority of waste, if not recycled, is used for energy production, and only a minor fraction of the waste is deposited in landfill. Biomass was transformed as a key source for heating after a political agreement in 1993, which specified that centralized power and CHP plants should use 19.5 PJ/year of biomass by 2000, with certain shares from wood chips and straw.

Solar heating was also massively developed. Between 2005 and 2014, 500,000 solar collectors were installed. Today, the regulation requires that thermal solar systems should be installed in buildings outside district heating areas for any new construction and major renovation (Engelund et al., 2016). The overall strategy of Denmark is oriented toward sustainable buildings. As an illustration of the success of their policy, Denmark has one of the most stringent definitions of nZEB in Europe with voluntary standards down to 20 kW/m^2/year for residential and non-residential buildings.

Finland is also paving the way for heat recovery in Europe. The country's vision set a target of 1 million heat pumps in 2020 for a population of 5.4 million inhabitants. According to the Finnish heat pump association (Hirvonen, 2016), an average of 60,000 additional heat pumps are installed every year. The implementation of this policy is supported by a strong incentive system including tax deductions for renovation work (€2000–3000 for labor costs) and a subsidy program providing up to 20% off the costs when oil and electric-heating systems are replaced by a heat pump, biomass or a district heating system (De Groote et al., 2017).

4 Conclusion

Policymakers in the EU are becoming increasingly aware of the opportunities offered by the sustainable transformation of their building stock. With the support of the European institutions, policies of Member States are evolving fast, and many different paths are being explored. Denmark has developed expertise in district heating, France and Italy are exploring demand-response and Germany supports residential PV connected to the grid with battery storage. Soon, and according to the European Energy Performance Building Directive, all new constructions should be nZEB. They will produce part of their energy and connect to electric cars.

The largest challenge faced by the European countries will be the renovation of the existing building stock. In a region where States are already highly indebted, this process may represent a significant burden for public finances. This is all the more pertinent since the EU counts about 15% of the energy poor in its population (40% in some countries) and there is no business model that yet allows for the energy renovation of low-income housing without the support of public grants. The split incentive in countries with high tenure rates (30–50%) will also require some creative financing schemes. However, the emergence of new and low-cost technologies for renovation, illustrated by the Energiesprong concept of isolated prefabricated facades, will hopefully facilitate the refurbishment process of European buildings.

With the rollout of smart meters taking place in most Member States, it is expected that a large share of European building stock will be connected to the grid by 2020. But the ultimate challenge may be behavioral, as European consumers have shown limited responsiveness to dynamic pricing to date. The development of smart appliances and user-friendly control devices may be critical to the success of this policy.

To conclude, the construction and renovation sectors are working toward an increase in energy efficiency and connectivity of buildings. However, several aspects of "sustainability" have been lost in translation. As the building stock starts its transformation, it is critical that European countries think of "buildings" in a holistic way that integrates water, waste, vegetation and material. "Sustainable buildings" must also be considered in relation to their environment and in connection with their districts and cities, where inhabitants move and live. "Sustainable buildings" must transform into "sustainable real estate".

References

ACER/CEER. (2015). *Annual Report on the Results of Monitoring the Internal Electricity Markets in 2015*. Retrieved July 7, 2017, from http://www.acer.europa.eu/official_documents/acts_of_the_agency/publication/acer%20market%20monitoring%20report%202015%20-%20key%20insights%20and%20recommendations.pdf

Arcipowska, A., Anagnostopoulos, F., Mariottini, F., & Kunkel, S. (2014). *Energy Performance Certificates Across the EU*. Building Performance Institute Europe. Retrieved July 7, 2017, from http://bpie.eu/publication/energy-performance-certificates-across-the-eu/

Atanasiu, B., Kontonasiou, E., & Mariottini, F. (2014). *Alleviating Fuel Poverty in the EU: Investing in Home Renovation, a Sustainable and Inclusive Solution*. Buildings Performance Institute Europe. Retrieved July 7, 2017, from http://bpie.eu/wp-content/uploads/2015/10/Alleviating-fuel-poverty.pdf

Bertoldi, P., Zancanella, P., & Boza-kiss, B. (2016). *Demand Response status in EU Member States*. Joint Research Center. Retrieved July 7, 2017, from http://publications.jrc.ec.europa.eu/repository/bitstream/JRC101191/ldna27998enn.pdf. https://doi.org/10.2790/962868

Boermans, T., Dinges, K., Grözinger, J., Sonja, M. S., Förster, S., Hermelink, A., ... Von Manteuffel, B. (2015). *Public Consultation on the Evaluation of the EPBD, Final Report*. Ecofys. Retrieved July 7, 2017, from https://ec.europa.eu/energy/sites/ener/files/documents/Task2_final%20report_Public%20Consultation%20on%20the%20Evaluation%20of%20the%20EPBD.PDF

Bouzarovski, S., Petrova, S., & Sarlamanov, R. (2012). Energy Poverty Policies in the EU: A Critical Perspective. *Energy Policy, 49*, 76–82 https://doi.org/10.1016/j.enpol.2012.01.033

BPIE (Building Performance Institute Europe). (2011). Europe's Buildings Under the Microscope. A Country-by-Country Review of the Energy Performance of Buildings. Retrieved July 7, 2017 http://bpie.eu/publication/europes-buildings-under-the-microscope/

BPIE (Building Performance Institute Europe). (2015). *Nearly Zero Energy Buildings Definition Across Europe*. Retrieved July 7, 2017, from http://bpie.eu/uploads/lib/document/attachment/128/BPIE_factsheet_nZEB_definitions_across_Europe.pdf

Build Up Skills. (2017). Build Up Skills Website. Retrieved July 7, 2017, from http://www.buildup.eu/en/skills

CEER. (2013). *Status Review of Regulatory Aspects of Smart Metering*. Retrieved July 7, 2017, from http://www.ceer.eu/portal/page/portal/EER_HOME/EER_PUBLICATIONS/CEER_PAPERS/Customers/2013/7-1_C13-RMF-54-05-Status_Review_of_Regulatory_Aspects_of_Smart_Metering_FOR_PUBLICATION.pdf

Concerted Action EED. (2013). *Good Practice Factsheet, KfW Energy Efficiency Construction and Refurbishment – Germany*. Retrieved July 7, 2017, from http://www.epbd-ca.eu/countries/country-information

Concerted Action EED. (2016). *National EED Implementation Reports*. Retrieved July 7, 2017, from http://www.esd-ca.eu/outcomes/national-eed-implementation-reports

Crisp, J. (2015). 27 Member States Hit with EU Legal Action Over Energy Efficiency. Euractiv. Retrieved July 7, 2017, from https://www.euractiv.com/section/energy/news/27-member-states-hit-with-eu-legal-action-over-energy-efficiency/

D'Agostino, D., Zangheri, P., Cuniberti, B., Paci, D., & Bertoldi, P. (2016). *Synthesis Report on the National Plans for Nearly Zero Energy Buildings (NZEBs) Progress of Member States Towards NZEBs*. Joint Research Center. Retrieved July 7, 2017, from https://doi.org/10.2790/659611. https://ec.europa.eu/jrc/en/publication/eur-scientific-and-technical-research-reports/synthesis-report-national-plans-nearly-zero-energy-buildings-nzebs-progress-member-states

Danish Energy Agency. (2016). *Regulation and Planning of District Heating in Denmark*. Retrieved July 7, 2017, from https://stateofgreen.com/files/download/1973

De Groote, M., Volt, J., & Bean, F. (2017). *Is Europe Ready for the Smart Buildings Revolution?* Building Performance Institute Europe. Retrieved July 7, 2017, from http://bpie.eu/publication/is-europe-ready-for-the-smart-buildings-revolution/

DEEP Platform. (2017). De-Risking Energy Efficiency Platform. Retrieved July 7, 2017, from https://deep.eefig.eu/

EIB (European Investment Bank). (2017). ELENA. Retrieved July 7, 2017, from http://www.bei.org/products/advising/elena/index.htm

Energies Posit'IF. (2017). Energies Posit'IF. Retrieved July 7, 2017, from http://www.energiespositif.fr/

Energiesprong. (2017). Energiespong Website. Retrieved July 7, 2017, from http://energiesprong.eu/

Energy Programs Consortium. (2013). *Qualified Energy Conservation Bonds (QECBs)*. DSIRE. Retrieved July 7, 2017, from https://energy.gov/sites/prod/files/2014/06/f16/QECB_memo_12-13-13.pdf

Engelund, K., & Wittchen, K. B. (2015). *Energy Performance Requirements Using Cost-Optimal Levels, Overview and Outcomes*. Retrieved July 7, 2017, from http://www.epbd-ca.org/Medias/Pdf/Cost_optimal_summary_document_final.pdf

Engelund, K., Wittchen, K. B., Ostertag, B., Varming, N. B., Egesberg, L. T., & Hartung, T. (2016). *Implementation of the EPBD in Denmark, Status in December 2014*. Concerted Action EPBD. Retrieved July 7, 2017, from http://www.epbd-ca.eu/outcomes/2011-2015/CA3-2016-National-DENMARK-web.pdf

Erhorn, H., & Erhorn-Kluttig, H. (2015). *Towards 2020, Nearly Buildings Overview and Outcomes*. Concerted Action EPBD. Retrieved July 7, 2017, https://www.epbd-ca.eu/outcomes/2011-2015/CA3-CT-2015-5-Towards-2020-NZEB-web.pdf

European Building Stock Observatory. (2014). EU Buildings Renovation Rate. Retrieved July 7, 2017, from https://ec.europa.eu/energy/en/eu-buildings-factsheets

European Building Stock Observatory. (2017). *Building Stock Characteristics*. Retrieved July 7, 2017, from https://ec.europa.eu/energy/en/eu-buildings-factsheets

European Commission. (2016). *Commission Staff Working Document, Good Practiced in Energy Efficiency Part 1/4*. https://doi.org/SWD(2013)93. Retrieved July 7, 2017, from http://ec.europa.eu/energy/sites/ener/files/documents/5_en_autre_document_travail_service_part3_v4.pdf

European Commission. (2016a). *Commission Staff Working Document, Evaluation of Article 6 and 7 of the Energy Efficiency Directive*. Retrieved July 7, 2017, from https://doi.org/SWD(2013)93. Eur-Lex, http://eur-lex.europa.eu/legal-content/EN/TXT/?uri=SWD:2016:0403:FIN

European Commission. (2016b). *Commission Staff Working Document, Good Practices in Energy Efficiency Part 3/4*. Retrieved July 7, 2017, from https://doi.org/SWD(2013)93. http://ec.europa.eu/energy/sites/ener/files/documents/5_en_autre_document_travail_service_part3_v4.pdf

European Commission. (2016c). Communication from the Commission to the European Parliament, the Council, the European Economic and Social Committee, the Committee of the Regions and the European Investment Bank; Clean Energy for all Europeans. Retrieved July 7, 2017, from http://eur-lex.europa.eu/legal-content/en/TXT/?uri=CELEX:52016DC0860

European Commission. (2016d). Communication from the Commission to the European Parliament, the Council, the European Economic and Social Committee and the Committee of the Regions, an EU Strategy on Heating and Cooling. Retrieved July 7, 2017, from https://doi.org/10.1017/CBO9781107415324.004., https://ec.europa.eu/transparency/regdoc/rep/1/2016/EN/1-2016-51-EN-F1-1.PDF

European Commission. (2016e). EU Construction & Demolition Waste Management Protocol. Retrieved July 7, 2017, from http://ec.europa.eu/growth/tools-databases/newsroom/cf/itemdetail.cfm?item_id=8983

European Commission. (2016f). Proposal for a Directive of the European Parliament and of the Council Amending Directive 2010/31/EU on the Energy Performance of Buildings, 381 §. Retrieved July 7, 2017, from Eur-Lex http://eur-lex.europa.eu/procedure/EN/2016_381

European Union. (2009). Directive 2009/125/EC of the European Parliament and of the Council of 21 October 2009, Establishing a Framework for the Setting of Ecodesign Requirements for Energy-Related Products (recast). *Official Journal of the European Union*. Retrieved July 7, 2017, from https://doi.org/10.1016/j.cirp.2012.03.121. Eur-Lex. http://eur-lex.europa.eu/legal-content/EN/ALL/?uri=CELEX%3A32009L0125

European Union. (2010a). Directive 2010/30/EU of the European Parliament and of the Council; on the Indication by Labelling and Standard Product Information of the Consumption of Energy and Other Resources by Energy-Related Products (recast). *Official Journal of the European Union*. Retrieved July 7, 2017, from https://doi.org/10.1017/CBO9781107415324.004. Eur-Lex. http://eur-lex.europa.eu/legal-content/EN/ALL/?uri=CELEX%3A32010L0030

European Union. (2010b). Directive 2010/31/EU of the European Parliament and of the Council of 19 May 2010 on the Energy Performance of Buildings (recast). *Official Journal of the European Union*, 13–35. Retrieved July 7, 2017, from https://doi.org/10.3000/17252555.L_2010.153.eng.Eur-Lex. http://eur-lex.europa.eu/legal-content/en/TXT/?uri=CELEX:32010L0031

European Union. (2012). Directive 2012/27/EU of the European Parliament and of the Council of 25 October 2012 on Energy Efficiency. *Official Journal of the European Union Directive*. Retrieved July 7, 2017, from https://doi.org/10.3000/19770677.L_2012.315.eng. Eur-Lex. http://eur-lex.europa.eu/legal-content/EN/TXT/?uri=celex%3A32012L0027

European Union. (2013). Council Regulation (EU, EURATOM) No 1311/2013 Laying Down the Multiannual Financial Framework for the Years 2014–2020, L 347/884. *Official Journal of the European Union*. Retrieved July 7, 2017, from Eur-Lex. http://eur-lex.europa.eu/legal-content/EN/TXT/?uri=CELEX%3A32013R1311

Giraudet, L.-G., & Finon, D. (2014). European Experiences with White Certificate Obligations: A Critical Review of Existing Evaluations. *Economics of Energy & Environmental Policy, 4*(1), 113–130. https://doi.org/10.5547/2160-5890.4.1.lgir

Govaert, M., Knipping, G., Mortehan, Y., Rouard, J.-H., & Squilbin, M. (2014). *Implementation of the EPBD in Belgium, Brussels Capital Region*. Concerted Action EBPD. Retrieved July 7, 2017, from http://www.epbd-ca.org/Medias/Pdf/country_reports_14-04-2011/Belgium_Brussels_Capital_Region.pdf

Green, G., & Gilbertson, J. (2008). Warm Front Better Health – Health Impact Evaluation of the Warm Front Scheme, 1–25. Sheffield Hallam University. Retrieved July 7, 2017, from http://www4.shu.ac.uk/research/cresr/warm-front-better-health-health-impact-evaluation-warm-front-scheme-0

Hirvonen, J. (2016). Heat Pump Market in 2016, PowerPoint presentation by SULPU. Retrieved July 7, 2017, from http://www.sulpu.fi/in-english

Ipsos MORI & University College London. (2014). *Process Evaluation of the Warm Front Scheme*. Retrieved July 7, 2017, from https://www.gov.uk/government/uploads/system/uploads/attachment_data/file/322901/Warm_Front_Evaluation_Report.pdf

Kaar, L. A., Turner, R., & Forster, D. (2017). *How Are Member States Implementing Articles 7 and 8 of the Energy Efficiency Directive?* Odyssee-Mure. Retrieved July 7, 2017, from http://www.odyssee-mure.eu/publications/policy-brief/member-states-energy-efficiency-measures.pdf

Kunde, J. (2016). *KfW-Förderreport 2015 Auswertung – Kurzfassung*. Retrieved July 7, 2017, from https://www.dena.de/fileadmin/dena/Dokumente/Presse___Medien/dena-KfW-Foerderreport2015-Analyse.pdf

Legifrance. (2015). Loi n°2015-992 du 17 août 2015 relative à la transition énergétique pour la croissance verte. Retrieved July 7, 2017, from https://www.legifrance.gouv.fr/affichTexte.do?cidTexte=JORFTEXT000031044385&categorieLien=id

Meijer, F., Visscher, H., Nieboer, N., & Kroese, R. (2012). *Jobs Creation Through Energy Renovation of the Housing Stock*. Neujobs. Retrieved on July 7, 2017, from http://www.neujobs.eu/publications/working-papers/jobs-creation-through-energy-renovation-housing-stock

Miladinova, G. (2015). *Energy Efficiency Financing: What Support from the European Structural and Investment Funds (ESIF)?* Not Accessible Online.

Naess-Schmidt, H., Bo Hansen M., & Von utfall Danielsson, C. (2012). *Multiple Effect of Investing in Energy Efficient Renovation of Buildings, Impact on Public Finances*. Copenhagen Economics. Retrieved July 7, 2017, from https://www.copenhageneconomics.com/publications/publication/multiple-benefits-of-investing-in-energy-efficient-renovation-of-buildings

PWC. (2015). Emerging Trends in Real Estate, a Balancing Act, Europe 2015. Retrieved June 7, 2017, from http://www.pwc.com/im/en/publications/assets/property/emerging-trends-in-real-estate-europe%2D%2D-2015.pdf

Region Bruxelles-Capitale. (2013). Arreté du Gouvernement de la Region de Bruxelles-Capitale modifiant l'arrêté du Gouvernement de la Région de Bruxelles-Capitale du 21 décembre 2007 déterminant des exigences en matière de performance énergétique et de climat intérieur des bâtiments. Retrieved July 7, 2017, from http://www.etaamb.be/fr/document-du-21-fevrier-2013_n2013031116.html

Renz, A., & Solas, M. (2016). *Shaping the Future of Construction. A Breakthrough in Mindset and Technology*. World Economic Forum. Retrieved June 7, 2017, from https://www.weforum.org/reports/shaping-the-future-of-construction-a-breakthrough-in-mindset-and-technology

Rothacher, T. (2016). *Energy Storage in Germany: Drivers Behind the Boom*. PowerPoint Presentation. Retrieved July 7, 2017, from https://www.gtai.de/GTAI/Content/EN/Meta/Events/Invest/2016/Reviews/Hannover-messe/smart-grids-forum-2016-presentation-tobias-rothacher.pdf?v=2

Saheb, Y., Bódis, K., Szabo, S., Ossenbrink, H., & Panev, S. (2015). *Energy Renovation: The Trump Card for the New Start for Europe*. Joint Research Center. Retrieved July 7, 2017, from https://doi.org/10.2790/39989. https://ec.europa.eu/jrc/en/publication/eur-scientific-and-technical-research-reports/energy-renovation-trump-card-new-start-europe

SEDC. (2015). *Mapping Demand Response in Europe Today. SEDC. Smart Energy Demand Coalition*. Retrieved July 7, 2017, from http://www.febeliec.be/web/infosessionstrategicdemandreserve_16_5_2014/1011306087/list1187970122/f1.html%5Cn

Thomson, H., & Snell, C. (2013). Quantifying the Prevalence of Fuel Poverty Across the European Union. *Energy Policy, 52*, 563–572 https://doi.org/10.1016/j.enpol.2012.10.009

Toleikyte, A., Kranzl, L., Bointner, R., Bean, F., Cipriano, J., De Groote M., …, Volt, J. (2016). *Nearly Zero-Energy Building Strategy 2020, Strategies for a*

Nearly Zero-Energy Building Market Transition in the European Union. Zebra 2020. Retrieved July 7, 2017, from http://zebra2020.eu/website/wp-content/uploads/2014/08/ZEBRA2020_Strategies-for-nZEB_07_LQ_single-pages-1.pdf

Vanstraelen, L., Marchand, J.-F., Casas, M., Creupelandt, D., & Steyaert, E. (2015). *Increasing Capacities in Cities for Innovating Financing in Energy Efficiency*. CITYnvest. Retrieved July 7, 2017, from http://citynvest.eu/content/review-local-authority-innovative-large-scale-retrofit financing-and-operational-models

PART II

Market-Driven Approaches

CHAPTER 6

Information or Marketing? Lessons from the History of Private-Sector Green Building Labelling

Jeremy Gabe and Pernille H. Christensen

1 Introduction

Amenities, architectural features, aesthetics, floorplate layouts, fit-outs, communal space quality, ownership titles, existing lease contracts, and forecasted cash flows are some of the visually or textually informative features prospective owners or occupiers of property can use when making buying or leasing decisions. Confidence in the local regulatory authority's ability to enforce building codes implies additional information associated with structural, health, and safety attributes. "Green" buildings are natural resource efficient spaces that do not pollute the biophysical environment. These attributes are invisible; thus, an absence of information on resource flows or pollutant emissions during the buying or leasing process may be

J. Gabe (✉)
University of Auckland, Auckland, New Zealand
e-mail: j.gabe@auckland.ac.nz

P. H. Christensen
University of Technology Sydney, Sydney, NSW, Australia
e-mail: Pernille.Christensen@uts.edu.au

T. Walker et al. (eds.), *Sustainable Real Estate*, Palgrave Studies in Sustainable Business In Association with Future Earth,
https://doi.org/10.1007/978-3-319-94565-1_6

responsible for local and global environmental degradation. "Sustainable" building advocates seek to expand the scope of information not available to the market to include social objectives such as human health, distributional economic justice, and community-building (Cole, 2012). One proposed solution is the same for both green and sustainable building: provide the missing information and the market will value and thus supply buildings with these attributes.

This market-based solution has developed into a private industry developing and managing third-party green building assessment tools. The general mechanism is that an applicant (i.e. building owner) pays a fee to the certifying firm and provides evidence within a pre-defined framework developed by the certifying firm to measure the invisible attributes of green buildings. Next, the certifying firm accredits auditors tasked with reviewing the application, verifying the supporting documentation, and establishing the credibility of the label. Sign-off from the review means the building owner can advertise a green building credential to all interested parties.

One purpose of this chapter is to argue that while there appears to be a wide diversity of private certification labels and schemes in the global property market (Christensen & Sayce, 2015; Reed, Bilos, Wilkinson, & Schulte, 2009), these can be simplified into two primary methods of certification based on the assessment strategy. We distinguish between "voluntary environmental building codes" and "measured building performance auditing". Voluntary environmental building codes reward applicants for exceeding statutory minimums associated with protecting the biophysical environment and, in most examples, human health. These systems seek to measure potential outcomes and apply to buildings pre-occupancy. This method was the predominant, often exclusive, method in the early years (1990s and 2000s) of green building labelling. Notable voluntary environmental building codes include the new construction modules of Leadership in Energy and Environmental Design (LEED), the Building Research Establishment Environmental Assessment Method (BREEAM), and Green Star.

Measured building performance auditing meets demand for continuous assessment during occupancy and facilitates labelling of the (much larger) population of existing buildings not undergoing major renovations. This approach typically involves a 12-month audit of operational data associated with direct or indirect environmental impacts.

The current state of green building labelling is shifting from conserving the biophysical environment to promoting human health and wellness. Such a pivot is not entirely novel; health is the reason many voluntary environmental building codes include credits for enhancing the indoor environment. However, a private firm, Delos Living, has recently demonstrated success with its WELL Building standard, which follows the voluntary environmental building code model but exclusively contains design guidelines associated with human health and wellness. A potential growth market for the labelling industry is for a building owner to undergo separate environmental and wellness assessments, as Delos Living suggests in its marketing materials.

A critical evaluation of the first two decades of the application of private green building assessment tools results in four findings. First, early pioneering users of a voluntary green building code behave as if they were complying with a statutory building code—an incentive to do the minimum required. Second, we review the widespread claim that labelled buildings are associated with increased market valuations. Third, data from Green Star Australia complements a robust literature demonstrating that post-occupancy evaluations in labelled buildings indicate these buildings are more average in-use than design-stage ratings imply. Finally, there is early research demonstrating how repetitive participation in a measured building performance auditing scheme produces rapid improvement in environmental outcomes.

We use our four findings from the critical evaluations above to reflect on the challenges facing green building labelling. Specifically, we reflect on how to improve effectiveness, increase adoption, harmonise benchmarking, and integrate design with operation. We argue that a life-cycle approach to green labelling built around a measured building performance auditing regime addresses these challenges. However, there are institutional and incentive barriers to this solution. The literature shows that the label itself is what delivers value; perception matters more than performance. In such a market, there is an associated cost to negative perceptions such as a rating downgrade or rating disqualification, so private certification firms eliminate this risk by allowing certification to be optional and, in most cases, last forever.[1]

[1] For example, should a building owner fail to obtain auditing sign-off, her building remains uncertified, a relatively neutral outcome. On the other hand, should the building have a bad year from a performance perspective, most measured building performance audit-

The emerging challenge for the private-sector is to champion commitment to a certification lifecycle (design → construction → operation) and create a marketing environment where such "deep" and continuous commitment stands out above those that only participate when the narrative or scheme suits their interests. However, given the private disincentive to integrate, we explain how mandatory disclosure regulation is the key to overcome these barriers and align incentives for successful integration between building designers and users.

2 Voluntary Environmental Building Codes

Beginning with the United Kingdom BREEAM in 1990, voluntary design- and construction-stage assessment schemes serve to differentiate buildings—usually commercial office buildings—that exceed local building code standards associated with the biophysical environment and human health. Using these optional standards, building owners obtain third-party certification for a building that conserves natural resources (energy, water, and materials), creates a healthy indoor environment, and enhances the quality of the biophysical environment. With differentiation in the market, economic theory suggests that if the market values enhanced environmental (or health and wellness) attributes, certified buildings will obtain value premiums (Fuerst & McAllister, 2011a).

There are hundreds of private green building certification systems in use today (Reed et al., 2009). We observe that most are regionally specific modifications of the framework established by BREEAM,[2] varying mainly through reference to regionally specific institutional and regulatory practices. We coin the term "voluntary environmental building code" to refer to the BREEAM framework and the hundreds of certification tools that follow its philosophy. This term recognises that the birth of the BREEAM framework was within a firm tasked with reviewing the building code; hence, it is unsurprising that its foundational philosophy was identifying buildings that exceed code minimums. In reviewing many of the schemes described in more depth by Reed et al. (2009) and Ding (2008), we

ing tools will award her building a low grade (say, 0 stars out of 6), conveying a negative, rather than neutral, message of differentiation.

[2] In this section, when we say "BREEAM" it more specifically refers to all BREEAM modules except In-Use.

observe that the following attributes are commonly associated with a voluntary environmental building code:

- Applicants receive a "point" (or "credit") for exceeding a building code or other statutory compliance requirement to a predetermined degree.
- Points are designed to maintain or enhance the quality of the biophysical environment, with a small fraction designed to enhance the quality of the internal environment for human health and wellness outcomes.
- Assessments occur at a pre-occupancy phase in the building lifecycle.
- Points associated with performance in-use are estimated using mathematical models or simulations to represent the potential of a building design.
- The majority of points are optional, with an overall "greenness" label determined by a randomly chosen percentage of optional points obtained.
- A "green building council"—a private firm supported by local design, construction, and property industry membership—typically manages the certification scheme and licences independent assessors to oversee compliance with the scheme.
- Participation in the certification process is not mandated by local building codes.
- Once issued by the independent assessor, a label has no expiration date.

The core philosophy of the voluntary environmental building code is to serve as an instrument for building designers to compare environmental (or health and wellness) **potential** between building designs. Potential in this context is best defined as "assuming normal or default patterns of occupant behaviour and building operation, making it easier to distinguish between improvements in the physical features and improved efficiencies in use and operation" (Cole, 1999).

Naturally, there are minor exceptions to the characterisation described earlier given the global diversity of assessment tools. The most common deviation occurs when local building codes mandate the achievement of a private green building certification, though Schindler (2010) finds this practice to be declining as governments learn that this practice effectively outsources management of the public building code to the private-sector. Another common deviation, which bridges the two frameworks discussed in this chapter, involves the treatment of existing buildings. When a voluntary environmental building code certifies an existing building—which occurred before BREEAM In-Use and other tools using a hybrid philosophy gained market traction—the subject building was assessed as if it was not occupied. This enabled the assessors to apply the philosophy that an assessment should evaluate building design potential, rather than building performance in-use. However, as we discuss later, the ability to measure actual existing building performance and the recognition that operational practice can result in significant deviations from design potential spurred on the development of separate hybrid labelling frameworks for existing buildings.

The following sections describe the scope of a voluntary environmental building code in more depth through the history of BREEAM and the LEED, the US-based tool. These two schemes are the oldest and most recognisable brands for voluntary environmental building codes and both are offered worldwide—the closest the industry has to a global standard for sustainable building design. Our discussion concludes with a section on other tools of note: Green Star, a BREEAM variant which dominates the market in Australasia, and PassivHaus, an early energy-efficiency specific tool that started in the residential, rather than commercial, sector.

2.1 BREEAM, the Archetype

In 1990, the United Kingdom government-owned Building Research Establishment (BRE) introduced BREEAM version 1/90. As one of the creators of BREEAM, Prior (1991) describes the growing public concern regarding damage to the global environment, poor indoor air quality, and the need to raise awareness of the large contribution by the property sector to these problems as motivation for developing the certification scheme. In the late 1990s, BRE was privatised, with management of BREEAM as one of its core businesses.

BREEAM assesses a building design by the degree to which it exceeds contemporary regulatory standards concerning "global-scale", "neighbourhood-scale", and "internal environment" indicators. Global- and local-scale concerns include enhancing the biophysical environment and mitigating ecological degradation while internal environment concerns included indoor air pollutants and their effect on human health

(Prior, 1991). It is important to understand that, because subsequent voluntary environmental building codes follow this framework, common understanding of green labelling as a holistic concept continues to include enhancement of human health and wellness, even though this has no impact directly on the biophysical environment.

Building developers seeking BREEAM certification use a checklist of compliance standards and gain one credit for meeting each individual standard. In BREEAM 1/90, the "greenness"—or depth of environmental quality—of the asset was measured by the total number of credits awarded; more credits indicated a "greener" asset. Later revisions to BREEAM increased the number of credits and created easy-to-understand adjective-based labels—"Pass", "Good", "Very Good", "Excellent", and "Outstanding"—that serve to communicate the depth of environmental quality based on the percentage of applicable credits awarded. Over the past 25 years, BREEAM has also grown in scope, expanding the list of standards associated with credits, the types of buildings that can be certi fied, sub-components of building structures that can be certified, where buildings could be certified, and the time in the design and construction process when certification can occur.

The first growth in the scope of BREEAM occurred through developing a larger list of environmental and health standards associated with credits. BREEAM 1/90 had a maximum of 25 credits, assessing potential greenhouse gas emissions from operational use, ozone depleting emissions, responsible wood product sourcing, provision of space for sorting recyclable materials, exposure to legionnaire's disease, site selection, indoor lighting quality, use of hazardous materials, and indoor air quality (Prior, 1991). In its current form, BREEAM 2016, there are a maximum of 150 credits across the suite of credit areas that includes building management practices, human health and well-being, hazard mitigation, operational energy efficiency, transport choices, water efficiency (including stormwater management), material selection, waste management, land use/ecology, pollution mitigation, and bespoke credits awarded for innovative design decisions (BRE Global, 2016). However, it is important to note that, while the list of standards has grown, the original three-tiered approach of global, neighbourhood, and internal environmental concerns remains the framework behind BREEAM.

Originally developed for office building designs, BREEAM has since developed a large portfolio of application methodologies to accommodate other building typologies. As of 2016, BREEAM has specific guidelines covering residential buildings (single-family, multifamily, long-term stay), commercial buildings (office, industrial, retail), educational campus buildings, and hotels (BRE Global, 2016). In addition, BRE offers to assess any building typology or civil infrastructure project in any global location on a bespoke basis.

The third growth strategy involved offering certification outside the United Kingdom. At first, BRE licenced their rating methodology for adaptation to firms in foreign countries. Hong Kong's Building Environmental Assessment Method (HK-BEAM) and Australia's Green Star are two frequently studied labelling schemes that began by licencing BREEAM and adapting it for local markets. Later, as BREEAM grew its own brand value, BRE created a BREEAM Europe rating scheme in 2008 (for systematic certification of buildings across the continent), followed by the launch of BRE Global, a division that offers to certify any building in any country with the BREEAM brand (BRE Global, 2013).

Another scope of growth involves offering certification for partial building components. BREEAM 1/90 could only assess a whole building, but to meet demand from developers that delivered speculative buildings with no fit-out, BREEAM developed a "Shell" and "Shell and Core" rating context. "Shell" refers only to the building envelope, internal partitions, and structural floors. "Core" includes centralised building services (lifts, mechanical systems, utilities) while excluding tenancy-specific fit-outs.

BREEAM also expanded when an assessment occurred in the building life-cycle: design, construction, in-use, or under refurbishment. Originally, BREEAM 1/90 was a checklist of design standards, so assessment occurred during the design phase. Prior (1991) describes the design assessment in BREEAM 1/90 as appropriate because this stage provided the best opportunity for improvements and changes. However, very few buildings are built exactly to design specification. It is common for significant changes to occur during construction management (e.g. perhaps the timber supplier no longer has sufficient stock of certified wood). To ensure delivery of green buildings in line with design expectations, BREEAM now refers to design-only ratings as "interim"; full certification is withheld until the assessor reviews documentation associated with the construction phase (BRE Global, 2016). Refurbishments and fit-outs do not have the same blank canvas as a new building, thus BRE offers a separate set of optional standards for this phase, which matches the project (say, an internal remodelling plan) with a subset of relevant BREEAM standards, much in the same manner as the Core and Shell certification scope operates.

Finally, the In-Use certification method for existing buildings not undergoing major refurbishment is a special exception to the voluntary building code model used by BREEAM. As is described later, BREEAM In-Use is a hybrid system that applies measured building performance audits when possible; it is not entirely a voluntary environmental building code.

The methodology, scope, and growth strategy of BREEAM serves as a template for the development of similar voluntary environmental building codes across the globe. Reviews of the emergence of green building certification in the 2000s narrate the breadth and depth of global market penetration for voluntary environmental building codes modelled on BREEAM (Cole, 2006; Ding, 2008; Reed et al., 2009; Sayce, Sundberg, & Clements, 2010). During this period of rapid growth, the success of BREEAM attracted its primary competitor in the global certification market, the LEED scheme developed in the United States.

2.2 LEED

Following its launch in 2000, the suite of tools under the LEED brand, developed by the industry-led United States Green Building Council (USGBC), began as the dominant voluntary environmental building code in the United States. Like BREEAM, it has since expanded to become a global brand.

LEED's earliest assessment method covered the construction of new office buildings. This flagship rating system, currently named LEED for Building Design and Construction (BD+C) is now in its fourth version (USGBC, 2017). It adopts the BRE philosophy of collating optional building standards associated with improving the quality of the global, local, and internal environment. It uses an increasingly precious metals scale of "Certified", "Silver", "Gold", and "Platinum" to label the relative sustainability of a building within the scheme. Like BREEAM's adjectives, these thresholds are associated with the percentage of optional credits met, with the lowest LEED benchmark consistently associated with meeting at least 40% of all optional credits along with a small number of required prerequisite actions.

Much of the earlier discussion on BREEAM also applies to LEED, particularly the agenda for incremental growth in optional credits, building types, construction phases, and global applications. Advocates of BREEAM or LEED may wish to engage in debate over which one was first to market with, say, the idea for an assessment just on the core and shell of a building, but in a market environment where it is easy to copy strategy, such claims are trivial to green building outcomes. However, there are three key areas where LEED has shaped the evolution of modern voluntary environmental building codes: the elimination of the design-only certificate for buildings, the expansion of scope into additional social outcomes through its Neighborhood Development module, and the hybrid approach to certifying existing buildings.

While BREEAM began with design-stage certification, LEED has never offered a building certification prior to completed construction. Version 1 of BD+C (then called "LEED for New Construction" or LEED-NC) in 2000 only offered certification on evidence associated with a building as-built. That philosophy continues, though the USGBC does allow aspiring projects in the design or construction phase to advertise that they have been "registered" for a particular certification that will be formally assessed upon completion.

The minor deviation from LEED's philosophy of as-built (or later) stage certification is the decision by the USGBC to expand the application of LEED into urban planning at the neighbourhood development scale. Owing to development timelines that can be much longer than the construction of a single building, the USGBC allows developers to obtain LEED for Neighborhood Developments (LEED-ND) certification once the developer has received full construction entitlements from a permitting authority. However, of greater interest to this narrative is the expanded scope of LEED-ND credits that contribute to the history of voluntary environmental building codes. LEED-ND expands the outcome scope of a voluntary green building code beyond the BREEAM building-archetype of global/local biophysical environmental quality and human health. Socioeconomic outcomes attract credits in LEED-ND, notably design attributes that promote universal accessibility, community engagement, food production, building type diversity, and the provision of affordable housing. This expanded scope is one of the earliest attempts at a built environment rating scheme applying the full traditional model of sustainability that includes environmental, social, and economic outcomes. BREEAM followed LEED-ND with its Communities scheme that mimics its expanded scope and, befitting the strategy of BREEAM, includes the option to certify earlier in the development process. Sullivan, Rydin, and

Buchanan (2014) review the emergence of neighbourhood-scale certification schemes in depth.

LEED has also been instrumental in offering certification to existing buildings not undergoing major renovations. Version 2 of LEED (USGBC, 2004) includes a certification scheme for existing buildings that was largely a voluntary environmental building code based on LEED-NC, but with a few credits rewritten to require in situ performance evaluations rather than simulated potential performance. Notably, buildings were required to undergo self-evaluation using the Energy Star methodology, a measured environmental performance audit, in lieu of simulating energy consumption. This strategy matured in LEED for Building Operations and Maintenance (LEED O+M), which was the earliest hybrid certification scheme that combines both philosophies of building certification discussed in this chapter and, importantly, provides the potential to inform the market across all stages of a building's life-cycle (Christensen, 2011).

Looking to future innovations, the USGBC has taken interest in the problem of operational deviation from design potential (see Sect. 5.3 later) and developed implicit incentives for building designers to work with future building users. In LEED BD+C 2009 (the third major revision), the USGBC encouraged building owners to share operational data with the USGBC. Operational data sharing became mandatory with the fourth major revision in 2016. Another innovative idea from the 2016 revision of LEED BD+C is the option for the design team to substitute a post-occupancy measured energy consumption audit as an alternative compliance path to simulating building energy consumption potential of the as-built structure. While this alternative compliance path may not entice many project teams (because waiting for the post-occupancy data can delay the final certification by up to two years post-construction), it provides a signal for designers to work with users, one of the major recommendations we make later in this chapter.

2.3 *Green Star Australia and New Zealand*

The Australian Green Star voluntary environmental building code began as a version of BREEAM licenced to the Green Building Council of Australia (GBCA). Following translation of the BREEAM credits to the professional and regulatory Australian building context, the GBCA rebranded the label as Green Star. Besides the translation, the key difference between BREEAM and Green Star is the labels; instead of the

BREEAM suite of adjective-based labels, Green Star takes its name from awarding a building between one and six "Green Stars" based on the percentage of relevant credits obtained. Zero stars signify statutory minimums for any building. Formal green building labels are offered to any building qualifying for 4, 5, or 6 Green Stars, representing compliance with 45%, 60%, or 75% of applicable credits.[3]

GBCA currently manages Green Star rating modules for new commercial buildings (Green Star Design, Green Star As-Built), commercial buildings in-use (Green Star Performance), commercial building fit-outs (Green Star Interiors), and community planning (Green Star Communities).[4] With the exception of Green Star Performance, a multi-attribute measured building performance auditing scheme, all Green Star labelling tools are voluntary environmental building codes.

GBCA licenced Green Star to the New Zealand Green Building Council (NZGBC), which manages its own suite of labelling tools referred to as Green Star NZ. NZGBC certifies new commercial buildings (design or as-built stages), new residential homes (Homestar), and commercial buildings in-use (office energy consumption only). Both green building councils only certify buildings in their respective countries as Green Star Australia and Green Star NZ are managed separately.

A particularly notable contribution in the evolution of voluntary environmental building codes is the Australian Green Star Communities rating system. Following the USGBC's novel attempt at integrating social, environmental, and economic outcomes in a single sustainability rating, GBCA borrowed from existing neighbourhood-scale certification systems, such as BREEAM Communities and LEED-ND, but sought to further expand the evaluation of social and economic outcomes associated with the planned neighbourhood (GBCA, 2015). Additions to the LEED-ND framework include credits for celebrating local heritage/cultural identity, planning for economic resilience through diverse employment/educational opportunities, measuring investment return, and the provision of digital infrastructure.

[3] 1, 2, and 3 Green Star achievements can be formally certified in the operational Green Star Performance scheme.

[4] The market for residential voluntary environmental building code certification in Australia is led by NatHERS (Nationwide House Energy Rating Scheme). This is an energy simulation similar to PassivHaus that estimates the energy efficiency of a housing design.

2.4 *Voluntary Environmental Building Codes for the Residential Sector*

BREEAM, LEED, and Green Star primarily serve the demand of the commercial-institutional (non-residential) building industry for voluntary environmental building codes. Though each has schemes available to certify residential property, these labels are not as widely adopted nor as widely studied in the literature. Instead, popular labelling schemes in green residential property, particularly single-family units, often take a much narrower, energy-centric, view that follows in the framework of the PassivHaus (Passive House) method developed in Germany around the same time as BREEAM.

Like the rating schemes described earlier, PassivHaus is a voluntary environmental building code, and the PassivHaus Institut (PHI) offers certification with its standard worldwide. But what makes it different from the BREEAM archetype is that PassivHaus only exists to evaluate energy efficiency, particularly demand for space conditioning. There are just three criteria for certification: a space conditioning (heating or cooling) demand of not more than 15 kWh/m^2/year (simulated), an airtightness performance threshold (measured on-site), and a total non-renewable primary energy consumption limit (<120 kWh/m^2/year originally). Certification was originally a binary outcome and a house must meet all three criteria along with less specific best practices on user controls and humidity. In 2015, PHI altered its renewable energy criteria to allow for differentiation between certified Passive Houses. Labels of "Classic", "Plus", and "Premium" now exist to identify properties that fall below specific thresholds of total non-renewable primary energy consumption and on-site renewable energy generation (PHI, 2016). PHI has also developed a rating scheme for labelling retrofits of existing houses and can amend their criteria for use in non-domestic commercial properties. In addition, a PHI "Low Energy Building Standard" was developed for buildings that fall shy of the strict space heating standard.

The PassivHaus approach to engineering standards for low energy buildings has become an archetype for residential energy certification in much the same manner as BREEAM became an archetype for voluntary environmental building codes in the commercial sector. Most notably, energy simulations of housing energy efficiency are being adopted as quasi-regulations by some governments. Members of the European Union (EU) must produce an Energy Performance Certificate (EPC) when offering residential property and, increasingly, certain types of non-residential property for sale. Despite the word "performance" in its name, an EPC is a simulation of an existing house structure that closely resembles the narrow scope of a PassivHaus certification. The objective of an EPC is not to mandate a stringent threshold like the PassivHaus but rather as a tool for prospective users to compare energy efficiency potential of houses on the market. Another example is NatHERS, the Australian Nationwide House Energy Rating Scheme. This rating system is managed by the federal Australian government for use by states, which apply NatHERS either on a voluntary basis, integrated into a state building code, or made quasi-mandatory in a similar manner to the European EPC directive. The institutional presence of NatHERS in the Australian market is one likely reason why Green Star Australia does not currently offer a voluntary environmental building code certification scheme for single-family homes.

3 Measured Building Performance Auditing

The philosophy of voluntary environmental building codes is the creation of a benchmark to compare the potential performance of buildings, an indicator of use to those in the design, development, and construction industry. However, this philosophy means little to those with an interest in how the building is operating. For example, facility managers, investment asset managers, and building occupants may wish to differentiate their businesses based on the actual performance of their building or tenancy. Importantly, not all high-spec buildings with great sustainability potential actually operate to such high standard. Vale and Vale (2009) discuss how user behaviour can quickly eliminate the best intentions of a building designer. Labelling schemes using a framework we call "measured building performance auditing" have emerged to fill the niche for assessing and informing the market on indicators of sustainable operation.

In theory, measured building performance auditing is an accounting exercise with three key steps. First, the firm (or, often, government agency in a quasi-private capacity) managing the labelling scheme produces a framework for the accounts, which is effectively a sustainability equivalent to a financial accounting framework such as the Generally Accepted Accounting Principles (GAAP) in the United States. Successful frameworks for measured building performance auditing enable fair comparison between building ratings, usually adjusting raw performance data by building use type (office, residential, industrial, etc.), building use intensity (hours of operation, occupant density, etc.), size, and location. Often, before certification can commence, there is a thorough market survey of average building performance across all adjustment categories used to calibrate the accounting framework. Second, the firm licences auditors to evaluate empirical performance data for buildings' that choose to apply for labelling using the accounting framework. Third, the results of the audit are relevant only to the period under audit, so regular audits, and re-benchmarking, are required to keep the public up-to-date. This final step in particular deviates from the assessment process associated with voluntary environmental building codes, which have no label expiration date and do not subject the building owner to future, more stringent, standards.

There are two archetypes popular for measured building performance auditing: single attribute and multi-attribute. A "single attribute" account assesses one performance outcome, most commonly operational energy consumption or greenhouse gas emissions resulting from operational energy consumption. Using a single performance indicator removes the issue of weighting between two dissimilar attributes, meaning the difficult decisions are limited to the data adjustment process, to enable fair comparison, and the boundary for data collection. The US Energy Star certification scheme is one of the earliest examples of this approach.

The other accounting framework is a "multi-attribute" account that behaves as a hybrid between voluntary environmental building codes and the single attribute accounts. This approach emerged via growth within the firms that manage voluntary environmental building codes and demand from industry for a broader scope than just a single attribute. In theory, the existence of a multi-attribute system on the market enables a building to be labelled at all three phases of the building life-cycle: design, construction, and operation.

To describe the practice of measured building performance auditing in more depth, this section describes three of the most widely used and researched single attribute labelling systems before discussing the structure of a multi-attribute system.

3.1 *Energy Star*

The Environmental Protection Agency of the US Federal Government (USEPA) manages a broad certification regime called Energy Star (often expressed in branding as ENERGY STAR) that covers consumer products (mainly domestic appliances), homes, commercial buildings, and industrial facilities. This section discusses the commercial building module, which is entirely based on measured building performance auditing.[5] The single attribute being assessed is annual primary energy use intensity, or the total primary energy consumption for a year divided by the total floor area of the building. Primary energy can be defined as the sum of energy consumed on-site plus the energy consumed in generation and transmission of that energy to the site. Whether the energy is from a renewable or non-renewable source is not considered. Energy Star only certifies efficiency in use. Commercial building certification, which began in 1999, is available to any building within the United States or Canada.

The accounting framework developed by USEPA has become typical of subsequent single attribute energy auditing labels and the operational energy consumption credits within multi-attribute systems. According to USEPA (2014), evidence of metered site energy consumption for the whole building is collected. The completeness of the data is confirmed by an auditor, who also gathers data on the building use type(s), hours of occupancy, number of computers (as a proxy for occupant intensity), climactic conditions over the auditing year (heating degree days and cooling degree days), and floor area of the building. These latter data are used to adjust metered energy use intensity and create a fair comparison to the national benchmark survey percentiles described later. If the building falls within the top quartile of the national benchmark survey associated with energy efficiency (i.e. lowest 25% of primary energy use intensity) for its building use type, it qualifies for certification, valid for one year. Energy Star is somewhat unique in that certification is a binary outcome only for those with the best performance; many measured building performance auditing tools use a full labelling scale to communicate both good and poor performance.

In order to convert adjusted raw performance data into an easy-to-understand label, USEPA must first apply its Energy Star accounting framework to a representative sample of the entire population of buildings in order to determine thresholds for certification. This benchmarking exercise is the Commercial Buildings Energy Consumption Survey

[5] The residential homes module offers a choice of certification based either on potential or on measured performance. The method for industrial facilities is very similar to that for commercial buildings, so this discussion also applies to the less popular practice of certifying industrial facilities. By May 2017, United States Environmental Protection Agency (USEPA) had issued just over 30,000 certificates to commercial buildings in 18 years but only 175 to industrial facilities.

(CBECS) conducted by the US Energy Information Administration. CBECS is supposed to occur every five years. All current 2017 Energy Star ratings are benchmarked against the 2003 survey, meaning that a decision to certify in 2017 is based on 12 months of recent data being compared with the top quartile of buildings in 2003. Hence, with increased attention to commercial building energy efficiency, it is probable that many more than 25% can qualify for the Energy Star label 14 years later. A revised CBECS was held in 2007, but data was discarded for statistical reasons according to an April 2011 press release from the Energy Information Administration. The most recent CBECS took place in 2012, but Zatz and Burgess (2016) claim the data is unlikely to be integrated into the Energy Star labelling framework until 2018 at the earliest. Canadian applicants for Energy Star labelling are benchmarked against the 2014 Survey of Commercial and Institutional Energy Use.

Energy Star has a very broad definition of who can qualify as the assessor with authority to audit raw energy consumption data and other data required to adjust raw consumption. Anyone who qualifies as a Professional Engineer or Registered Architect in the United States or Canada can act as an Energy Star assessor; USEPA does not run its own educational programme to certify independent assessors. Indeed, on the USEPA Energy Star website, under "tips for low-cost verifications", it suggests having an in-house Professional Engineer or Registered Architect sign off on the audit.[6] Thus, Energy Star offers the potential for self-certification in lieu of traditional "third-party" certification where the auditor is independent of both the certifying organisation and the applicant.

With the exception of the allowance for self-certification, the Energy Star assessment framework is a model for other single attribute measured building performance auditing systems. In some US state and local jurisdictions, notably California, Minneapolis, New York City, and Seattle, advertising the percentile of a building against the CBECS benchmark (i.e. the Energy Star method) is now mandatory for office buildings offered for lease or sale.

[6] https://www.energystar.gov/buildings/facility-owners-and-managers/existing-buildings/earn-recognition/energy-star-certification/tips-low [viewed 30 April 2017].

3.2 National Australian Built Environment Rating System

According to Bannister (2012), the New South Wales (NSW) state government in Australia sought to produce a voluntary market-based labelling tool in 1999 that measured both actual and potential greenhouse gas emissions from office buildings, but dropped the latter owing to the complexity involved. The measured building performance auditing methodology that was implemented became known as the Australian Building Greenhouse Rating (ABGR). Later, in 2006, the ABGR would be rebranded as the National Australian Built Environment Rating System (NABERS) Energy.

NABERS Energy uses a very similar accounting framework as Energy Star, with the major difference being an additional step that converts primary energy use intensity into a measure of greenhouse gas emissions intensity.[7] The NSW Office of Environment and Heritage (2013) manages NABERS and publishes the NABERS Energy accounting framework, which includes a 12 month audit of metred site energy conversion, measurement of "rateable" floor area (removing unoccupied areas from the denominator of energy use intensity), intensity of building use (hours of operation), and intensity of occupancy (number of computer workstations). Measured site energy use intensity is adjusted in a similar manner to Energy Star, with the one exception being that the climate adjustment occurs later, when referencing the benchmark survey for labelling purposes. Audits are conducted by independent third-party assessors licenced to conduct NABERS audits. Since NABERS Energy is interested in greenhouse gas emissions, adjusted site energy use intensity is translated into adjusted source greenhouse gas emissions intensity (CO_2-eq/m^2/year) before being compared with the benchmark survey to assign a label. Certification is then valid for one year from the date of the audit.

NABERS Energy star ratings reference a benchmark survey taken in 1999 when the ABGR was established.[8] The strategy is that a median

[7] Over 85% of energy used in Australian commercial buildings is sourced from electricity, so this difference is trivial from an operational energy-efficiency perspective, though it does allow fuel-switching as a strategy to improve labels.

[8] Adjustments in the primary-energy-to-greenhouse-gas-emission conversion factors in the benchmark sample changed in 2008 for some states to reflect updated knowledge of electricity emissions in those states (Mitchell, 2010).

building for each building typology in each Australian state in the survey is given a 2.5 star rating, with percentiles used to delineate intermediate half-star thresholds between 0 and 5 stars (expanded to 6 stars in August 2011). A building's adjusted source greenhouse gas emissions intensity is compared with the half-star thresholds for the comparable building type in the same state and assigned a star rating to communicate relative building performance. Unlike Energy Star, NABERS Energy assigns a star rating to all buildings undergoing the audit, good and poor, not just those in the top quartile of energy efficiency. As of early 2017, there is no publicly disclosed plan in place for an updated NABERS Energy benchmark survey, despite the most recent annual report showing that the average NABERS Energy rating (4.2), which covers over 80% of eligible office building stock (NSW Office of Environment and Heritage, 2016), is much higher than its intended calibration of 2.5. Building types eligible for NABERS certification include offices, retail centres, and hotels.

NABERS has expanded the scope of the single attribute measured building performance auditing tool in two key directions: non-energy related single attribute labels and the offer of sub-building scale audits. The original plan for NABERS was operational measurement of every category of the Green Star voluntary environmental building code (Bannister, 2012). When the NABERS labelling scheme was tendered on the market for implementation, the winning bidder (NSW Government), chose the single attribute approach as opposed to the integrated approach used by BREEAM and Green Star. As of early 2017, an existing building can be certified for its performance in four attributes: operational energy-related greenhouse gas emissions (NABERS Energy), potable water consumption (NABERS Water), waste generation (NABERS Waste), and indoor air quality (NABERS Indoor Environment). A NABERS Transport label has been proposed but has yet to be offered to the market. Only NABERS Energy and NABERS Water have achieved substantial market uptake.[9] Befitting its status as a single attribute assessment tool, ratings in each area of concern are independent and certified separately; there is no method to weight the various categories and produce a single multiple attribute NABERS rating.

[9] According to the New South Wales (NSW) Office of Environment and Heritage (2016), the number of unique Australian buildings certified at least once by the four single attribute NABERS labelling systems are 3017 in NABERS Energy, 1349 in NABERS Water, 93 in NABERS Indoor Environment, and 45 in NABERS Waste.

Three assessment boundaries exist for NABERS Energy. At the building scale, building owners can choose to disclose their greenhouse gas emissions from "Whole Building" energy use or "Base Building" energy use. The former includes all energy consumed in the building while the latter is limited to services under the owner's control: mechanical systems, space conditioning, lifts, hot water, and common area lighting. The third boundary is the "Tenancy" scope, which is limited to a particular tenancy to measure the services under the tenant's control: tenant equipment (computers and other plug loads), tenancy lighting, and supplementary air conditioning services specific to one tenancy. In theory, the energy consumption measured in a Whole Building rating equals the energy measured for the Base Building rating plus the sum of all energy consumption from a complete set of Tenancy ratings. Base Building is the most popular scope in the market. For the other attributes (Water, Waste, and Indoor Environment), NABERS only offers a Whole Building scope.

3.3 Display Energy Certificates

As mentioned in Sect. 2.4, member states of the EU must produce an EPC when transacting residential and some typologies of commercial property. An EPC is typically based on the framework of energy- and greenhouse gas emission-related credits in a voluntary environmental building code and thus measures design potential, not actual, energy performance or greenhouse gas emissions.

A government labelling scheme in the United Kingdom called the Display Energy Certificate (DEC) introduced a measured building performance audit label to the market in 2008 as an operational stage variant of the EPC. At the commencement of the DEC programme, valid DECs were mandatory in publicly owned buildings and offered on a voluntary basis to privately owned buildings. As far as we are aware, this arrangement remains in place as of early 2017. According Bruhns, Jones, Cohen, Bordass, and Davis (2011), the majority of the measured building performance audits (15,335) took place in "schools and seasonal public buildings", with office buildings (3230) and university campus buildings (2637)—the other popular building typologies—obtaining a DEC. This usage distribution implies a strong bias towards uptake only through the mandate for publicly owned buildings.

According to the Department for Communities and Local Government (2008), the process of producing a DEC is a local variant of the standard measured building performance audit methodology described earlier. As with Energy Star, an assessor collects data over a year of site energy consumption, local climate degree days, building floor area, and building occupancy over the year measured. The DEC assessor then adjusts the site energy consumption for building size and the local climate, then, like NABERS Energy, converts this adjusted site energy consumption to greenhouse gas emissions for comparison with a building use type benchmark figure for labelling. All DEC ratings are valid for one year.

The accounting benchmarks for a DEC rating are managed by the Chartered Institute of Building Services Engineers (CIBSE) and are based on "old data collected in the 1980s and 1990s" (Bruhns et al., 2011, p. 37). The Bruhns et al. (2011) report claims CIBSE will be using data collected from DEC audits to improve and update these old benchmarks where necessary. Unfortunately, the DEC benchmark methodology is not the same benchmark as is used in the design-based EPC, so a DEC and EPC in the United Kingdom are not directly comparable as design forecasts (EPC) and operational accounts (DEC) even though they both use nearly identical labelling aesthetics and letter grade labels.

3.4 *Multiple Attribute Rating Systems*

Voluntary environmental building codes effectively exclude existing buildings. Building stock replacement rates in developed countries range between 0.66% to 3% per year (Eichholtz, Kok, & Quigley, 2010; United Nations Environment Programme, 2007), meaning that a complete transition to current non-voluntary building code performance standards could take somewhere between 30 and 130 years. Forecasts of future energy consumption for an entire building stock conclude that existing buildings have a disproportionate effect on total consumption and greenhouse gas emissions (Coffey et al., 2009). Hence there is a large market for promoting operational behaviours that improve environmental and human health outcomes, irrespective of whether the building has high potential performance or not. In addition, single attribute labelling schemes do not produce an integrated green label often demanded in the market. To respond to this demand, managers of the major voluntary environmental building codes offer multiple attribute labelling schemes that integrate operational management policies (in-use "potential") and single attribute measured building performance auditing methodologies.

Despite the possibility of a larger market relative to new construction-only, multiple attribute labelling systems are relatively unpopular. As of early 2017 only LEED, BREEAM, and Green Star Australia offer multiple attribute certifications. In all three cases, the operational phase multiple attribute rating system was last to be offered to the market and, in all three schemes, has a lower number of publicly disclosed certifications or registrations relative to the traditional voluntary environmental building codes for new construction and major renovations.

The earliest hybrid certification was LEED for Building Operations and Maintenance (LEED O+M), originally LEED for Existing Buildings, described earlier. Currently, LEED O+M uses measured building performance auditing to evaluate transportation, potable water consumption, energy consumption (via Energy Star's accounting framework), renewable energy generation, waste generation, and daylight quality. In general, LEED O+M awards small numbers of credits (1 to 2) for the observance of written building management plans, purchasing contracts, and policies, with much larger numbers of credits awarded in the areas where measured building performance auditing is required.

BREEAM In-Use and Green Star Performance follow the LEED O+M strategy of translating their voluntary environmental building code credits into credits appropriate for measurement in-use. Christensen (2011) presents a detailed comparison between LEED O+M and BREEAM In-Use. Like LEED O+M, these multiple attribute operational labelling tools also involve a combination of stated/contracted intentions and measured building performance auditing. In particular, Green Star Performance benefits from the existence of NABERS. Green Star Performance credits on energy consumption, potable water consumption, and indoor environment quality align with NABERS Energy, Water, and Indoor Environment respectively. Another feature unique to Green Star Performance is while LEED O+M and BREEAM In-Use persist with a minimum threshold for labelling ("Certified" and "Pass" ratings, respectively), Green Star Performance removes the 4-star minimum required for official certification, allowing ratings of 0, 1, 2, and 3 stars.

Beyond restructuring credits, multiple attribute labelling systems closely follow the measured building performance auditing framework because certifications are issued with expiration dates. In LEED O+M, Green Star Performance and BREEAM In-Use, certifications expire after five years and must be renewed with up-to-date measurements and strategies.

4 WELL Building Rating

In 2016, the Global Real Estate Sustainability Benchmark (GRESB) expanded its report to include a separate Real Estate Health & Well-being module.[10] The report notes health and well-being are re-emerging as opportunity areas for the real estate industry as many property companies look for competitive advantage strategies, particularly in markets with a perceived market saturation of green building labels.[11] From the occupant perspective of green labelling, firms know that of all the inputs needed to produce office-based services, human resources are the most valuable. Gabe and Gentry (2013) report on the situation of Sydney office tenants, finding that office worker salaries are nearly ten times as costly per square metre as building rents, and hundreds of times more costly than building energy consumption. Just a small increase in worker productivity from building design could be a source of efficiency gains. These gains can be shared between occupants and owners through tenant's willingness to pay higher rents for occupancy of space where employees are more productive.

WELL is the first building labelling standard that focuses exclusively on building occupants' health and well-being. Established in 2014 by Delos Living, the WELL Building Standard[12] is now administered by the International WELL Building Institute (IWBI). Building on medical and scientific research, the standard aims to help building designers and managers integrate human health and well-being features into building design and operation with the goal of improving occupants' work quality, work productivity, and reducing absenteeism. While green building labels also address some aspects of human health and wellness, WELL certification excludes any credits associated with environmental sustainability. To ensure building professionals do not neglect environmental sustainability, IWBI is collaborating with the managers of LEED, BREEAM, and Green

[10] https://www.gresb.com/sites/default/files/2016-GRESB-Health-Module.pdf [viewed 4 July 2017].

[11] Prior (1991) discusses how the development of BREEAM 1/90 included consideration of voluntary building design standards associated with improving human health and well-being. Voluntary environmental building codes and multi-attribute measured building performance auditing continue to consider human health design guidelines as a prominent module for points/credits towards a green building label. Data and claims of market saturation for green building labels can be found in NSW Office for Environment and Heritage (2016) and Robinson and McAllister (2015).

[12] WELL in capital letters refers to the branding of the certification scheme. It is not an acronym.

Star ratings to promote international awareness of health and well-being with the aim of working synergistically with these voluntary environmental building codes. As of July 2017, over 480 projects across 30 countries are registered for certification under the WELL standard.[13]

When placed in this chapter's typology of green building labelling tools, the WELL building certification is unique as the first hybrid rating tool—with some points resembling voluntary environmental building code credits (i.e. credits associated with design process, building material specifications, construction methods, and performance simulations) and some points requiring measured verification in-use (i.e. airflow rates, water quality, food offered for occupant consumption, on-site fitness opportunities, and occupant surveys). Perhaps the most notable deviation from the voluntary building code frameworks is the validity of the label. WELL certificates are required to be renewed every three years (compared with never for LEED BD+C, a voluntary building code, and five years for LEED O+M, a multi-attribute measured performance tool). Projects can register their intent to certify during design, but final audits to verify the certification can only occur once the building is in operation with at least 50% of expected occupancy (IWBI and Delos Living, 2017).

Borrowing from LEED, WELL has adopted the precious metals scale of "Silver", "Gold", and "Platinum" to identify the relative health and wellness of a building (there is not a base-level "Certified" label). Also in harmony with the LEED scale, these thresholds are calculated based on the total number of voluntary points achieved. But that is where similarities in rating strategy end. There are significantly more prerequisite features that must be achieved for a WELL certification. This means that a WELL-certified building is more homogenous in its design and operational management than a building with one of the flexible green building labels, like LEED, which have few prerequisite credits and thus more choice for the designer and/or building manager. A New or Existing Building certification includes 41 of 100 WELL points as mandatory prerequisites, while Core and Shell has 26 pre-conditions and New and Existing Interiors has 36. A WELL Silver certification can be achieved by meeting only the prerequisite points. WELL Gold requires achieving all the prerequisite features plus at least 40% of the remaining optimisation points (i.e. 24 of 59 for a new and existing building certification), while WELL Platinum requires 80% (i.e. 48 of 59 for a new and existing building certification).

[13] https://wellonline.wellcertified.com/community/projects [viewed 4 July 2017].

Currently, WELL v1 certification is available only for commercial and institutional buildings. As of mid-2017, certification was available for office, retail, educational facilities, multifamily residential and commercial kitchens (IWBI and Delos Living, 2017). It is not a requirement to certify a whole building. IWBI has identified points that apply specifically to the base building structure ("core and shell") and points that associate specifically with the design and management of occupied space ("interiors"). Combining the parts together (allowing for some overlap) results in a "whole building" WELL certification. There is no distinction between a new construction or existing building—the requirements are the same and address the full scope of project design, construction, and building operations—but whole building certifications for office buildings do require at least 90% of the total floor area to be occupied by the building owner.

Led by LEED co-founder Rick Fedrizzi, IWBI has developed a strategic array of industry alliances and collaborations to help capture international market share for the WELL Building certification and, uniquely, has invested in producing intellectual capital in an effort to understand and empirically measure the relationship(s) between building design, management, and human health. In April 2016, Delos and the Mayo Clinic launched the Well Living Lab,[14] a reconfigurable research facility built to investigate the real-world impacts of indoor environments on human health and well-being and generate evidence-based information that can be used in practical ways to create healthier indoor spaces and increase the robustness of the WELL standard. This in-house approach to certification development is unique; most green building label management bodies solely use committees of external technical experts to write scheme credits. The IWBI has also enlisted the support of major property development and management firms. In February 2016, CBRE, a global property services firm, announced plans to pursue WELL certification for at least 100 buildings associated with CBRE worldwide. This commitment to implementation has begun to influence several of the local markets in which CBRE has committed to achieving WELL standard in buildings they manage. For example, in Sydney, Australia, major property developers, managers, and occupants including Grocon, Macquarie Bank, Mirvac, DEXUS, Lendlease, and Frasers Property have all registered their intent to pursue WELL certification for some of the buildings in their portfolio.

[14] http://welllivinglab.com/ [viewed 4 July 2017].

5 Critical Review on the Efficacy of Current Systems

Fuerst (2009) and Kok, McGraw, and Quigley (2011) have documented the rapid rise in green building labelling around the world, particularly the rise of voluntary environmental building codes. Their data imply that the invention of voluntary environmental building codes has met a formerly latent demand in the market. While not as popular in the private market, the accounting frameworks of measured building performance auditing have led to the creation of a new regulatory tool in the private market: mandatory disclosure (Gabe, 2016b; Kontokosta, 2013). Hence, both labelling frameworks have a captive market and must be recognised as having contributed to reducing information asymmetries between owners, users, and potential purchasers of labelled property.

Importantly, these labelling systems enable researchers to understand how labelling frameworks are used and to evaluate resulting improvements in the health of the biophysical environment.[15] This section explores four key arguments that have emerged from empirical research on outcomes from green building labelling. First, users of a voluntary environmental building code behave as if they were complying with minimums in a statutory building code, suggesting that the label is more important than the actions performed obtaining it. Second, labelled buildings are associated with increased financial performance, though deeper investigations face a challenge to separate the marketing value of the label from the inherent value resultant from the actions performed to obtain the label. Third, potential environmental outcome estimates of buildings in the design phase are often too optimistic relative to environmental outcomes measured in use. Finally, measured building performance auditing labels have demonstrated that repetitive participation in the auditing scheme produces surprisingly rapid improvement in environmental outcomes in-use and reduction in building-to-building variance.

[15] Epidemiological studies on the relationship between green building design (or performance) and human health (or business productivity) outcomes are either anecdotal in nature or find it difficult to disentangle the number of exogenous determinants of human health (or business productivity) sufficiently to discuss the marginal effect of building design (Fisk, 2000). Hence, we discuss the much easier to measure effect of green building design on biophysical environmental quality.

5.1 *Striving for the Minimum*

One goal of the voluntary environmental building code model is to create an incentive for designers to exceed code minimum standards. While the presence of BREEAM's framework around the world has provided such incentive, research finds that labelling applicants behave in a manner befitting regulatory compliance; they strive for the minimum number of credits required to obtain a particular label.

Management scholars propose the phenomenon of "misdirected attention" that is discussed in the study of institutional motivations within regulatory schemes targeted at environmental stewardship (Hoffman & Henn, 2008). Researchers observe that regulations to fix environmental externalities can misdirect attention away from the problem and towards compliance with the written standards and codes that can result in suboptimal outcomes and potential barriers to innovative solutions (Tenbrunsel, Wade-Benzoni, Messick, & Bazerman, 1997). Anecdotes on the practice of "point mongering" (where a building design team sets its objective as the most LEED points at the lowest cost) and similar behaviours suggest users of voluntary environmental building codes have directed their attention towards the credits, rather than towards the environmental or health performance outcomes of certified buildings (Schendler, 2009).

Empirical evidence of misdirected attention and point mongering comes from our own research on the first 450 projects[16] that have been certified using early versions of LEED BD+C. There is a clear bias towards achieving the minimum number of points for the desired level of certification (Fig. 6.1). If maximising environmental and human health outcomes were the market driver of using LEED, one would expect there be no trend in Fig. 6.1 as points would vary with resource allocations, not the random thresholds of 40%, 50%, 60%, and 80% of points created by the

[16] While there are now thousands of LEED BD+C-certified buildings worldwide, studying early adopters in the context of point-scoring behaviours is most insightful because one expects this cohort to be biased towards maximising environmental outcomes. We use the first 450 buildings because from late 2006 the USGBC stopped releasing scorecards from all projects, creating potential bias in the population of LEED buildings with known point scores. To confirm that Fig. 6.1 is not aberrant from average behaviour today, a random sample of the population of all BD+C certifications with disclosed LEED scorecards up until May 2017 reveals no material change in the pattern.

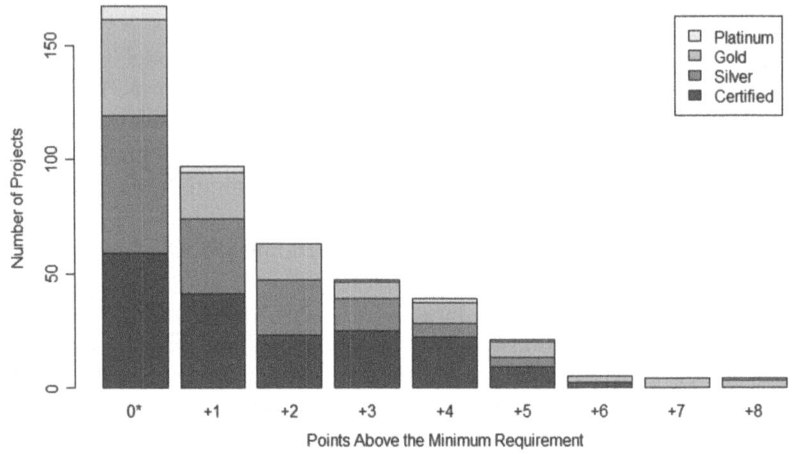

Fig. 6.1 Number of points over the minimum required for LEED certification for the first 450 certifications. Notes: Based on data from the US Green Building Council. *Includes two Silver-certified buildings that obtained less than the minimum points for a Silver certification

USGBC for labelling purposes. While Fig. 6.1 involves only the US LEED system, we find similar patterns exploring BREEAM and Green Star assessments.[17]

5.2 *Financial Returns to Labelling*

Many empirical studies have used green building labels as a "treatment" to assess a wide range of outcomes resulting from that treatment, particularly financial returns. While this research design appears sensible, it includes an important, usually unstated, limitation when applied to any multiple attribute auditing scheme. The term LEED Silver, for example, is a useful summary of a certification outcome, but it refers to a very heterogeneous label. The structure of a voluntary environmental building code like LEED

[17] LEED is more suitable for this research because it has a fixed total number of points (credits) available. BREEAM and Green Star, for example, allow designers to remove credits from the total and thus the total number of credits earned is not predictive of the label. Exploratory work from the authors on Green Star Design and Green Star As-Built disclosures in Australia confirms that early users of those labelling systems also skew to the minimum percentage of credits required.

is such that designers have wide latitude in selecting the points/credits they wish to pursue. As a hypothetical example, one building can obtain the minimum LEED Commercial Interiors points for a Silver rating by concentrating on indoor environment attributes while another building gains Silver status in LEED Building Design and Construction by designing one of the most energy-efficient building envelopes in the market. Both would be LEED Silver certified and appear to share the same label, but the intrinsic value they offer to the market is inherently different. Furthermore, the rapid scope expansion observed in BREEAM and LEED (and other voluntary environmental building codes)—particularly into partial building systems, refurbishments, interior fit-outs, and hybrid performance auditing—creates a need for the market to understand the boundaries of each rating system. Studies on financial performance have an implicit limitation that their results only measure the marketing value of a certification label, as that is the only commonality between certified projects without addressing particular activities or boundaries.

With that limitation in mind, the common narrative on the financial returns to owners of labelled buildings supports the claim that possessing a green building label enhances asset value. Most of this research has been conducted on commercial office markets and includes both voluntary environmental building codes and measured building performance audits. Research in the United States finds evidence of average/asking rent premiums, occupancy rate premiums, cap rate reductions, and sales price premiums for LEED and Energy Star labelled buildings (Eichholtz et al., 2010; Fuerst & McAllister, 2011a; Miller, Spivey, & Florance, 2008; Pivo & Fisher, 2010). In general, value premiums are higher for LEED (voluntary environmental building code) than Energy Star (single attribute measured building performance audit). Outside North America, studies finding value premiums for green labelled office space have been conducted in the United Kingdom (Chegut, Eichholtz, & Kok, 2014; Fuerst & McAllister, 2011b), the Netherlands (Kok & Jennen, 2012) and Australia (Newell, MacFarlane, & Walker, 2014).

However, deeper research into office markets indicates it is not clear that enhanced asset value results from occupiers of certified space paying higher rent. When the scale of data analysed shifts from the building scale to the tenancy scale, rental price premiums disappear or causality becomes impossible to disentangle with other building attributes. Gabe and Rehm (2014) find no rent premiums from NABERS Energy ratings when modelling office rental contracts in Sydney, Australia. Fuerst, van de

Wetering, and Wyatt (2013) find the rent premium for a labelled building in the United Kingdom difficult to disentangle from the rent premium for a new building.

Outside of commercial office markets, Freybote, Sun, and Yang (2015) finds that LEED for Neighbourhood Development certification does not offer additional premiums beyond those observed for certified housing units within the certified neighbourhood. Robinson, Singh, and Das (2016) found mixed results in regards to the financial performance of LEED labelled hotels. Sale price premiums for certified homes have also been reported using European Energy Performance Certificates (Fuerst, McAllister, Nanda, & Wyatt, 2015) and an aggregation of various green ratings in California (Kahn & Kok, 2014). Measured building performance auditing is not widely used outside the office sector, so these non-office studies involve voluntary environmental building code certifications. Human health-only certification schemes such as the WELL Building label are too new to the market for robust research into their impact on financial value.

To summarise, while most research finds support for the claim that the presence of an eco-label such as a voluntary environmental building code or measured building performance audit leads to higher capital values, there is an ongoing academic debate on the exact source of that value. Furthermore, awareness of the heterogeneity associated with many eco-labels, especially those using the voluntary environmental building code methodology, leads to a more accurate conclusion that these studies measure the marketing value of the label, not necessarily the specific actions involved in acquiring the label. Of course, this would not matter if there was a strong correlation between the presence of a label and resulting environmental or human health outcomes. But as the next section describes, that is not a widely accepted conclusion.

5.3 *Environmental Returns to Design- and As-Built-Stage Labelling*

The environmental performance outcomes of voluntary environmental building code-certified green buildings have been mixed, but most research concludes that certified buildings do not perform to their full potential. Empirical data on energy consumption is a common metric used to examine the performance of labelled buildings objectively, since energy efficiency is a central component of voluntary environmental building codes (Newsham, Mancini, & Birt, 2009). All voluntary environmental building codes require projects to simulate anticipated energy consumption, usually to some optimal use pattern and often excluding non-core building services. The typical research approach used to compare potential energy performance with measured energy performance is to amend the simulated potential to reflect a whole building consumption estimate.

From a self-selected distribution of 121 of the first 552 LEED certified buildings, Turner and Frankel (2008) examined post-occupancy energy consumption data relative to simulated expectations. On average, the set of 121 buildings met expectations of around 25% reduced energy consumption relative to a regulatory minimum, but the distribution was highly scattered; over half of the projects deviated more than 25% from this mean, including some resulting performance outcomes that would not be deemed compliant with the regulatory minimum. Therefore, at the individual building scale, the outcome of an early-stage green building certificate on building operations can be highly variable, even when the heterogeneity of voluntary environmental building codes are removed by constructing fair comparisons between potential and actual performance.

Further studies attempt to remove the self-selection sample bias associated with Turner and Frankel (2008). These later studies conclude that there is systematic underperformance as a group rather than actual equalling potential on average. For example, Oates and Sullivan (2012) studied 19 office buildings in Arizona, finding that 18 underperformed relative to their LEED rating while, surprisingly, 15 of those 18 failed to meet the baseline building code specification for energy efficiency. Their small sample size and unique arid climate into consideration could lead to a regional sample bias if extrapolating this result to a wider asset population outside the sampling frame. However, similar bias towards underperformance in small samples has been observed in the United Kingdom (Bordass, Leaman, & Ruyssevelt, 2001) and New Zealand (Gabe, 2008). The latter study identifies potential causes as the tendency to specify complex building systems in green buildings that are innovative but challenging to simulate during design and manage during operation.

With the introduction of Green Star Performance, we identify an opportunity to take a census of certifications across multiple building life stages. Descriptive data from Green Star certification data provides further evidence that performance in-use is more average than performance potential indicates. Figure 6.2 is a series of three histograms counting the number of Green Star Australia certifications by certification type and star

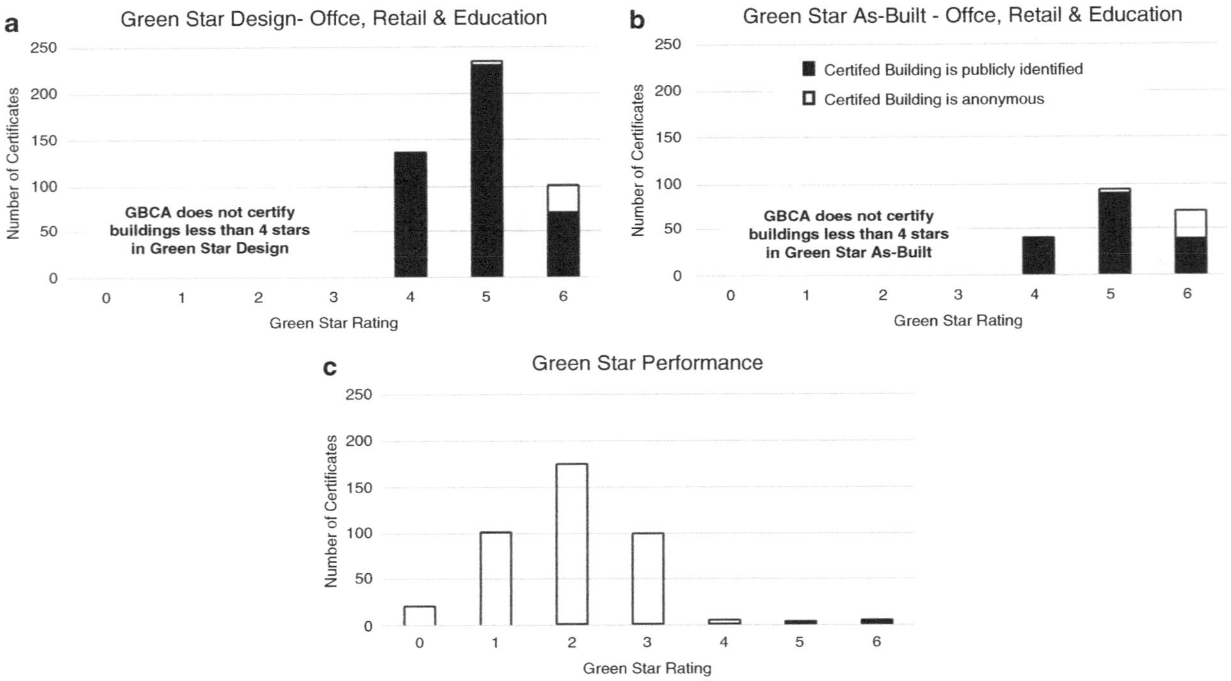

Fig. 6.2 Histogram of the number of buildings certified in Australia by (**a**) Green Star Design, (**b**) Green Star As-Built, and (**c**) Green Star Performance. Note: Design and As-Built counts include the three most popular building typologies (office, retail centre, and educational building) while Performance does not separate buildings by use type. Based on data from the Green Building Council of Australia

rating in the most popular building types (office, retail, and education) from the founding of Green Star to early 2017. The GBCA offers building owners the choice to make identifying characteristics of a labelled building publicly available on the GBCA database (dark shading in Fig. 6.2) or to withhold identifying information from the GBCA database (outline shading in Fig. 6.2). Looking at the histograms in Fig. 6.2 with the caveat that this is not a true panel data set,[18] it appears that buildings perform best on paper during the design and as-built phase, though there is a large drop in the number of buildings that pursue as-built certification as a complement to design certification. However, the more interesting aspect of Fig. 6.2 is the noticeable drop in star ratings when measured in-use. Only a very small fraction of Green Star Performance certifications meet the traditional certification threshold of 4 stars and nearly all of them (95%) choose to remain anonymous behind ratings that would be perceived as poor, even though 1 star or higher represents improvement above the benchmark standard.

In response to a growing consensus that voluntary environmental building code-certified buildings tend to underperform their on-paper potential, the USGBC has taken the opportunity with the latest revision of LEED BD+C (v4, 2016) to better understand why this is the case. As introduced earlier, one of the mandatory requirements of certification under Version 4 of LEED BD+C is to share performance data in-use with the USGBC. While this data is unlikely to be made public, nor will it affect the past award of a LEED BD+C certificate, it will enable the certification agency to better understand causes of systemic underperformance and the risks involved with a life-cycle model of building certification.

5.4 *Early Outcomes from Repetitive Measured Building Performance Auditing*

One potential cause of the systemic underperformance of buildings certified using voluntary environmental building codes may be the lack of an

[18] Meaning certification activity for the same sample of buildings is not observed at each phase in the building life-cycle. With the near-universal decision to make Green Star Performance certifications anonymous, we cannot construct a sub-sample of histograms that feature the same buildings through their lifecycle. However, we can conclude that, except for an unknown fraction of the design-certified cohort that was never built or has not yet finished construction, each building owner has the opportunity to certify using all three systems.

established framework for ongoing performance assessment. Studies of NABERS Energy, one of the few measured building performance auditing labels that has been around long enough to produce repetitive certification data for research, reveal that repetitive audit participation leads to rapid reductions in measured energy use. By tracking 14 years of NABERS Energy/ABGR disclosures, Gabe (2016a) constructs a sequential series of raw site energy use intensity measurements from over 800 buildings in Australia that have certified more than once. As seen in Fig. 6.3, repetitive certification is associated with both a reduction in the variance between buildings and a statistically significant reduction in the average site energy use intensity. Expectation of a future audit is also important; long time periods between re-certification events lead to statistically significant increases in energy use intensity. In aggregate, the average building undergoing repetitive NABERS Energy audits reduces energy use intensity by 20–30% from the initial audit. A tangential study (Gabe, 2016b) found

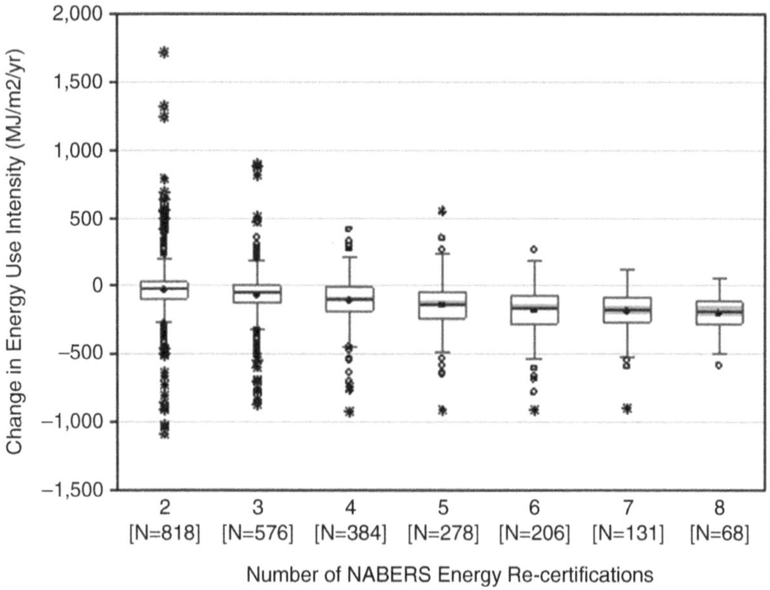

Fig. 6.3 The distribution of change in EUI between first NABERS Energy audit and each subsequent audit (re-certification). Based on data from Gabe (2016a)

that the mechanism of entry (voluntarily or via mandate) had no influence on these outcomes.

Further research on the non-financial outcomes of repetitive labelling activity is likely to increase over the next decade. The accounting framework behind Energy Star has enabled local and state policymakers across the United States to implement mandatory disclosure laws, which rapidly increases the data available for assessing measured performance (Kontokosta, 2013). Multiple attribute labelling systems have a longer time between audits, usually five years, but over the next decade, data on repeat certifications from LEED O+M may be rich enough to evaluate early empirical outcomes associated with a broader scope of measured building performance auditing. In Europe, Bruhns et al. (2011) describe a database of Display Energy Certificates in the United Kingdom, but do not investigate the effects of repetitive audits. The mandatory EPC labelling scheme is an environmental building code framework, but it has a ten-year expiration. Many of the earliest adopting member states have recently reached their second decade of the mandate in the residential property context. Future research on repetitive EPC labelling outcomes will provide an interesting look into how expectations of future labelling assessment affect building design potential.

6 Recommendations

Moving forward, what can be learnt from our review to improve the market for private green building labelling and better integrate sustainability considerations into market transactions? We discuss four recommendations that will improve effectiveness, increase adoption, harmonise benchmarking, and integrate design with operation. There is a general theme in these proposals: the need for a building life-cycle approach to labelling involving design forecasts and operational audits. Standing in the way of this future is the private-sector's hesitancy to introduce downside risk that follow-up disclosed audit information may be perceived negatively. Our review finds market perception matters more than proof of performance when it comes to the financial rewards associated with labelled buildings. Thus, we see a critical role for the public-sector to drive this integration using the tool of mandatory disclosure.

6.1 Improving the Effectiveness of Green Labelling and Reporting Tools

In our review, we find two contrasting narratives on "effectiveness". The first is a positive story on the financial effectiveness of labelling; many empirical studies have demonstrated that the label itself has marketing value. While researchers continue to question the source of that marketing value, there is no support for a claim that obtaining a building eco-label negatively affects the market value of a building. Thus, we find no grounds on which to recommend improvements in the financial effectiveness of green building labelling.

The second narrative on the environmental effectiveness of green labelling is less palatable and signals opportunity for improvement. Empirical evidence on measured environmental outcomes from voluntary environmental building codes largely finds a building stock that performs below its operational design potential. Researchers and labelling firms continue to investigate the causes of underperformance. Encouragingly, early evidence from measured building performance auditing labels reverses this narrative; ongoing re-certification leads to observable environmental performance improvements.

Improving environmental effectiveness is important because a mismatch between marketing messages and in-use performance creates a significant credibility risk for the labelling firms, whose business capital rests on their credibility and independence. Misleading information on the current performance of a building enhances, instead of removes, the information asymmetry market failure that provides an economic rationale for the existence of labelling tools.

Understandably unpopular in a market that values perception over performance, dynamic eco-labels are needed to reflect information appropriate to the current stage of the building's life-cycle. During the design phase, it is sensible for a design team to use Green Star Design, for example, to market a building to construction contractors and potential users. After construction, there is a "settling in" period with insufficient data for a performance audit. However, transitioning to a Green Star As-Built rating for marketing to prospective owners, users, and property managers makes use of the most relevant information available. Lastly, once the building is in use for sufficient time to measure performance, marketing needs to use Green Star Performance to communicate with prospective users and buyers. One can even take this concept further to advocate real-time operational performance management where possible. For example, the USGBC are currently trialling a "LEED Dynamic Plaque" labelling interface wherein real-time operational data is used to create a visual display of the building's current performance across five categories of measurement (energy, water, waste, transportation, and human experience).

Our recommendation for marketing to match the phase of the building life-cycle introduces two important incentives into the property market. First, integration provides the expectation of future auditing, which, importantly, places costs on decisions during construction or operation that may affect environmental or health potential later on in the building's life-cycle. Research has shown expectations of future building performance audits to be effective at maintaining and enhancing performance in use (Gabe, 2016a). Second, our recommendation improves communication, and perhaps legal contracting, between designers and users; knowing that future occupants will need to operate efficiently means designers must consider usability in design.

Dynamic labelling faces an important challenge. It introduces an element of downside risk into the market for green labelling. With private green labelling tools being voluntary, there is only upside risk. Should a building not achieve the goals its designers set, the designers can simply choose not to certify (or remain anonymous), a neutral outcome. If successful, the building gains a label that has improved its marketing value, a positive outcome. The possibility of a negative outcome in dynamic labelling—declining ratings or the loss of a label, for example—is likely to deter voluntary participation, which has two effects. One is that with performance and perception aligned, buildings that excel in this system should be appropriately recognised with higher financial returns. But the other is a result of reduced demand for certification; a private firm in the business of certification may not remain profitable. Therefore, our recommendation implies that research into adoption rates may become more important.

6.2 *Increasing Adoption and Use of Voluntary Ratings in Regulation*

Besides acknowledgement of rapid adoption rates early in the market for voluntary green building codes (Fuerst, 2009; Kok et al., 2011), researchers are only just beginning to explore adoption rates empirically. Unsurprisingly, regulatory pressures—either the threat of or legislation of mandatory disclosure—are the primary determinants of adoption rates once the novelty of green labelling wears off (Fuerst, Kontokosta, & McAllister, 2014; Gabe, 2016b). Other studies support the environment-as-luxury-good narrative, indicating adoption rates are positively associated with income and market conditions (Kok et al., 2011; Sanderford, McCoy, & Keefe, 2017).

Redistributing or growing income and intervening in real estate markets in the service of increasing voluntary green labelling tool adoption is unlikely. We therefore anticipate that mandatory disclosure policies (Kontokosta, 2013) will be the primary means of targeting increased adoption.

Through research on Australia's mandatory energy performance disclosure regime for commercial office buildings (Gabe, 2016b), we can elaborate on two context factors that have made mandatory energy disclosure successful in Australia. First, single attribute measured building performance auditing tools are the best fit for mandatory disclosure. The cost of compliance—auditing site utility bills, for example—is very low, particularly in the case of repeat audits. Without needing to weight non-comparable credits, single attribute systems provide fair and comparable accounting frameworks and benchmarks for measured building performance auditing. Labelling thresholds and credit weightings within hybrid rating systems (e.g. LEED O+M, Green Star Performance) are typically random round numbers.

Second, Australian success is partially attributed to NABERS Energy being a voluntary labelling tool for a decade before it became mandatory in commercial office building transaction advertisements. For policymakers, this is an important context that enables a three-step process observed in Australia to be adopted elsewhere. First, a group of private asset owners saw sufficient value in differentiation to enable significant uptake of a voluntary disclosure scheme. Second, a market for building retrofits emerged to improve ratings for these pioneering owners. Third, a mandatory disclosure regime provided the incentive for disinterested owners to engage in improving performance at a much faster rate given the presence of the market for building retrofits.

6.3 *Harmonising Benchmarking*

While we have argued that understanding of green building labelling tools can be simplified into two key genres—voluntary environmental building codes and measured building performance auditing—potential remains for continued market confusion. One example is how certification thresholds are not comparable. For example, a "Pass" in BREEAM involves meeting 30% of applicable credits while the equivalent "Certified" level in LEED involves meeting 40% of all possible credits, and the credits in each are not identical. The most confusing example of disharmony is the use of a 0 to 6 star scale by both Green Star and NABERS in Australia. It appears as if there is harmony in measurement, but Green Stars are based on an ambiguous collection of voluntary environmental building code standards while NABERS stars are based on measured single attribute performance relative to consumption benchmarks from a 1999 benchmarking survey. NABERS and Green Star Australia "stars" are not comparable at all despite sharing the same marketing label. A similar story can be told for the relationship between Energy Performance Certificates and Display Energy Certificates in the United Kingdom. Both use an A to G letter grading system as the label to communicate potential (EPC) or measured (DEC) building energy efficiency, but the EPC is not a forecast of a DEC because the letter grades have a different methodology and different benchmarking thresholds. Furthermore, voluntary environmental building codes and multiple attribute auditing schemes face the challenge of weighting the relative value of compliance with optional building standards that make up scheme credits/points. Some, like LEED, weight credits implicitly while others, notably BREEAM and Green Star, have both implicit and explicit weightings.

We suggest harmonising design- and construction-stage labelling with the accounting benchmarks developed by measured building performance auditing labels is a sensible, but challenging, opportunity to address the confusion. Design- and construction-stage use of these accounting frameworks then become "forecasts" of performance to be directly compared with subsequent performance audits. The survey-based percentile labelling thresholds used by Energy Star, NABERS, and the United Kingdom DEC become rational grounds for meaningful comparisons within a local or national market. Finally, with a design rating directly comparable to an in-use rating, the dynamic labelling process recommended here would ensure harmony across all stages of the building life-cycle. This will work for both single and multiple attribute auditing frameworks, though the latter face an additional challenge in harmonising the inter-credit weighting used to arrive at a single label.

Currently, this is not how voluntary environmental building code credits that could be comparable, such as those for operational energy consumption, are written. BREEAM, LEED, and Green Star reward potential, not actual, consumption targets in these credits. By assuming static use patterns and climate models, designers maximising potential have an incentive to optimise their design to this static use pattern. Our recommendation would require those designers to simulate their design against a range of plausible use patterns to arrive at an expected value of consumption given the resulting probability distribution of simulated outcomes. This changes the incentive of the designer from optimising the building in a particular scenario to optimising the resilience of the design to changes in use patterns.

A further need is to address the heterogeneity that exists in voluntary environmental building code labelling. This can occur in many ways. One is to have an organisation such as the World Green Building Council collaborate with its global network of green building certification firms to agree on performance-based accounting frameworks and survey percentiles that could apply to any market. Another opportunity is to increase disclosure of raw data behind each rating, enabling consultants to provide translation services across markets.

Should markets harmonise labelling via operational auditing frameworks for a range of sustainable building attributes, the next challenge will involve regularly updating the benchmark survey. If a market is becoming more environmentally efficient, a benchmark update will lower, or possibly disqualify, marketing labels specific to a particular building. The literature on the financial rewards from green building studies only the labelling value; until research can better inform markets about the value of measured environmental performance outcomes, marketing perceptions are arguably more important to the market than the activities required to obtain the label. Furthermore, legal frameworks based on labels mean an old benchmarking survey becomes implicitly entrenched in the market. For example, it is common for government agencies to set label minimums for government accommodation; most Australian government agencies state that they prefer tenancies in buildings with at least 4 NABERS Energy stars. Such soft regulation has likely helped inflate the current NABERS Energy population to an average of 4.2 stars. However, the accounting framework is designed such that the average building in the benchmark survey is to be awarded 2.5 stars. With no updates since 1999, such “ratings creep” is unsurprising, but an update would mean a 4-star building becomes 2 or 2.5 stars and, thus fall afoul of government tenancy preferences.

Updates of voluntary environmental building codes face a similar legal disincentive to increase the stringency of credit requirements over time. Since design or as-built Green Star, BREEAM, or LEED labels do not have an expiration date, buildings that certified under the older, less stringent, versions of the voluntary building codes could obtain valuable government leasing agreements instead of potentially better performing, but less distinctively labelled, newly certified buildings. To complement the challenge of progressing benchmarks in both labelling frameworks, we anticipate a challenge for policymakers to keep their public procurement policies up to date and relevant within a rapidly changing industry.

6.4 *Integrating Design and Operation*

We are certainly not the first to collect or present evidence of the need to align incentives between building designers and users.[19] Others have written of the need to overcome an institutional divide where designers' contractual involvement ends with the commissioning of a new building, resulting in no incentive to learn from the user experience (Way & Bordass, 2007). The development of voluntary environmental building codes reinforces these institutional boundaries; designers prefer to be assessed on potential performance as it removes the cost and limitations of cooperating with property managers. Furthermore, the offering of certification for partial building systems such as LEED Core and Shell, LEED for Commercial Interiors, NABERS Energy Base Building or NABERS Energy Tenancy, demonstrates a willingness to accept institutional boundaries, rather than challenge them by requiring greater multi-disciplinary coordination and cooperation over longer periods of time.

Earlier, we argued that a life-cycle based framework could increase the environmental effectiveness of green building labelling. However, we also acknowledged a further barrier to such a solution: the introduction of downside risk. Private firms offering a life-cycle certification regime will likely find a few elite and well-integrated projects to certify voluntarily but soon find themselves out of business due to competition from certification firms that continue to offer single-stage static labelling. As long as the market continues to value financially the perception (i.e. marketing) value of the label, it appears unlikely for a life-cycle based framework to align the

[19] For example, the same recommendation was the central finding of a multi-year research study nearly 20 years ago in the United Kingdom (Bordass et al., 2001).

incentives of designers and users. Tales of the gap between certified buildings' potential performance and their in-use failure to meet that potential have been known for almost a decade (Oates & Sullivan, 2012; Turner & Frankel, 2008), so we can only assume users are collectively disinterested or inadequately informed.

Trivial private financial benefits of environmental efficiency in operation may be a good reason why users are disinterested. Enhancing the value of the biophysical environment is the production of a "public good", or something available to be enjoyed by all irrespective of whether a particular individual or firm paid for its production. Gabe and Gentry (2013) demonstrate that the private cost savings of natural resource efficiency is very low in comparison to other occupancy-related costs, particularly employee labour and building rent. Interestingly, enhancing the indoor environment to promote human health is not a public good but rather a "club good", or a benefit that can be restricted to those paying rent for space in the building "club". Unsurprisingly, most cost-benefit analyses associated with voluntary environmental building codes (e.g. the well-known Kats, Alevantis, Berman, Mills, & Perlman, 2003, report) rely on labour productivity gains, which can be directly associated with indoor environment design, not energy efficiency (Fisk, 2000). Therefore, it is perhaps unsurprising that the system closest to integration between designers, operators, and users is the emergence of the WELL Building Certification; this health-and-wellness-only framework better aligns with a private accounting of costs and benefits.

While the WELL certification scheme is too young to have produced empirical research on its impact in the market, we have included it within this chapter because its unique design supports the recommendation for an integrated labelling system. Although WELL is targeted primarily at new building design, its hybrid structure, with three-yearly performance verification audits always required to maintain certification, provides an incentive for designers to consider building operations. The challenge that may soon face IWBI will be how to maintain its market leadership should a competitor emerge offering a less integrated health and wellness building certification.

Absent coordination between green building labelling firms or collective demand from users, engendering market interest in conserving the biophysical environment in operation is likely to require public regulation, specifically mandatory disclosure using measured building performance audits. The Australian case study provides an optimistic narrative on how this action feeds back to adjust designers' incentives. Once a NABERS Energy label became mandatory in transaction advertising, the Green Building Council of Australia amended the energy performance credit in Green Star Design & As-Built to include an alternate compliance pathway for a building to allow a NABERS Energy Commitment Agreement to obtain credits for energy-efficient design. These agreements require designers to simulate expected energy efficiency in use as opposed to potential energy efficiency in use, with the modelling result becoming a direct forecast of the building's operational NABERS Energy rating. According to the online NABERS database of Commitment Agreements as of May 2017, 60 of 105 eligible Commitment Agreements have been confirmed with an operational NABERS Energy audit at or above the expected rating. A 57% success rate appears low, but when compared with the apparent systematic disconnect between Green Star Design/As-Built and Green Star Performance, the NABERS Commitment Agreement framework is a significant improvement to the integration of design and operation.

7 Conclusion

Green building labelling has evolved into two dominant forms: voluntary environmental building codes and measured building performance auditing. The former, created for and used by building designers, is a collection of voluntary building standards primarily associated with assessing the potential for a building to preserve the biophysical environment. The latter is accounting frameworks for measuring environmental performance in use. A review of empirical studies into the use of these labelling systems reveals a consensus that the market is willing to pay for labelled buildings, but that buildings certified with voluntary environmental building codes often do not perform to their full potential in use.

In response, we propose that a life-cycle-based labelling system is needed to match the incentives of designers with the needs of building users. Such a system faces barriers within the private-sector because private financial value associated with green buildings is primarily associated with marketing value, not intrinsic environmental performance value. The introduction of mandatory non-financial performance disclosure using measured building performance auditing labels introduces a non-financial accounting framework into the market that can successfully align the incentives of designers and users, opening the pathway for life-cycle building labels.

Appendix: Summary of Rating Schemes Reviewed

Scheme name	*Managing firm*	*Labels (lowest to highest)*	*Location of certified buildings*	*Building typologies*
A. Voluntary environmental building codes				
BREEAM New Construction; BREEAM Refurbishment & Fit-out	BRE Global	Pass, Good, Very Good, Excellent, Outstanding	Global	Any
BREEAM Communities	BRE Global	Pass, Good, Very Good, Excellent, Outstanding	Europe and Africa	Masterplanned neighbourhoods
LEED Building Design and Construction	US Green Building Council	Certified, Silver, Gold, Platinum	Global	Any
LEED Interior Design and Construction	US Green Building Council	Certified, Silver, Gold, Platinum	Global	Offices, Retail, Hotel
LEED for Neighborhood Development	US Green Building Council	Certified, Silver, Gold, Platinum	Global	Masterplanned neighbourhoods
Green Star Design; Green Star In-Use	Green Building Council Australia	4, 5, 6 stars	Australia	Any non-residential building
Green Star New Zealand	New Zealand Green Building Council	4, 5, 6 stars	New Zealand	Any non-residential building
Green Star Communities	Green Building Council Australia	4, 5, 6 stars	Australia	Masterplanned neighbourhoods
Homestar	New Zealand Green Building Council	1, 2, 3, 4, 5, 6, 7, 8, 9, 10	New Zealand	Any residential building
PassivHaus	PassivHaus Institut	Classic, Plus, Premium	Global	Residential, Office
NatHERS	Australian Federal Government	1, 2, 3, 4, 5, 6, 7, 8, 9, 10	Australia	Any residential building
Energy Performance Certificate	All EU member state governments	G, F, E, D, C, B, A	Europe	Primarily residential buildings, but some commercial buildings depending on the member state.

(*continued*)

(continued)

Scheme name	*Managing firm*	*Labels (lowest to highest)*	*Location of certified buildings*	*Building typologies*
B. Measured building performance auditing, single attribute schemes				
Energy Star	US Environmental Protection Agency	75 to 100 by integer	USA and Canada	Commercial and Industrial
Display Energy Certificate	UK Government	G, F, E, D, C, B, A	UK	29 types of commercial buildings
NABERS Energy, Water, Indoor Environment, Waste	NSW State Government	0, 1, 1.5, 2, 2.5, 3, 3.5, 4, 4.5, 5, 5.5, 6 stars	Australia	Office, Retail, Hotel
C. Measured building performance auditing, multiple attribute schemes				
BREEAM In-Use	BRE Global	Pass, Good, Very Good, Excellent, Outstanding	Global	Any non-residential building
LEED for Building Operations and Maintenance	US Green Building Council	Certified, Silver, Gold, Platinum	Global	Office, Retail, Education, Hotel, Warehouse
Green Star Performance	Green Building Council Australia	0, 1, 2, 3, 4, 5, 6 stars	Australia	Any non-residential building
D. Health and wellness certifications				
WELL Building Certification	International WELL Building Institute	Silver, Gold, Platinum	Global	Office, Retail, Education, Multifamily Residential

References

Bannister, P. (2012). *NABERS: Lessons from 12 Years of Performance Based Ratings in Australia*. Paper presented at 12th International Conference for Enhanced Building Operations, 23–26 October 2012, Manchester, United Kingdom.

Bordass, B., Leaman, A., & Ruyssevelt, P. (2001). Assessing Building Performance in Use 5: Conclusions and Implications. *Building Research & Information, 29*(2), 144–157.

BRE Global. (2013). *BREEAM International New Construction 2013 FAQs*. Watford: BRE.

BRE Global. (2016). *BREEAM International New Construction 2016*. Watford: BRE.

Bruhns, H., Jones, P., Cohen, R., Bordass, B., & Davis, H. (2011, May). *CIBSE Review of Energy Benchmarks for Display Energy Certificates—Analysis of DEC Results to Date*. Report for the CIBSE Benchmarks Steering Committee.

Chegut, A., Eichholtz, P., & Kok, N. (2014). Supply, Demand and the Value of Green Buildings. *Urban Studies, 51*(1), 22–43.

Christensen, P. H. (2011). *LEED-EB: O+M and BREEAM In-use: Implications for commercial real estate*. Paper presented at European Real Estate Society Annual Conference, June 15–18, 2011, Eindhoven, the Netherlands.

Christensen, P. H., & Sayce, S. L. (2015). Sustainable Property Reporting and Rating Tools. In S. J. Wilkinson, S. L. Sayce, & P. H. Christensen (Eds.), *Developing Property Sustainably* (pp. 203–234). New York: Routledge.

Coffey, B., Borgeson, S., Selkowitz, S., Apte, J., Mathew, P., & Haves, P. (2009). Towards a Very Low-Energy Building Stock: Modelling the US Commercial Building Sector to Support Policy and Innovation Planning. *Building Research & Information, 37*(5–6), 610–624.

Cole, R. J. (1999). Building Environmental Assessment Methods: Clarifying Intentions. *Building Research & Information, 27*(4–5), 230–246.

Cole, R. J. (2006). Shared Markets: Coexisting Building Environmental Assessment Methods. *Building Research & Information, 34*(4), 357–371.

Cole, R. J. (2012). Transitioning from Green to Regenerative Design. *Building Research & Information, 40*(1), 39–53.

Department for Communities and Local Government. (2008). *The Government's Methodology for the Production of Operational Ratings, Display Energy Certificates and Advisory Reports*. Wetherby: Communities and Local Government Publications.

Ding, G. K. C. (2008). Sustainable Construction – The Role of Environmental Assessment Tools. *Journal of Environmental Management, 86*(3), 451–464.

Eichholtz, P., Kok, N., & Quigley, J. M. (2010). Doing Well by Doing Good? Green Office Buildings. *American Economic Review, 100*(5), 2492–2509.

Fisk, W. J. (2000). Health and Productivity Gains from Better Indoor Environments and Their Relationship with Building Energy Efficiency. *Annual Review of Energy and the Environment, 25*, 537–566.

Freybote, J., Sun, H., & Yang, X. (2015). The Impact of LEED Neighborhood Certification on Condo Prices. *Real Estate Economics, 43*(3), 586–608.

Fuerst, F. (2009). Building Momentum: An Analysis of Investment Trends in LEED and Energy Star-Certified Properties. *Journal of Retail & Leisure Property, 8*(4), 285–297.

Fuerst, F., Kontokosta, C., & McAllister, P. (2014). Determinants of Green Building Adoption. *Environment and Planning B: Planning and Design, 41*(3), 551–570.

Fuerst, F., & McAllister, P. (2011a). Green Noise or Green Value? Measuring the Effects of Environmental Certification on Office Values. *Real Estate Economics, 39*(1), 45–69.

Fuerst, F., & McAllister, P. (2011b). The Impact of Energy Performance Certificates on the Rental and Capital Values of Commercial Property Assets. *Energy Policy, 39*(10), 6608–6614.

Fuerst, F., McAllister, P., Nanda, A., & Wyatt, P. (2015). Does Energy Efficiency Matter to Home-Buyers? An Investigation of EPC Ratings and Transaction Prices in England. *Energy Economics, 48*, 145–156.

Fuerst, F., van de Wetering, J., & Wyatt, P. (2013). Is Intrinsic Energy Efficiency Reflected in the Pricing of Office Leases? *Building Research & Information, 41*(4), 373–383.

Gabe, J. (2008). *Design Versus Performance: Lessons from Monitoring an Energy-Efficient Commercial Building in Operation.* Proceedings of the 3rd International Conference on Sustainability Engineering and Science, 9–12 December 2008, Auckland, New Zealand.

Gabe, J. (2016a). Successful Greenhouse Gas Mitigation in Existing Australian Office Buildings. *Building Research & Information, 44*(2), 160–174.

Gabe, J. (2016b). An Empirical Comparison of Voluntary and Mandatory Building Energy Performance Disclosure Outcomes. *Energy Policy, 96*, 680–687.

Gabe, J., & Gentry, R. (2013). Government. In R. Vale & B. Vale (Eds.), *Living Within a Fair Share Ecological Footprint* (pp. 134–146). New York: Routledge.

Gabe, J., & Rehm, M. (2014). Do Tenants Pay Energy Efficiency Rent Premiums? *Journal of Property Investment & Finance, 32*(4), 333–351.

Green Building Council of Australia [GBCA]. (2015). *Green Star Communities: National Framework.* Sydney: Green Building Council of Australia.

Hoffman, A. J., & Henn, R. (2008). Overcoming the Social and Psychological Barriers to Green Building. *Organization & Environment, 21*(4), 390–419.

International WELL Building Institute [IWBI] and Delos Living. (2017). *The WELL Certification Guidebook, Version 1.* New York: Delos Living.

Kahn, M. E., & Kok, N. (2014). The Capitalization of Green Labels in the California Housing Market. *Regional Science and Urban Economics, 47*, 25–34.

Kats, G., Alevantis, L., Berman, A., Mills, E., & Perlman, J. (2003). *The Costs and Financial Benefits of Green Buildings: A Report to California's Sustainable Building Task Force.* Sacramento, CA: California Department of Resources Recycling and Recovery.

Kok, N., & Jennen, M. (2012). The Impact of Energy Labels and Accessibility on Office Rents. *Energy Policy, 46*, 489–497.

Kok, N., McGraw, M., & Quigley, J. M. (2011). The Diffusion of Energy Efficiency in Building. *The American Economic Review, 101*(3), 77–82.

Kontokosta, C. E. (2013). Energy Disclosure, Market Behavior, and the Building Data Ecosystem. *Annals of the New York Academy of Sciences, 1295*(1), 34–43.

Miller, N., Spivey, J., & Florance, A. (2008). Does Green Pay Off? *Journal of Real Estate Portfolio Management, 14*(4), 385–399.

Mitchell, L. M. (2010). Green Star and NABERS: Learning from the Australian Experience with Green Building Rating Tools. In R. K. Bose (Ed.), *Energy Efficient Cities: Assessment Tools and Benchmarking Practices* (pp. 93–130). Herndon, VA: World Bank Publications.

Newell, G., MacFarlane, J., & Walker, R. (2014). Assessing Energy Rating Premiums in the Performance of Green Office Buildings in Australia. *Journal of Property Investment & Finance, 32*(4), 352–370.

Newsham, G. R., Mancini, S., & Birt, B. J. (2009). Do LEED-Certified Buildings Save Energy? Yes, But…. *Energy and Buildings, 41*(8), 897–905.

NSW Office of Environment and Heritage. (2013). *NABERS Energy and Water for Offices: Rules for Collecting and Using Data, Version 3.0.* Sydney: NSW Government.

NSW Office of Environment and Heritage. (2016). *NABERS Annual Report 2015/16. 30 September 2016 Version.* Sydney: NSW Government.

Oates, D., & Sullivan, K. T. (2012). Postoccupancy Energy Consumption Survey of Arizona's LEED New Construction Population. *Journal of Construction Engineering and Management, 138*, 742–750.

Passive House Institute [PHI]. (2016). *Criteria for the Passive House, EnerPHit and PHI Low Energy Building Standard. Version 9f.* Darmstadt: Passive House Institute.

Pivo, G., & Fisher, J. D. (2010). Income, Value, and Returns in Socially Responsible Office Properties. *Journal of Real Estate Research, 32*(3), 243–270.

Prior, J. J. (1991). BREEAM–A Step Towards Environmentally Friendlier Buildings. *Structural Survey, 9*(3), 237–242.

Reed, R., Bilos, A., Wilkinson, S., & Schulte, K. W. (2009). International Comparison of Sustainable Rating Tools. *Journal of Sustainable Real Estate, 1*(1), 1–22.

Robinson, S., & McAllister, P. (2015). Heterogeneous Price Premiums in Sustainable Real Estate? An Investigation of the Relation Between Value and Price Premiums. *Journal of Sustainable Real Estate, 7*, 1–20.

Robinson, S., Singh, A. J., & Das, P. (2016). Financial Impact of LEED and Energy Star Certifications on Hotel Revenues. *The Journal of Hospitality Financial Management, 24*(2), 110–126.

Sanderford, A. R., McCoy, A. P., & Keefe, M. J. (2017). Adoption of Energy Star Certifications: Theory and Evidence Compared. *Building Research & Information.* Published Online in early access on 5 January 2017.

Sayce, S., Sundberg, A., & Clements, B. (2010). *Is Sustainability Reflected in Commercial Property Prices: An Analysis of the Evidence Base.* London: Royal Institute of Chartered Surveyors.

Schendler, A. (2009). *Getting Green Done: Hard Truths from the Front Lines of the Sustainability Revolution.* New York: PublicAffairs.

Schindler, S. B. (2010). Following Industry's LEED: Municipal Adoption of Private Green Building Standards. *Florida Law Review, 62*(2), 285–350.

Sullivan, L. J., Rydin, Y., & Buchanan, C. (2014). *Neighbourhood Sustainability Frameworks—A Literature Review*. UCL Working Paper Series. London: UCL Centre for Urban Sustainability and Resilience.

Tenbrunsel, A., Wade-Benzoni, K., Messick, D., & Bazerman, M. (1997). The Dysfunctional Effects of Standards on Environmental Attitudes and Choices. In M. Bazerman, D. Messick, A. Tenbrunsel, & K. Wade-Benzoni (Eds.), *Psychological Perspectives to Environmental and Ethical Issues* (pp. 105–121). San Francisco: New Lexington.

Turner, C., & Frankel, M. (2008). *Energy Performance of LEED for New Construction Buildings*. White Salmon, WA: New Buildings Institute.

United Nations Environment Programme. (2007). *Buildings and Climate Change: status, challenges and opportunities*. Paris: United Nations Environment Programme.

United States Environmental Protection Agency [USEPA]. (2014). *Energy Star PortfolioManager Technical Reference: Energy Star Score*. Washington, DC: USEPA.

United States Green Building Council [USGBC]. (2004, October). *Green Building Rating System for Existing Buildings, Upgrades, Operations and Maintenance*. Washington, DC: United States Green Building Council.

United States Green Building Council [USGBC]. (2017). *LEED v4 for Building Design and Construction. April 14 2017 Version*. Washington, DC: United States Green Building Council.

Vale, R., & Vale, B. (2009). *Time to Eat the Dog? The Real Guide to Sustainable Living*. London: Thames & Hudson.

Way, M., & Bordass, B. (2007). Making Feedback and Post-Occupancy Evaluation Routine 2: Soft Landings – Involving Design and Building Teams in Improving Performance. *Building Research and Information, 33*(4), 353–360.

Zatz, M., & Burgess, M. (2016). *CBECS 2012: Update on EPA's Schedule and Methodology*. Washington, DC: US Environmental Protection Agency.

CHAPTER 7

Global Real Estate Sustainability Benchmarking: An Essential Tool for Real Estate Management

Willem G. Keeris and Ruben A. R. Langbroek

1 Sustainable Real Estate

1.1 Introduction: Historically Based Benchmarking and Future Focused Scenarios

This chapter examines the theme of benchmarking in general, specifically the Global Real Estate Sustainable Benchmark (GRESB). Taking into account that sustainability hereby stands for a balanced policy on all economic, social, and governmental (ESG) issues. Contributed to scenarios, it delivers a very useful tool for the necessary productivity improvement of the real estate management organization.

W. G. Keeris (✉)
Delft University of Technology, Delft, The Netherlands

GRESB Asia Pacific, Sydney, NSW, Australia

R. A. R. Langbroek
GRESB Asia Pacific, Sydney, NSW, Australia

T. Walker et al. (eds.), *Sustainable Real Estate*, Palgrave Studies in Sustainable Business In Association with Future Earth,
https://doi.org/10.1007/978-3-319-94565-1_7

Benchmarking can be described as the technique of achieving continuous improvement of one's own performance, by comparing against gained insight into the performance of other organizations and peers. So it concerns a process of consistently systematic collecting all needed (historical) data and the thorough analysis of it in its context to compare. This provides an idea of the effectiveness of the organization in sub-areas, in terms of results, productivity, quality, and practice. In addition, it provides the opportunity to translate opportunities for improvement into action, based on new ideas and insights having emerged from the benchmarking process. Benchmarking is therefore always conducted with multiple participants in that process, based on comparisons in areas of performance, including the context of underlying operational and management skills. While the focus should be on outperforming peers, whose methods, policies, and procedures can be sources of inspiration in operational improvements, the average performance of the peers can also serve as an objective performance target. As such, the findings are in a way influenced by the frame of the past, while the main purpose is future focused decision-making.

Given that the future is not predictable, one needs an image of the years to come making it possible to anticipate upon the possible upcoming developments during that period. In that case, by lack of effective causal insight and quality data, scenarios are the highest attainable level of forecasting those developments. Scenarios serve merely as support to create that wanted future picture. Although no scenario predicts the actual future market situation, the way of working with these gives useful illustrations of what is 'maybe'. Say as awakening to a coming 'climate change' in the market. Scenarios keep users on their toes about upcoming or possible changes and which signal is valuable, given the scale of risks involved.

However, scenarios are not only used to implement future expectations, they also depict the effects on the operations of real estate investments through their earning potential. This potential can be used by investment managers and appraisers to calculate the value of real (estate) assets.

So starting from the actual point of view, scenarios lay the foundation for the representation of what possibly might happen in the future, with premises for the probable chance and presupposed impacts of the developments. The starting point for this purpose is on the one hand the availability of a sufficient minimum on causal cohesion, based on images and characteristics. And on the other hand the availability of enough reliable, relevant, and historically representative data to underpin these pointed out relations. With regards to both these issues, benchmarking delivers the most useful information.

Benchmarking usually considers multiple data series, and therefore performance results are affected by this historical frame of reference. However, handled within scenarios, this information is used for future decision-making, since the evaluation of the quality and value of real estate assets is fully future focussed. This is the weak spot in the decision-making process involved in the development of any future-oriented policy. One has to address that gap between projections founded on historically based benchmarking and future operational and management performances. Given that use, those benchmarking results as such must first be adapted to the personal and subjective future expectations. One also needs the use of scenarios to transform those results from the passed to future possibilities. The impacts of those subjective transformations are of vital importance for real estate management organizations, as well as concerned brokers and/or appraisers. This chapter focuses on this and other critical issues relating to current ESG-focused real estate benchmarking practices. The GRESB is used as the example of how one can address these issues. Recommendations are made for further improvement of the quality of similar real estate benchmarking in the future.

1.2 *Sustainable Real Estate Investing: A Need When 'Going Concern'*

When determining the value of real estate assets, the 'going concern' scenario must be taken as a starting point, on portfolio base as well as for the separate properties of it. The 'going concern' concept is applied to this setting because it is also used as an accounting concept, due to the similarity as well as the essential difference in meaning between them. In both cases that concept expresses autonomous continuation from the actual reality. However, in accounting everything is focused on the concerned financial year. Thus as an accounting concept it doesn't really imply the future; that the concern has a future, of at least the next year, is sufficient information to ground the handled accounting principles. The assumption with that is that a policy without taking sweeping reforms, placed within the context of the real estate market, includes a static policy and in that way none drastic operational changes in the future. Although it doesn't directly imply extrapolation of the obtained last results, that is often the habit. Nevertheless, given the dynamic, what is typical for the real estate market: standstill means decline. Seen in that light, when realistic, one can interpret such a going concern scenario as in time leading to the loss of market position, next positive perspective and in the end losing the foundation for further going. That is not what investing is about. The use of the same concept (going concern) in the context of the real estate market gives now the impression that this is not a risk. By that, the accent is laid on the actual situation of really going and doing well as if it concerns also the future. It is on the contrary the case: it means just an active policy by the management concerned, which is aware of the risks of not timely reacting on the dynamic developments in the market. And thus has that management not only to be constantly focused on improving the market position, the quality of the real estate assets, and operational results, but equally important is the focus on her organization, and the alignment of the policies with the material ESG issues, which implies the possibilities of needed changes. Because typically, real estate is a means of investments, as well as a business asset, of which the return on investment depends on the operational management.

So the real estate management is responsible for the realization of that so meant going concern process and must use newly acquired knowledge, experiences, and potential opportunities to its full advantage; and implement it in its policies. Including the analysis of ESG issues as part of the investment valuation and decision-making process, as being identified as opportunities for outperformance. While there is strong evidence that thoughtfully designed and operated buildings can provide practical solutions to the most challenging ESG issues, while creating value for stakeholders.

The aim for GRESB is to measure and benchmark ESG performance of real estate management organizations around the globe. The GRESB results provide useful insight into what future potential might be in terms of improvement on ESG performance, as it assesses the achievements of local, national, and international ESG policies in the real estate sector. This is crucial information, because climate change and unstable communities are major system risks. These risks require an adequate reaction from the individual real estate management organization. The ESG philosophy must be carried out correctly. Not only will this lead to reduced risks and improved returns on capital that is invested in real estate assets, but it will also result in an enhanced market position, because it forces GRESB participants to have an open mind regarding new developments with concern to ESG policies. Furthermore, it will create a realistic view on future ESG-related developments.

1.3 *Background of GRESB: Stimulating Responsible Real Estate Investing*

The recognition of the link between ESG performance and the ability to enhance and protect shareholder value has increased the commitment of real estate investors to responsible investing. Consequently, an increasing number of investors are incorporating responsible investing principles into their investment and management processes. In line with the United Nation's Principles for Responsible Investment (PRI), the responsible investing approach must incorporate ESG factors to better manage risks and generate sustainable long-term returns. This approach recognizes that the generation of returns depends on stable, well-functioning, and well governed social, environmental, and economic investments and portfolios.

Responsible investing requires that investors take a wider view, acknowledging the full spectrum of ESG-related risks facing society as a whole. Though not always considered in conventional real estate investment decision-making, because of these risks are material economic issues, which makes them relevant to investment risk and return. Investors are concerned that sustainability-related risks, as well as the policies that are increasingly being put in place by governments and policy makers to avert those risks, will have negatively impact on the value of their real estate portfolios. Increasingly, real estate investors are using a combination of approaches, such as direct corporate engagement, positive screening (or best-in-class screening), ESG integration and sustainability-themed investing, including investing in green bonds.

These different strategies share one powerful principle, namely that in the end institutional investors hold the key to market transformation, that is because they have the money. By using that firepower to allocate their capital to real estate companies and fund managers, which are working the hardest to improve their ESG performance, investors create bottom-up commitment. Besides the social aspects for the community as a whole, this is needed to transform the built environment into an energy-efficient, low-carbon, and climate-resilient sector. In addition, it may be also more social minded as result of that.

In order to allocate their capital responsibly, investors need to know which real estate companies and fund managers are performing well, while those seeking investment need to know where they stand, both in absolute terms and relative to their peers. Furthermore, all stakeholders stand to gain from understanding how ESG performance can be improved. Benchmarking ESG performance of real estate companies and funds provides all parties with business intelligence that helps identify best practices, highlight organizational strengths and improvement opportunities, and inform implementation action plans.

Market needs motivate GRESB to provide institutional investors with clear, actionable information about the ESG aspects of their real estate investments around the world. GRESB seeks to offer investment decision-makers the tools they need to understand the positive and negative impacts of their investments, recognize leadership, and engage effectively with real estate companies, fund managers, and operating partners.

At the same time, benchmarking the ESG performance of property companies and funds provides these parties with business intelligence that helps identify best practices, highlights organizational strengths and improvement opportunities, and informs implementation action plans.

Early studies show that relative outperformance on the GRESB benchmark translates into higher total returns for private equity funds and higher returns on assets and equity for listed property companies. Conversely, there is also increasing evidence that more traditional, conventional approaches to property development and management often have the opposite effect.

This line of ESG thinking should effectively be disseminated. It is proven that ESG policy leads to better returns on invested capital. In 2015, researchers from Oxford University and asset management firm Arabesque Partners published a report that demonstrated the economic relevance of sustainability parameters for corporate management and for investors (Clarke, Feiner, & Viehs, 2015). That meta-analysis research investigates over 200 academic studies and sources on sustainability, to assess the economic evidence on both sides. The main findings of the report are:

1. 90% of the studies on cost of capital show that sound ESG standards lower the cost of capital;
2. 88% of the studies show that solid ESG practices result in better operational performance;
3. 80% of the studies show that stock price performance is positively influenced by good sustainability practices.

Alongside this, the organization's management should constantly utilize potential for performance improvement from a discretionary authorization and responsibility point of view. Discretionary asset management implies that the management is responsible for full compliance with the previous commitments to the fiduciary relationship. This fiduciary relation is based on two judicial grounded principles: proper diligence and loyalty.

The first associated principle of proper diligence legally demands that one should provide professional, specialist knowledge, and skills to competently represent the interests of the client(s). If needed through external support, and through delegation of tasks and responsibilities. Current lack of knowledge thus cannot be seen as an argument for lack of an ESG policy.

In addition, the second associated principle of loyalty emphasizes that it's the interest of the real estate investor—in fact better formulated all stakeholders—that should be the main focus. That requirement of unconditional loyalty should be accepted as the absolute norm of the wholehearted commitment to the objectives of the client. The principle of loyalty means that the interests of the client must outweigh their own personal or business interests, or any other interests that are deemed worthwhile pursuing. This means that profit-focused targets should be seen in the context of providing profits to the client(s) of the management. However, this does not mean that these interests can only be expressed financially. For example, a good reputation and market position are also in the interest of clients and other stakeholders. Indirectly, such interests can contribute to meeting the financial targets. The management should take these interests into account, and act in compliance with them, because a well implemented ESG policy will also serve financial aspects, as shown in multiple studies. Regarding the latter, one could say that such an ESG policy is an essential component of raising the productivity for which the property management should continuously strive for.

Apart from all those situations with the private use of the properties, real estate is perceived as a means of investment, as well as a business asset, as stated before, whose return on investment depends on the quality of operational management in addition to the underlying quality of the asset itself. Considering a broader range of factors, including ESG issues, is perceived by the market as an operational improvement that translates into improved market positioning of the real estate asset and, in turn, its management organization. Conventional real estate asset valuation is mostly based on the extrapolation of the current situation into the future situation. If that is the case, this simple method does not take into consideration continued efforts to improve the quality of the assets and their operational management. That creates an increasingly disadvantaged market position for those assets over time, that reflects neither the evolution of the organization's management policies and practices nor their increasing alignment with material ESG issues. What is not in the interest of the investor(s).

When determining the value of properties, appraisers usually take the aforementioned going concern scenario in accounting as the base case scenario. However, these appraisers are free to use any number of scenarios to describe the developments. With that, they should incorporate how the management organization specifically will develop in the future with regard to operational improvements in the line of the real going concern scenario. As such, that chosen scenario is based on the actual achieved progress in terms of ESG performance, as well as the forecasted opportunities, and thereby also taking into account the needed reliable estimates of market evidence on those ESG issues, which are provided in terms of what is profitable and feasible. The earning potential of the asset can be derived from that sketched market level.

2 Benchmarking

2.1 History and Background of Benchmarking

The term benchmark originated from geodesy, which refers to a certain point in the landscape that can be used over time as a reference point in cartography. Distances from that mark determine the positioning of each subsequent point and are thus relative to all other points in space.

Similarly, within the context of business management, benchmarking refers to using external points of reference to determine the position of the organization or business. The results, obtained through the systematic process of benchmarking (acquisition, analysis, and assessment), are used as support for improving the efforts to realize the objectives of the organization, with its hard and soft goals.

Over time, benchmarking has become synonymous with a successful learning process, by way of looking at reference points within an effective but binding cooperation among like-minded other parties by grouping compatible focused professionals for analyses of the perceived results of their operations as well as the context in which these are to be placed.

Through splitting into ever-lower aggregation levels, the comparison enhanced in expressiveness and broadened the approach from the relatively low, most simple level of being product-oriented to the strategic point of view at the global level. Subsequently, for gaining more new information each time, all of these ongoing processes had to be tested and compared again, as a result of the dynamic development of the context. In addition, the available results were, in turn, input for analyses related to certain elapsed periods, which gave benchmarking a continuous character.

However, with time, the obtained set of benchmarking results shows that this alone is not sufficient for the process of gaining knowledge and insights into how to realize the aimed performance. Certainly, sufficiently adequate data is indispensable. Nevertheless, of more interest, and a key factor, is getting a broad orientation and meaningful interpretation of those benchmark results, including awareness of the context in place as well as having consciousness and appreciation of the spirit of the age. Furthermore, transparency and communication within the peer group, as much as outside that group, is important because sharing information leads to multiplying knowledge. The 'what's in it for me?' question must be answered by the individual parties themselves.

After the results of the peer group are mapped, benchmarking is above all focused on the question what was it, hidden behind the single figures, which expresses the performances. In this context, it should be noted that only looking at the achieved results is insufficient, because it does not include the mentioned important context. For example, the obtained return is meaningless without proper understanding of the experienced risks profile during the same period. Also, too little attention is often paid to the physical, social, institutional, and especially emotional aspects that have contributed to those results. Results are always a consequence of the historical context, and as such, they are always lagging behind the current situation and actual facts. These are crucial because real estate is focused on future expectations, both in terms of lessons learnt and as a reflection for the future. The relative benchmarking analysis should illustrate this, however, deeper analysis in time and context are conditions to do so.

2.2 Future Focused Use of Benchmarking

The findings in the last paragraph are certainly true when the benchmark is used for determining future policies. Firstly, it is about the context in which the results were realized, while secondly, it is about translating that to the context in which the targeted results should be realized. Certainly, when the benchmark is used to determine future policies, it is necessary to have an eye for that context, on the one hand, to know in which context the results obtained were achieved. And, on the other hand, to transform that into the context within which the intended results to be achieved should be achieved. This also feeds into market positioning, amongst others.

It should also be noted that since each organization has an individualized mission, vision, and strategic/tactical insights, as well as operational qualities, which are all different aggregation levels, benchmarking should be individualized and reflect the specificities of each organization. When this line of thought is followed, comparison between results and processes only provide marginal advantage. Although that first point is correct, the second is not because of the following three remarks.

Firstly, participants with similarities included in the benchmark are, more often than not, simply coincidental. When speaking about being 'more or less comparable', being more comparable simply isn't feasible.

Secondly, it must be kept in mind that the different identified effects of evolving developments do provide valuable input, even though the context wasn't the same. Benchmarking is always about transposing the results to their own situation, not plain copying. Although the results of benchmarking are given in absolute terms, they must actually be seen as relative values.

And thirdly, benchmarking and analysing the obtained results has another important benefit for real estate management as it controls a very human behavioural aspect, namely the tendency to quit search immediately, once an acceptable alternative has been found to solve a problem. Benchmarking provides value by looking beyond the surface and considering aspects and/or innovations that might otherwise be overlooked in favour of more obvious short-term solutions.

2.3 Criteria for Benchmarking

Permanent self-reflection and learning curves via benchmarking can only be extended over time if the set-up of the benchmark is kept consistent. This requires a fixed structure that meets the following nine criteria (Table 7.1).

Table 7.1 The nine criteria a benchmark must meet

1. *Acceptance*: The benchmark should be generally accepted as the point of reference for the assessment, by the external and/or internal users.
2. *Collecting and analysing data*: The benchmark must allow for comparing the calculated results through analysis. In addition, it must be possible to explain the differences between those results.
3. *Feasibility*: Benchmarking should be easy to implement, in terms of timely and sufficient frequency of availability of the required data, with sufficient expertise for processing and interpretation, supported by a clear conceptual framework, uniform design, and used principles.
4. *Representativeness*: Benchmarking should be based on 'apples to apples' comparison of representative, meaningful data, which means that the data to be processed must be obtained under similar circumstances, both physical and policy-wise. It should provide sufficient coverage to give the results meaning at the intended target level of the participants, in respect of which contribution of each participant in the peer group of the benchmark should correspond to the characteristics of the whole of said frame of reference, referred to as the 'universe'.
5. *Clarity, homogeneity*: The conceptual framework should be based on good, clear, market conforming, and generally accepted clear definitions or descriptions, including uniformity in terms of methods and method of calculation.
6. *Reliability of design and execution*: The entire design and execution of the benchmarking process should be reliable and controlled, through quality assurance and transparency, simple and quick audit trails of results, and so on.
7. *Reliability of calculations*: The results of the benchmark must be reliable, ensured by basing the calculation on the correct choice of the calculation method, considering in particular the purpose of calculation and the characteristics of the depicted image. In addition, calculations should be correctly executed, with an equally rated input. With that also taking into account the current contextual and influencing factors and corresponding frequency of execution.
8. *Consistent as seen over time*: A prerequisite for the use of separate benchmarks within a systematic entirety is that the set-up (in outline) is the same, since 'apples' should be added to 'apples' in one basket. This is important because each benchmark is by itself only a snapshot. What can be valuable in itself does not necessarily reflect the development of that result, seen over a certain period of time. Therefore, it must be derived from a contiguous data time series of nearly fully comparable benchmark results. The result, the derived index, provides insights into the developments during the period.
9. *Specific results*: The benchmark should be applicable in practice, at acceptable costs, and representative for the intended purposes, corresponding to functional lines of responsibility among the participants.

2.4 Indicators for Benchmarking

Benchmarking is based on data collection and the analysis of that data. It is necessary to identify factors that are not only part of the process, where the benchmarking is focused on, but also have a certain influence on the progress of that process. That influence must be measurable, of course. The results of those measurements can then be compared to corresponding reference values for comparison. On this basis, progress and quality can be measured unambiguously. These factors are referred to as the term 'indicators' or 'influencing factors'.

Those points within the critical processes are identified as 'critical success factors' because they are crucial to the success of the business process. As such, they form the basis for the benchmark study, because it is impossible to separately identify within the benchmarking process all the points that hold influence of any kind within each part and sub-process within that whole of the process. The focus should be on what is critical of the success and for the entire company, which usually results in a limited and clear number of factors. That does not alter the fact that first the process in question should have been fully transparent, to know the forces acting behind the signal information and to be able to determine the data points.

It must be taken into account that the choice of the indicators is dependent on the purpose of benchmarking and thereby on the type of benchmark. These influencing factors give only clues—sometimes only indirectly—that their influence is exercised. The measured values relating thereto can thus only provide a sense of how much impact has been encountered, and if possible, what kind of influence exists (Table 7.2).

The measurement results from benchmarking provide the performance at the appropriate level, which is then introduced into the company's present situation and that of the peer group in terms of development. However,

Table 7.2 The criteria which indicators must meet

1. *Acceptance*: They must be generally accepted as a factor, so that there is no discussion beforehand about the results of the benchmarking.
2. *Discoverability*: They should generally be clearly recognizable, have their place within the known processes, and thus be simple in nature.
3. *Influential*: They must be influential at what they represent, offering the potential to improve processes.
4. *Stimulating*: They must be inspiring and motivating, to encourage improvement.

these results have real meaning only after they have been compared with their reference value, such as a corresponding norm, average, or signal value. A norm can be that corresponding with a, mostly minimal, level of a set task, or term of reference, such as a Target Return (TR). The Minimal Accepted Return (MAR) can be seen as a signal value, in which case the result must be mostly of a higher value. The signal is given a sign, so that underspending below that signal level is not allowed because of the related financial consequences for the investor, such as there being insufficient liquidity to cover the costs. But the average of the data series is most often used, for instance like the achieved Average Total Return of the Market Portfolio. That benchmark result is for common use, while the mentioned other two are for individual practice.

The results that are coupled to the indicators only have a (first) signalling function in practice. The derived signal is also often considered to be an indicator. At that point within the process, at a higher aggregation level, the influence is measured based on the obtained signal. For example, in real estate, vacancy rate, mutation rate, and average remaining lease duration all have signal functions to assess the lease situation of an asset. This can then be compared with the vacancy and absorption rate of the rental market data at the higher level of aggregation and at the relevant local market. This can provide an image of the positioning of that asset in the marketplace.

Indicators should be the points which one needs to generate the output data required to bring into picture the development of a certain process. The aim is to determine the points in the different phases of the overall process where improvement by adjustments is desirable and feasible. In that respect, there are hard and soft targets for quality improvement. These are indicators that say over time something about those parts of the process to which they are related, and the direction of development of the results, as well as the achieved and/or to be achieved level with regards to the previously stated objectives. With these objectives, it is about providing direction to the actions in conformity to that process, adjusting this when necessary for the effectiveness of the actions that should be taken.

Indicators are therefore directly linked to the steps to perform the work within the organization, and therefore linked to organizational aspects. This is closely related to the type of benchmark.

2.5 *Benchmark Types*

Based on their literature about the different applications and the types of benchmarks on the organizational level, Waalewijn, Hendriks, and Verzijl (1996) created in their time a structure for the classification of benchmark types. That work resulted in the first four types of benchmarks included in the following, more comprehensive, table (Table 7.3).

In direct relation to those four types, a fifth type is added, which in practice is often used as an overall type for them.

Subsequently, two more types, numbers six and seven, were added.

The sixth type is a benchmark which is based on realizing set targets, in combination with actual results, as explained before by the theme norm indicators. With that the comparison takes place internally and externally among the participants, and the results are placed relative to that set target, which as a goal is set at a higher aggregation level. The GRESB benchmark is an example of this type.

Table 7.3 The seven types of benchmarking

1	*Internal benchmarking*: Comparing and explaining the results of a certain division of the business to other business divisions.
2	*Competitive benchmarking*, also called *peer group comparisons benchmarking* and *statistical universe benchmarking*: This type compares the performance results at the level of (more or less) similar assets and/or portfolios.
3	*Functional benchmarking*, also called *activity type benchmarking*: Comparing and explaining the performance results of (more or less) similar functional processes amongst, for example, non-competing, organizations.
4	*Generic benchmarking*: Comparing and explaining the processes within various process functions from multiple organizational divisions and departments.
5	*Best-use benchmarking*, also called *best-in-practice benchmarking* and *world-class operations benchmarking*: In fact, a collective name for the combined use of the first four specific types of benchmarking.
6	*(International) standards benchmarking*, also called *carrot and stick benchmarking*: The difference between this method and the previous benchmark types is the fact that a theoretical, but realistically considered achievable, objective is used as a target, instead of a proven best practice based on actual peer performance.
7	*Indexes*: Indexes can be seen as a derivative product of the benchmark. To determine the performance results, the organization's own position and the position of its peers are taken into account with respect to the absolute benchmark value. It is not only the position of the benchmark that is of interest but also the structure and composition of the market portfolio as well as the development of the average score, measured over a specific historical period.

The seventh type refers to the indexes derived from benchmarks. This is especially an important benchmark, due to mostly working with average results when noted as a time series of achieved results. Instead of using the total range of results from those series to get a good overview of the development of it, one uses the successive differences from chosen time period to period, mostly year-to-year, expressed in terms of percentage.

2.5.1 *Considering the Competitive Benchmarking*

Determining the representativeness of the compared information, as well as the confidentiality of the shared information, should be paid particular attention. Comparing and explaining an organization's performance results with those of its peers is referred to as performance attribution. A specific form of this type is risk-adjusted performance measures benchmarking, also called risk-adjusted returns benchmarking, whereby this benchmark type is based on the assumption that a high risk should correspond to a higher expected (average) return. To assess whether a portfolio, given its risk profile, could provide a sufficiently high return, a number of return/risk ratios have been developed. However, the problem is that on one hand, for the system, specific and management risks must be recognized and expressed in the risk profile. On the other, the challenge is to determine the reference frame in terms of accepted return/risk profile for real estate as an asset class. (This isn't the place to go in depth; more information is offered in publications by the authors (Keeris, 2007; Keeris & Langbroek, 2007)).

2.5.2 *Considering the Functional Benchmarking*

A specific form of this is portfolio opportunity distribution benchmarking, also called normal portfolio benchmarking. The purpose of this type of benchmarking is to measure the value of the involved management of the portfolio. The comparison is relative to an arbitrary composite universe portfolio to which a specific policy view is assigned. This approach focuses on asset selection, while other factors are kept equal. It is a quantitative research method that needs a significant amount of information to get an adequate picture of the different activities and their mutual relations. The challenge lies in the ability of organizations to collect this information reliably and over a longer time period.

2.5.3 Considering the Best-Use Benchmarking

This approach is based on comparing the organization's own performance results with the best performing peer for each indicator in question. This peer can be a direct competitor from the own business division, or can be chosen from the viewpoint of functional relevance for benchmarking. The best achievable performance level is proven in practice and within its context (at the time).

2.5.4 Considering the (International) Standards Benchmarking

This objective is the 'raised bar', or the 'dot on the horizon'. Setting such objectives puts pressure on the organization, as it hasn't been proven that the performance level can be achieved, and as such, it could adversely impact the organization's reputation. But on the other hand, collectively knowing that the set goals are realistic and reachable brings in good spirit amongst the peers, creates motivational effects, and gives inspirational impulses. Similar to the proverbial carrot and stick, the carrot might never get caught, because new developments could raise the bar even higher, like the dot on the horizon which never can be reached, resulting in more challenging objectives that provide the new norm. As such, there will always be a distance between the organization and the carrot, and there will always be the same stick chasing those organizations.

2.6 The Multiple Kinds of Information from Benchmarking

Multiple functions can be assigned to benchmarking depending on the points of view the results of it could be used.

2.6.1 Considering the Market Information

As such, benchmarking has become a crucial tool for investors in determining the structure and composition of their investment portfolio, also known as asset allocation. Based on benchmarks and indices derived therefrom, both the required market information generated for external use, and information about their own portfolio, are obtained.

2.6.2 Considering the Entrepreneurial Information

Benchmarking also provides the necessary entrepreneurial support for policy proposals and decision-making, while allowing these elements to be placed in a framework. The investment policy that is put in place sets the framework for tactical policy and operational implementation.

2.6.3 *Considering the Competitive Information*

In addition, benchmarking is also necessary to place the actual performance within the context of the competitive environment, as well as to assess the quality of the management involved, especially because of the pressure on management to always outperform the benchmark, in terms of performing better than the average of the relevant (partial) market or market segment. This relates directly to the accepted risk profile of the investment portfolio.

This issue of data sensitivity from a competitive perspective can be partially eliminated by benchmarking with participants from outside the real estate market. This point is deepened when the different types of benchmarking are highlighted.

2.6.4 *Considering the Context Information*

It is well known that in assessing actual performance results, there may be both a certain effect of chance, due to the occurrence of specific exogenous market factors, as well as of endogenous factors. Regarding the latter, namely the management's own qualities and skills, it is also known that even the most professional and experienced management teams go through some periods of lesser performance. In order to make an acceptable judgement regarding the performance, it is important to understand to what extent these exogenous factors (possibly) had influenced the used benchmarking results. That judgement is important for the relative comparisons of the company's results to those of its competitors, and as such, for the future outlook and expectations, which is what benchmarking is about. That is just why a distinction has been made between real investment portfolios based on the return/risk profile by moving them into the categories Core, Value Added, and Opportunity. And even this made difference is too rough for the right use. In the end, it's the context that needs to be considered.

With regard to the context, there is another point to be aware of, namely an extra problem with real estate management with regards to the fact that the general used processes are still not mapped. It is conveniently ignored in practice, so that the judgement is based directly on acquired signals. This is not only incorrect but also short-sighted, because other factors of influence may be missed or excluded. For example, probably most managers know, or have at least heard, about 'knowledge management' and what can be gained by bringing it into practice. Nevertheless, it is not implemented as a useful tool in any real estate organization. Due to the lack of a good theory and generally accepted best practice rules, the processes in the real estate market are particularly based on personal insight of the manager involved.

Thus, the importance of the context in which this is placed is relevant in order to better understand the results from the benchmarking process, particularly as the processes, that are hidden behind these results, are mostly non-financial. Often, the 'human factors' plays an important role. For example, take good notice of the many expressions of the influence of the psychological phenomenon of 'cognitive dissonance', such as collectively sharing behind the alpha in the pack, mostly while there is no evidence for the storytelling. So it is crucial when selecting indicators to also take into account the level of perception of the involved people, both internally and externally.

2.6.5 *Considering the Information's Representativeness*

It should also be noted that a group of like-minded participants is required in the benchmarking process. For example, it makes a big difference on a strategic policy level when the shareholders have a short-term and quick profit-making point of view compared to the point of view of a long-term investor, such as institutional investors like pension funds. However, in practice, that formed group of participants always concerns a relatively small sample size likening to the market as a whole, and therefore, such a benchmark can never be sufficiently representative for the aggregation level of the total market, but only for the benchmark and its constituents.

Although it is unrealistic to assume a high degree of reliability, the presented benchmark results can be placed, in the absence of better information, as an image for the whole of the real estate market. In that case, they will be used outside of the area of their original scope of action and only as an approximation of what might have been also the case at that same time at market level.

There are three reasons for that lack of representability of the benchmark in the last case when used at market level.

First, and perhaps the most important reason for the unwillingness of market parties to participate in benchmarking, is the unwanted attendant effect it creates with concern to transparency. The main reason for that attitude is closely connected to the kind of real estate investments, whereby the properties are not only an investment vehicle but at the same time capital equipment for the enterprise.

Second, benchmarking involves spending resources, which should be covered by the benefits of the benchmarking process. Because normally the management strives to minimize the operational costs for the sake of creating more shareholder value, which is also in its own interest, so upfront there is an unwanted uncertainty if the connected costs can be earned back by participating in the benchmark.

And finally, a lack of interest in benchmarking can be attributed to a lack of knowledge in terms of which information is included and what to do with that information that can be derived from the benchmarking process. An example of this, in another context already mentioned, is the lack of applicability if the benchmark results are limited to the analysis of financial return, without including the corresponding risk profile. Always real estate investments had to be tuned to the aimed return/risk profile and risk-adjusted returns. As such in this case, the benchmark must address both return and risks in order to be meaningful. Although all real estate professionals ought to realize that point, the achieved returns are what it's always all about in publications and even for the remuneration.

2.6.6 Considering the Information's Transparency

The point of co-created transparency is also relevant in a competitive market. Mainly due to the fact that more authorities in many countries are strongly focused on promoting competition. Sharing important information amongst a sub-group within a market segment can be seen in those situations as forbidden cartel formation, especially when financial information is involved. In practice, this is dealt with by anonymizing the input data and output results for non-directly involved organizations and publishing only realized average values, or only non-financial information. However, this is at the expense of the benchmark's strength, as averages exist only arithmetically.

Otherwise, can one question the added value of having a larger number of participants? If with that benchmark's strength is decreased by an increased mass around the average (or mean) by the included individual results? After all, the risk is measured based on the spread of the used data whereby the nuances of aberrant scores disappear from the picture by a growing critical mass around the mean. These nuances of aberrant scores can otherwise be very informative.

The loss of expressiveness of the benchmark is connected to the inclusion of the benchmark results with the specific individual situations of the participants. And the most important characteristic of real estate is that each property is unique compared to all the other properties. As such, numerically comparing an average, without actually providing comparative material, yields little or no useful information. This applies to all aggregation levels and focuses of benchmarking, whether it is concerned with operational quality aspects, such as realized returns or organizational aspects, such as quality of management.

2.7 *Benchmarking and Real Estate Investment*

The choice of the type of benchmark used has significant implications and, therefore, merits attention. As demonstrated by Goslings, this choice is specific to each participant in the selected benchmark (Goslings, 1995). The reason being that the benchmark results must be applicable and relevant to each participant's specific situation, and, moreover, to the participant's objectives regarding future policy and its implementation. After all, different types of benchmarks focus on different quality aspects within the overall process, as business activity of the organization.

Furthermore, commonly used forms of benchmarking, as presented by the seven types in Table 7.3, are not applicable in some cases. For example, when it comes to listed real estate, the development of the share price is only relevant for shareholders, in combination with their (possible) personal expectations and perspectives on the development in the (near) future. The price that is continuously determined by the stock market provides the latest benchmark but doesn't provide fundamental information pertaining to the actual operations of the organization.

Various indexes that can benchmark the stock price development of listed real estate entities are available. However, these are not very reliable for the national market situation, mainly because the composition of the constituents does not meet the aforementioned criteria for benchmarking, with respect to representativeness, comparability, uniformity, and minimum number of constituents. In particular, the imbalance in regards to size of the invested capital and the composition of the portfolio (geographic spread and focus, property type, management style) results in a complex progress of objective comparison of performance results. Additionally, stock prices are mainly determined by the 'sentiment' in the stock market, and market sentiment is influenced by previously obtained performance results and those expected to be achieved by the listed entity. Besides, they are expressed in terms of actual return, with respect to the universe, and (more or less) similar entities. Finally, when determining the mood of the stock market, a number of aspects must be taken into account, such as the appreciation of management quality, corporate governance, presented vision, mission and outlook, and relationships between management expectations and actual realization, and so on.

On the basis of these influencing factors, it may occur that the value of the stock, expressed as the 'market value', can be lower or higher than the so-called intrinsic value of the underlying assets. This is because value is determined by the assigned market value of the assets. Benchmarking achieved returns or performance results alone are therefore not conclusive.

3 GRESB as an International Standards Benchmark

3.1 Global Real Estate Sustainability Benchmark: A New Type of Benchmarking

With the introduction of GRESB, a new benchmark type was created. It is comparable with the other benchmarks as it takes historical data series into account and is therefore plagued by the same limitations with respect to future projections. The main difference between GRESB and other benchmarks is the fact that the contemporary achieved average performance level isn't the only target. That means, there is also the level determined by the forward-looking GRESB experts, whom real estate investors and management organizations can make use for their investment decision-making. As such, those experts implicitly state that this level for the ESG issues that are of concern should realistically be achievable at that moment. This is certainly true for the early adopters, but in the near future also for the fast followers; and even the laggards are able to follow that crowd for the time being. So the GRESB benchmark doesn't only take the achieved best practice level of the peer group into account, as is common, but it also relates all the diagnostic findings on how it could and should have been. Exactly this reference of the achievable performance level in the future results in real estate managers having to pay attention to their ESG policy.

The last item presented in Table 7.3 is benchmark type, the (International) standards benchmarking, which also covers GRESB, is relatively new. It is a particular type of benchmark because its purpose is two-fold. In the case of GRESB, the results provide both the best method and achievable performance as proven in practice, as the relation to the theoretical but realistically considered achievable maximum (by experts knowledge of that moment). As such, performance is measured according to both theoretical and proven best practices.

The primary goal of GRESB's analysis is to provide insight into how one can achieve the more ambitious theoretical performance level. Performance improvement typically is about progressing to the 'dot on the horizon' but equally typical is the forward movement of the horizon, including that placed dot, with every successful attempt to get nearer to that point of reference. However, this does not mean that the pursuit of progress lacks result. The point of reference indeed can be an ideal, but the achieved results must be weighed within their own context. Making progress step by step can be a good strategy, while the way to that ideal also delivers relatively constant better performances.

Still, the imagery of the dot on the horizon is appropriate. This image adequately expresses the dynamic nature of the objective to achieve the theoretical maximum. The objective itself is, in this type of benchmark, never really achieved. It always adapts to the new insights which are immediately incorporated into the definition of the new norm. This continuous process of improvement should not be seen as an issue because benchmarking is aimed at knowing the difference between these theoretical levels, and benchmark participants themselves relate thereto.

3.2 GRESB's Benchmarking Characteristic

GRESB's benchmark covers more, compared to the other benchmarking types, though it appears similar, for example a benchmark focus on the achieved average return against the level of sustainability. Indeed, GRESB focuses on sustainability but from a by far broader context, namely that of corporate social responsibility (CSR). Nowadays, this is more commonly referred to as ESG. Basically, they refer to the three main ways to measure a company's commitments to ecological sustainability, to its community, and to corporate governance.

GRESB takes into account the unique characteristics of different property types, not only in benchmarking absolute scores but also in the scoring of a selection of questions. A selection of indicators is scored based on each portfolio's main property types.

In the GRESB framework, the three main aspects of ESG are divided into seven sub-aspects. Therefore GRESB Real Estate Assessment is structured into those seven sustainability themes, formulated as questions to be answered, so-called aspects or sub-aspects, with a separate Aspect for New

Construction & Major Renovations. The assessed data is collected via an online questionnaire, containing 42 main indicators. Each of those aspects has been judged, assigning it a certain number of points. The weighted combination of scores for each aspect generates the overall GRESB Score. The maximum score for each aspect is a weighted element of that overall GRESB Score. The sum of the scores for each question adds up to a maximum of 137 points, being that overall GRESB Score. The achieved scores are then expressed as a percentage—from 0 to 100. That score illustrates how well a participant has performed, in absolute terms and compared to the market. As such, the term 'relative benchmarking' is applicable.

That market comparison is preferably done at the local level, as that is the level where portfolios can be compared best. In addition, comparison occurs within certain property types, for example, office portfolios, retail portfolios, or a combined or diversified portfolio. Lastly, the legal status of the entity is considered, listed or non-listed.

The GRESB Score is used to provide the different rankings. The most relevant ranking is the ranking within the peer group, as that result provides an idea of the relative performance on ESG in comparison with similar real estate portfolios. Additional rankings are provided as well. To illustrate, when looking at a non-listed real estate fund that has mainly investments in US offices, the peer group is ideally composed of non-listed US office portfolios. Besides this comparison, the fund is also compared to all other US portfolios, regardless of the property type they are invested in. Furthermore, a comparison is also made with all other office portfolios, regardless of their geographic allocation.

In addition to these rankings, GRESB provides a performance breakdown at different levels. At the highest aggregation level, the overall GRESB Score is divided into two dimensions: Management & Policy (MP) and Implementation & Measurement (IM). MP is defined as 'the means by which a company or fund deals with or controls its portfolio and its stakeholders and/or a course or principle of action adopted by the company or fund'. IM is defined as 'the process of executing a decision or plan or of putting a decision or plan into effect and/or the action of measuring something related to the portfolio'.

A further breakdown is provided at the level of the three main ESG aspects of the benchmark. At the most granular level, a comparison is made based on the seven sub-aspects: 'Management', 'Policy & Disclosure', 'Risks & Opportunities', 'Environmental Management Systems & Monitoring', 'Performance Indicators', 'Building Certifications', and

'Stakeholder Engagement'. For each sub-aspect a score is provided alongside an indication of the increase or decrease in score compared to the previous year. The sub-aspect scores are also compared with the peer group average, just like the global average. Furthermore, the comparison with the peer group is expressed via a distribution histogram, which provides additional insights into the relative performance.

Last, at the individual indicator level, an overview is provided for the participant's response, how that translates into a score, and how the response compares to the peer group's response. In this respect, a 'best practice' result is provided, based on what the majority of the peer group has answered, thus not on what the best performing peer has answered. As such, it would be better to refer to the provided information, instead of 'best practice', as 'most common practice'.

The amount of provided information could be overwhelming, even though it is based on self-reported data. However, it is necessary to understand the professional context of that information, as is the case with knowledge management. In this regard, knowledge alone is not sufficient because the point is how that knowledge is used. This was also the clear conclusion in a study by Runhaar, Iron Mountain and PwC (Runhaar, Iron Mountain and PwC, 2015). Their findings showcase how three out of four organizations hardly benefit from the information they have about their business. The study looked at how companies and organizations use their own information and was held amongst 1800 European and North American business leaders of medium-sized (over 250 employees) and large-sized (over 2500 employees) organizations. Too often, the organization's management predominantly has an overly positive image about its own functioning. The clear message was understand what information is available, and use it! Benchmarking should be an essential part of that process.

4 Productivity Improvement and GRESB

4.1 A Sketch of How It Is Today

Benchmarking is not only used to assess the performance results. That assessment certainly is valuable because the provided image tells if the organization is on the right track to meet the hard and soft targets and set objectives within the competitive arena. However, this always concerns an objective that was set in the past based on a strategy that was determined at that specific moment. As such, the applicability should periodically be evaluated, taking into considerations the dynamic developments in the market, and—not at least—within the organization. This also includes the benchmarking results, via the derived indices.

When it comes to drawing up a vision of the possible future developments, trends of various influencing factors are introduced. The indices show the picture of the former developments of these factors in which trend lines should be extended to the future. For their interpretation, scenarios at the macro, medium, and micro level can be applied.

The basis is established by the combination of the absolute data from the internal benchmarks, compared with the data from external relative benchmarks. In the case of GRESB, the results from the most common practice benchmark analysis are then added, otherwise the best practice or the average result is used. This provides a baseline assessment of the current situation and determines the starting point for the development of the scenarios that estimate the future developments in each factor. These scenarios can be split into autonomous occurrences and picture-based providers on the effect of the organization's own actions. A non-negligible scenario of the first order, for example, is the occurrence of the real estate cycle, or the development of crucial factors as currency rates, interest rates, and inflation. The whole of these activities is called 'forecasting'.

The generic image of the estimated future developments, obtained via forecasting, should be made more concrete in terms of effects on the company's operations and the achieved and expected performance results. This is where appreciation and valuation comes in. It involves the use of calculation models which define the assigned earning capacity of the real estate asset(s) in question. Based on the determined baseline situation for each parameter of the calculation model, the combined benchmark results and scenarios are processed into numerical data for the observed period. At the same time, it also provides the basis for the obtained results.

4.2 *How to React on the Placed Dot on the Horizon*

The above description of the process is generally considered a common practice in which the management's focus and policies are future oriented. However, a key factor should be taken into account: the inclusion of the future development of the degree of improvement in labour productivity of the company as a whole and on specific operational components.

Real estate is not only an investment asset but also an operational asset within this context of a real estate investor in pursuit of returns. Within a commercial approach, extrapolation of financial assumptions at the start of the asset's utilization simply isn't suitable. After all, investors expect the property manager to continually strive to improve the investment result.

To determine an asset's value, real estate appraisers cannot just take their client's position and determine what kind of investment policy should be instated in each situation. This directly affects the image of the asset's earning capacity. Alternatively, the appraiser is the expert who knows the effects of cyclical market trends and shifts in the market, as well as potential incidents. At the same time, the appraiser isn't the party who should hold the view that the client's organization should strive for productivity improvement from the viewpoint of business continuity. After all, the evaluation is based on going concern in conformity to the accounting interpretation of that concept, as previously mentioned. The same applies for investing in real estate and the real estate asset's valuation.

This ongoing aim for productivity improvement, when applied to real estate, means improving the market positioning of the asset, alongside management organization. This not only requires constant commitment in terms of the quality offered; equally important is that the policy is aligned with corporate responsibility. This is exactly the point where GRESB shows its added value, as it analysed the ESG policy that was put in place.

After all, these are the main components of GRESB, for which the dot on the horizon was set. No other benchmark involves the future developments in its structural approach, while that future is crucial. As such, it should be mapped nationally and internationally by the different stakeholders. This is important because the international risks, associated with climate change, water shortages, and other environmental factors, as well as the increasing instability within communities, have been identified as large systemic risks. Appropriate response is needed, again both nationally and internationally but also at the level of the individual investor.

This line of ESG thinking should effectively be disseminated. First, because it is clearly proven that it leads to better returns on invested capital as already mentioned. As mentioned earlier, the research was conducted by Oxford University and Arabesque Partners, and they present the found results (Clarke et al., 2015) that demonstrate the economic relevance of sustainability parameters for corporate management and for investors, with a spin-off for the other stakeholders.

GRESB reports in accordance with the nature of all benchmarks, that is, by looking back. As a result, in drawing up a vision for the pursuit of productivity improvement, the absolute and relative results cannot be used for the entire duration of the considered future period. However, the resulting baseline for the initial situation can be compared to the available quality level of the benchmark as GRESB provides a view of what is realistically achievable in the future, thus providing a basis to the organization to plot a policy-based trajectory for the first phase of its future operations.

This is needed, firstly, to mitigate any gap between the performance results, and what should have been possible according to the most common practice results. Secondly, the subsequent steps in the direction of the dot on the horizon can be derived from the results. Doing so ensures that the assumed potential for improvement of the future performance results is based on sound information. This is often lacking with overly optimistic future expectations that are based on 'gut feeling'.

As stated above, the difference between GRESB and other types of benchmarks is that with GRESB, the proven best quality isn't decisive for future targets. Instead, it is about the level of quality which the experts believe it is (theoretically) feasible at that moment. That means feasible for real estate investors, including any additional investments to meet the targets and the preceding objectives. Regarding these additional investments, any decisions should take cash flow, earning capacity, and ascribed value into account.

GRESB raises the bar for the management organization and provides the 'carrot'. This is not without obligation, as indirectly, pressure is applied. For example, if the targets aren't met, reputational damage might follow. As such, GRESB also provides the 'stick'.

When determining the value of real estate assets, the developments on international ESG policies should explicitly be taken into account. If this is not the case, then the effect of the occurring additional economic ageing, or obsolescence, of the assets should be considered when determining the earning capacity. Think of it as a form of 'policy obsolescence'. In fact, any disconnect with the global approach to consider ESG issues implicitly means accepting a position amongst the laggards—with all consequences for the performance.

That may be accepted, if the asset is already at the end of its life-cycle. In that case, the investment decisions are highly speculative, and as such, won't be valued on a going concern basis. However, if it concerns continuation of the operations, a position must be picked in the competitive (local) real estate market. That doesn't fit into accepting a laggard position, while that also is the starting point for further future operations. Plus, in case of discretionary asset management on behalf of one or more real estate investors, providing the necessary efforts are part of the fiduciary obligations, as stated before.

5 GRESB Remarks

Without devaluing GRESB and its approach, three points for improvement are discussed in this and next paragraph. Firstly, the benchmark only considers non-financial information. A number of market parties are still reluctant to provide financial information to external parties, outside the existing group of shareholders. This is the lack of transparency issue, specifically regarding sustainability aspects and what in those specific fields has been and/or could be achieved. Including financial indicators could adversely impact global response rate, which in turn would make the comparison of global performance results less valuable. Besides, GRESB specifically focuses at the level of both the real estate organization and the portfolio.

Moreover, a large number of industry parties already gather and measure financial performance of real estate management organizations, such as Morgan Stanley Capital International—Investment Property Data, MSCI-IPD; European Association for Non-listed Real Estate Vehicles, INREV; European Public Real Estate Association, EPRA; National Association of Real Estate Investment Trusts, NAREIT; and National Council of Real Estate Investments Fiduciaries, NACREIF; to name a few. In addition, there are numerous specific real estate indices available. As such, the need to include financial information in the GRESB benchmark is less crucial, although these other sources could be used to try to link non-financial performance to financial performance of real estate management organizations.

It should be noted that some research, regarding the relationship between the financial performance of real estate management organizations and their overall ESG performance, has been conducted. In 2015, a study conducted by Cambridge University and commissioned by Carbon War Room looked at the relationship between investing in sustainability and financial returns of REITs, by using GRESB data (Carbon War Room, 2015; Fuerst, 2015). These studies showed that, adjusted for risk, there is a significant link between corporate- and portfolio-level sustainability indicators and REIT stock market performance. Both the returns on assets and returns on equity of REITs with high GRESB scores appear to outperform the rest of their cohort. The evidence is less clear-cut regarding absolute stock market performance; however, adjusting for risk using a basic Sharpe ratio measure reveals a significant link between sustainability and stock market performance.

Secondly, (international) standards benchmarking provides a complex challenge when it concerns determining the theoretical, but realistically considered, achievable maximum. Best practice benchmarking provides a clear target: the actual proven highest or best level. Because it's proven, it provides conviction. However, when the dot on the horizon is the target for all benchmark participants, more is needed. Certainly at the global level, where differences in standards, cultures, and market approaches play a decisive role. Besides physical and technical aspects, the non-physical must be taken into account. The question arises if a global standard fits within the dominant local culture. The same accounts for the way in which the target should be met. This is specifically true for the desirability of the measures regarding environmental aspects that should be taken, followed by the effects on the social and governance aspects of ESG. Therefore, instead of following a generally applicable example, there should be room for interpretation according to the own local views of what is generally regarded as desirable, given the context of the own culture and social conditions.

The GRESB experts, who contribute to use the formulation of the dot on the horizon, should be open for such an approach. In any case, the possible cultural differences are also taken into account and thereby the extent of alignment with the desired global level. This is exactly why it is important for GRESB to provide local comparisons within the peer groups. After all, it is important for parties with a different culture to understand why these differences exist and because fostering understanding is a strong foundation for further cooperation. The collective participants in the benchmark are therefore broken down into smaller entities. At the local level, participants can push and pull each other towards the next target at a higher aggregate level but at the same time also provide an example for other peer groups.

That point relates to the different comparisons and rankings that are provided on an increasing scale. The main determinant is the local benchmark within the peer group, on which all results are based. The following comparisons provide additional information, but these cannot affect the previously obtained image of the performance results at that first level.

There appears to be a need for this additional information by the GRESB participants because some prefer to be compared at the global level, regardless of the differences in portfolios, while others prefer to be compared at the level of their local market. GRESB's approach is very accommodating in this regard, but it also provides considerably more information. The ranking can actually be seen as a performance attribution analysis.

In this way of comparing performance results, cultural differences play a decisive role, more specifically, the cultural differences between the national real estate markets. For example, different national accountancy rules influence the reported data, the reporting boundaries, and organization accountability. The assessment at the peer group level also includes the local or regional sustainability standards, best practice recommendations, and guidelines as developed by industry associations and bodies.

The issue with these cultural differences also affects the organizational, administrative, and legal aspects of the management. Every culture has its own execution characteristics for the real estate management process. As a result, the manner of determining the gross and net income level varies, and as such, returns and assigned values also vary. Such a comparison would therefore not be completely applicable if it concerned financial performance results.

Partly for that reason, the INREV provides the financial performance results of their constituents 'triple net'. This is the most granular level of aggregation: the financial rewards provided to the investor, based on the invested capital after deduction of taxes, paid fees, and so on. That level of reporting makes it possible for investors to compare performance results of their managers, at least, if currency and financial effects are accounted for. However, such a benchmark comparison says nothing about the operational level, where cultural differences directly affect the performance of the real estate management processes. So, a combination with the results of GRESB is preferable.

6 Why GRESB Should Be Further Developed

Although, GRESB is doing well, yet it needs to step up its acts. Presented is the most common practice, for understandable reasons as explained before. With that, the example, operational realized, of the best practice is lacking as guide line. While the best operational approach on ESG performance improvements is unknown, one cannot implement such improvements within their own organization.

Thus an alternative is needed instead of the best-use benchmarking, which looks at if and how peers meet the desired level of quality. In that case, the needed practice information can be offered by presenting elucidating documentations on the different ESG issues as shown by example. After all, it's about the best practice knowledge, not the level of the achieved benchmark results. The implementation focuses on the maximum achievable result for the year under consideration, and the years after. GRESB is ideally suited to deliver, in an appealing way, information of proven performance improvements, like case studies about sustainable real estate assets or from GRESB participants. That knowledge is needed on a yearly basis to determine the strategy to get to the set theoretical, but realistically considered, achievable maximum level of performance. This is a very important part of marketing the current ESG achievements and line of thinking. The knowledge needs to be delivered in such a way that it positively influences value, fully supported by the International Valuation Standards.

7 To Conclude

A focus on the context and moment in time is crucial for all real estate-related disciplines, especially for appraisers, asset managers, and property management. Those represent processes that involve assigning interests because it offers a basis for real estate asset valuation, appraisal, and operation.

Also it contributes to benchmarking and the broader development of knowledge and understanding, simply because they are the source of the data that should be collected, as well as required for weighing the importance of that data. Their behaviour is linked to that basic set of data. It therefore concerns a permanent self-reflection and learning organization. Participation in GRESB contributes greatly to this development. It offers a basis for continuous productivity improvement, which is necessary from the going concern perspective in a strong competitive market.

Furthermore, it allows the involved real estate management organization to meet its fiduciary obligations regarding the full deployment of its knowledge and services in the interest of the client(s) to the best of its ability, including possibly having to attract external expertise.

Finally, a recommendation to improve GRESB is made, namely to offer yearly inspirational examples of the needed practice information by presenting elucidating documentations on the different ESG issues as shown by the model. After all, it's about the best practice knowledge, not the level of the achieved benchmark results. GRESB is ideally suited to deliver, in an appealing way, information of proven performance improvements like case studies about sustainable real estate assets from GRESB participants. That knowledge is needed to determine the strategy to get to the set theoretical, but realistically considered, achievable maximum level of performance. It positively serves by getting fellow workers support, needed to create focus on the set goals, and working as a team to achieve the set targets.

References

Carbon War Room. (2015). Building Returns: Investing in Sustainability Pays Off.

Clarke G. L., Feiner, A., & Viehs, M. (2015). *From the Stockholder to the Stakeholder: How Sustainability Can Drive Financial Outperformance.* Oxford University and Arabesque Partners.

Fuerst, F. (2015). *The Financial Rewards of Sustainability: A Global Performance Study of Real Estate Investment Trusts.* Cambridge: Cambridge University.

Goslings, J. H. W. (1995) Prestatiemeting: theorie en praktijk. *VBA Journal.*

Keeris, W. G. (2007). *The Diversifying Power of Real Estate Investments: You Never Can Tell.* Paper for the 14th ERES Conference 2007, London, 26–30 June.

Keeris, W. G., & Langbroek, R. A. R. (2007). *Measuring Stability of Performance by Means of the Volatility Ratio.* Paper for the 14th ERES Conference 2007, London, 26–30 June.

Runhaar, P. (2015, December). Onderzoek toont aan: bedrijven hebben enorme slag te maken bij benutten eigen informatie. *Facility Management Magazine* (in Dutch).

Waalewijn, Ph., Hendriks, A., & Verzijl, R. (1996). Benchmarking in Nederland: op zoek naar het ideale proces. *Holland/Belgium Management Review*, nr. 51 (in Dutch).

CHAPTER 8

Business Case for Green Buildings for Owner-Operators

Philippe St-Jean

1 Introduction

The oil embargo of 1973 thrust the burgeoning green building movement into the public spotlight ('White Paper on Sustainability', 2003). At the time, sustainable development focused primarily on energy efficiency ('White Paper on Sustainability', 2003). Starting in the 1980s, the green building movement began to consider a wider range of environmental and social issues (Kibert & Kibert, 2008). However, it is only as of the 1990s that the return on investment of various sustainable building strategies has become more clearly understood ('White Paper on Sustainability', 2003). Although the results can vary significantly from project to project, the underlying trends are undeniable, and as it turns out, the greatest return on investment is not achieved through those measures traditionally believed to be the most profitable.

P. St-Jean (✉)
McGill University, Montreal, Canada
e-mail: philippe.st-jean@mcgill.ca

T. Walker et al. (eds.), *Sustainable Real Estate*, Palgrave Studies in Sustainable Business In Association with Future Earth,
https://doi.org/10.1007/978-3-319-94565-1_8

2 Understanding the Lifecycle Cost of Ownership

2.1 *Lifecycle Cost Defined*

To understand the financial benefits of sustainable building practices, one must first understand the lifecycle costs of owning and operating a building. The lifecycle of a project can be broken down into seven stages: project development; planning; implementation; commissioning; operation; modernization and deconstruction (Hugger, Fuchs, Stark & Zeumer, 2007). During the first stage, project development, the business case for the project is defined, including the use, financing mechanisms and targeted service life of the building. This is followed by the planning stage, which starts with the preliminary design of the project, the implementation plan, the final design and ends with the tendering process. The third stage, implementation of the project, consists of the construction process up to the pre-occupation of the building. Commissioning, the fourth stage of the building lifecycle, includes the optimization of the building's systems and the training of building operators. Commissioning closes out the construction process through the verification of the functionality of construction elements such as the building envelope, mechanical systems and electrical systems. Ongoing commissioning, however, would continue until the end of the building's service life. The operation stage follows commissioning and is defined as the period during which the building is occupied and maintained. For owner-occupied buildings, the costs associated with this phase include the wages and salaries of building occupants.

Although the importance of both initial and ongoing commissioning has only recently gained widespread recognition (Barnes, Noerika, Bruceri, Summers, et al., 2012), the first five stages of the lifecycle of a project are for the most part taken into consideration by real estate owners, and their implications are well understood by the market.

Modernization is the penultimate stage of a building's lifecycle wherein it is recognized that the building, or a portion of it, will eventually reach the end of its useful life. This can be driven by numerous factors such as the obsolescence of the building's materials or systems, or changing market desires with respect to building design. Regardless of the driving force behind modernization, it is imperative to consider its implications as early as the development stage. Otherwise, inherent features of the initial design of the building might impose costly and wasteful limitations on any future retrofitting project. By recognizing the inevitability of a future renovation of a building, the initial project should be designed so as to optimize the balance between the first cost of the project, including its environmental impact, and the future financial, operational and environmental impacts of retrofitting the original design. Of course, the same logic would apply to the optimization of the design of the retrofitting project as well. Materials, equipment and assemblies should be chosen in such a way as to minimize the lifecycle impact of their eventual replacement and disposal.

The seventh and final stage of a building's lifecycle is deconstruction. No building will last forever. As such, it remains important at the project development phase to take into consideration the eventual environmental, economic and social impacts of demolishing the building.

Employing a holistic analysis of the cost implications of decisions at each stage of a building's lifecycle, portfolio managers and building owners can more accurately target the most advantageous design, construction, operation and maintenance strategies.

2.2 *Impact of Sustainability on the Lifecycle Cost*

To maximize the potential return on investment from sustainable building practices in the commercial sector, it is important to consider the lifecycle cost of a commercial building. By the mid-1990s it had already been determined that land acquisition, project design and construction costs represent only approximately 2 percent of the 30-year lifecycle cost of a commercial building, followed by a mere 6 percent for all operating costs, including heating, cooling, maintenance and cleaning services (Romm, 1994). Most surprising, however, was the finding that 92 percent of all the money spent on owning, operating and occupying a building over a 30-year period goes to the salaries of the people working within its walls (Romm, 1994). A 2002 study of state employee-occupied buildings in California (Kats, Alevantis, Berman, Mills, & Perlman, 2003), and a 2015 analysis of business costs for offices in the United Kingdom (Property Data Report, 2016), reaffirmed these ratios of operating costs to building occupant salaries.

The implications of the disproportionate lifecycle cost of building occupants' salaries versus construction, operations and maintenance costs are significant. Whereas traditional sustainable building practices attempted to justify the construction cost premium of going green for owner-operators with the resulting savings from energy and water efficiency (Kats et al., 2003), the true savings were hidden in the productivity of the building occupants. Even with the knowledge that building occupant efficiency represents the largest potential return on investment, construction professionals and developers still gravitate toward the 'hard' savings that can be calculated for every joule of energy and liter of water saved through improvements in building efficiency. When the true lifecycle costs of different sustainable design measures are considered, the scale tips heavily toward the less tangible building occupant productivity gains resulting from the sick day that is not taken (Miller, Pogue, Gough, & Davis, 2009), or the increase in employee focus, creativity and attention (MacNaughton et al., 2017). Leadership in Energy and Environmental Design (LEED) certification for new buildings, for example, has been associated with a 0–3 percent increase in construction cost (Mapp, Nobe, & Dunbar, 2011), a 13 and 16 percent reduction in energy and water use respectively (Kuzimeko, 2014), and a 5.24 percent increase in building occupant productivity (Miller et al., 2009). A 2011 study of 6153 buildings found LEED certification to contribute to a real estate sales premium of as high as 26 percent (Fuerst & McAllister, 2011). When considering these numbers, the decrease in operating costs would be enough to justify the premium paid for a LEED certified construction. Similarly, the increased sales value of the building would also be enough to offset the additional construction costs of a certified project. It is, however, the 5.24 percent increase in employee efficiency, documented by Miller, Pogue, Gough and Davis, which represents the most interesting return on investment for an owner-occupied building. Using Romm's 30-year lifecycle cost of ownership of a building, a 3 percent construction premium resulting in a 5.24 percent increase in employee productivity would represent an 8.035 percent return on investment.

For existing buildings, it is possible to see similar benefits to those of a new construction built to the LEED standard. Simple and cost-effective strategies such as improving the quality of natural and artificial light can produce significant returns on investment. A 2004 comparison of 11 studies by Carnegie-Mellon University attributed a 3.2 percent increase in employee productivity to an improvement in lighting design (Carroll, 2013). Similarly, improvements to indoor air quality can be achieved by increasing ventilation rates and upgrading air filters at little to no cost, while potentially doubling the cognitive performance of building occupants (Allen et al., 2015). In the proceedings of the Fifth International Conference for Enhanced Building Operations, an analysis of four buildings pursuing LEED Existing Buildings Operations and Maintenance certification found that the cost of improving the sustainable performance of the buildings to meet the certification requirements was offset by the resulting operational savings alone in as little as six months (Iczkowski, 2005).

2.3 *Financial Tools to Accurately Assess Return on Investment*

To properly assess and compare the initial and future cost implications of decisions affecting each phase of a building's lifecycle, it is important to use the appropriate financial formulas. Most financial equations are based on the simple principle that an amount of money available today is worth more than that same amount available tomorrow, also known as the time value of money. How much more that money is worth depends on the discount rate, a percentage value which incorporates interest rates, inflation and uncertainty risk. Two commonly used equations when assessing the value of a design decision in a construction project are the 'Discounted Payback Period' (DPP) and the 'Net-Present Value' (NPV). The DPP is a formula that evaluates the period of time needed for the return on investment to equal the sum of the initial investment, or in other words, the time it would take for a cost-savings measure to pay itself off.

$$DPP = \ln\left(\frac{1}{1-\frac{O_1 \times r}{CF}}\right) \div \ln(1+r)$$

$$O_1 = \text{Initial Investment}(\text{Out flow})$$

$$r = \text{rate}$$

$$CF = \text{Periodic Cash Flow}$$

(Finance Formulas, n.d.-a)

This equation does not account for the lifecycle of the investment and so does not consider the period of time after the breakeven point. Put differently, after the initial investment has paid itself off, its residual annuity is not considered. An acceptable payback period is usually set arbitrarily based on what the market considers acceptable for a given type of investment (Besley & Brigham, 2016). Conversely, NPV is an equation that calculates the present value of an investment based on the return over the lifecycle of that investment.

$$NPV = -C_0 + \frac{C_1}{1+r} + \frac{C_2}{(1+r)^2} + \ldots + \frac{C_T}{(1+r)^T}$$

$$-C_0 = \text{Initial Investment}$$
$$C = \text{Cash Flow}$$
$$r = \text{Discount Rate}$$
$$T = \text{Time}$$

(Finance Formulas, n.d.-b)

As such, the NPV of an investment gives a more realistic assessment of the actual value of a design decision.

To better understand the difference between DPP and NPV, take, for example, the choice between two options to replace a building's ventilation unit. Unit A costs $15,000, has annual operating savings of $3000 when compared to the existing unit and has a useful life of ten years. Unit B costs $19,000, has an annual operating savings of $2500 when compared to the existing unit, and has a useful life of 18 years. Assuming the client considers eight years to be the maximum acceptable DPP, which unit would represent the most sound investment? At an annual discount rate of 5 percent, the DPP for Unit A is 5.9 years and for Unit B is 9.8 years. If a building owner were to base their decision on the acceptable market DPP, Unit A would be the obvious choice. However, if the building owner were also to consider the NPV of the savings from Unit A versus Unit B, their decision would not be as clear-cut. Over Unit A's ten-year useful life, its $3000 annual savings would be worth $23,165.20 today. For Unit B, the $2500 annual savings, over its 18-year useful life, would be worth $29,223.97 today. Unit B, however, costs $4000 more than Unit A. Unit A's lifecycle cost, when the NPV of its annual savings is considered, would be $15,000–$23,265.20= –$8265.20 versus Unit B's lifecycle cost of $19,000–$29,223.97= –$10,223.97. As such, when considering the NPV of the savings from each unit, instead of the DPP, Unit B is the clear winner.

As the example above illustrates, the DPP does not present the full picture on which to base an investment strategy. Why should a ventilation unit with an 18-year useful life be required to pay off its additional cost in under 8 years simply because that is what the market deems to be acceptable? When taking a lifecycle approach to investment strategies, the focus shifts from a short-term perspective to a long-term perspective and the door opens to truly sustainable decisions.

3 Challenges Posed by Regional Economics

The prices of utilities vary greatly from region to region and often do not reflect the true cost of their production and distribution (Casten & Meyer, 2004). When pursuing energy and water conservation measures in jurisdictions where prices are low, and therefore direct financial returns are also low, it can be hard to defend any additional investment required based purely on the social and environmental arguments for resource conservation. A more pragmatic approach would be to identify synergies between energy or water efficiency and operating costs or revenues. When a financial argument can be made for measures to improve the efficient use of resources, there is little room for debate as to whether to integrate them into a project's design. The difficulty lies in identifying and quantifying the return on investment of a decrease in water or energy use when it is not directly linked to the cost of the utility itself.

It is important to consider water and energy efficiency not only based on their present-day financial and environmental merits but also on their ability to reduce exposure to the risks associated with climate change. As global weather patterns shift, consistent and relatively inexpensive access to potable water and energy may no longer be commonplace (Finley & Schuchard, 2011). As such, reducing the operational resource requirements of a building may be an effective way of buffering against future resource scarcity.

3.1 Low Energy-Cost Regions

There are numerous regions around the world where the cost of energy remains relatively inexpensive. Montreal, for example, has the lowest cost of electricity of any major North American city at an average residential rate of $0.0722 CAD per kWh (Hydro Quebec, 2016). When compared to New York City (NYC) at an average of $0.295 CAD, or San Francisco at $0.310 CAD (Hydro Quebec, 2016), it is evident that a cost-effective measure to improve energy efficiency in NYC has no guarantee of being profitable in Montreal. In such low energy-cost regions, the argument for energy efficiency may be weak if considering the savings in energy alone. However, as previously presented, measures to improve energy efficiency are often accompanied by other benefits.

When focusing on the quality of the building envelope to reduce heating and cooling requirements, the benefits of improving thermal performance can extend far beyond energy savings. Strategies like airtightness, over-insulation and high-performance windows and doors should outlast the efficiencies of high-performance mechanical equipment simply by virtue of their comparative service lives. The airtightness of a building will also contribute to the longevity of the building's envelope and structure by reducing the accumulation of vapor in the envelope assembly, thereby reducing the risk of mold growth and of the premature decomposition of the building materials (Sandberg, Bankvall, Sikander, Wahlgren, & Larsson, 2007). Additionally, improvements in airtightness can improve indoor air quality by reducing the infiltration of outdoor contaminants such as airborne particulate matter and radon. Airtightness also improves the acoustic performance of the envelope and reduces drafts, contributing to higher levels of occupant comfort (Sandberg et al., 2007). When combining an airtightness strategy with the over-insulation of the building envelope and high-performance windows and doors, the interior surface temperature of the envelope can be maintained within 4 °C of the ambient room temperature and further contribute to occupant comfort by eliminating the sensation of temperature differences within the room, also known as radiative thermal asymmetry (Olesen, Fanger, Jensen, & Nielsen, 1972). The most interesting application of these strategies is to pursue Passivhaus levels of envelope performance where the resulting space conditioning requirements drop to a level for which heating and cooling can be supplied uniquely by conditioning the minimum fresh air requirements of the building. In such a scenario, not only can the space conditioning energy demand of the building drop by upward of 80 percent ('Energy Efficiency of the Passive House Standard', 2015) but the initial construction and ongoing maintenance costs can be significantly reduced by eliminating all of the decentralized heating and cooling systems that would normally be required to guarantee occupant comfort in a traditional building.

In low energy-cost regions it is important to consider both the 'hard' savings calculated from reduced energy demand and the simplification of mechanical systems, as well as the less tangible savings and revenue streams that result from increased occupant comfort, higher rates of employee productivity, better tenant retention rates and reduced risk exposure to the impacts of climate change.

3.2 *Low Water-Cost Regions*

Many jurisdictions, such as the city of Guadalajara in Mexico, still provide potable water to local businesses and residents at little to no cost ('International Statistics for Water Services', 2016). However, even for buildings in these areas, there is still a business case to be made for water saving measures. It is important to recognize that water conservation can also contribute to energy conservation. In residential projects, domestic hot water can represent an energy demand of 21 kWh per square meter of treated floor area per year (Hastings & Wall, 2007). For projects targeting Passivhaus levels of performance, or in locations having low space heating and cooling requirements, this can represent more than the energy required to heat or cool the building. As such, introducing water saving measures such as low-flow showerheads and faucets can help reduce both water consumption and energy consumption simultaneously. Similarly, by optimizing the size, length and insulation of hot water distribution pipes, standby heat losses through the pipes can be reduced, which in turn would reduce the volume of water wasted while awaiting hot water to reach the point of use.

In commercial and industrial buildings, cooling towers represent the largest source of water consumption (Henderson, 2015). This water requires costly chemical treatment to avoid corrosion, scale formation, fouling and microbial contamination of the cooling tower. Reducing water losses from drift, poorly managed blowdown, basin leaks and overflows ultimately results in a reduction in makeup water and the costs associated with its treatment (U.S. Department of Energy, n.d.). To further reduce the operating costs and water consumption of cooling towers, water can be recycled from sources in the building that require little or no pre-treatment, such as air handler condensate. This strategy is particularly effective given that air handlers usually generate the greatest volume of condensate when cooling tower loads are at their highest (U.S. Department of Energy, n.d.).

Depending on the nature of a given building and its operations, a variety of synergies can be applied to reduce operating costs through water efficiency measures, as illustrated by the domestic hot water and cooling tower examples earlier. To make an effective business case for water efficiency in low water-cost regions, it is important to take a holistic view of the resource consumption by both the building and the activities within it to maximize the return on investment of any measure to improve efficiency.

4 Sustainability for New Versus Existing Building Stock

The most sustainable building is the one that is never built. In Europe, buildings represent 47 percent of greenhouse gas emissions, with just under 11 percent of emissions attributed to their construction (Eurostat, 2016) and the remaining 36 percent to their ongoing operation (Directorate-General for Energy, 2017). New construction methods, materials and equipment, however, can create increasingly efficient buildings. As such, the challenge for developed countries lies in leveraging the embodied energy of existing buildings by improving energy efficiency, water efficiency and indoor environmental quality, to achieve a lifecycle environmental impact inferior to that of constructing new buildings. Although building construction and operation represent 25 percent of total global emissions (Lucon et al., 2014), less than one third of the 2015 Paris Agreement signatories included details of how more ambitious performance targets for the building sector would contribute to meeting their greenhouse gas emission targets (Olear, 2016).

4.1 Implications of Improving Sustainability of Existing Buildings

Working with existing buildings is significantly more complex than building from the ground up. In an existing building, the homogeneity of the composition of the elements making up the structure and building envelope can be difficult to ascertain with 100 percent accuracy. Moreover, the technologies and methods used at the time of original construction can be incompatible with newly developed technologies and strategies that would significantly improve energy performance, or reduce water consumption. It is therefore critical for building professionals to have both a deep understanding of building science and a sound knowledge of common issues arising in high-performance retrofits.

When deciding between renovating a building or replacing it with a new one, owners are often confronted with difficult environmental, economic and social considerations. While conserving the majority of the building elements may prove to be the most environmentally sustainable decision with respect to the embodied energy and resources that went into its construction (National Trust for Historic Preservation, 2011), it may prove uneconomical when considering the long-term maintenance and operation costs of a building well into its service life (Gorse & Highfield, 2009). Conversely, the most economical choice may be to conserve the majority of the building when factoring in both construction and operation costs but prove to be disadvantageous when considering the revenue stream dictated by the market rental rates of a building with an outdated design or infrastructure (Gorse & Highfield, 2009). It is therefore important for building owners to perform a lifecycle analysis to assess both the environmental impacts as well as the lifecycle cost of ownership of retrofitting a building versus constructing a new one.

Depending on the size of the building, its age, structure and the general condition of the building envelope, it may be more cost effective and efficient to do away with the existing building entirely and rebuild from the ground up. This may be attributed to a variety of factors, such as the investment of time and money associated with modeling and understanding the existing building, structural modifications required to meet new design requirements and constant adjustments to the design and timeline to account for surprises discovered during a renovation. However, for taller buildings made of steel or concrete, where the structure represents between 20 percent and 25 percent of the project construction cost ('Cost Challenges of Tall Buildings', 2010), it is often more cost effective to conserve an existing building's structure and to transform it to meet the new project's needs rather than to demolish the building entirely. With the structure representing upwards of 90 percent of the embodied energy of these types of buildings ('Tall Buildings in Numbers', 2009), the benefits of reuse extend beyond the financial advantages. The challenge rests in making the business case to conserve building elements that are either not cost effective to reuse or recycle or that have an impact on the aesthetics of the final project.

Improvements to the thermal performance of an existing building envelope can present a host of issues. For example, when increasing the insulating value of a roof, it is imperative to verify that the roof structure has been adequately sized to bear the full weight of the seasonal snow load. The original structural design may have assumed a constant melting of the snow resulting from heat loss through the roof assembly and may consequently have been undersized. Similarly, improvements to the thermal performance of a load bearing masonry wall may compromise the structural integrity of the wall assembly if the original design depended on the heat lost through the wall to dry the assembly and avoid interstitial condensation.

Similarly, when addressing water efficiency in existing buildings one must consider that the drainage pipes may have been designed for toilet drainage volumes as high as 26 liters per flush (U.S. Environmental Protection Agency, 2015) and can lack the necessary slope to ensure the adequate displacement of sewage when low-flow fixtures at 4.8 liters per flush are installed ('Can Your Plumbing System Handle a Low-Flow Toilet?', n.d.). This can result in recurring blockages and the resulting blame being placed on the functionality of the low-flow toilet as opposed to the drainage system of the building. When replacing traditional urinals with waterless, or ultra-low flow models, care must be taken to ensure that either the maintenance staff has the knowledge and capacity to guarantee the proper ongoing maintenance of the urinals, or that the drainage pipes are regularly flushed out with volumes of water great enough to avoid blockages caused by the crystallization of uric acid or sludge build-up. In a new construction, this would simply involve designing the urinals' drain downstream from a toilet or sink. In a renovation project, however, this might entail completely redoing the drainage lines for the entire washroom.

4.2 Commissioning

Commissioning is the process for achieving, evaluating and documenting that a building's systems and assemblies meet the objectives and criteria of the owner (ASHRAE, 2012). In other words, commissioning ensures that the components of a building are designed, installed, tested and can be operated in such a way as to meet the operational needs of the building occupants. Proper commissioning starts early in the design phase of a new project and should continue at least ten months into the occupancy of the building to ensure that systems continue to operate as designed and benefit from the initial warranty period if ever they do not (U.S. Green Building Council, 2016). Retrocommissioning is a term used for the commissioning of a building that had not previously been commissioned. Recommissioning is the reapplication of the commissioning process to a building previously commissioned and is normally carried out every 3–5 years (United States Environmental Protection Agency, 2008). Conversely, ongoing commissioning refers to real-time, or near real-time, tracking of the performance of building systems. Both recommissioning and ongoing commissioning are ways of ensuring that commissioned building systems continue to operate optimally over their service lives. Regardless of the stage or frequency at which commissioning is performed, it can represent the most cost-effective way to improve energy efficiency (United States Environmental Protection Agency, 2008).

Commissioning of buildings is important because their operational and occupancy patterns change over time and influence the optimal performance parameters of their mechanical, electrical and control systems. Buildings occupied for as little as two or three years can be the best candidates for retrocommissioning ('Retrocommissioning for Better Performance', 2006). A 2004 case study conducted by the Energy Systems Laboratory at Texas A&M University found that the heating and cooling requirements of buildings increased by 12.1 percent over as little as two years due mainly to component failure and control changes (Claridge et al., 2004). Issues related to the functionality of the overall HVAC system are the most common deficiencies, with air handling and distribution being the most prevalent (Mills et al., 2004).

The benefits of commissioning have been well documented and can extend beyond energy savings. Commissioning has been shown to extend equipment life, reduce maintenance costs, improve the thermal comfort of building occupants and enhance indoor air quality (United States Environmental Protection Agency, 2008). A study of 22 buildings, published in 2011 by Michaels Energy, found a 15 percent savings in electricity consumption resulting from retrocommissioning. Similarly, a 2004 study of 150 existing buildings of various usage types found that commissioning led to average energy savings of 18 percent, with a 15 percent median savings and a simple payback period of 0.7 years (Mills et al., 2004). The same study found that energy savings were not strongly correlated with the energy intensity of the building prior to commissioning. This indicates that buildings did not have to be inefficient to show significant improvements following commissioning. The size of the building, however, was shown to be positively correlated with the return on investment of commissioning and although the smaller buildings were able to achieve cost-effective commissioning, it was more challenging (Mills et al., 2004).

4.3 Deep Retrofits

The challenge with improving the sustainability of existing buildings is that improvements in energy consumption and water consumption rarely involve replacing only one component, whereas ongoing maintenance and renovations rarely require working on more than one element of the building at any given time. The service lives of each building components making up an assembly can vary significantly. As such, it can be difficult to take a linear approach to improving the sustainable performance of a building. It is rare, for example, that the exterior siding of a building requires replacing at the same time as the windows. It is therefore important to plan accordingly in order to leverage the end of life of each building component and obtain the most interesting lifecycle return on investment. Furthermore, any work performed on the building should be designed such that the service life of the work be at least equal to that of the entire building, or so that the work be easily replaced. This will facilitate future retrofits, helping reduce both their cost and environmental impact.

Existing building renovation projects do not normally benefit from the budgetary largesse or logistical freedom to vacate a building, strip its envelope and mechanical systems and retrofit from scratch. It can be extremely costly, or impossible, to relocate existing building occupants without disrupting business operations and services. For this reason, deep retrofits may be most pragmatic if performed in planned stages. To minimize the financial and environmental lifecycle impact of the retrofit, the stages should be primarily based on the service life of those building elements targeted for improvement. Each stage should consider the other building components affected by the modification of the building element in question, as well as contribute to the future overall performance of the building above and beyond the improvement of the replaced element itself. A building owner looking to improve the energy efficiency of their property would first assess the remaining service life of the building elements that primarily affect energy consumption, such as windows, opaque envelope assemblies, ventilation systems and lighting. Similarly, a building owner targeting improved water efficiency would assess the remaining service life of building elements such as washroom fixtures and water towers.

For example, take a developer that has just acquired a poorly insulated building in which the windows have reached the end of their service life. The developer would like to take the opportunity to improve the energy efficiency of the building by properly insulating the envelope, but can only access sufficient funding to replace the windows this year, and then insulate the building in two years. Given that the windows are failing, the developer has no choice but to proceed with their replacement and chooses a higher performing model to help reduce thermal losses. To fully benefit from the better performance of the windows and contribute to the future performance of the building, the developer should use the optimal window installation detail based on the future insulated envelope. As a general rule, a window assembly's thermal performance is maximized when the window is centered in the wall assembly's insulating layer (Hines et al., n.d.). As such, if the developer's future plans are to insulate the building from the outside, the windows should be stepped toward the outside of the envelope in an effort to place them closer to the center of the future insulation layer. This strategy might sacrifice the short-term thermal performance of the window installation due to the less than optimal location in the existing wall assembly; however, the long-term performance of the building envelope will be significantly improved once the new insulation is installed.

To facilitate a staged retrofit, Passivhaus, through its EnerPHit certification program, provides an energy-modeling tool to evaluate the performance of the building for each state of its development. Care must be taken to structure the retrofit's interventions in such a way as to ensure the integrity of the building's assemblies and the health of its occupants are not compromised by the staggered nature of the modifications to the building.

4.4 Retrofits and Green Certification Rating Systems

The challenges of working with existing buildings versus designing from scratch are well recognized by the construction industry, and the sustainable certification bodies are no exception. LEED BD + C certification distinguishes between new construction projects and major renovations by setting higher energy performance targets for new builds in both the Minimum Energy Performance prerequisite and the Optimize Energy Performance credit. The Passivhaus certification makes a similar distinction with its EnerPHit certification program for existing buildings. Given the extremely demanding minimum performance criteria for a Passivhaus new build of an energy demand of 15 kWh/m^2 per year, or a 10 W/m^2 energy load, the EnerPHit targets are significantly more forgiving at 25 kWh/m^2 per year for projects in cool temperate climates and 30 kWh/m^2 per year for those in a cold climate. Additionally, EnerPHit offers an alternative compliance path based solely on the prescriptive thermal performance of the windows, ventilation system and opaque assemblies of the building envelope.

The disparity between the energy performance requirements of new construction projects versus major renovations can be mainly attributed to the limitations imposed by both the building envelope, if it is conserved, and the building structure. The orientation, shaping, massing and shading of the building can be the most cost-effective design strategies for optimizing energy performance, and, in a major renovation, are for the most part unchangeable. Moreover, the existing structure often includes major thermal bridges that are nearly impossible or too costly to eliminate, such as cantilevered concrete balconies or the junction between structural concrete columns and their footings. By adjusting the performance requirements of the certification to recognize the limitations of a retrofit project, the green certification programs avoid penalizing owners and developers working with existing buildings. To this, programs like LEED and Building Research Establishment Environmental Assessment Method (BREEAM) also encourage the reuse of buildings by awarding points for projects looking to retrofit historic buildings, refurbish abandoned buildings or to conserve large percentages of an existing building's structure and envelope. Passivhaus takes a slightly different approach by allowing projects to pre-certify through the EnerPHit program for a multi-phased retrofit with the end goal of achieving the required performance levels. These approaches not only encourage more building owners to pursue a green certification of their buildings, they also promote more sustainable development by rewarding projects in a way that considers their lifecycle impact and cost of ownership, as opposed to only their operational efficiency.

5 Conclusion

The green building movement has come a long way since the 1970s. Over the years, numerous green certification programs have been developed to guide building professionals, owners and developers through the process of constructing sustainably. Additionally, new tools, such as lifecycle analysis, have enabled building professionals to more accurately weigh the environmental, social and economic impacts of various building strategies.

In developed countries, working with existing buildings has become an ever more important strategy to mitigate the effects of the built environment on resource depletion and greenhouse gas emissions. However, strategies to significantly improve the sustainability of existing buildings can be complex, costly and risky if not properly executed. Properly designing and staging deep retrofits can help reduce costs and mitigate exposure to risk. Similarly, cost-effective actions such as commissioning have shown disproportionately large impacts on the functionality, comfort and resource consumption of buildings.

Whether working with existing buildings or designing new ones, the business case for sustainable construction has been strengthened by an increasing pool of research, with the productivity of building occupants now taking center stage. As the market comes to consider the true lifecycle cost of various construction approaches, the once altruistic pursuit of environmentally sustainable building practices is being driven to an ever-greater degree by economic forces.

References

Allen, J. G., MacNaughton, P., Satish, U., Santanam, S., Vallarino, J., & Spengler, J. D. (2015). Associations of Cognitive Function Scores with Carbon Dioxide, Ventilation, and Volatile Organic Compound Exposures in Office Workers: A Controlled Exposure Study of Green and Conventional Office Environments. *Environmental Health Perspectives.* doi: 10.129/ehp.1510037

ASHRAE. (2012). *Commissioning Process for Buildings and Systems.* Retrieved from https://osr.ashrae.org/Public%20Review%20Draft%20Standards%20Lib/202P_2ndPPRDraft(ChairApproved).pdf

Barnes, J., Noerika, M., Bruceri, M., Summers, H., et al. (2012). Retrocommissioning Program Toolkit for Local Governments. *California Sustainability Alliance.* Retrieved from http://sustainca.org/sites/default/files/Alliance_LG_Rcx_Toolkit.pdf

Besley, S., & Brigham, E. (2016). *CFIN.* Boston, MA: Cengage Learning.

Can Your Plumbing System Handle a Low-Flow Toilet? (n.d.). Retrieved from https://www.lowes.com/cd_Can+Your+Plumbing+System+Handle+a+LowFlow+Toilet_1350913159827_

Carroll, B. J. (2013). *Exploring the Business Case for LEED EBOM Certification of a "Mixed Use" Facility* (Master's thesis, Massachusetts Institute of Technology). Retrieved from https://dspace.mit.edu/bitstream/handle/1721.1/80989/857788659-MIT.pdf?sequence=2

Casten, S., & Meyer, J. (2004, December). Cross-Subsidies: Getting the Signals Right. *Fortnightly Magazine.* Retrieved from https://www.fortnightly.com/fortnightly/2004/12/cross-subsidies-getting-signals-right?page=0%2C0

Claridge, D. E., Turner, W. D., Liu, M., Deng, S., Wei, G., Culp, C., Chen, H., & Cho, S. Y. (2004). Is Commissioning Once Enough? *Energy Engineering, Vol. 101, No. 4.* pp. 7–19. Retrieved from http://oaktrust.library.tamu.edu/bitstream/handle/1969.1/153718/ESL-PA-04-07-01.pdf?sequence=1

Cost Challenges of Tall Buildings. (2010, April). *LS Dynamics.* Retrieved from http://www.langdonseah.com/en/bn/files/download/220

Energy Efficiency of the Passive House Standard: Expectations Confirmed by Measurements in Practice. (2015, November 16). In *Passipedia.* Retrieved from https://www.passipedia.org/operation/operation_and_experience/measurement_results/energy_use_measurement_results

European Union. Directorate-General for Energy. (2017). *Buildings*. Retrieved from https://ec.europa.eu/energy/en/topics/energy-efficiency/buildings

European Union. Eurostat. (2016). *Greenhouse gas emissions by industries and households*. Retrieved from http://ec.europa.eu/eurostat/statistics-explained/index.php/Greenhouse_gas_emissions_by_industries_and_households

Finance Formulas. (n.d.-a). *Discounted Payback Period*. Retrieved from http://financeformulas.net/Discounted-Payback-Period.html

Finance Formulas. (n.d.-b). *Net Present Value*. Retrieved from http://financeformulas.net/Net_Present_Value.html

Finley, T., & Schuchard, R. (2011). *Adapting to Climate Change: A Guide for the Energy and Utility Industry*. Retrieved from https://www.bsr.org/en/our-insights/report-view/adapting-to-climate-change-a-guide-for-the-energy-and-utility-industry

Fuerst, F., & McAllister, P. (2011). Green Noise or Green Value? Measuring the Effects of Environmental Certification on Office Values. *Real Estate Economics Vol. 39* (No. 1, 2011) p. 45–69. Retrieved from http://immobilierdurable.eu/images/2128_uploads/Fuerst_article_autoris_.pdf

Gorse, C., & Highfield, D. (2009). *Refurbishment and Upgrading of Buildings*. New York, NY: Spoon Press.

Hastings, R., & Wall, M. (2007). *Sustainable Solar Housing: Volume 1—Strategies and Solutions*. London, UK: Earthscan.

Henderson, S. (2015, April 28). The Business Case for Investments in Water Efficiency. *GreenBiz*. Retrieved from https://www.greenbiz.com/article/business-case-investments-water-efficiency

Hines, J., Godber, S., Butcher, B., Siddall, M., Jennings, P., Grant, N., Clarke, A., Mead, K., & Parsons, C. (n.d.). *How to Build a Passivhaus: Rules of Thumb*. Passivhaus Trust. Retrieved from http://www.passivhaustrust.org.uk/UserFiles/File/Technical%20Papers/ROT/How%20to%20build%20a%20Passivhaus_Chapters%201%20to%204(2).pdf

Hugger, M., Fuchs, M., Stark, T., & Zeumer, M. (2007). *Energie Atlas*. Munich, Germany: Birkhäuser.

Hydro Quebec. (2016). *Comparison of Electricity Prices in Major North American Cities*. Retrieved from http://www.hydroquebec.com/publications/en/docs/comparaison-electricity-prices/comp_2016_en.pdf

Iczkowski, E. (2005, October). *LEED-EB: How to achieve certification and reduce operating costs*. Paper presented at Fifth International Conference for Enhanced Building Operations, Pittsburgh, Pennsylvania. Retrieved from oaktrust.library.tamu.edu/bitstream/handle/1969.1/5134/ESL-IC-05-10-39.pdf?sequence=4&isAllowed=y

International Statistics for Water Services 2016. (2016). The International Water Association. Retrieved from www.iwa-network.org/wp-content/uploads/2016/10/Water_Statistics_SCREEN.pdf

Kats, G., Alevantis, L., Berman, A., Mills, E., & Perlman, J. (2003). *The Costs and financial benefits of Green buildings: A Report to California's Sustainable Building Task Force*. Retrieved from https://noharm-uscanada.org/sites/default/files/documents-files/34/Building_Green_Costs_Benefits.pdf

Kibert, N. C., & Kibert, C. J. (2008). Sustainable Development and the U.S. Green Building Movement: Profitable Development Projects Can Be Good for the Planet, Too. *Probate & Property, Vol. 22 No. -2* (March/April). Retrieved from http://www.americanbar.org/publications/probate_property_magazine_home/rppt_publications_magazine_2008_ma_sustainable_kilbert.html

Kuzimeko, J. (2014, December 4). Do LEED Buildings Perform? Indeed They Do!. Retrieved from http://insight.gbig.org/do-leed-buildings-perform-indeed-they-do/

Lucon O., Ürge-Vorsatz, D., Zain Ahmed, A., Akbari, H., Bertoldi, P., Cabeza, L. F., …, Vilariño, M. V. (2014). Buildings. In O. Edenhofer, R. Pichs-Madruga, Y. Sokona, E. Farahani, S. Kadner, K. Seyboth, A. Adler, I. Baum, S. Brunner, P. Eickemeier, B. Kriemann, J. Savolainen, S. Schlömer, C. von Stechow, T. Zwickel, & J. C. Minx (Eds.), *Climate Change 2014: Mitigation of Climate Change. Contribution of Working Group III to the Fifth Assessment Report of the Intergovernmental Panel on Climate Change*. Cambridge and New York, NY: Cambridge University Press. Retrieved from https://www.ipcc.ch/pdf/assessment-report/ar5/wg3/ipcc_wg3_ar5_chapter9.pdf

MacNaughton, P., Satish, U., Laurent, J. G. C., Flanigan, S., Vallarino, J., Coull, B., Spengler, J. G., & Allen, J. G. (2017). The Impact of Working in a Green Certified Building on Cognitive Function and Health. *Building and Environment, Vol. 114* (March 2017) p. 178–186. Retrieved from http://www.sciencedirect.com/science/article/pii/S0360132316304723

Mapp, C., Nobe, M. C., & Dunbar, B. (2011). The Cost of LEED: An Analysis of the Construction Costs of LEED and Non-LEED Banks. *The Journal of Sustainable Real Estate, Vol. 3* (No. 1, 2017) p. 254–273. Retrieved from http://www.josre.org/wp-content/uploads/2012/09/Cost_of_LEED_Analysis_of_Construction_Costs-JOSRE_v3-13.pdf

Miller, N., Pogue, D., Gough, Q., & Davis, S. (2009). Green Buildings and Productivity. *Journal of Sustainable Real Estate: 2009, 1(1), 65–89.*

Mills, E., Friedman, H., Powell, T., Bourassa, N., Claridge, D., Haasl, T., & Piette, M. A. (2004). *The Cost-Effectiveness of Commercial-Buildings Commissioning*. Lawrence Berkeley National Laboratory. Retrieved from http://evanmills.lbl.gov/pubs/pdf/cx-costs-benefits.pdf

National Trust for Historic Preservation. (2011). *The Greenest Building: Quantifying the Environmental Value of Building Reuse*. Retrieved from https://living-future.org/wp-content/uploads/2016/11/The_Greenest_Building.pdf

Olear, G. (2016, May 4). Nations to leverage building efficiency to meet Paris commitments. *USGBC*. Retrieved from https://www.usgbc.org/articles/nations-leverage-building-efficiency-meet-paris-commitments

Olesen, S., Fanger, P. O., Jensen, P. B., & Nielsen, O. J. (1972, September). *Comfort Limits for Man Exposed to Asymmetric Thermal Radiation*. Paper presented at CIB Commission W45 (Human requirements) Symposium: THERMAL COMFORT AND MODERATE HEAT STRESS, London. Retrieved from www.cbe.berkeley.edu/research/other-papers/Olesen%20et%20al%201972%20Comfort%20limits%20for%20man%20exposed%20to%20asymmetric%20thermal%20radiation.pdf

Property Data Report. (2016). *Facts and Figures About the UK Commercial Property Industry to Year-end 2015* (2016). Property Industry Alliance. Retrieved from www.bpf.org.uk/sites/default/files/resources/PIA-Property-Report-2016-final-for-web.pdf

Retrocommissioning for Better Performance. (2006, March). *Building Operating Management*. Retrieved from http://www.facilitiesnet.com/energyefficiency/article/Retrocommissioning-for-Better-Performance%2D%2D-4097

Romm, J. J. (1994). *Lean and Clean Management: How to Boost Profits and Productivity by Reducing Pollution*. New York: Kodansha International.

Sandberg, I., Bankvall, C., Sikander, E., Wahlgren, P., & Larsson, B. (2007). The Effects and Cost Impact of Poor Airtightness—Information for Developers and Clients. Retrieved from http://web.ornl.gov/sci/buildings/conf-archive/2007%20B10%20papers/047_Sandberg.pdf

Tall Buildings in Numbers. (2009). *CTBUH Journal*, (Issue III). Retrieved from http://www.ctbuh.org/LinkClick.aspx?fileticket=mtjd4j7fG1s%3D&tabid=1211&language=en-US

U.S. Department of Energy. (n.d.). *Best Management Practices #10: Cooling Tower Management*. Retrieved March 15, 2017, from https://energy.gov/eere/femp/best-management-practice-10-cooling-tower-management

U.S. Environmental Protection Agency. (2015). *WaterSense Labeled Flushometer-Valve Toilets*. Retrieved from https://www.epa.gov/sites/production/files/2017-01/documents/ws-products-factsheet-fv-toilets.pdf

U.S. Green Building Council. (2016). *LEED Reference Guide for Building Design and Construction*. Washington, DC.

United States Environmental Protection Agency. (2008). *ENERGY STAR Building Upgrade Manual*. Retrieved from https://www.energystar.gov/sites/default/files/buildings/tools/EPA_BUM_Full.pdf

White Paper on Sustainability. (2003, November). *Building Design & Construction*. Retrieved from https://www.bdcnetwork.com/sites/default/files/BD+C%202003%20White%20Paper%20on%20Sustainability.pdf

CHAPTER 9

Sustainability as an Organizational Effectiveness Tool

Sara Levana Schoen

Sustainability initiatives are widely recognized to impact both costs and revenues via corporate value drivers including reputation, operating expenses, tenant attraction and retention, and risk management. Eccles, Ioannou, and Serafeim (2014) present evidence that sustainability adoption improves stakeholder engagement and long-term financial performance. Savitz and Weber (2013) discuss ways sustainability enhances innovation, collaboration, and employee engagement. When companies connect employees' work to a positive social mission, morale and motivation improve (Winston, 2014).

For real estate companies with organizational structures that disconnect firm leaders from the front lines, sustainability can also help improve organizational dynamics and effectiveness. Executives who are removed from the rank and file often can't see organizational issues or the associated profit-enhancing opportunities, and sustainability professionals with

S. L. Schoen (✉)
Schoen Sustainability, Washington, DC, USA

First Potomac Realty Trust, Bethesda, MD, USA
e-mail: sara@schoensustain.com

T. Walker et al. (eds.), *Sustainable Real Estate*, Palgrave Studies in Sustainable Business In Association with Future Earth,
https://doi.org/10.1007/978-3-319-94565-1_9

strong soft skills are well-positioned to help them understand and strengthen organizational function to maximize value creation.

Real estate companies hugely impact the built and natural environments, human communities around the world, and millions of employees. Their optimal function and the wellness, actualization, and performance of their employees have the potential to significantly improve public health and general societal welfare. A holistic approach to sustainability that includes a broad range of social and governance issues, including organizational excellence, maximizes the financial and social benefits from sustainability adoption.

This chapter discusses ways the sustainability enterprise can, in addition to highlighting a company's social purpose, help address organizational inefficiencies that reduce productivity. After two real-world examples, this chapter describes several features of sustainability work that make it a strong tool for improving organizational effectiveness and then discusses additional real-life examples from companies in the building sector.

Nicholas Stolatis held leadership positions with one of the world's largest real estate investment managers for more than 30 years, but it wasn't until he became head of sustainability 22 years in that he was able to systemize organizational effectiveness. In the asset and portfolio management roles Stolatis held during his first two decades with the firm, he was responsible for quarterly financial results. When his responsibilities were shifted to create a new sustainability program, his capacity to work on non-urgent but important priorities that impacted long-term investment performance increased. In addition to achieving an impressive 22% reduction in energy use and $102 million in avoided energy cost during his nine years as global head of real estate sustainability (N. E. Stolatis, personal communication, March 29, 2017), he essentially became his company's de facto head of operational excellence.

Stolatis developed a property management governance platform that standardized operating practices across the firm and thereby improved returns and pleased compliance auditors. The platform addressed the full spectrum of management activities from acquisitions to dispositions, including building operations, risk management, tenant satisfaction, and environmental reporting. It encouraged active management of properties and monitored and improved timeliness and accuracy of operating reports. The platform also spurred best practices sharing and continuous improvement of the firm's policies and procedures manual: eliminating extraneous content and simplifying operating policies and procedures improved their usability and effectiveness.

At its core, the effort was about extracting maximum value from existing resources by learning how to operate more effectively. The standardization of firm-wide operational excellence caught the attention and earned the approval of internal compliance auditors. The firm's research team evaluated how the program impacted financial performance and validated absolute improvement in total returns. As this example illustrates, utilizing sustainability learnings to improve organizational effectiveness can dramatically increase the value sustainability brings a company.

In a second example, a real estate owner's human resources staff was kept so busy with payroll administration and legal matters that it lacked capacity to address bigger-picture needs such as orienting new employees or helping them integrate into the culture of the firm. The company's sustainability director created an employee onboarding program that included telling new hires the company's founding story. The program's success led firm leaders to expand the sustainability role to include oversight of internal and external communications and some employee relations activities (personal communication, March 17, 2017).

With the assumption of these additional responsibilities, the sustainability director was promoted to Vice President, Strategy and Sustainability, and formally added to the firm's Executive Committee. In this hybrid strategy and sustainability role, he guides initiatives ranging from legislative affairs to corporate mission and visioning. His influence on corporate strategy and operations increased, allowing him to impact organizational decisions and processes.

At one location, he observed challenges with coordination and communication among a group of extremely diverse operations professionals. Property managers, accountants, maintenance technicians, construction managers, building engineers, and leasing agents worked in silos and had difficulty communicating effectively. Each function had different goals and priorities, making it difficult for the property manager to lead the group as a cohesive team. There were even some personality conflicts and relational tensions that were keeping staff from doing their jobs effectively.

The property management role is complex and challenging even without such interpersonal friction. In addition to managing staff, keeping up with tenant needs requires much leg work and human interaction. It is a demanding and physically active job at which individuals can remain successful only if they maintain high levels of engagement. A step removed from this complexity and daily grind, those focused on sustainability remain or become semi-outsiders and can often more easily see coordination and communication challenges and formulate potential improvement strategies. If a sustainability leader's station within an organization affords him sufficient power to act upon the opportunities he sees, he can put his insight to work.

This sustainability executive conceived an idea to rotate employees to shadow functions very different from theirs. For example, an accountant would spend a day in the field shadowing property and facilities managers. Accountants usually have nine-to-five desk jobs in which they sit in a company's corporate office. This rotation would allow them to experience the daily challenges field staff face in a way they never could from their desks. Increasing an accountant's understanding of the pressures of an on-property job would help them work better with individuals in such roles. In this manner, inviting sustainability practitioners to share their observations and recommend solutions can be a powerful method for company leaders to improve organizational effectiveness.

1 Features That Make Sustainability a Strong Organizational Effectiveness Tool

Sustainability is long-termism regarding all aspects of human welfare, including financial, workforce, community, and environmental health. For those interested in long-term financial performance, sustainability is good business. Sustainability efforts can help companies function better at a basic level. They promote good management; considering the long-term impacts of business decisions builds management capacity and improves operational efficiency, quality, and profitability.

When executives examine company processes through the lens of sustainability, challenges with those processes and opportunities to improve them become apparent. Sustainability work has a way of shedding light on areas of suboptimal function and possibilities to improve overall organizational effectiveness. Those who work on sustainability thus have unique insight into organizational inefficiencies and potential solutions. This extends to systems, relationships, and leadership. The following sections discuss several ways in which sustainability work is uniquely suited to both identify and address organizational issues.

1.1 Long-Term Orientation

Many policies and best practices, including those related to environmental management but also in other areas, benefit the bottom line if fully implemented but are rarely managed closely. Increasing attention on these non-urgent but return-impacting priorities can improve long-term financial performance (O'Dell & Grayson, 1998). Real estate firm leaders who are focused on delivering quarterly and annual financial performance have limited capacity for time-consuming efforts that pay off only over the long term (Davies, Haldane, Nielsen, & Pezzini, 2014).

Adding the energies of a professional, whether internal or consultant, who has real capacity to invest in long-term organizational improvement efforts can correct this inefficiency that firms experience. Sustainability employees and consultants are essentially champions of long-termism. No one is better positioned to see and articulate the value of general management improvement than a professional with responsibility for long term rather than quarterly performance.

1.2 Change Agency

Sustainability work is organizational change work. Its core function is to change corporate behavior to increase long-term value creation. There has been a tendency, encouraged by the individual building certification model developed by the U.S. Green Building Council in the 1990s, for real estate companies to focus resources on the sustainability of a subset of "lowest hanging fruit" buildings at the expense of doing the more difficult and impactful work of altering organizational processes to design and operate entire real estate portfolios sustainably. But there is untapped long-term business value in changing company systems and processes. Doing so is an excellent way to not only integrate sustainability considerations but also improve organizational effectiveness.

Doing sustainability right requires revising company systems, processes, and procedures to include environmental, governance, and other social considerations. This takes significantly more upfront time than adopting separate policies and developing independent processes and systems to address sustainability issues. But the former uncovers operational improvement opportunities that can be leveraged across the entire organization while the latter creates redundancies and consumes more organizational resources over the long term.

Pursuing efforts to, for example, operate buildings more resource-efficiently leads sustainability practitioners to examine companies' general operational management practices. Those driving sustainability change efforts delve into existing policies, processes, and systems and gain intimate knowledge of them, including knowledge of ways in which they are inefficient or ineffective. Addressing such issues can increase time- and cost-efficiency, reduce employee stress, and improve firm performance (Allen, Rogelberg, & Scott, 2008; Altinkemer, Ozcelik, & Ozdemir, 2014). The normal course of sustainability endeavors thus brings opportunities to improve productivity across business functions.

The time and effort required to study policies, systems, and processes to integrate sustainability considerations makes it efficient for sustainability practitioners to lead policy, system, and process optimization. This approach expands the scope of sustainability, but the additional value it creates can more than offset the increased volume of work (Altinkemer et al., 2014).

Change is hard, and sustainability efforts ask a lot of people within companies. Pursuing sustainability goals requires learning new terminology, systems, and processes, collecting new data, trying new technologies, and significantly altering job responsibilities. Those implementing change therefore encounter challenges and issues early and often. As sustainability attempts to alter existing processes to include new considerations, it easily comes across organizational weaknesses and tensions. Some departments are open-minded, responsive, and easy to work with. Others resist change. By driving change, sustainability tests and learns about each department's capacity to deal with challenges. Because change brings tensions and inefficiencies to the surface, sustainability initiatives can be potent catalysts for organizational improvement.

An organization's ability to integrate sustainability initiatives is a litmus test for management capacity. The ease and speed with which a group or organization adopts new processes or technologies reveals important information about its resilience and ability to learn and improve (Pinkse & Dommisse, 2009). Slowness to, for example, begin tracking newly needed data can indicate low adaptability.

Likewise, the success of sustainability efforts is a strong indicator of agility. Organizations with high levels of interpersonal respect and accountability and low overextension and burnout are much more able to adopt new efforts seamlessly and without resistance or interpersonal struggle. If challenges are encountered, they can become opportunities to make companies more agile and capable. Attending to pockets of resistance can allow executives to address underlying issues and lead their firms to operate more efficiently and profitably.

Sustainability work requires its practitioners to raise uncomfortable questions and challenge existing practices and modes of thinking. Sustainability leaders who can serve as agitators while retaining the trust of executives and workers are most effective at improving environmental and social performance. This prepares sustainability practitioners well to lead organizational change efforts. It is a natural step to extend the sustainability role to include development and execution of strategic agendas beyond the classic scope of environmental, governance, and other social issues.

1.3 Presence on the Dance Floor and the Balcony

Most senior executives spend little time performing front-line tasks, working through processes, or interacting with software systems or property teams. For this reason, it is common for firm leaders to develop blind spots in areas of organizational dysfunction (Geiger & Antonacopoulou, 2009; Sala, 2003). Sustainability efforts require digging into policies, processes, and data systems as well as working with employees up and down the ladder.

George Washington University School of Business professor Jennifer Griffin describes sustainability as "on both the dance floor and the balcony" (personal communication, March 24, 2017), borrowing language from Harvard Kennedy School Center for Public Leadership founder Ronald Heifetz (Heifetz & Linsky, 2002). Interacting with workers and processes can increase senior executive awareness of organizational issues such as role clarity and process deficiencies. Working directly with rank-and-file employees can shed light on cultural and psychological issues such as dissatisfaction and fear of job loss. In this way, taking on sustainability initiatives can bring firm leaders onto the dance floor and help them better understand and manage organizational function.

Sustainability professionals who are not at the senior executive level, and are treated accordingly, receive the same responsiveness and quality other rank-and-file workers commonly experience in working with each department. Further, employees of all levels are more likely to share frustrations and observations with those outside their reporting chain of command, which includes many sustainability practitioners. Most with access to senior firm leaders interact only with lower-ranking employees for whom they have management responsibility, whether directly or several steps up the ladder. In contrast, sustainability practitioners work closely with employees up and down the ladder over whom they do not have management authority. These factors put sustainability practitioners more fully on the dance floor than most senior executives, lending them an advantage in learning about and helping improve organizational weaknesses.

Sustainability also provides its practitioners, from dedicated sustainability professionals to front-line workers and even middle managers, a firm-wide perspective that can help them see organizational challenges and opportunities they otherwise wouldn't. Tactical workers and managers don't normally view a firm from the vantage point from which sustainability operates, so sustainability provides these employees a unique "balcony" perspective.

Because sustainability professionals inherently inhabit both the dance floor and the balcony, they can provide a useful link between the C-suite and the front lines. Translating between the two is a natural role for many sustainability professionals but one that few firm leaders ask them to play. Chief executives can dramatically increase the value sustainability professionals provide by asking them what they hear and see on the front lines and seeking their input on broad organizational health and strategy.

1.4 *Need for Data*

To conduct sustainability reporting, real estate sustainability professionals require vast amounts of data that are generally not utilized by anyone else within a company. Interacting heavily with company data management systems leads sustainability professionals to develop a thorough understanding of weaknesses in such systems and opportunities to improve them. Reliance on company data collection processes and general management mechanisms to obtain data needed for sustainability purposes also gives sustainability professionals a window into strengths and weaknesses in those areas.

In line with the "dance floor and balcony" nature of sustainability work described earlier, those who manage sustainability are often uniquely in touch with both data systems and firm leadership. Senior executives rarely utilize data management systems directly, but sustainability leaders usually have relationships with top executives. Sustainability professionals also interact with data systems more intimately than most others with connections to the C-suite, positioning them to share insights about data systems with firm leaders. Because others with direct contact with data systems are usually either responsible for data system performance or don't interface with chief executives, this type of information sharing may not occur as efficiently through other organizational chains of command.

Improving corporate data quality, efficiency, accessibility, and ease of use has implications far beyond environmental management and can improve the capabilities and agility of companies across the real estate lifecycle from acquisitions due diligence to marketing assets for sale. This is another way in which sustainability is uniquely positioned to help improve organizational effectiveness.

1.5 Cross-Functional Nature

Contributing to the "balcony" perspective they cultivate is the fact that sustainability efforts by nature require working with nearly all departments within a company as well as with all regions and a variety of project and building sites. Corporate sustainability expert Andrew Winston sees sustainability as "the most cross-functional role in an organization, giving it an uncommon firm-wide view of what works and what doesn't," (personal communication, February 23, 2017).

Sustainability both requires collaboration with and serves as a resource to accounting, finance, marketing, legal, leasing, asset management, property management, operations, engineering, information technology, development, construction, and service providers. By interacting with such a wide range of business areas, sustainability practitioners gain unique insight into interdepartmental dynamics and the capability, responsiveness, and agility of each department. Exposure to a diversity of functions allows those carrying out sustainability efforts to see tensions and relative strengths and weaknesses between departments. A company-wide view of business practices, communication, and how departments interface with each other is a powerful tool in improving organizational effectiveness.

Such understanding has proven so valuable to companies that Winston considers Chief Sustainability Officer roles excellent CEO training grounds. In the words of Hugh Welsh, President of DSM North America (personal communication, April 7, 2017), "Smart companies are working to future-proof their organizations by adopting sustainable practices in operations and strategic planning, applying circular economic principles in deciding how to deploy capital, develop new products, and do mergers, acquisitions, and divestitures. As a consequence, future CEOs will come not necessarily with a finance, operations, or sales background, but with a sustainability background."

Beyond sustainability practitioners, the parties that need to collaborate to achieve sustainability goals often aren't accustomed to doing so, such as accountants and building engineers. Sustainability asks departments to work together in new ways, often coordinating cross-functional efforts larger than ever undertaken previously. This kind of change has the side effect of forcing increased and eventually improved communication between departments.

Along the way, sustainability change focuses attention on interdepartmental tensions and then provides opportunities to iron them out. This is a chance to increase trust between departments. Sometimes the involved parties are aware of tensions before sustainability comes along. But often they have accepted tension as inevitable and buried their awareness of it. People commonly give up on improving imperfect situations. The introduction of new sustainability efforts presents a large opportunity to boost interdepartmental cooperation.

1.6 *Insider-Outsider Perspective*

It is natural for rank-and-file workers and senior executives alike to become accustomed to whatever norms exist within a company. Because sustainability work necessitates focusing on externalities from business activities as well as the impacts of global issues on a company, it naturally helps employees of all levels and functions understand how those outside the company see it. Savitz and Weber (2013) refer to this as "outward focus" and note that sustainability can inspire closer collaboration with customers, suppliers, distributors, and other stakeholders (p. 23). The outsider perspective can expand senior executives' view beyond internal business pressures, allowing them to see opportunities that are less visible from the inside. This is related to the long-term orientation and balcony perspective described earlier.

Even longtime employees who lead sustainability efforts operate to a degree like external consultants, working closely with employees who don't report directly to them, struggling to understand others' challenges and motivations, and collaborating with various departments to implement initiatives. This can provide a perspective on an organization that's closer to the way an external consultant would see it than the way employees typically do. Thus, sustainability practitioners, whether focused fully on sustainability or integrating sustainability into preexisting roles, bring a fresh set of eyes that more easily see organizational issues, including relational, structural, and leadership tensions.

1.7 Inclusion of Personnel Issues

While many firms initially focused on sustainability as encompassing only environmental issues, the term is now widely used to describe a broader set of social issues including employee and occupant health and wellness as well as corporate governance. As firms have moved beyond a strict environmental sustainability scope, the function has begun to address employee relations, benefits, and satisfaction as well as leadership diversity and pay equity.

This chapter generally argues for expanding the role of sustainability to include advising on organizational challenges and improvements. But if sustainability covers social issues by definition, adding organizational effectiveness to its purview is less a departure than a natural maturing as the function comes to assume its full responsibilities. Workplace culture, communications, relationships, stress, leadership capacity, emotional intelligence, role clarity, process efficiency, and reporting structures greatly impact employee health and well-being. Involving sustainability professionals in efforts to improve "human resource sustainability" is an appropriate development (Savitz & Weber, 2013).

2 Opportunities for Sustainability to Improve Organizational Effectiveness

The features described earlier allow the sustainability function to provide a comprehensive organization-wide lens that can help sustainability professionals and firm leaders understand and strengthen a company. Integrating sustainability concerns and approaches into business practices can lead to improved organizational efficiency and benefit employee well-being and firm profitability.

The integrated design process (IDP), one of the hallmarks of the green building movement, is itself an organizational fix: it corrects a communication disconnect in the standard design and construction process by encouraging collaboration between all stakeholders, including owners, occupants, architects, engineers, and builders, in the very early stages of a project's life. Many other sustainability efforts can improve organizational function. To round out the examples at the start of this chapter, additional real-world scenarios follow.

2.1 *Process Improvement*

One Real Estate Investment Trust (REIT) was plagued by utility invoice late fees due to inefficiencies in its accounts payable process. While totaling to a somewhat significant amount of money across hundreds of buildings, the late fees were far from the most pressing business matter. Managers had given up on addressing the issue and were focused on other priorities, but the company was unnecessarily losing money to late fees (personal communication, March 15, 2017).

While exploring the possibility of automating energy and water consumption data upload to ENERGY STAR Portfolio Manager, the company's sustainability director learned of the late fee situation. Some of the automation providers the company was considering also offered utility bill pay services. Bundling bill pay with benchmarking automation services would eliminate the late fees paid to utility companies.

The sustainability director's goal was not to reduce non-consumption related energy costs. But pursuing environmental benchmarking led him to delve into the REIT's utility bill processes, which revealed an opportunity to reduce general, unrelated costs. The late fee problem went unaddressed until sustainability refocused attention on utility bills in general. Sustainability encourages proactive management that can improve general business operations beyond the social issues that typically fall under its purview.

2.2 *Productivity Impediment Removal*

There was more to the bill pay story at the REIT described in the immediately preceding section. The accounts payable employees who worked directly on seeking approvals and issuing payments for utility invoices had been aware of cost-effective bill pay services for years. The bill pay systems would have reduced costs for the REIT and would have also altered the invoice approvals process to eliminate late payments and therefore late fees. But the accounts payable administrators had not pursued or shared such options with higher-level staff out of fear that adopting these systems would lead to the elimination of accounting jobs (personal communication, March 15, 2017).

Fear that improving productivity could lead to layoffs prevented this company from taking advantage of an efficiency-improving solution. Accounting employees saw better systems as a threat to their job security. So, when they encountered software that would improve their team's performance, they looked the other way. The company's accounting managers wanted to innovate but were not aware of the bill pay solutions or the culture of fear among their staff members.

The firm's sustainability executive began discussing utility bill processing with accounts payable staff as part of his effort to automate upload of utility data to ENERGY STAR Portfolio Manager. By interacting directly with rank-and-file staff, he became aware of the dynamics in the department. Insight into the thought processes of their team members allowed accounting leadership to address their anxieties and explicitly assure employees that improving productivity would not lead managers to shrink the team. Managers explained that reducing manual data entry would allow existing staff to spend their time on more productive and engaging activities such as identifying and correcting billing errors and working with property managers to reduce utility costs.

In this example, intelligence collected by sustainability in its normal course of business allowed a company's large accounting group to clear a cultural and communication barrier that was keeping it from operating more effectively. It was the sustainability director's ability to be "on the dance floor" with the accounts payable administrators that allowed him to learn about the personnel anxieties. His connection to senior managers, his "balcony" access, enabled him to put the knowledge he gained to use to improve his company's performance.

2.3 *Tenant Service*

For as long as employees could remember, their property management company spent thousands of dollars each year on holiday decorations in office building lobbies. This expensive winter holiday cheer was so ingrained and taken for granted that employees assumed that building occupants valued it highly. When the sustainability group observed how wasteful of materials the annual effort was, they asked how much the company spent on it (personal communication, April 3, 2017).

At first, their inquiries were dismissed as non-starters for questioning a practice held dearly by executives, occupants, and property management employees. But a curious property manager began raising the issue with tenants in casual conversation. She discovered that many occupants, especially corporate real estate decision-makers, found the holiday decorations annoying and judged them as wasteful. It turned out that tenant representatives were happy, and in some cases enthusiastic, to forego elaborate decorations for the sake of cost savings and environmental-friendliness. Lease structures at many properties were such that ownership did not benefit in a direct financial way from the resulting cost savings, but the change generated tenant goodwill and loyalty.

The experience led the property management firm to develop a formal process for collecting information on which building services tenants most valued and aligning operational spending with tenant priorities. The company created an electronic survey that included actual amounts spent on various amenities and asked tenants how they would reallocate dollars. The firm then began to make spending decisions based on gathered information rather than assumptions and old ways of doing business.

This made the company more responsive to customer desires. It also increased cost-efficiency; the firm could spend less while keeping tenants happier. At some properties, this change freed up budget dollars for energy efficiency projects that further reduced operating expenses and generated more tenant goodwill and loyalty (personal communication, April 3, 2017). This is an example of a sustainability initiative that not only reduced waste but also improved fundamental organizational performance by leading the company to become more efficient and effective at serving its customers.

2.4 Occupant Satisfaction

A residential developer assigned an employee the task of reviewing and integrating efficiency technologies into home designs. As a high-end developer with a reputation for quality, the firm was concerned about user experience with systems such as motion-activated lighting, water-efficient showerheads, and tank-less water heaters. The company's culture of focus on occupant satisfaction led the job to evolve into a hybrid resource conservation and user experience role. Making the same professional responsible for both these priorities alleviated concerns that the former would be sacrificed for the latter (personal communication, April 13, 2017).

When defined broadly to include social issues, sustainability encompasses customer satisfaction. Occupant experience, natural resource costs, and environmental impacts all affect customer satisfaction and therefore long-term value creation. Focusing on all these factors upfront improves firm reputation and profitability. Considering diverse sustainability issues in concert can maximize organizational effectiveness.

2.5 *Policy Usability and Compliance*

The opening of this chapter described Nicholas Stolatis' efforts to shorten and simplify operating policies and procedures to improve their use and effectiveness. Similarly, a nationwide construction company's new Director of Corporate Responsibility quickly found herself working to streamline company policies. When she joined the firm, it had four different Code of Conduct documents, some up to 20 pages in length (personal communication, March 24, 2017). No one within the firm had been attending to them. The senior executive overseeing corporate responsibility tasked the new director with managing the codes of conduct. She consolidated them into one highly readable, four-page document that is now used much more frequently and effectively.

Ethics policies are outside the purview of the traditional energy or environmental manager but included when sustainability is defined broadly to include corporate governance or personnel issues. When human resources, legal, or compliance departments lack capacity to manage such policies, a sustainability professional can be the first that is able to give them the attention they deserve.

Corporate policies are crucial to the healthy functioning of companies. Efforts to make them relevant and accessible are a powerful way for firm leaders to improve organizational effectiveness. Assigning someone responsibility for maintaining and optimizing policies is an investment in long-term corporate welfare. Because traditional functions are often consumed by pressing business priorities and sustainability practitioners exist expressly to manage long-term priorities, the latter can be a natural fit.

2.6 *Dumb Money to Smart Money*

Many large investment managers, which collectively manage hundreds of billions of dollars of real estate on behalf of institutional investors, want to impact the environmental performance of development projects in which they invest (personal communication, March 28, 2017). But investment managers typically play a "dumb money" role in these projects, leaving the decision-making to trusted development partners.

Assigning responsibility for managing development projects to partners benefits investment managers and their investor clients. But transferring authority along with that responsibility does not serve investment managers or investors well. Relinquishing authority diminishes the ability of investors and investment managers to pursue their own priorities and desires for development projects. Some employees of investment managers think that investors and their agents abdicate more power to development partners than is in their interests.

Pursuing sustainability involvement is an opportunity for investors and investment managers to reclaim their authority over development projects. Elevating investment managers' roles in these projects would allow them to contribute more value throughout the development process. More active management would improve general development project outcomes and performance. This is an example of a sustainability issue offering an opportunity to correct an organizational inefficiency to the benefit of investors.

2.7 *Leadership and Compensation Issue Identification*

The sustainability department of a privately held real estate owner and operator asked multiple departments to collect employee travel data so they could calculate scope 3 climate emissions. Three departments did it with no problem but a fourth submitted incomplete and error-ridden data (personal communication, March 15, 2017). The head of sustainability mentioned it to the firm's Chief Financial Officer (CFO) in a routine meeting. The CFO decided to investigate.

After examining records and talking with members of the team that submitted inaccurate data, the CFO discovered that employees in that group were submitting exaggerated vehicle mileage reports to increase the reimbursements they received. It turned out that the department head informally encouraged this practice to boost what he perceived as unfair compensation discrepancies between his group and others in the firm. The financial loss was relatively minimal but obviously represented a leadership issue and the department head was let go.

The sustainability team, performing its routine work, implemented change and uncovered a leadership issue that needed to be addressed. By simply requesting new information, sustainability drew attention to travel reimbursement data and a normally overlooked administrative process and organizational weaknesses were swiftly addressed and improved. This work also highlighted potential issues with respect to the perceived fairness and equitability of the compensation structure that may have broader implications on retention, employee engagement, and overall productivity.

2.8 Interdepartmental Teamwork

When a publicly traded REIT hired its first sustainability manager in 2011, the firm's property management group was extremely decentralized. Each of several regions had its own Director of Property Management (DPM), but there was no corporate property management executive. Each DPM reported directly to the firm's Chief Operating Officer (COO).

The company's construction group, on the other hand, was highly coordinated across all regions. A Vice President (VP) of Construction led the 20-person team from the company's headquarters. Construction managers, located in each region, traveled to headquarters for monthly team meetings.

The discrepancy in central coordination between the property management and construction groups led to interdepartmental friction. The VP of Construction had strong ideas regarding how property and construction managers should work together. He had a clear vision of the tasks property managers should handle, what the role of construction managers should be, and how the two should work together. He consistently communicated this vision to his own staff, but coordinating with property management was more difficult.

Coordinating with property management required communicating with four different leaders, one in reach region. Keeping up with four busy individuals was challenging, and the difficulty was compounded by turnover in the DPM positions. Structural issues thus prevented the VP of Construction from effectively communicating protocols to property managers. Consistency in expectations among property managers across regions remained elusive even while the VP of Construction instilled clear expectations in his own staff. This resulted in much frustration in both departments.

Construction managers began to anticipate difficulty every time they worked with property managers. The clear vision they shared with their boss and teammates created expectations that were dashed when they tried to coordinate with property managers. A culture of prejudice toward the property management group developed within the construction group.

Construction staff aired frustrations with each other behind closed doors. They complained openly in construction team meetings that property management did not follow processes and procedures. Their assessment was accurate, but they lacked a productive outlet for their criticisms. Without a healthy way to express concerns directly, construction manager discontent spilled out in interactions with property managers. They acted annoyed, condescended, and sometimes treated property managers with disrespect. They often became rigid, insisting that property managers follow processes they had not agreed to or worked to create.

Property managers concluded that construction managers were inflexible and unhelpful. They described construction managers as "not being team players." Relationships deteriorated further from there, with each side judging and criticizing the other, unable to find a way to improve the situation.

The COO and CEO were either unaware of the situation or did not know the full extent of it. But the friction between these two departments was costing the company in employee motivation and productivity. Because the sustainability manager worked closely with both departments, she was privy to the murmurings and complaints on each side. She could easily describe and explain the situation and articulate the views and needs of each department. If utilized as such by senior management, sustainability is a valuable source of insight into organizational tensions and methods for ameliorating them.

2.9 Agility

A REIT's sustainability manager completed lighting retrofit projects within months of beginning her employment with the firm. But after three years, she was still struggling to impact lighting choices made as part of tenant fit-outs. Installing high-performance lighting as part of a larger renovation that is occurring anyway is more time- and cost-efficient than conducting a project solely to upgrade lighting. But construction managers, who controlled the tenant construction process, resisted making changes to their processes to consider more efficient lighting. And because retrofit projects addressed only lighting, they moved forward independent of the firm's construction managers. The complexity and challenge of coordinating construction managers thus prevented the firm from installing high-performance lighting efficiently and consistently even though doing so would have benefitted its long-term bottom line.

Similarly, a large retailer orchestrated multiple solar installations on existing buildings with a real estate partner but missed opportunities to integrate solar into newly developed properties with the same real estate partner. This occurred even though designing a solar system into a new roof is both safer and more cost-effective than adding solar panels to an existing roof that was not designed to carry their weight. The retailer's construction managers had little capacity to attend to changing priorities. They were so overwhelmed with their regular duties that they did not read procedure manuals and thus missed crucial points at which solar would be considered during the design process (personal communication, January 28, 2017).

The REIT's sustainability manager and the retailer's solar manager, a member of its sustainability team, both encountered a weakness in adaptation capacity. They each witnessed low agility lead to missed opportunities and suboptimal decision-making. Inability to adapt to sustainability change is the tip of an iceberg. It indicates much broader and deeper potential performance issues. Sustainability professionals routinely have insight into such organizational dysfunction and can serve as valuable assets to firm leadership in identifying opportunities to improve their companies.

2.10 *Lifetime Cost Over Low-Bid Procurement*

A vertically integrated owner-manager's sustainability director reported into its construction department. He managed lighting retrofits according to the firm's standard three-bid construction process and noticed change orders leading lowest bids to result in final project costs that exceeded higher bidders' total fees. He suggested tracking final project costs and comparing them with proposal costs. His team found that actual costs from low bidders often exceeded projected costs from higher bidders (personal communication, March 8, 2017). This applied not only to efficiency-improving sustainability projects but also to general construction projects managed by others on the construction team.

Sustainability encourages analysis of lifetime rather than upfront costs, which calls into question the lowest-bidder procurement convention. The downsides of lowest-bidder procurement go far beyond energy efficiency but are nonetheless ingrained in many real estate organizations. Environmental advocates easily see financial losses resulting from lowest-bidder approaches and can drive examination of such practices, shedding light on their long-term costs and driving organizational change.

2.11 Talent Attraction and Retention

Commercial real estate companies' commitment to valuing their own product—physical space that employees inhabit every day to perform their work—may lead them to resist the remote work arrangements that many industries now embrace. This can cost real estate firms access to some of the best and brightest millennial workers, who value flexibility more highly than previous generations.

The environmental benefits of telecommuting make it attractive to sustainability practitioners. If sustainability proponents contend with resistance to telecommuting, they can help shift real estate organizational culture to meet modern professional norms and reduce this talent attraction disadvantage.

Sustainability initiatives such as the California State Teachers' Retirement System's Responsible Contractor Policy (2015), which aims to ensure fair wages and benefits for workers, may help establish industry-wide compensation levels that enable sufficient attraction and retention of workers in trades with labor shortages. This represents a correction to an organizational challenge and market inefficiency that can affect companies across the building sector.

3 Integrating Sustainability and Organizational Effectiveness

As the earlier examples illustrate, sustainability efforts can be potent tools for improving organizational function and companies can benefit from the organizational insights of sustainability practitioners. Firm leaders can access these insights by inviting sustainability practitioners to share the full range of what they see, beyond the issues that are typically under the purview of sustainability. Seeking recommendations on organizational matters from sustainability, practitioners can unlock tremendous organizational effectiveness value that is currently underutilized. Interacting with those who are in the trenches on sustainability can provide a CEO or board member an edge in knowing and improving their company.

A powerful positive feedback loop exists between sustainability and organizational effectiveness: pursuing better consideration of the long-term implications of business activities is a potent method for effecting positive organizational change. Sustainability initiatives can increase quality and effectiveness across a company, in all functions and departments. In turn, improving organizational effectiveness makes companies more sustainable both financially and socially: well-run companies are more profitable and perform better on environmental and other social issues. The more that company leaders, including board members, fully recognize this interplay, the more highly they will prioritize sustainability efforts and the more they will capture the full business value of sustainability.

References

Allen, J. A., Rogelberg, S. G., & Scott, J. C. (2008). Mind Your Meetings: Improve Your Organization's Effectiveness One Meeting at a Time. *Quality Progress, 41*, 48–53. Retrieved from digitalcommons.unomaha.edu/cgi/viewcontent.cgi?article=1091&context=psychfacpub

Altinkemer, K., Ozcelik, Y., & Ozdemir, Z. D. (2014). Productivity and Performance Effects of Business Process Reengineering: A Firm-Level Analysis. *Journal of Management Information Systems, 27*(4), 129–162. https://doi.org/10.2753/MIS0742-1222270405

California State Teachers' Retirement System Responsible Contractor Policy. (February 2015). In *CalSTRS.com*. Retrieved July 24, 2017, from https://www.calstrs.com/general-information/responsible-contractor-policy

Davies, R., Haldane, A. G., Nielsen, M., & Pezzini, S. (2014). Measuring the Costs of Short-Termism. *Journal of Financial Stability, 12*, 16–25. https://doi.org/10.1016/j.jfs.2013.07.002

Eccles, R. G., Ioannou, I., & Serafeim, G. (2014). The Impact of Corporate Sustainability on Organizational Processes and Performance. *Management Science, 60*(11), 2835–2857.

Geiger, D., & Antonacopoulou, E. (2009). Narratives and Organizational Dynamics: Exploring Blind Spots and Organizational Inertia. *The Journal of Applied Behavioral Science, 45*(3), 411–436. https://doi.org/10.1177/0021886309336402

Heifetz, R., & Linsky, M. (2002, June). A Survival Guide for Leaders. *Harvard Business Review*. Retrieved from https://hbr.org/2002/06/a-survival-guide-for-leaders

O'Dell, C., & Grayson, C. J. (1998). If Only We Knew What We Know: Identification and Transfer of Internal Best Practices. *California Management Review, 40*(3), 154–174. https://doi.org/10.2307/41165948

Pinkse, J., & Dommisse, M. (2009). Overcoming Barriers to Sustainability: An Explanation of Residential Builders' Reluctance to Adopt Clean Technologies. *Business Strategy and the Environment, 18*(8), 515–527. https://doi.org/10.1002/bse.615

Sala, F. (2003). Executive Blind Spots: Discrepancies Between Self- and Other-ratings. *Consulting Psychology Journal: Practice and Research, 55*(4), 222–229. https://doi.org/10.1037/1061-4087.55.4.222

Savitz, A., & Weber, K. (2013). *Talent, Transformation, and the Triple Bottom Line: How Companies Can Leverage Human Resources to Achieve Sustainable Growth*. San Francisco, CA: Jossey-Bass.

Winston, A. S. (2014). *The Big Pivot: Radically Practical Strategies for a Hotter, Scarcer, and More Open World*. Boston, MA: Harvard Business School Publishing.

PART III

Delivering Affordable, Reliable, Sustainable Energy

CHAPTER 10

Building Energy Simulation and the Design of Sustainable and Resilient Buildings

Bruno Lee

Building energy simulation provides an effective means of evaluating the energy performance of buildings. Over the years, the simulation tools have evolved from a piecemeal calculation that represents just one physical phenomenon to computer software that considers the building as a whole in both space and time (Clarke, 2001; Crawley et al., 2001). Starting in the mid-1990s, due to the rapid advancement in computational technologies, modern-day building energy simulation tools began to take shape and represent every dynamic interaction between different factors, across different domains. A detailed simulation model, with high-resolution inputs, can resemble the actual energy operation of buildings quite faithfully (Henninger, Witte, & Crawley, 2004; Judkoff & Neymark, 1995; Neymark & Judkoff, 2004). Depending on the stage of the design, building energy simulation can be used in a variety of ways, from proposing design alternatives at the early stage to offering energy performance estimation and supporting financial propositions. Echenagucia, Capozzoli, Cascone, and

B. Lee (✉)
Concordia University, Montréal, QC, Canada
e-mail: bruno.lee@concordia.ca

T. Walker et al. (eds.), *Sustainable Real Estate*, Palgrave Studies in Sustainable Business In Association with Future Earth,
https://doi.org/10.1007/978-3-319-94565-1_10

Sassone (2015) used energy simulation tools to determine the optimal window-to-wall ratio (WWR), for each orientation, to minimize heat, cooling and lighting energy consumption. With similar design parameters and objectives, Samuelson, Claussnitzer, Goyal, Chen, and Romo-Castillo (2016) investigated from an urban design perspective and suggested that different design goals such as reducing peak-loads or decreasing energy-use intensity could result in different solutions. Other than energy consumption, thermal comfort is also an important aspect and was studied by Nembrini, Samberger, and Labelle (2014) with different architectural typologies. The work of Attia, Hamdy, O'Brien, and Carlucci (2013) promoted the use of building performance optimization at the early design stage and highlighted uncertainty as one of the main issues needing to be addressed.

Building energy simulation facilitates the design of a building and the decision-making process by offering effective assessments of different design alternatives and strategies. Such assessments may range from the simple one-time evaluation of a design to a parametric study of different design options or even to a large-scale simulation that simultaneously and holistically investigates multiple domains. Simulation tools combined with the appropriate automation tools can cover vast design spaces with different design parameters and can inform decision-making at all stages in the design process.

In present-day society, sustainability has become a household term and a part of life. Sustainable development is also on the agenda of many corporations. A commonly used definition of sustainable development is "development that meets the needs of the present without compromising the ability of future generations to meet their own needs" (Brundtland, 1987, p. 41). Two key implications arise from this definition. The first is that there are limited resources (e.g. energy resources) and therefore, we must sustain our needs (e.g. consume energy) by using a reduced amount of those resources. The second implication is that the fulfillment of these needs must be able to withstand anticipated but unexpected future contextual changes, such as occurred during the 1970s oil crisis.

To many, buildings are simply part of the immovable landscape; yet, in developed countries, they are responsible for as much as 40% of the total energy consumption (Pérez-Lombard, Ortiz, & Pout, 2008) and approximately 30% of carbon emissions (Ürge-Vorsatz, Danny Harvey, Mirasgedis, & Levine, 2007). While increasing efficiency in other areas such as transportation and power generation are part of the solution, increasing the energy efficiency of buildings represents a cost-effective and proven path to sustainability and contributes to a reduction in overall carbon emission. Thus, strategies to lower the energy consumption of buildings, or to supplement it with renewable energy, help meet energy efficiency and carbon emission targets. Together with an automated scheme, building energy simulation offers a systematic way to increase the energy efficiency of buildings.

1 Building Energy Simulation and Its Application

Many engineering designs can be implemented and tested with prototyping, while they are being refined and simultaneously made into marketable products. Because of the physical size of buildings and the monetary and material resources that they demand, buildings are not amenable to this process of prototyping and testing in multiple rounds. On the other hand, in building energy performance, extensive piecemeal investigations are conducted to study building components or systems, for example, investigations into the construction of the building envelope, the configuration of multiple heating, ventilation and air-conditioning (HVAC) systems, lighting arrangements and photovoltaic (PV) energy generation.

These components and systems do not act individually and can have significant interactions with each other. Once installed, two individual components that offer energy savings of 10% each, even if all other factors remain the same, are unlikely to guarantee a 20% energy saving. Their effects could be contradictory to each other and could even result in a total saving of less than 10%. For example, insulation offers significant energy savings in buildings in cold climates by increasing thermal resistance and thus reducing heat loss through building surfaces. Well-insulated glazing offers the additional benefit of providing solar heat gain to warm the house during the day. A concrete floor next to a window can act as a thermal mass, absorbing solar heat gains and slowly releasing them back to the space at nightfall. This building setup is quite common in high-performance residential buildings. However, if there are high internal heat gains in the building (e.g. an industrial building with energy intensive manufacturing processes), such a configuration will most likely lead to overheating and thus introduce a cooling energy penalty.

The above example illustrates the dynamics among different design considerations. Elements such as insulation value, glazing type and thermal

Table 10.1 An abridged list of common design parameters for building energy simulation

Design parameter	*Common range (units)/types*	*Building designers*
Shape	–	Architects
Dimension	–	Architects
Window-to-wall ratio (WWR)	20–90%	Architects/ engineers
Skylights (% of roof area)	0–20%	Architects/ engineers
Lighting type	Fluorescent, LED	Architects/ engineers
Reflectance (surfaces)	0.2–0.8	Architects/ engineers
Construction type	Steel frame or concrete structure	Architects/ engineers
Insulation (wall and roof)	3.0–8.0 m^2K/W (for cold climates)	Engineers
Insulation (glazing)	0.5–2.5 m^2K/W (for cold climates)	Engineers
Cooling/heating equipment	Chiller, cooling tower, boiler, air source heat pump, ground source heat pump and so on	Engineers
Air distribution system	VAV, CAV, DOAS and so on	Engineers

capacity are often categorized as design parameters. Table 10.1 lists common design parameters with their respective range of values for building energy simulations in typical building designs. Building designers (in many cases, the architects and engineers) qualify and quantify their design in appropriate formats, such as graphical representation or tabulated values, for other stakeholders. The choices of the decision-makers depend on design objectives such as the achievement of specific energy performance goals (e.g. net-zero energy building—NZEB).

Quantities such as internal heat gain and solar radiation are often referred to as environmental variables. Building designers should have knowledge of the approximate range of their potential values but can never be certain of exact values since they are ever-changing and scholastic in nature. Table 10.2 gives some examples of environmental variables.

Table 10.2 An abridged list of common environmental variables for building energy simulation

Environmental variable	*Type*	*Stakeholders*
Building end use	Residential, commercial, industrial, institutional and so on	Developers, building owners
Occupancy patterns	Daily routines, work schedules, retail opening hours and so on	Business operations, occupants
Weather	Weather station dependent (possibly adjusted by local microclimate)	

2 A Typical Building Energy Simulation Process

There is a significant difference in complexity between a residential building and a commercial development, as well as in size between a single-family house and an industrial complex. Most building types can be modeled with building energy simulation tools having more or less the same set of design parameters (as partially listed in Table 10.1) differing only in their values which are subject to the same set of environmental variables. To simplify the discussion, the examples given throughout this chapter involve warehouses, as their occupancy is determined by distinct work shifts, meaning that the space is either occupied or not occupied. In such cases, we can safely ignore the uncertainty in the occupancy pattern, which is a broad topic in itself. In contrast to warehouses, if the building is for retail, one can imagine that unspecified numbers of shoppers will enter and leave. For offices, variations in the 9–5 pattern commonly arise, due to meetings, events and overtime. For residential units, no single family occupies the space in the same way, as each individual has their own style of living.

Most warehouses are large, single-story structures that are spaced some distance apart in suburban industrial areas. They are usually flat in order to accommodate the layout of manufacturing equipment and to facilitate logistics. Unlike high-rise buildings in city centers, which cast a shadow over or block the wind to other buildings, a single-story warehouse on a sparsely populated site does not have an interactive relationship with neighboring buildings in terms of its energy performance. This simplified setting allows the discussion to focus on the applications and limitations of the simulation without going into site-specific details.

The single-story warehouse used in this example is located in the city of Montreal. It has a 4000 m^2 floor area, skylights and is designed to have an internal heat gain (due to workers, logistics and office equipment) of 5 W/m^2. Figure 10.1, a graphical representation of such a warehouse, illustrates some of the modeling concepts in building energy simulations.

While the simulation model reflects the actual construction and operation of the building, certain simplifications and abstractions need be made to reduce the potential uncertainty introduced by model details that are not well supported. For example, while warehouses are normally fitted with an array of loading docks (as indicated in the bottom oval of Fig. 10.1), they are not considered in the current simulation model. This is because the gates are only opened for a limited time when freight trucks are fully backed up against the loading docks. Thus, no significant effect on energy performance arises from this type of gate operation. An uneducated assumption about air leakage does not support a more conservative design but rather makes the results unreliable. Handling this type of uncertainty should rely on site measurement and experimental testing of gate operation devices.

A further abstraction is related to the skylights, which in reality might take the form of domes installed across the whole roof (as indicated in the top oval of Fig. 10.1), but in the model are represented by long strips

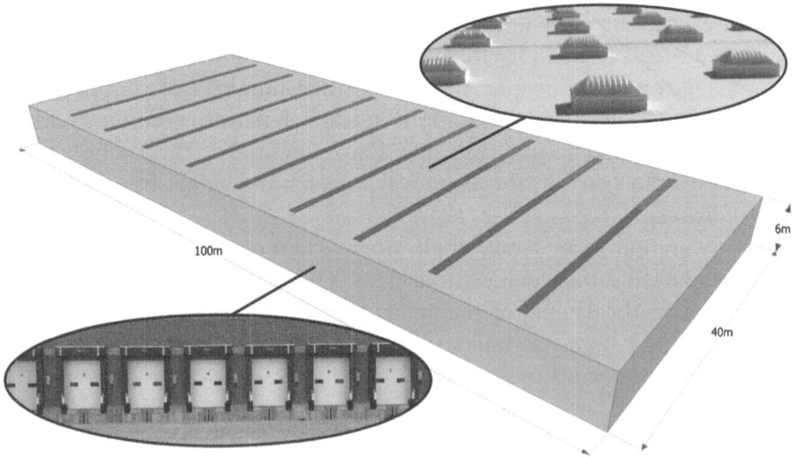

Fig. 10.1 Graphical representation of a building energy simulation model for a typical warehouse with omission of loading docks and abstraction of skylights

(shown on the roof in Fig. 10.1). In a real building, the particular shapes and spatial configurations of the skylights are chosen to introduce an even distribution of natural daylight into the space. However, the long-strip pattern in the building energy simulation model results in the same daylight distribution and does not affect the energy performance. In fact, the sole parameter of interest is the percentage of the roof area fitted with skylights (see Table 10.1).

The simplifications illustrated above imply that some design parameters have a greater influence on energy performance than others. Figure 10.2 presents a tornado chart, which is commonly used to illustrate the sensitivity of design parameters and thus to reduce the size of the variable space by including only the most influential design parameters. In Fig. 10.2, the sensitivities of 11 design parameters are shown for a particular project. If, for each design parameter, there are 3 possible choices (e.g. a thick layer of insulation, a thin one and one specified by the building code), then almost 200,000 (3^{11}) possible design solutions are available, where each solution is a combination of design parameters with values within the suggested ranges of the investigation. With current computational power, such large-scale simulations are possible but are not necessarily effective. In practice, most buildings are designed only according to the require-

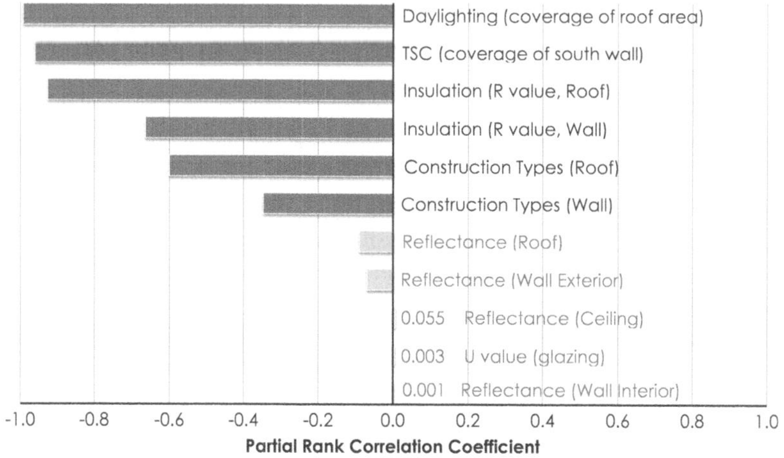

Fig. 10.2 Tornado chart showing the sensitivity (ranking based on partial rank correlation coefficient) of design parameters

ments of the building code, which corresponds to just 1 of the 200,000 possible solutions. However, if comparison between a number of potential solutions is required, the most efficient way to achieve this is to systematically explore only the most influential design parameters, that is, parameters for which a small change in value leads to a large difference in energy consumption. Thus, sensitivity analysis renders the energy performance problem solvable with limited resources (e.g. computational power).

For an extensive exploration of sensitivity analysis, the reader is referred to Saltelli, Chan, and Scott (2000). However, it is important to note that the partial rank correlation coefficient (PRCC) is a more appropriate metric for ranking the sensitivity of parameters that are monotonically but nonlinearly related with energy performance. The previous example of solar heat gain suggests that there is an interdependency between different design parameters when considering their effect on the energy performance of buildings. Having carried out (a) a rank transformation to linearize the relationship between the values of the design parameters and energy performance and (b) the removal of correlation that is due to mutual association among parameters, PRCC offers proper sensitivity ranking for these interdependent parameters. Readers interested in this topic should explore the difference between PRCC and other common metrics, such as the standardized regression coefficient (SRC), which in most cases is being misused for ranking building design parameters. Certain design parameters, such as the WWR can only be appropriately ranked through analysis of variance (ANOVA). Lam, Ge, and Fazio (2016) present this approach in detail.

As mentioned above, the purpose of performing sensitivity analysis in this example is to identify influential design parameters. The absolute values of the coefficients carry no physical meaning and therefore there is no absolute cutoff point to differentiate influential parameters from non-influential ones. However, as may be observed from Fig. 10.2, the coefficients of the top six design parameters are much larger than those of the other design parameters. In fact, it is quite often the case that there is a sharp decline in the numerical value of the coefficient between two adjacent design parameters (when plotted in rank order), which offers a clear means of identification of the influential parameters.

Having identified the six most influential parameters (from Fig. 10.2), Table 10.3 lists their respective ranges of values for investigation. For example, insulation, represented by the thermal resistance (commonly referred to as R_{SI}) is investigated at seven values ranging from 1.5 to

Table 10.3 List of influential design parameters with their ranges of values

Parameter	*Design range*	*Number of levels of investigation*
Insulation (thermal resistance, roof)	1.5–4.5 m^2K/W (3.5)	7
Insulation (thermal resistance, wall)	1.5–4.5 m^2K/W (3.5)	7
Construction type (roof)	Steel or concrete	2
Construction type (wall)	Steel or concrete	2
Daylighting (% of roof area)	0–15% (5%)	4
Transpired solar collector (% of south wall)	0–100% (0%)	6

4.5 m^2K/W (increasing in increments of 0.5 m^2K/W). The ranges listed in Table 10.3 are typical of values used in construction depending on the types of projects. The values in brackets are either the values stipulated by the building code for Montreal's climate or the default values used when, for a given specification of the simulation, the parameter in question is held constant.

Based on these design parameters and their corresponding resolutions, approximately 4000 (4704) possible design solutions exist. Figure 10.3 presents the energy performance result of one of those design solutions. Monthly energy consumption data are presented according to their end-uses (i.e. lighting, heating and cooling), thereby indicating how the energy is consumed. In this example, a significant amount of energy is consumed consistently for all 12 months on lighting, which could potentially be reduced through the selection of a more efficient lamp type. While cooling is only needed during the summer months, heating is needed for almost every month. Even during the shoulder season months such as May and October, a small amount of heating is needed, most likely for a limited number of hours at night. These kinds of heating and cooling profiles help building designers select an efficient system that can achieve specific energy performance goals. Careful inspection of the hourly data for each of the "zones" (spaces within the building that have particular heating and cooling needs) may reveal that the optimum heat-pump system is one consisting of multiple tanks, since during the summer months the energy extracted from the spaces that need cooling could fulfill the heating needs of other areas of the building. If high heating needs arise during the winter months, the application of passive solar technologies that harness the free

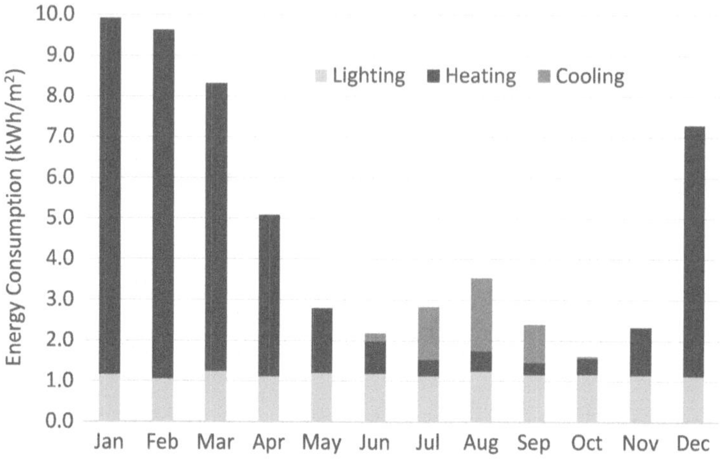

Fig. 10.3 Predicted energy consumption according to energy end-uses (lighting, heating and cooling)

energy from the sun might be suitable. The exact energy saving potential due to such measures can then be evaluated by incorporating the new design features into the simulation model. Whole-system improvements could be made through successive and iterative simulation runs or by implementing a parametric study with different design options (e.g. the 4704 possible design solutions suggested in Table 10.3) through an automated process.

Figure 10.3 shows energy consumption on a monthly basis. In reality, simulation results are commonly reported for each hour or sometimes for even shorter intervals. Hourly reporting is particularly useful for locations or buildings where feed-in tariffs (FIT) or differential energy pricing is available. As an incentive to promote the integration of renewable energy technologies, some regions offer FIT, meaning that payments are made to customers who generate their own energy. Differential energy pricing (tiered time-of-use pricing) is also used as a means of encouraging or discouraging the use of electricity at certain points in time. As one of the green building rating systems, LEED v4 (Leadership in Energy and Environmental Design; USGBC, 2013) certification gives credit for energy cost savings rather than energy savings. Hourly performance data illustrating the energy cost savings potential of certain technologies that can take advantage of differential energy pricing schemes are therefore important. In fact, whole-building energy simulation is a requirement in order to achieve maximum points under the LEED Energy and Atmosphere (EA) credit category "Optimize Energy Performance", for example, 18 points by demonstrating 50% energy cost savings for a new construction as compared to the baseline building. An additional two points can be obtained under the "Demand Response" category by designing the building and equipment such that they shed or shift the load at times when the grid is at peak demand. For example, many jurisdictions offer reduced electricity rates at night, meaning that it could be advantageous to generate ice at night and cool the building during the day with chilled water from the stored ice.

3 Objectively Achieving Sustainable Building Design Goals in Energy

Today's society values sustainable, high-performance buildings and expects developers to move toward sustainable practices. Simply put, a high-performance building is one that reflects state-of-the-art energy performance, cost-effectiveness and reduced environmental impact. These values do not imply a reduction in the quality of the building or the comfort of its occupants to meet energy goals. Instead, such a building aims to maximize the usability of its floor space, as well as the productivity and comfort of its occupants, while minimizing its energy consumption and environmental footprint.

Several design standards and guidelines have been proposed to define and shape sustainable building designs. Though achieving low energy is the common goal, the different philosophies behind the standards and guidelines have driven the designs in different directions. These design philosophies are briefly presented here for the purposes of illustrating how they impact the energy design of buildings and the simulation approaches that lead to these designs.

The Passivhaus standard (PHI, 2015) sets ambitious criteria with regard to lowering the energy demand of buildings. While in common parlance, the terms "energy demand" and "energy consumption" are used interchangeably, they represent quite different concepts. The heating and cooling energy demand of a building is the energy added to the space (for heating) and removed from the space (for cooling). The energy consumption for heating and cooling, on the other hand, is the energy that must be spent in order to achieve such heating and cooling effects. In other words, the energy demand is independent of the method of heating or cooling the building, while the energy consumption considers the efficiency of the heating and cooling equipment. The current Passivhaus standard specifies a very low annual energy demand of 15 kWh/m^2 for either heating or sensible cooling. In general, this low energy demand can be achieved through thick insulation, high airtightness and other passive means such as properly timed solar heat gain. For locations at higher latitudes, an awning can be used to block the summer sun while still allowing the winter solar gain from the sun at a lower angle. Thermal mass is also commonly deployed to control the absorption and release of heat at appropriate times. Building energy simulation can be used to evaluate these different options (e.g. location and depth of awnings), optimize the design and fulfill the stringent criteria of Passivhaus.

An NZEB might come with many of the same energy saving measures as a Passivhaus but must generate an amount of energy equal to what it consumes and must do so via renewable means. Whether that energy balance is recorded on-site or off-site and whether it is conducted hourly, annually or on some other timescale depends on the NZEB definition (NIBS, 2015; NREL, 2006). However, in theory, an NZEB does not need to have a low energy demand. It simply needs to produce as much energy as it consumes and therefore, the focus can shift to achieving efficient heating and cooling equipment, sophisticated control schemes and sufficiently large renewable energy-generation capacity. An example of a strategy that could be used in this case is that mentioned above for large buildings that have simultaneous heating and cooling needs: heat removed from one area for cooling could be used to heat another area that requires heating. Such a design feature is often not considered for buildings that meet the Passivhaus standard, as their focus is on passive measures (e.g. insulation).

Referring to Fig. 10.3, high heating energy consumption during the winter months might suggest that there is a lack of insulation. Designing the building to be airtight with thick insulation might drastically reduce this source of consumption, but at the same time will increase (albeit most likely to a lesser degree) the cooling energy consumption in certain areas of the building. An integrated design approach that considers both passive measures (e.g. insulation, airtightness, solar heat gain) and active measures (e.g. redistribution of heating and cooling, conversion of energy sources) truly exploits the full energy savings potential of a building. A building's energy savings potential is unique depending on its architectural features and forms and other site-specific characteristics.

Carbon-neutral buildings represent yet another design goal. Instead of accounting for energy savings and generation in terms of the amount of energy or its cost, carbon-neutral buildings consider the carbon footprint of the energy sources and possibly also the embodied carbon of the building materials, depending on the definition of carbon neutrality in use. Figure 10.4 demonstrates how deploying a multi-objective optimization by means of building energy simulation can help achieve carbon neutrality.

As demonstrated in the previous section, an investigation of six design parameters with reasonably detailed resolutions could result in several thousand design solutions. An integrated platform is used to automate the simulation process in which combinations of design parameters at defined resolutions are generated, energy performance is evaluated through the simulation tool of choice and performance results are analyzed and presented. Figure 10.4 plots every design solution (based on the design parameters presented in Table 10.3 and additional design parameters for energy generation) that was produced for our example. Each light gray diamond presents a unique design solution, which is represented by the

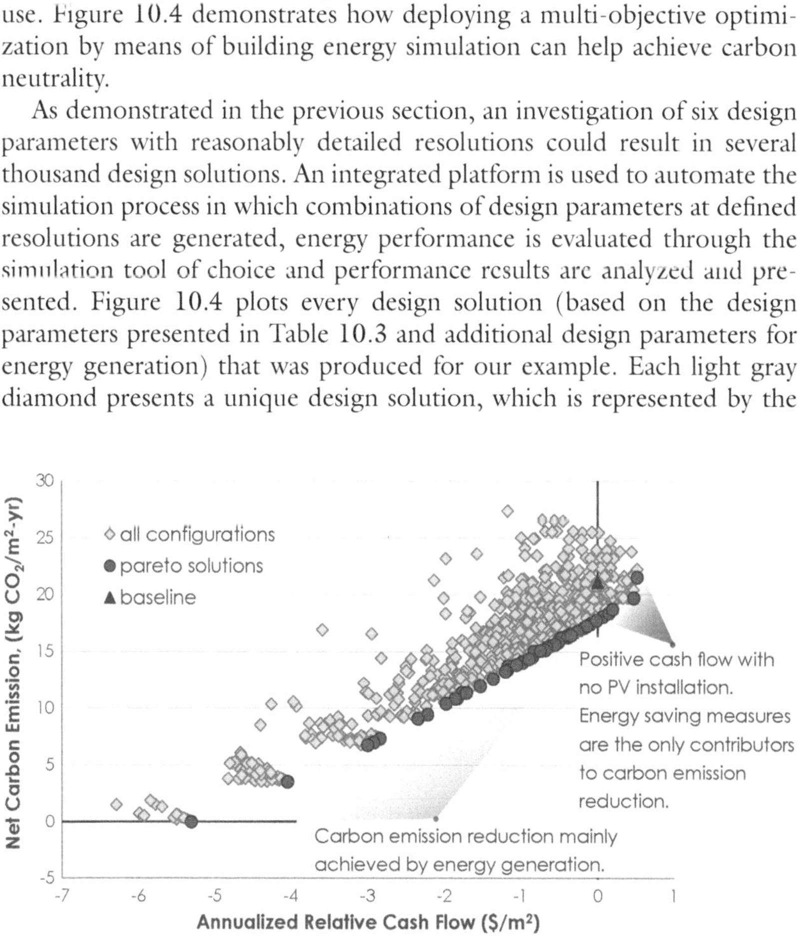

Fig. 10.4 Design solutions from building energy simulations categorized into two groups—with and without photovoltaic (PV) installations

corresponding values of net carbon emission and annualized relative cash flow. The dark gray circles represent the optimized design solutions, also known as Pareto solutions, which cannot be improved in one performance aspect without worsening another. In this example, there can be no lower net carbon emission solution without reducing the annualized relative cash flow. Selection among the solutions involves a trade-off between the desired environmental impact (in terms of carbon emissions) and the desired cash flow. The dark gray triangle represents the default solution, yielded by adhering to minimum building code requirements. Thus, the relative cash flow is zero, since this solution is a baseline configuration with which the other solutions are compared.

The design solutions are categorized into two groups. One group of solutions does not include PV installations. Thus, carbon emission reduction is purely a result of energy saving measures. The positive annualized relative cash flow in these solutions suggests that the corresponding design options are cost-effective, in the sense that the energy cost savings offer a positive return over the investment. The second group includes PV energy generation. While PV installations offer significant carbon emission reductions and even enable design solutions to achieve carbon neutrality, a high-capacity installation incurs a large cash flow penalty. When the information in Fig. 10.4 is combined with energy performance predictions, decision-makers can base their decisions on objective evaluations and select solutions that simultaneously satisfy both their desired performance level and their carbon emission goals.

4 Resilient Buildings in a World of Uncertainty

As illustrated in previous sections, building energy simulation can offer an effective means of evaluating the feasibility of different design options. However, previous studies have suggested that the actual performance of buildings in operation might not correspond to their predicted (simulated) performance. Goldman, Osborn, Hopper, and Singer (2002) showed that 30% of the buildings that were studied consumed 15% more energy than had been predicted and this percentage increased with high-performance buildings (Scofield, 2013). One reason for such a discrepancy in performance is that many assumptions and parameters made in a deterministic simulation are, in reality, stochastic in nature and end up affecting the entire design and simulation model (Brohus, Frier, Heiselberg, & Haghighat, 2012; Sun, Kensek, Noble, & Schiler, 2016). Furthermore, building energy simulation models are effectively an abstraction of reality (i.e. an oversimplification), meaning that important parameters or details might be omitted.

Uncertainty reflects the inability of the model to accurately describe the system's "true" characteristics. The solutions identified through building energy simulation depend largely on the assumed design conditions, which more often than not are subject to uncertainty. By contrast, the current design practices are fundamentally deterministic. For example, in building energy simulations, the temperature setpoints of different units of a residential building are, at best, set on a single schedule (very much like a programmable thermostat), while at worst they are set at a fixed value regardless of the time of year or the function of the space. However, in reality, different units are likely to have different combinations of setpoints not only across seasons but also on different days (e.g. weekdays, weekends, holidays). Furthermore, the settings are likely to be tailored to different spaces (e.g. bedrooms vs. living rooms). In addition to the fact that these nuances are often not included in the simulation (oversimplification), there may be stochastic changes in the temperature settings over time, for example, due to occupants' preferences. The incorporation of statistical data on people's preferences with regard to temperature settings could reduce this source of inaccuracy.

The temperature setpoint is just one of the many assumptions in a simulation model. The number of hours people stay home, the period of time for which the windows are open and the duration and frequency of cooking activities represent just a small subset of the many assumptions that may need to be made in a model, each of which can have a multitude of effects. For example, cooking activities induce energy consumption (which is determined by the efficiency of the various appliances) and have energy cost implications that may be more severe in areas where there is differential energy pricing (i.e. depending on the time of day). The accompanying kitchen exhaust has the potential to greatly increase heating for homes in cold climates. The use of a fan partly mitigates this process and heat recovery from kitchen exhaust is usually not an option since the exhaust is too oily and flavorful (note that the fan itself does not consume much energy). On the other hand, depending on the season, the heat and moisture added to the space through cooking activities can be problematic. Thermal comfort is an issue and if the moisture is not properly treated, it has the potential to cause damage to the building in the form of mold growth (a health issue) and deterioration (a structural issue).

Under current practices, the only aspect in the above discussion that is considered in an energy simulation model is the energy consumption of the appliances. All other direct and indirect consequences of cooking activities are either ignored or improperly modeled, not to mention the aforementioned stochastic nature of these activities. For example, suppose that a kilogram of moisture is added to the space due to a specific amount of electric heat. The moisture increase might be spread across ten hours through slow cooking, dispensed within an hour with a streamer, or any other scenario in between. Each of these processes would impose different kinds of stress on the space and ideally, the simulation model would need to be adapted to handle these diverse possibilities. Due to the large number and variety of potential scenarios, this would be easiest to achieve using stochastic modeling. Later in the chapter we discuss two major sources of stochastic uncertainty—economic and meteorological input parameters—and investigate their effects on energy cost and energy performance, respectively.

An important goal of sustainable real estate is to design buildings to be "resilient". This term refers to buildings that perform in accordance with their intended design under varying conditions. Measures for achieving building resilience can be categorized into three subgroups: robustness, adaptivity and flexibility (Bhamra, Dani, & Burnard, 2011).

A *robust* design can weather a wide range of uncertainties, while still maintaining the intended performance. The above example describing the diverse ways of dispensing a given amount of moisture into a space represents the kinds of uncertainties that may exist in real-world living. A robust building design process takes into account these potential uncertainties. In contrast, an *adaptive* design allows the building to return to its intended performance levels when there is a change in operating conditions that negatively affects performance. In many cases, those changes are the result of a disaster or extreme weather scenarios. Finally, a *flexible* design allows for future design changes that still maintain the original performance levels of the building. In these designs, there is the threat of a permanent reduction in performance level (as opposed to a temporary aberration) that can be averted by a design change (retrofitting). In the remainder of this chapter, the examples of using building energy simulation to increase resilience will be taken from the first category—robustness.

Risk analysis is the name given to the process of quantifying the expected difference in performance of a building between the design/simulation phase and real-world implementation. Minimizing design risk plays an important role in maintaining the performance of buildings in an ever-changing world. However, there is no consistent definition of risk. In this chapter, risk is defined as the product of the magnitudes of the possible adverse consequences and the likelihood of occurrence of each of the consequences (DHA, 1992; Melching & Pilon, 2006; Stamatelatos, 2000; Wreathall & Nemeth, 2004). In mathematical terms, it is the product of the consequence of the failure (e.g. loss in revenue) and the probability of failure. Presuming the parameter of interest is revenue; the corresponding risk carries the same unit for revenue.

5 Evaluating Design Risk to Achieve Resilient Building Design: An Economics-Based Example

The stochastic nature of input assumptions and their impact on performance are illustrated in this economics-based example. Calculations of cash flow and energy cost saving involve input assumptions about interest rates (due to the financing of the development project) and energy prices. Figures 10.5, 10.6 and 10.7 present historical probability distributions of the discount rate (an interest rate used in cash flow calculations), electricity prices and gas prices for the past ten years.

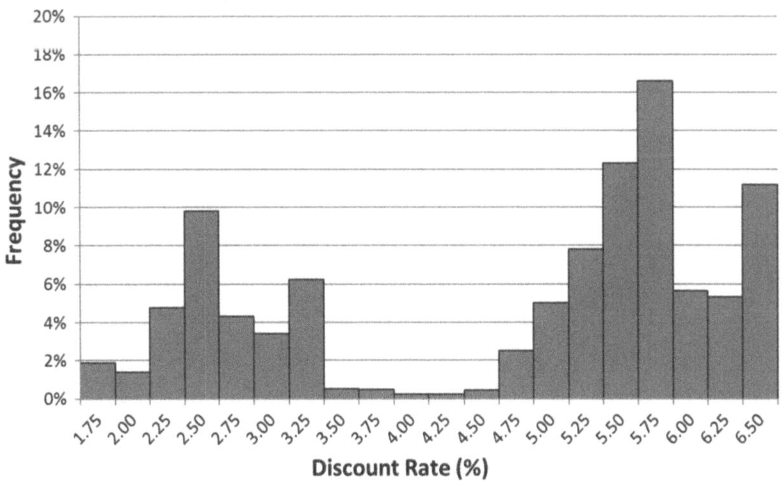

Fig. 10.5 Discount rate probability distribution over the past ten years

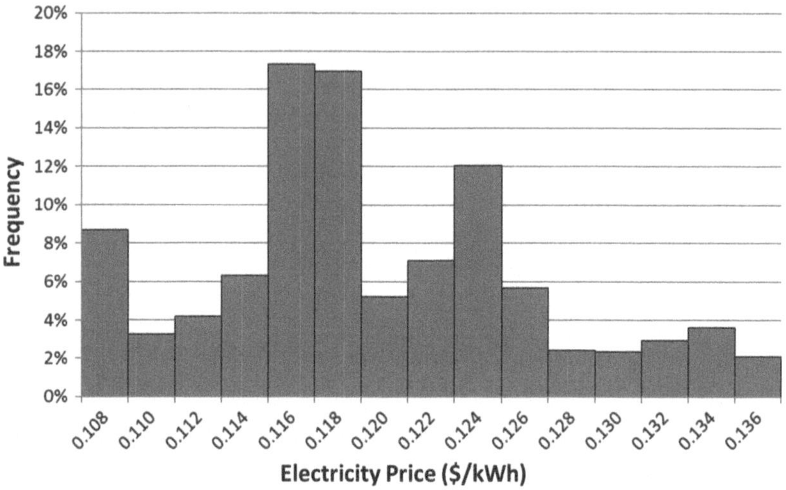

Fig. 10.6 Electricity price probability distribution over the past ten years

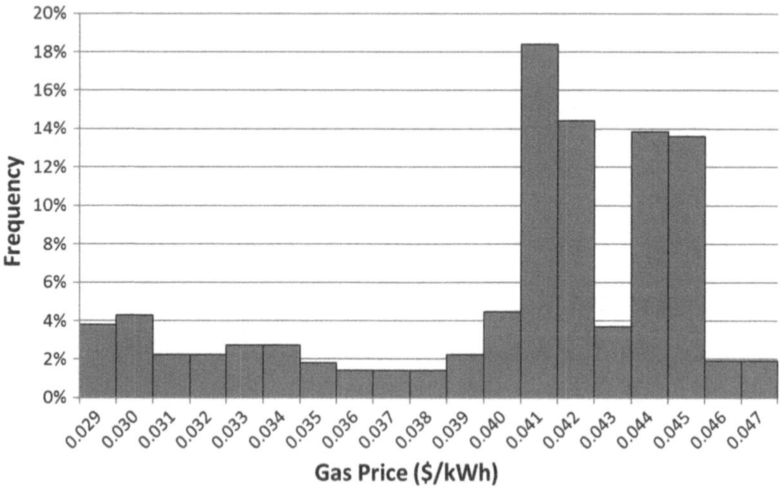

Fig. 10.7 Gas price probability distribution over the past ten years

Figure 10.5 indicates that it is more likely for the discount rate to be higher (as opposed to lower) than 4.75%. In a long-term view, the higher the discount rate, the greater the financial cost and thus the lower the investment return. From a design perspective, a design that offers the same level of performance but involves a lower investment cost is less likely to be affected by the uncertainty in discount rate. Viewed differently, for two designs with the same annualized return, the design with lower investment cost is subject to greater energy operating expenses, in which case the uncertainty in utility prices becomes important. When considering uncertainty in any of these input parameters, the likelihood of the occurrence of the uncertainty values should be considered.

To evaluate the impact of uncertainty in the input parameters, building designers often study the "worst-case scenario". In most business events, such as investing in a piece of machinery or operating a production line, the highest interest rate for the investment combined with the highest energy cost for the operation comprises the "worst-case scenario". Therefore, intuitively and understandably, historically high rates (a combination of high discount rates, high electricity prices and high gas prices) might be identified as a "worst-case scenario". However, this would be mistaken. Table 10.4 presents a comparison between two different design solutions with their respective annualized relative cash flows under two different scenarios: one with ten-year high rates and one with ten-year low rates.

Table 10.4 A comparison between two different design solutions under two different scenarios: high and low interest and energy cost rates

Parameter	*Design solution 1*	*Design solution 2*
Insulation (thermal resistance, roof, m^2K/W)	1.5	3.5
Insulation (thermal resistance, wall, m^2K/W)	3.5	3.5
Construction type (roof)	Concrete	Steel
Construction type (wall)	Concrete	Steel
Daylighting (% of roof area)	0	15
Transpired solar collector (% of south wall)	0	100
	Outcome (annualized relative cash flow, $/m²)	
Ten-year high-rate scenario	0.25	(0.73)
Ten -year low-rate scenario	0.09	0.35

For design solution 1, the high-rate scenario yields a better relative cash flow. For design solution 2, the high-rate scenario yields a much poorer relative cash flow (negative return). The relationship between the economic performance of the design solutions and the economic input parameters is not straightforward. That is, higher rates do not necessarily reduce economic performance and there is no clear "worst-case scenario". Therefore, it is not possible to evaluate the impact of uncertainty in the input parameters using a deterministic approach (e.g. with one set of assumed "worst-case" scenario inputs). Furthermore, some design solutions are more susceptible to uncertainties than others, meaning that they show much wider variation in the predicted performance.

The data in Table 10.4 illustrate that there is no simple, objective means of predicting whether a particular combination of input parameters is likely to represent the "worst-case scenario". Therefore, the decision as to whether to apply the highest historical rates, the average historical rates or some other values is a matter of subjective judgment or personal preference. However, there is an alternative approach. Provided that the input parameters are independent from one another, a Monte Carlo simulation can be used to estimate the likely impact of uncertainties. This procedure involves randomly selecting values for the input parameters according to the probabilistic distributions of occurrence and feeding different combinations of these values into the simulation model to evaluate the outcomes. Since input parameters are assumed to be independent, extreme combinations of input parameters are possible, for example, a very high discount rate with a very low electricity price. A large number of random combinations ensure that values are adequately sampled. In this economic performance study, 1000 different outcomes (annualized relative cash flow values) were obtained, each corresponding to a different economic scenario (combination of the economic input parameters). Figure 10.8 presents the probability distribution of the annualized relative cash flow for design solution X in Table 10.4 (i.e. the input parameters in the first six rows).

Figure 10.8 reflects the distribution of economic performance outcomes that might occur. However, in practice, it may be useful to cite a single value for the predicted performance, which is often based on a reference scenario. The reference scenario could be the ten-year average rates or some other set of rate values that the decision-makers (e.g. development investors) deem to be appropriate. From an investment perspective, the decision-makers can treat the predicted relative cash flow for this reference scenario as the expected outcome.

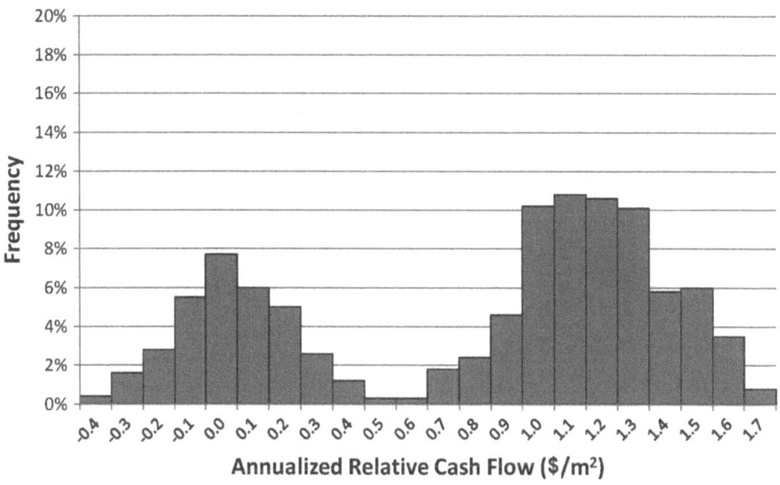

Fig. 10.8 Probability distribution of annualized relative cash flow for a single design solution

The adverse consequence of a risk, in economic performance terms, is the potential shortfall from the predicted performance. That is, the decision-makers would be satisfied with any outcome equal to or better than the predicted performance, while any shortfall would be regarded as an adverse consequence. Figure 10.9 depicts a case in which decision-makers opt for the ten-year average rates as a reference scenario. This particular design solution yields an annualized relative cash flow of 0.731 $\$/m^2$. The set of outcomes located to the left of 0.731 $\$/m^2$ in Fig. 10.9 represents the potential shortfall scenarios. The risk is the potential shortfall multiplied by the frequency of occurrence. The risk acts as a performance indicator to objectively quantify the economic impact of uncertainties. Decisions are not only based on the predicted cash flow but also based on the acceptable level of quantified risk.

Table 10.5 presents an example in which risk exposes hidden pitfalls in design solutions and serves as the decisive factor in making informed choices between different design options. It can be observed that even though both design solutions provide almost the same relative cash flow, the risk incurred by design solution 2 is two orders of magnitude greater than that of design solution 1. There could be many factors contributing to an elevated risk for a particular design solution. For example, if there is

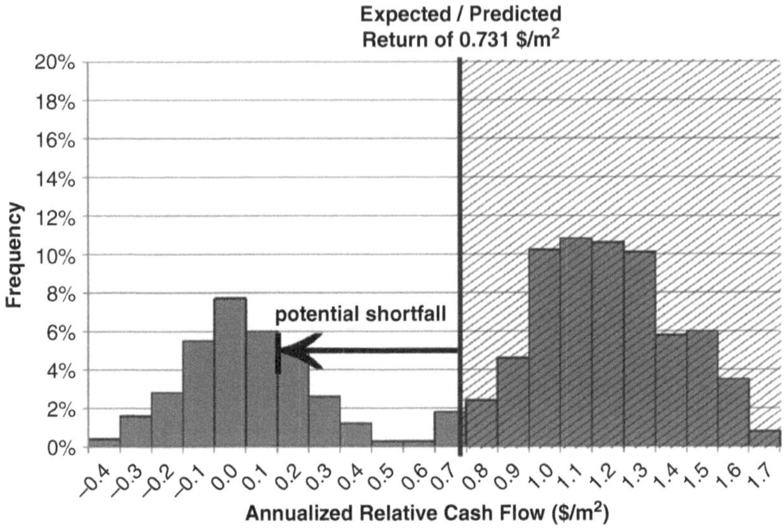

Fig. 10.9 An example depicting the relationship between the expected return, potential shortfalls and risk with respect to the expected return

Table 10.5 A comparison between two different design solutions with very similar economic performances but different levels of risk

Parameter	*Design solution 1*	*Design solution 2*
Insulation (thermal resistance, roof, m^2K/W)	3.0	2.0
Insulation (thermal resistance, wall, m^2K/W)	2.0	2.0
Construction type (roof)	Steel	Concrete
Construction type (wall)	Steel	Concrete
Daylighting (% of roof area)	0	15
Transpired solar collector (% of south wall)	60	20
Predicted annualized relative cash flow ($\$/m^2$)	0.173	0.172
Risk ($\$/m^2$)	(0.002)	(0.152)

large uncertainty in gas prices, then any design solution that relies on gas equipment will incur greater uncertainty and thus higher risk. In addition to emphasizing the added importance of quantified risk information, this example once again illustrates that economic performance evaluation using a deterministic approach does not provide sufficient information to inform design decisions.

6 Evaluating Design Risk to Achieve Resilient Building Design: A Weather-Based Example

In any discussion of weather, it is important to acknowledge the impact of climate change and global warming, which are now household terms and no longer restricted to scientific debate. However, the discussion here focuses on how to conduct building energy simulations so as to take account of the uncertain nature of weather. The goal is to achieve "resilient" designs that maintain the desired energy performance of buildings despite uncertainties in the weather.

The Resilient Design Institute (2017) defines resilient design as "*the intentional design of buildings, landscapes, communities, and regions in order to respond to natural and manmade disasters and disturbances—as well as long-term changes resulting from climate change—including sea level rise, increased frequency of heat waves, and regional drought*". Unexpected changes in the weather, particularly those due to climate change and global warming, can have a significant impact on the energy performance of buildings due to a variety of mechanisms. One of the most direct effects of a weather-related disaster (such as an ice storm or hurricane) on energy performance is the corresponding power outage. Note that the discussion here is limited to energy performance; thus it excludes other types of consequence such as the collapse of houses (related to structural performance) or the flooding of communities (related to urban planning and water management).

Figure 10.10 illustrates that in the case of an ice storm, it is not just the power outage that contributes to the degradation of energy performance. The drop in temperature for a significant period of time after the ice storm results in a large increase in the demand for energy to heat buildings (quantified by the metric "heating degree days"). The ice storm in January 1998 was considered one of the largest natural disasters in Canada's history causing 35 casualties and considerable material damage. From January 5–9, over 100 mm of precipitation in the form of ice and freezing rain caused extensive power outages affecting over one million people in Quebec. From Fig. 10.10, it can be observed that temperatures dropped significantly for almost a week following the precipitation. This same pattern of low temperatures was observed after a storm of shorter duration on January 23. Such conditions have multiple implications for energy performance and resilient building design. During power outages, the generation of localized renewable energy should help ease the situation, albeit to

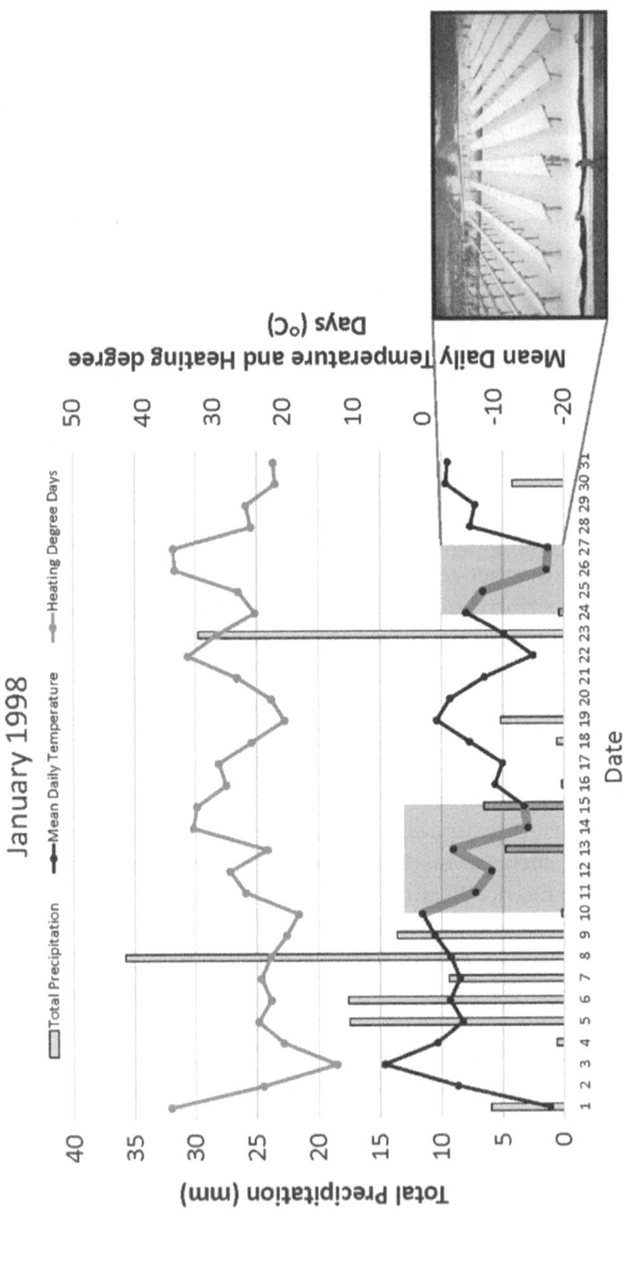

Fig. 10.10 Periods of relatively low temperatures after the Canadian ice storms of January 1998, where power supply from both the electric grid and local generators failed

an extent dependent on the generation capacity of the system. However, in reality, PV systems are fully covered and wind turbines may become locked in ice. Consequently, the situation can only be improved when the temperature increases. As discussed earlier, a building can achieve NZEB status if the energy generated can cover the energy consumed. In this particular example, a potential NZEB design with large energy-generation capacity fails to withstand the ice storm.

The concept of robustness, that is, maintaining the intended performance amidst the ever-changing weather conditions, offers a direction for resilient design. Lechner (2014) explicitly suggested that resilient building strategies should focus on passive survivability instead of active systems (e.g. energy generation or mechanical systems). In fact, the major cause of death during the 1998 ice storm was hypothermia. Without power and with a consistently low outside temperature over a prolonged period of time, many buildings were at sub-zero temperatures. Passive means, such as increased levels of insulation and solar heat gain (an inspection of the weather data reveals that it can be cold but sunny) potentially extend the number of hours for which buildings can maintain survivable temperatures.

With respect to weather, climate change effectively refers to two intricate phenomena, one being a global temperature increase and the other being a more frequent occurrence of unpredictable and extreme weather (Easterling et al., 2000; Meehl et al., 2000; Murphy, Sexton, Barnett, & Jones, 2004). A common misconception about global warming is the belief that there is a uniform increase in temperature regardless of the time of year and location. This misconception results in building energy assessments that account for global warming by adding a fixed number of degrees uniformly for each of the 8760 hours of a year. Such assessments may result in designs with inappropriate recommendations, such as the lowering of insulation values or the increasing of cooling equipment size. There is a substantial body of research into the prediction of future weather based on different climate change scenarios. Readers interested in this topic should refer to the works of Jentsch, James, Bourikas, and Bahaj (2013) and Murphy et al. (2009).

The rest of this section is devoted to the assessment of energy performance under uncertainty in the weather. Building energy simulations, regardless of the specific tools being used, rely on weather files to perform the analysis. The Typical Meteorological Year (TMY) weather file or the Canadian variant—Canadian Weather year for Energy Calculation

(CWEC)—are both commonly used. The TMY weather file is a synthetic file of hourly weather data (including temperature, solar radiation, humidity, and wind speed and direction) based on actual historical weather data recorded over the last 30 years. For each of the 12 months, a statistically representative month from the last 30 years was selected. For example, the TMY file (which covers the period from 1960 to 1989) for Montreal Internal Airport composes of January 1966, October 1986, December 1978. Since the weather files are meant to represent the typical weather, extreme weather conditions were intentionally excluded. The use of TMY weather files presupposes that the resulting predicted energy performance reflects the average performance over an extended period of time. Thus, on an annual basis, the predicted performance will either overestimate or underestimate the actual energy performance.

Figure 10.11 shows the simulated heating, cooling and total energy demand based on actual meteorological year (AMY) weather data of the last 30 years versus CWEC data (Hosseini, Lee, & Vakilinia, 2017) for 2 different roof designs. The building design employs values suggested by the National Energy Code of Canada for Buildings (NRC, 2011) with the exception that roof design 1 has a solar reflectance of 0.9 (cool roof) and a thermal resistance of 2.4 m^2K/W (thinner insulation), while roof design 2 has a solar reflectance of 0.1 (dark roof) and a thermal resistance of 15.4 m^2K/W (thicker insulation).

It can be observed from Fig. 10.11a that over the 30-year period, CWEC generally overestimates the heating demands and the overestimation can be up to 16 kWh/m^2 and 21 kWh/m^2, respectively, for the two roof designs. For the years in which heating demands are underestimated, the predicted heating energy consumption difference amounts to 3 kWh/m^2 and 13 kWh/m^2, respectively. Figure 10.11b indicates that in most years, CWEC also tends to overestimate the cooling energy demand. It is noteworthy that CWEC overestimates both the heating and cooling energy demand to a greater extent for roof design 1 than for roof design 2. As a result, and as can be seen in Fig. 10.11c, CWEC grossly overestimates the total energy demand for almost every year for roof design 1, while reflecting reality more accurately over the long run for roof design 2 (i.e., a more equal mix of overestimation and underestimation).

From the above example, it can be seen that the current practice of performance building energy simulation based on a TMY/CWEC weather file may offer reasonable energy performance predictions for certain building designs (such as roof design 2). However, the predictions for the cool

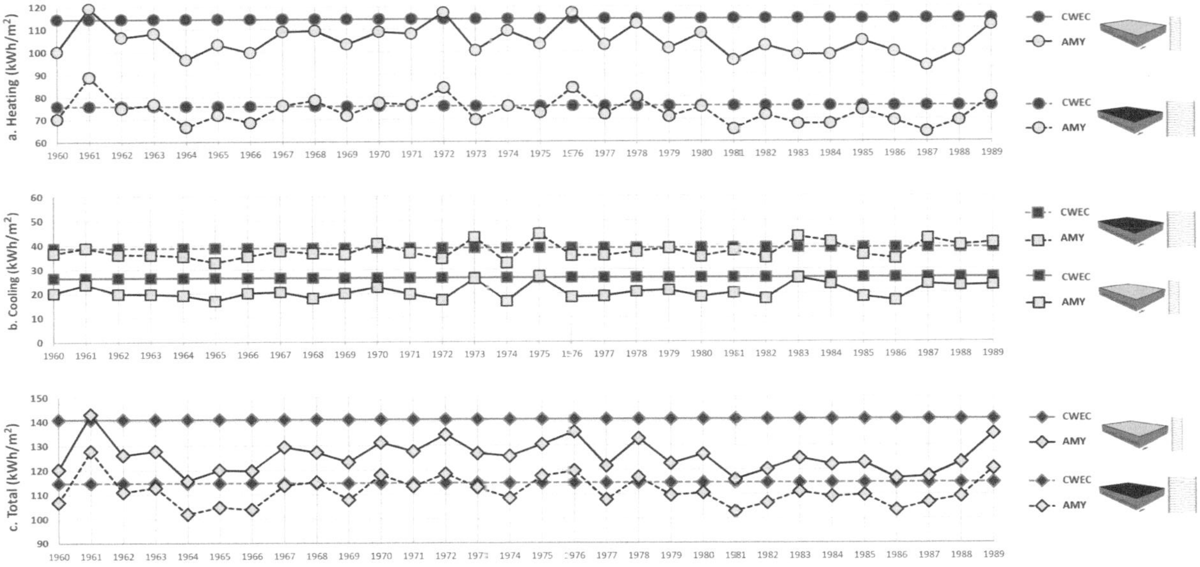

Fig. 10.11 Heating, cooling and total energy demand of the prototypical building based on actual meteorological year (AMY) weather data versus CWEC data for two different roof designs

roof design in this example overestimate both the heating and the cooling energy demand by a large margin. In this particular example, the energy performance predicted through CWEC tends to be more conservative than that achieved in reality. However, if the predicted value were to consistently underestimate the true value, then this shortfall would need to be accounted for. The Monte Carlo simulation approach described in the previous economics-based example could be applied here as well. Instead of a deterministic prediction based on typical weather conditions (such as in the CWEC weather file), a Monte Carlo simulation could reflect the stochastic nature of weather and present the energy prediction as a probability distribution. Any energy performance shortfalls from the expected performance would be considered as design risk; that is, if the design risk is high, there is a high probability that the design will consume more energy than predicted.

Interest rates, energy prices and weather are just some of the major sources of uncertainty in any building design. The above example further supports the notion that the design should be represented both by the predicted performance and by the corresponding risk. Deterministic assumptions, which ignore the stochastic nature of real-case scenarios, will result in a design that either cannot maintain its performance or is not optimal.

7 Resilient and Sustainable Building Design: An Attainable Goal

Building energy simulation offers a means to predict the energy performance of buildings with a model that very closely represents reality rather than using a prototype scaled model. With the deployment of large-scale simulations, building designers can systematically select design solutions that fulfill desired performance requirements. However, a discrepancy always exists between the predicted performance and actual performance through years of operation. This chapter has proposed that the main source of discrepancy results from the fact that input assumptions made during the design phase do not accurately reflect real-case scenarios due to uncertainties in the input parameters, which in most cases, are stochastic in nature in the real world.

Input uncertainties and their potential impacts on energy performance were demonstrated using two examples: the economic climate and the weather. These examples serve to illustrate the concepts of design risk and resilient building design. By incorporating and considering design risk in the performance-based design process, sustainable building designs that maintain performance levels over time are indeed attainable.

References

Attia, S., Hamdy, M., O'Brien, W., & Carlucci, S. (2013). Assessing gaps and needs for integrating building performance optimization tools in net zero energy buildings design. *Energy and Buildings, 60*, 110–124.

Bhamra, R., Dani, S., & Burnard, K. (2011). Resilience: The Concept, a Literature Review and Future Directions. *International Journal of Production Research, 49(18)*, 5375–5393.

Brohus, H., Frier, C., Heiselberg, P., & Haghighat, F. (2012). Quantification of Uncertainty in Predicting Building Energy Consumption: A Stochastic Approach. *Energy and Buildings, 55*, 127–140.

Brundtland, G. H. (1987). *Report of the World Commission on Environment and Development: "Our Common Future."* United Nations.

Clarke, J. A. (2001). *Energy Simulation in Building Design*. London: Routledge.

Crawley, D. B., Lawrie, L. K., Winkelmann, F. C., Buhl, W. F., Huang, Y. J., Pedersen, C. O., ... Glazer, J. (2001). EnergyPlus: Creating a New-generation Building Energy Simulation Program. *Energy and Buildings, 33(4)*, 319–331.

Easterling, D. R., Meehl, G. A., Parmesan, C., Changnon, S. A., Karl, T. R., & Mearns, L. O. (2000). Climate Extremes: Observations, Modeling, and Impacts. *Science, 289(5487)*, 2068–2074.

Echenagucia, T. M., Capozzoli, A., Cascone, Y., & Sassone, M. (2015). The Early Design Stage of a Building Envelope: Multi-objective Search Through Heating, Cooling and Lighting Energy Performance Analysis. *Applied Energy, 154*, 577–591.

Goldman, C. A., Osborn, J. G., Hopper, N. C., & Singer, T. E. (2002). *Market Trends in the US ESCO Industry: Results from the NAESCO Database Project*. Berkeley, CA: *Lawrence Berkeley National Laboratory*.

Henninger, R. H., Witte, M. J., & Crawley, D. B. (2004). Analytical and Comparative Testing of EnergyPlus using IEA HVAC BESTEST E100–E200 Test Suite. *Energy and Buildings, 36(8)*, 855–863.

Hosseini, M., Lee, B., & Vakilinia, S. (2017). Energy Performance of Cool Roofs Under the Impact of Actual Weather Data. *Energy and Buildings, 145*, 284–292.

Jentsch, M. F., James, P. A., Bourikas, L., & Bahaj, A. S. (2013). Transforming Existing Weather Data for Worldwide Locations to Enable Energy and Building Performance Simulation Under Future Climates. *Renewable Energy, 55*, 514–524.

Judkoff, R., & Neymark, J. (1995). *International Energy Agency building energy simulation test (BESTEST) and diagnostic method (No. NREL/TP--472-6231).* Golden, CO: National Renewable Energy Laboratory.

Lam, T. C., Ge, H., & Fazio, P. (2016). Energy Positive Curtain Wall Configurations for a Cold Climate Using the Analysis of Variance (ANOVA) Approach. *Building Simulation, 9*(*3*), 297–310.

Lechner, N. (2014). Heating, Cooling, Lighting: Sustainable Design Methods for Architects. Hoboken, NJ: *John Wiley & Sons.*

Meehl, G. A., Zwiers, F., Evans, J., Knutson, T., Mearns, L., & Whetton, P. (2000). Trends in Extreme Weather and Climate Events: Issues Related to Modeling Extremes in Projections of Future Climate Change. *Bulletin of the American Meteorological Society, 81*(*3*), 427–436.

Melching, C. S., & Pilon, P. J. (2006). Comprehensive Risk Assessment for Natural Hazards. *World Meteorological Organization, WMO/TD, 955.*

Murphy, J. M., Sexton, D. M., Barnett, D. N., & Jones, G. S. (2004). Quantification of Modelling Uncertainties in a Large Ensemble of Climate Change Simulations. *Nature, 430*(*7001*), 768.

Murphy, J. M., Sexton, D. M., Jenkins, G. J., Booth, B. B., Brown, C. C., Clark, C. M., … Wood, R. A. (2009). *UK Climate Projections Science Report: Climate Change Projections.* Exeter: Met Office Hadley Centre.

Nembrini, J., Samberger, S., & Labelle, G. (2014). Parametric Scripting for Early Design Performance Simulation. *Energy and Buildings, 68*, 786–798.

Neymark, J., & Judkoff, R. (2004). International Energy Agency Building Energy Simulation Test and Diagnostic Method for Heating, Ventilating, and Air-Conditioning Equipment Models (HVAC BESTEST): Volume 2: Cases E300-E545 (No. NREL/TP-550-36754). *National Renewable Energy Laboratory, Golden, USA.*

NIBS. (2015). *A Common Definition for Zero Energy Buildings.* Washington, DC: National Institute of Building Sciences.

NRC. (2011). *National Energy Code of Canada for Buildings.* Ottawa, Canada: National Research Council of Canada.

NREL. (2006). *Zero Energy Buildings: A Critical Look at the Definition.* Golden, CO: National Renewable Energy Laboratory.

Pérez-Lombard, L., Ortiz, J., & Pout, C. (2008). A Review on Buildings Energy Consumption Information. *Energy and Buildings, 40*(3), 394–398.

PHI. (2015). *Criteria for the Passive House, EnerPHit and PHI Low Energy Building Standard.* Darmstadt: Passive House Institute.

Resilient Design Institute. (2017). Defining Resilient Design [Online]. Retrieved July 25, 2017, from http://www.resilientdesign.org/what-is-resilient-design/

Saltelli, A., Chan, K., & Scott, E. M. (Eds.). (2000). *Sensitivity Analysis* (Vol. 1). *New York: Wiley.*

Samuelson, H., Claussnitzer, S., Goyal, A., Chen, Y., & Romo-Castillo, A. (2016). Parametric Energy Simulation in Early Design: High-rise Residential Buildings in Urban Contexts. *Building and Environment, 101*, 19–31.

Scofield, J. H. (2013). Efficacy of LEED-Certification in Reducing Energy Consumption and Greenhouse Gas Emission for Large New York City Office Buildings. *Energy and Buildings, 67*, 517–524.

Stamatelatos, M. (2000). Probabilistic Risk Assessment: What Is It and Why Is It Worth Performing It? *NASA Office of Safety and Mission Assurance, 4*(05), 00.

Sun, S., Kensek, K., Noble, D., & Schiler, M. (2016). A Method of Probabilistic Risk Assessment for Energy Performance and Cost Using Building Energy Simulation. *Energy and Buildings, 110*, 1–12.

UN DHA. (1992). Internationally Agreed Glossary of Basic Terms Related to Disaster Management. *UN DHA (United Nations Department of Humanitarian Affairs), Geneva.*

Ürge-Vorsatz, D., Danny Harvey, L. D., Mirasgedis, S., & Levine, M. D. (2007). Mitigating CO2 Emissions from Energy Use in the World's Buildings. *Building Research & Information, 35*(4), 379–398.

USGBC. (2013). *LEED Reference Guide for Building Design and Construction, LEED V4.* Washington, DC: U.S. Green Building Council.

Wreathall, J., & Nemeth, C. (2004). Assessing Risk: The Role of Probabilistic Risk Assessment (PRA) in Patient Safety Improvement. *Quality and Safety in Health Care, 13*(3), 206–212.

CHAPTER 11

Driving Investment in High-Performance Commercial Buildings

Molly J. McCabe

1 Driving Investment

In 2007, the US Congress defined high-performance buildings as ones which "integrate and optimize all major high performance attributes, including energy conservation, environment, safety, security, durability, accessibility, cost-benefit, productivity, sustainability, functionality, and operational considerations."[1] In recent years the attributes have organically expanded to include resiliency and incorporate the experience of building occupants. While there are numerous mechanisms (policy, rating systems, codes, standards, and design guidelines) to define high performance, as shown in Fig. 11.1 from Legrand's June 1, 2016, white paper on High-Performance

[1] https://www.nibs.org/?page=hpbc.

(Adapted from "High-Performance Buildings—Value, Messaging, Financial, and Policy Mechanism" by MJ McCabe, for the US Department of Energy and the Pacific Northwest National Laboratory, February 2011, PNNL-20176 http://www.pnl.gov/main/publications/external/technical_reports/PNNL-20176.pdf)

M. J. McCabe (✉)
HaydenTanner, LLC, Bigfork, MT, USA
e-mail: mmccabe@haydentanner.com

T. Walker et al. (eds.), *Sustainable Real Estate*, Palgrave Studies in Sustainable Business In Association with Future Earth,
https://doi.org/10.1007/978-3-319-94565-1_11

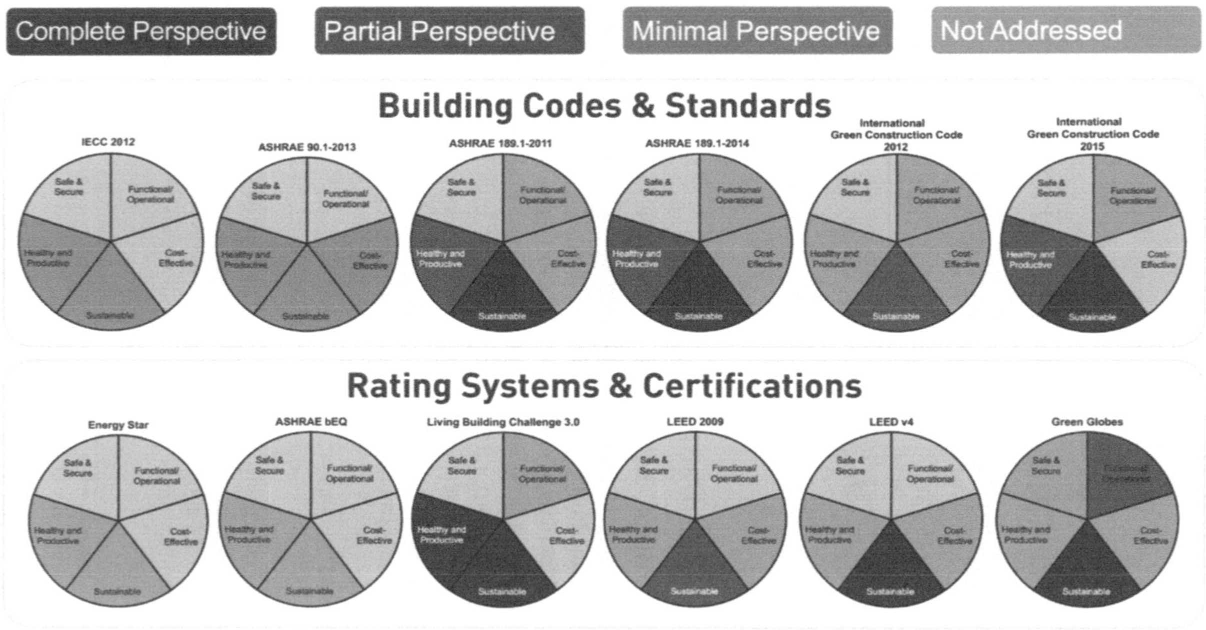

Fig. 11.1 The High Performance Building (HPB) landscape: How comprehensively do performance mechanisms address the full scope of HPB attributes? (Based on Legrand's June 1, 2016, white paper on High-Performance Buildings. In particular, Legrand assessed the degree to which each mechanism addresses these attributes: (1) sustainable, (2) healthy and productive, (3) safe and secure, (4) functional/operational, and (5) cost-effective.)

Buildings,[2] no one encompasses the full range of variables, and there is no definitive determination as to when a building has passed the threshold into "high performance." That said, mechanisms such as Leadership in Energy and Environmental Design (LEED) v4, The Living Building Challenge, The WELL Standard, EnergyStar, code changes, and energy disclosures provide benchmarks and a clear roadmap for property owners and investors. In the context of this chapter, high performance is defined as the optimization and integration of building systems (e.g., energy and water efficiency), leveraging technology and human behavior and the buildings' ability to enhance the well-being of its occupants.

In an environment where concepts such as *green*, *sustainable*, and *high performance* seem to be in the forefront, many property owners and investors have not jumped on the bandwagon. We continue to face challenges in financing such projects. Despite the available technology and the sheer amount of information on hand, actual investment in high-performance building, particularly in the US, continues to lag expectations. Why?

Despite many studies to the contrary, for many, the perceived market risks of deep energy and water efficiency and other high-performance features outweigh any potential benefits.[3] Many in the commercial building sector continue to believe that there is a significant cost premium associated with the design and construction of high-performance buildings, deep efficiency is difficult to attain, retrofits are disruptive to occupants, and cost premiums are not recovered when the buildings are sold or leased.

How do we change this perspective and get a wide array of building owners, investors, and lenders, not only engaged but excited about high-performing buildings and motivated to modify investment strategies, deploy capital, and upgrade operations and maintenance (O&M) to achieve significant resource efficiency? The short answer—it's got to make economic sense and be readily financeable. We must quantify the outcomes, both environmental and economic, and demonstrate high-performance elements are a sound investment opportunity.

This chapter is centered on the financial impact to the property and/or portfolio, specifically risk and return. The allocation of capital and financing remain critical components in deploying the necessary technology and are significant impediments to seeing substantial investment in

[2] http://go.legrand.us/hpb-whitepaper

[3] Updated and adapted from the US Department of Energy (DOE) Building Technologies Program (BTP) *Commercial Buildings Integration Multi-Year Program Plan FY 2010–2015 Opportunities and Gaps*, excerpt on Financing.

high-performance attributes. Hurdles can be pivotal and include a lack of data, first cost, capital versus operating budgets, risk exposure, the low ratio of energy costs to total operating expenses, high transaction costs, discount factor issues, and the inadequacy of traditional financing underwriting and mechanisms for energy efficiency projects. Further complicating investment decisions are the large number of small- to mid-sized buildings, wide geographic dispersion, and varying regional incentives. While some companies and property owners see the value of energy efficiency and choose to finance projects from their own budgets/accounts, others look at their available capital and make a different choice. The decision to invest is not necessarily tied to the decision to seek outside financing.

High-performing buildings are a hedge against future risks such as competitive obsolescence, energy price volatility, resource availability, and pending regulatory changes.[4] There is an increasing recognition of a link between higher-performing buildings and health of occupants and the corresponding impact on risk/return and value.[5] Ultimately, there is a need to assist property owners, investors, and lenders in evaluating the true risks associated with a given property in concert with the opportunities for return. Overall, high-performing properties save money—money that will increase net operating income and consequently the value of the property.

1.1 Value Analysis

The factors that go into making the decision to invest in a specific sustainable property or high-performance measures are inherently no different than looking at any other property type or capital investment. However, what is different is that the assessment needs to take into account the net impact of all costs and benefits related to the high-performance attributes after synergies and risk mitigation measures are considered. Sustainability-related development or retrofit costs might be higher than conventional properties due to costs related to a number of items, including energy modeling and commissioning. Further, in some markets, lack of an integrated design and construction team along with a limited availability of

[4] Energy consumption benchmarking and disclosure mandates exist in 24 cities across North America, 2 states, and 1 province, covering approximately 10.7 billion, s.f. (*www.buildingrating.org*). All enacted since 2008.

[5] Associations of Cognitive Function Scores with Carbon Dioxide, Ventilation, and Volatile Organic Compound Exposures in Office Workers: A Controlled Exposure Study of Green and Conventional Office Environments https://ehp.niehs.nih.gov/wp-content/uploads/124/6/ehp.1510037.alt.pdf

products and materials can increase costs. New modes of operation require a learning curve to get everyone from the contractor through the maintenance team up to speed. These costs can be offset through integrated operational systems as well as utility and governmental rebates and incentives.

Looking at the long-term operational aspects of the property means evaluating the resource use and potential cost reductions resulting from the efficiency measures. Putting the inherent challenges of accurate energy modeling aside, energy forecasts can be difficult—energy price volatility, changing weather, use type, and occupancy factors all impact the quality of the estimate and say nothing about the ongoing durability of the savings. Rigorous monitoring and verification along with robust commissioning, staff and tenant education and training, and an alignment of performance measurements can mitigate this risk.

The financial performance of a property is determined by a number of inputs including rent, occupancy, tenant renewals, operating costs, insurance, and a market estimation of the risk of the property investment (discount rate). The relative impact of each of these factors is critical to the overall analysis. For example, rent and revenue-related components would have a more significant impact than operating expenses. However, high-performance attributes that reduce operating expenses have a twofold impact. First, even small reductions in energy, water, and maintenance costs add up and increase net operating income. Second, persistent reductions in those same expenses reduce the operating risk of the property and can have a large impact on the discount rate and resulting value. Further, this limited look does not take into consideration the potential market value of future proofing against regulatory changes or increased marketability due to sustainable attributes.

A reasonable reduction in energy use and accordingly, operating expenses can be much easier to achieve than increased rents and still have a substantive impact on value. One way to analyze the impact is to use a discounted cash flow (DCF) model over a ten-year horizon. (The DCF is the most likely analysis tool for commercial property investors.) By using a DCF, the investor is able to compare, over time, the relative value of the reduced expenses to the annual cash flow and to the ultimate value of the property. Thus a modest reduction in energy efficiency—say 20% or 30%, which can be fairly easily achieved through simple and low-cost improvements—can yield a substantial return equivalent to increases in rent, which may be far more difficult to obtain. A simple proxy for the impact of these efficiencies on the value of the property is to capitalize ("cap") the annual net operating income of a property before and after an efficiency retrofit. Let us look at an example of a 50,000-square-foot office building before and after a retrofit that yields a 30% reduction in energy costs. In this example a reduction in electricity alone results in reduced operating expenses and an increase in Net Operating Income (NOI) (and cash flow) over $21,000. Using a 6% cap rate, this savings increases the value of the building by just over $350,000.

Box 1

Hypothetical Office Building 50,000 s.f.		Base Case	30% reduction in energy cost
Revenues			
	Rent	$1,875,000	$1,875,000
	Less: 10% vacancy	-$187,500	-$187,500
	Effective Gross Revenue	$1,687,500	$1,687,500
Operating Expenses			
	Cleaning/Janitorial	-$49,613	-$49,613
	Maintenance	-$50,794	-$50,794
	Utilities		
	Electricity	-$70,875	-$49,613
	Water & other	-$64,969	-$64,969
	Adminstrative/Insurance	-$106,313	-$106,313
	Real Estate Taxes	-$248,063	-$248,063
	Total Operating Expenses	-$590,625	-$569,363
Net Operating Income		$1,096,875	$1,118,138
Annual Cash Flow Savings			**$21,263**
Value (NOI/cap rate*)		$18,281,250	$18,635,625
Value Difference			**$354,375**

*Assumes capitalization rate of 6%.
A quick way to estimate a property's value is to "cap" (i.e., apply a "cap rate") its net operating income. The capitalization rate ("cap rate") is the percentage number used to determine the current value of a property based on estimated future operating income. Net operating income divided by property value = the cap rate. The higher the cap rate, the greater risk the investor perceives with the property returns.

2 Challenges

Studies, such as those conducted by the World Business Council for Sustainable Development (WBCSD) and McKinsey & Company, show that vast reductions in resource use are possible, even in the face of an increasing absolute number of buildings (Granade et al., 2009; WBCSD, 2009). However, this is clearly not happening on a wide-scale basis. Why are we not deploying that which we know we have the technology to accomplish and that makes sense to deploy? The obstacles to achieving this level of performance and efficiency in the building sector take many forms, many of which derive directly from the investment side of the equation:

- first costs and short-term investment horizons
- inadequate awareness of and interest in efficiency including risks associated with the impact of future regulation and energy prices
- low priority of energy issues as compared to other factors (such as tenancy, rental income, short-term returns on investment, competing capital needs)
- difficulty in "seeing" actual energy usage or its costs in real time
- practical limitations on obtaining a complete picture of energy consumption for the entire building (i.e., lack of sub metering, lack of access to tenant data, "ownership" of energy consumption data)
- cultural inertia driven by standard practices in design, construction, and operation that enable inefficient energy use and equipment applications over the building life
- financial transaction costs that create agency issues, inherent conflicts between stakeholders; for example
  - utility incentives that reward kilowatt-hours used instead of kilowatt-hours saved
  - financial structures and investment horizons that typically do not go beyond 3–5 years and consequently do not accommodate the longer-term payback (>3 years and frequently much longer) often needed to reach deep efficiency[6]

[6] In reality, this may not be as substantial a hurdle as it appears on the surface. The issue really drives toward the nature and depth of the improvements. Amory Lovins has posited that when you reach significant efficiency, you "tunnel through the cost barrier," whereby "when designed as whole systems, the superefficient [building] can often cost less than the

  - principal-agent problems (the split-incentive), such as a difference between who pays for the investment and who benefits from the performance
  - who pays the costs of getting people up the learning curve—upfront training and education
  - societal benefits that do not translate into individual owner benefits
- operational and budgetary fragmentation that divides the analysis and decision-making regarding capital investments from operating costs
- shortage of skilled service providers
- regional differences that require capacity building among building professionals
- the imprecision of energy modeling as a tool—actual results often do not meet the modeled results, leading to skepticism about efficiency outcomes.
- inadequate persistence and performance of efficiency measures
- limited historical, comprehensive, and reliable financial data on investment returns for high-performance components.

2.1 *Short-Term Focus and Unaligned Solutions*

In 2007, the Swedish utility company Vattenfall AB and the consulting firm McKinsey published a very influential study comparing the greenhouse gas abatement potentials of various strategies and technologies to their respective costs, including those in the transportation, industrial, and building sectors. In January 2009, McKinsey updated this widely circulated and heavily discussed analysis (McKinsey & Co., 2009). The

original, unimproved version" (Hawken, Lovins, & Lovins, 2008, p. 114). Among others, property owners along with researchers at the New Buildings Institute have confirmed that their research and pilot projects support this conclusion. However, this presumes a **holistic and whole-building approach and creative architects and engineers, incorporating tenant engagement**—not typical of today's construction or retrofit process. One of the key challenges in reaching this point is a limited design budget that incentivizes design professionals to use existing plans as the basis for new and retrofit projects, consequently limiting overall cost and a risk factor resulting from new modes of design (one engineer mentioned that the cost of his liability insurance increases if the design is not the tried and true standard). One way to enhance deep efficiency design could be by providing technical assistance to the design team.

analysis evaluates the potential magnitude of savings in carbon dioxide (CO_2) emissions versus cost of each abatement measure. Many of the positively correlated strategies include a variety of "cost-effective" building-related changes—lighting, insulation, and retrofitted Heating, Ventilation and Air Conditioning (HVAC) systems. The report implies that future energy savings could potentially pay for the upfront costs. The International Energy Agency's World Energy Outlook for 2016[7] notes "government policies, as well as cost reductions across the energy sector [will] enable a doubling of both renewables ... and of improvements in energy efficiency over the next 25 years." There are clear winners—natural gas, wind, and solar. However, the future of global energy production remains to be written. Government policies across the globe will determine where we head and under what time frame.

However, as the McKinsey authors point out, it is one thing to have significant potential and another thing entirely to implement the necessary changes. Massive behavior modification and major capital resources are required. Further, the benefits and the cost of abatement are calculated from a societal perspective rather than from an individual investor point of view. Few property owners will invest their hard-earned dollars on a philanthropic basis simply for the public good, highlighting some of the challenges inherent in making broad assumptions on the ease of implementing the technology available today. As a building owner, it would be difficult to use McKinsey's data to make investment option decisions on an individual level. Hence, it is necessary to develop a full range of tools that can be deployed in concert to maximize performance for any given building.

Integrated solutions start with a whole-building (or even district-wide)[8] approach that incorporates advanced technology, ongoing commissioning, education, and training (operations staff and occupants), along with universally agreed-upon benchmarks, measurement standards, and mandated improvements in efficiency. When supported by financial incentives, modified lease structures, and cost/benefit-sharing that align stakeholder interests, these integrated solutions result in more rapid deployment of measures and in meaningful and persistent performance, thereby facilitating investment decisions.

[7] http://www.iea.org/newsroom/news/2016/november/world-energy-outlook-2016.html

[8] www.buildingrenewal.org; IEA. *Transition to Sustainable Buildings- Strategies and Opportunities to 2050.* 2013 https://www.iea.org/publications/freepublications/publication/transition-to-sustainable-buildings.html

2.2 *Stakeholder Diversity and Market Fragmentation*

First, we need to define the audience. There are various categories and subcategories of commercial real estate owners and investors. Owner/users are those who use buildings to house their own employees to meet their own business needs—these may be corporate, institutional, or government entities. Then there is a broad category of "real estate investors"—institutional, private, core, opportunistic, large, and small—each with differing motivations, experience, and capacity.

According to the 2012 Commercial Building Energy Consumption Survey[9] Energy Information Administration (EIA), 2016), only 6% of commercial buildings are larger than 50,000 square feet. These large properties account for more than 50% of the total space by square footage and are generally owned by institutional investors. The vast majority, 72%, of the total number of commercial buildings in the US are 10,000 square feet or less. These figures reflect a highly fragmented ownership market.

Generally speaking, some of the more difficult groups to interest in deep efficiency are polar opposites—on one hand, the smaller, less well-capitalized investors, lacking in expertise and capacity, and on the other, large aggregated pools of funds whose institutional owners have allocated a portion of their investment monies to asset managers and investment advisors in the real estate sector. These large portfolio owners are focused primarily on the real estate return compared to the return on their other investments. They typically only look at investments with a discrete payback period of three years or less. Fortunately, within the institutional and private capital group, there is an increasingly large subset of investors who do understand the benefits of high performance and efficiency and have been doing a good job maintaining and upgrading their properties. Many of these have embraced high-performance attributes particularly in new construction. On their existing properties, they make capital improvements when the timing is right (i.e., when equipment has reached the end of its useful life or a retrofit is necessary) and actively manage their buildings to maximize operational efficiency. They track their performance through Green Real Estate Benchmark (GRESB), GreenPrint, and EnergyStar and report out to their investors. These firms are forward thinking, have weathered the real estate cycles fairly well, and have positive and long-standing relationships with tenants. They often will look

[9] https://www.eia.gov/consumption/commercial/

toward utility and government incentives and rebates to offset the costs of efficiency improvements.[10]

Then there are investors who may be interested in efficiency but who do not have ready access to capital. Either they are too small or their real estate exposure is in less desirable markets, capital availability is more limited and contractor expertise and capacity is lacking. Finally, there are those smaller owners and investors who have never considered energy efficiency or high-performance attributes and for whom the issue is a low priority. There are other investor-related participants, such as tenants, lenders, real estate brokers, and rating agencies, each of which have a stake in a property's performance and returns and have significant influence on the owner/investor's decision.

3 Building the Tools and Measures

Moving from talk into meaningful action means increasing investment in deep energy savings[11] (e.g., 30–50% in the US, >75% in the European Union (EU) as compared to current state), not simply going after the "low-hanging fruit." Emerging ideas and solutions thus far are clustered around education and information transparency; codes, standards, and policies; and incentives and financing mechanisms. Crucial in ensuring ongoing success are measurement, verification, transparency, and ongoing monitoring and active management.

Cities such as New York, San Francisco, and Seattle are leading the way on benchmarking and transparency. In 2007, California approved legislation that required benchmarking and limited disclosure as of 2010. In 2008, the District of Columbia went further and required phased-in public disclosure, also starting in 2010. And in what has been called the most sweeping commercial building energy efficiency legislation, New York City passed the Greener, Greater Buildings Plan[12] in December 2009. The legislation increases energy efficiency requirements for renovations and requires most properties to undergo energy use audits and retrocommissioning[13] every ten years. The audit process will identify

[10] http://www.dsireusa.org

[11] http://www.gbpn.org/sites/default/files/08.DR_TechRep.low_.pdf

[12] http://www.nyc.gov/html/planyc2030/html/plan/buildings_plan.shtml

[13] Retro commissioning involves retuning measures that ensure building systems are operating efficiently.

capital improvements that will pay for themselves in a "reasonable" period. Perhaps most significant is the requirement that all commercial buildings greater than 50,000 square feet benchmark and publicly report their energy use. The city of Seattle followed suit in January 2010. Since then a total of 24 cities, 2 states, and 1 province have passed building rating and/or disclosure laws.[14]

3.1 *Market Linkage*

There is a need to link high performance and energy efficiency to the value of the property beyond that which can be achieved in operating savings. In the private-sector, efforts to capture these data are centered on linkages between properties that achieve certain levels of Energy Star and LEED ratings and their corresponding rent and sale values. According to a recent study by Dodge Analytics, building owners report that green buildings—whether new or renovated—command a 7% increase in asset value over traditional buildings.[15] This and other reports provide some compelling directional data but are still limited in the size and scope of their results. The US Green Building Council (USGBC) now requires submittal of performance data on properties that receive LEED certification. CoStar, a firm that collects real estate information on the sales and lease rates for commercial properties, has added a screen to its database that includes a check for properties rated as LEED or Energy Star.[16] The CoStar database notes if a property has received a designation but does not collect data related to property performance. As of April 2017, there were 37,300 LEED-certified projects[17] and as of year-end 2015 around 29,700 Energy Star-labeled buildings,[18] which compare to the EIA 2012 estimate of 5.5 million commercial buildings nationally. Clearly, these still account for only a small proportion of properties.

[14] http://www.imt.org/resources/detail/map-u.s.-building-benchmarking-policies, Retrieved May, 2017.

[15] The World Green Building Trends 2016 SmartMarket Report http://www.saint-gobain.co.uk/media/18079/world-green-building-trends-2016f_europe.pdf

[16] www.costar.com. www.costar.com

[17] http://www.usgbc.org/articles/usgbc-statistics

[18] https://www.energystar.gov/buildings/about-us/facts-and-stats

3.2 Validating Energy Efficiency

Supporting efforts to develop more accurate methods of verifying energy use provides clarity around efficiency results and allows private-sector capital to finance improvements. A nationally agreed-upon standard for determining energy baseline, measurement, and verification, akin to ISO 50001[19] and that targets protocols aimed at ensuring strong persistence of savings, also would help. Certainty around actual energy performance and savings requires increased focus on analytic tools that allow for accurate measurement and transparency of information.

Two equally important elements play a role here—metering and operations. Simply getting the design "right" is not enough. There must be measurable performance standards to confirm that the building works and to allow benchmarking against other buildings. The building must be operated and maintained, discrepancies immediately reported and fixed, over its whole life if we are to achieve persistent and meaningful energy efficiency.

Critical in defining which mechanisms are most practically applicable in a given region or for a specific property type are the characteristics of the building stock:

- Who are the major property owners (government, owner/user, long-term or short-term investors)?
- What percentage is leased versus owned?
- What are typical lease structures and terms?
- What is the energy makeup in a specific region in the country, and how expensive is it?
- And how much capacity building (of engineers, contractors, builders, architects) is necessary?
- Some mechanisms will be more successful in urban office building markets and some in rural retail, some in the investor markets, and others with corporate owner/users.

[19] International Organization for Standardization (ISO) International Standard 50,001. https://www.iso.org/iso-50001-energy-management.html

3.3 Tools

To monetize energy savings, the savings must be bankable. To be bankable, the investment community must believe in the level of efficiency and that it will be persistent over time, or else they will not invest in or finance the improvements. The notion of savings is predicated on the credibility and credence of a valid baseline. To achieve legitimacy, we need to:

- understand and agree on the baseline;
- validate the baseline, prove out the energy models, via measurement and verification;
- track efficiency over time; monitoring and verification equate to transparency; and
- proactively manage efficiency measures through robust operations and maintenance protocols (O&M).

Tools that facilitate this level of transparency, increase awareness, reduce risk by alleviating uncertainty, and set standards upon which appropriate benchmarks may be based by property type and region. Monitoring and verification, ongoing commissioning, and robust maintenance are critical. Through metering and response, they provide both feedback and transparency and enable persistent efficiency, increasing stability and continuity, and reducing uncertainty over time. These in turn give comfort to tenants, owners, and investors that the savings are achievable and credible and allow for the efficiency to be monetized and the benefits allocated.

3.3.1 Industry Consensus Metrics, Third-Party Standards, and Reporting

Industry consensus metrics verified by a credible third party will ensure transparency and enable sustainability value to be incorporated into value and financing decisions. There is presently no universal benchmark system. The real estate industry in the US has embraced Energy Star, but additional work is necessary to enhance and create standards that meet all property types and allow for local, national, and global comparison.

3.3.2 Access to Real-Time Numbers

Providing the technology and the means to "see" and track the consumption metrics allows owners and tenants to modify activities in ways that avoid peak pricing use and allow for rapid deployment of maintenance staff to fine-tune systems and identify and address operational failures.

One means of increasing the visibility of energy use and transparency to building owners and occupants would be some type of "dashboard" akin to that on the Prius vehicle. Metering provides transparency to the owner, the tenant, the investor, and the lender.

3.3.3 *Robust Operations and Maintenance*

Ensure the persistence of the efficiency results through active and effective O&M protocol. Retrocommissioning, ongoing commissioning, and the means to correct problems as they arise are critical for durable results. Consistent feedback and correction ensures the property is operating at peak levels and enables investment and financing to proceed with greater assurance of returns.

3.3.4 *Monetizing Energy Efficiency*

There must be a market for energy efficiency through which efficiency measures can be monetized—such as carbon and/or energy efficiency trading, policies that place energy efficiency at the same level as energy supply, white certificates, or energy performance certificates (EPCs). This market is yet unproven and considered risky. An agreed-upon baseline methodology to measure energy use and a means to consistently track performance are required. A greater amount of certainty and transparency is needed before private actors will be willing to engage further. *Investors, owners, tenants, brokers, and appraisers are pivotal to the market's development.* Through its EPCs, whereby property owners are required to measure and disclose energy use of their buildings to potential purchasers and tenants, the EU is poised to make significant progress.

3.3.5 *Tenant Engagement*

A key efficiency driver is a tenant who identifies high-performance attributes as a best practice. Increasingly, an investor's decision to integrate efficiency and/or high-performance attributes can be directly linked to tenant demand. The Urban Land Institute's Tenant Energy Optimization Program directly engages tenants by providing a returns-based approach via a ten-step process to integrate energy efficiency into space design and construction.[20] Tenants who have used the process have demonstrated substantial energy savings and positive returns. Once energy demand in tenant spaces is reduced, central systems can be replaced with smaller

[20] http://tenantenergy.uli.org

equipment, thus reducing first costs and the overall energy use of the building. However, the timing must be synchronized with existing business plans, capital improvement plans, and equipment replacement cycles to leverage the opportunity with the property owner.

Leases that allow the landlord and tenant to share in the efficiency gains can further enhance owner motivation. Without modification, many lease structures exacerbate what is often called the "split-incentive." "In many commercial lease structures, the party expending capital for an energy efficiency upgrade does not sufficiently benefit from the energy savings created by that upgrade. This occurs most frequently in leases where tenants pay for utilities but the landlord is wholly responsible for capital improvements, as is the case in many net leases. The split-incentive barrier is frequently cited by property owners as a key roadblock to energy efficiency projects."[21]

In a typical lease structure such as a Full Service Gross (FSG) lease, the landlord pays all capital improvements (including energy efficiency/high-performance upgrades) and the stated rent includes the operating expenses (including utilities) and taxes for the building. In this case, the landlord benefits from reduced operating costs, but the tenant does not, giving the tenant little incentive to modify behavior to enhance savings. In contrast, in a triple net lease (NNN), the landlord pays all capital expenses, and the tenant, in addition to rent, pays all expenses of the property, such as utilities, taxes, insurance. In this case, the tenant reaps any benefits of lower property expenses, giving the landlord little incentive to invest in the capital costs of efficiency measures that may be harder to recoup. A Modified Gross Lease muddles the incentives. In some cases the landlord reaps the benefits of the efficiency improvements and in other cases, the tenant does. Regardless, any lease can incorporate green provisions, which align the financial incentives of sustainability and/or energy measures between the landlord and tenant.

With reporting standards for energy efficiency leaning toward increased transparency, property owners who have benefited from utility pass-throughs through a Full Service Lease as an additional revenue source likely will see increasing pressure to modify their agreements. (Without recognition of this issue and care in drafting new lease structures, these property owners may resist efficiency measures and/or transparency.)

[21] What's in a Green Lease? Measuring the Potential Impact of Green Leases in the US Office Sector. Andrew Feierman, Institute for Market Transformation. May 2015.

The Green Lease Library[22] maintained by the Institute for Market Transformation is a useful compendium of tools and resources to aid in crafting appropriate lease language.

3.3.6 *Public/Private Partnerships*

To leverage private-sector participation, governments at all levels need to reach further to create mechanisms that enable more public/private partnerships, risk sharing, and certainty. By linking multiple components in one initiative, public-private partnerships offer strong opportunities to move the market rapidly. One example is the C40 Climate Leadership Group, a network of world's largest cities committed to addressing climate change by sharing best practices, peer to peer exchanges, and city-to-city collaboration. The C40 recently launched the Cities Finance Facility (CFF) to facilitate access to financial means for climate change mitigation and resilience projects in developing countries and emerging economies and has published several best-practices reports.[23] Other possibilities include loan guarantees/credit enhancement provided by a government entity to leverage private capital investment; requirements by government-sponsored enterprises (i.e., Fannie Mae/Freddie Mac), the US Department of Housing and Urban Development (HUD), rating agencies, financial institutions, and investors for energy efficiency certification; and municipalities and utilities offering fiscal incentives for the use of specific green products or reaching and maintaining specific efficiency benchmarks.

These types of partnerships tackle multiple hurdles and leverage the policy impact, driving larger and more sustainable changes.

3.4 *Communication Strategies, Messaging, and Transparency*

Communication strategies must be developed and tailored to investors, owners, managers, and tenants. Delivery must be made by trusted partners and industry leaders. Partnerships that leverage key industry organizations and stakeholders to deliver targeted education, training, and information around specific incentives, financing structures, and tools will

[22] http://www.greenleaselibrary.com/guidance.html

[23] http://www.c40.org/c40_research—*Urban Efficiency II: Seven Innovative City Programmes for Existing Building Energy Efficiency, February 16, 2017,* outlining the characteristics and impact of innovative city programs emerging across the C40 cities, and that advance operational energy efficiency and retrofitting in existing, privately owned buildings.

reach a far greater audience than through one medium or strictly from one entity. Messaging that educates and looks at high-performance attributes in the context of property operations and the real-life impact on occupants, operations, cash flow, and net operating income is effective—risk and return, health, and safety.

3.4.1 Messaging

A study by Attari, DeKay, Davidson, and Bruin de Bruin (2010) surveyed 505 individuals on their perceptions of energy consumption. Results showed participants consistently and substantially underestimated energy use and savings and believed that curtailment (turning lights off) was a more effective strategy than efficiency improvements (new light bulbs). The authors posit that the lack of focus on efficiency improvements was due to the fact that efficiency improvements involve research, effort, and out-of-pocket costs. Further, participants were unable to accurately estimate the magnitude of energy use across devices and activities.

Attari et al. (2010, p. 1) concluded "The serious deficiencies highlighted by these results suggest that well designed efforts to improve the public's understanding of energy use and savings could pay large dividends." The study suggests that understanding the knowledge gaps and misconceptions will enable credible and understandable messages to be crafted that can influence better-informed decisions.

The nonprofit Technology, Entertainment, and Design (TED, www.ted.com) is a great example of successful messaging that leads to action. The TED motto is "Ideas Worth Spreading." At its core is an annual conference featuring 18-minute talks by leading-edge thinkers and innovators on a variety of topics ranging from green energy to global social issues and culture. What makes it successful in spreading ideas broadly is that in addition to live participation, the talks are available online for free. The ideas are spread by word of mouth, via online videos, and through a variety of social networking tools, including blogs, tweets, and discussion groups. The talks showcase innovative ideas with the potential for far-reaching impact—the messages are successful because they link to individual values by making an emotional connection while providing information. The participants are directly engaged and act as influencers in bringing the concepts to a wider audience.

Information leads to awareness, and awareness leads to action. Messages and mechanisms that link multiple components are likely to have wider-ranging impact and be more durable and sustainable by bringing together stakeholders for a common goal. Incorporating meaning that ties to a common goal encourages a viral component to messaging, which is critical to widespread adoption.

So, how can this be successfully applied to incentivizing property owners and investors to invest in high-performance measures?

1. Information must reach the investors most likely to take action and act as influencers.
2. Market research is necessary to better understand the demand patterns going forward. Creating transparency around performance metrics will strengthen both the desire to achieve high performance and facilitate investment by creating certainty around results.
3. Models, programs, and standards that facilitate benchmarking[24][25]and help firms identify and set efficiency targets will elevate awareness, enhance competition among properties, and increase investor confidence.
4. Incentives that incorporate both a carrot and a stick to move investors toward certain behaviors.
5. Communication strategies that influence companies and corporate leaders and dispel misinformation. Messaging that concretely links sustainability and high performance with risk and return will prove more impactful than broad concepts.

To scale, messaging must close the gap between the innovators/early adopters (15.5% the market) and the early majority (34%).[26] Bridging this

[24] The EPA Energy Star program and American National Standards Institute (ANSI)/ American Society of Heating, Refrigerating and Air-Conditioning Engineers (ASHRAE)/ Illuminating Engineering Society (IES)/US Green Building Council (USGBC) Standard 189.1–2014, Standard for the Design of High-Performance Green Buildings are good examples. Standard 189.1 is modeled after LEED. Like typical codes, it provides specific requirements for energy efficiency in buildings but extends to other "green building" considerations such as materials selection. The resulting building might look and behave much like a LEED-certified building but is not labeled as such.

[25] Performance Metrics for Commercial Buildings, 2010. Pacific Northwest National Laboratory and the National Renewable Energy Laboratory. These metrics include energy, water, indoor environmental quality, transportation, maintenance, and waste and recycling. http://www.pnnl.gov/main/publications/external/technical_reports/PNNL-19830.pdf

[26] In *Diffusion of Innovations*, Everett Rogers outlines a study by Bruce Ryan and Neal Gross that provides a well-documented examination of the diffusion and spread of hybrid seed corn in Iowa in the 1930s. Rogers defines diffusion as "the process by which an innova-

gap brings the idea to the mass market. The innovators and early adopters are comfortable making gut decisions and utilizing an imperfect model. The early majority needs more proof—they want more evidence and will try something after the opinion leaders or respected members of the community have tried it. Messaging must link beyond the "what" (energy efficiency) and "how" (lighting, building orientation) to the "why" (the cause, purpose, or belief). This increases the level of confidence in the decision beyond the rational—"I think this is the right decision" and the gut—"this feels like the right decision" to one that incorporates both. "The decision both feels right and can be justified by facts and figures"—"I know this is the right decision" (Sinek, 2009). Few people make decisions solely on facts and figures. Their fundamental values such as security, freedom, and responsibility play into their decision significantly. Property owners and corporations also operate under fundamental values such as safety, responsibility, and reliability, respect for their workers and clients, innovation, and in increasingly more cases, environmental sustainability and community commitment (with the awareness that being a good corporate citizen engenders trust and ongoing corporate sustainability and profitability).

Messages that will resonate with investors will target two key areas—risk and return. Investments by their nature have some inherent risk—some deviation from expected returns—be it opportunity cost, risk of failure, risk of default, and lower return. An investment that yields a higher return than another is not necessarily better than the other. One needs to evaluate the overall risk associated with that return and the risk tolerance of the investor. In the case of a property owner, as we move toward an energy-conscious market, the risks associated with an inefficient building can be significant. These include regulatory risk, energy price risk,[27] energy availability and security, health and well-being of occupants, and competitive obsolescence (companies and buildings that are no longer as desirable as others—the perception of being behind the times/not cutting edge or lower performance; workers who look for "cutting-edge firms" and socially conscious firms; occupants/tenants who require sustainable properties).

tion is communicated through certain channels over time among the members of a social system" (Rogers, 2003, p. 6). The concept has been expanded by Malcolm Gladwell in *The Tipping Point* (Gladwell, 2002) and Simon Sinek in "How Great Leaders Inspire Action" (Sinek, 2009), a TEDx, Puget Sound, lecture filmed September 2009 available from http://www.ted.com/talks/lang/eng/simon_sinek_how_great_leaders_inspire_action.html (September 2010).

[27] Johnson Controls (2010b) reflects that property owners anticipate an average annual increase in energy prices of 7%.

3.4.2 Communication Strategies and Transparency

Communication strategies may subtly encourage transparency and raise the bar. Look at the results of car labeling and the Corporate Average Fuel Economy (CAFÉ) standards enacted after the 1973–1974 oil crisis.[28] The sticker is a visible announcement of a vehicle's fuel economy and allows for easy comparison between cars.

This concept is supported by a study done on Los Angeles County restaurants. In 1998, Los Angeles County introduced hygiene-quality grading cards that each restaurant was required to display in its window. As reported in Thaler and Sunstein (Thaler & Sunstein, 2008, p. 190), "[t]he researchers found that the grade cards caused the restaurant health inspection scores to improve, consumers' sensitivity to hygiene in restaurants to increase, and hospitalizations for food-borne illnesses to decrease."[29]

The two examples just presented highlight the positive implications inherent in transparency and reporting. From an energy perspective, this underpins reporting in the UK, which compels both commercial and residential property owners to provide EPCs to prospective buyers (and tenants). In addition, public buildings must post display energy certificates (DECs) of their energy usage.[30]

EPCs became compulsory on all commercial properties constructed, rented, or sold within the UK effective October 1, 2008. With the introduction of EPCs into the commercial sector, details of the energy efficiency and environmental impact of a rental property are made available to prospective tenants/buyers at the earliest opportunity. The energy certificate provides a rating of the energy efficiency and carbon emissions of a building from A to G, where A is very efficient and G is very inefficient. For rental property, an EPC is currently valid for ten years and can be reused as many times as required within that period. Landlords do not have to commission a new EPC each time a new tenancy starts, but they are required to provide a copy of the latest EPC to new tenants. Furthermore, although landlords are not obliged to make any of the changes suggested on the EPC, measures that could be taken to improve

[28] http://www.nhtsa.gov/cars/rules/cafe/overview.htm

[29] As reported in Thaler and Sunstein (Thaler & Sunstein, 2008, p. 190) who reviewed a 2003 paper by Ginger Zhe Jin and Philip Leslie.

[30] Available through the UK National Archives: http://webarchive.nationalarchives.gov.uk/+/http://www.communities.gov.uk/planningandbuilding/theenvironment/energyperformance/

the property's energy efficiency and environmental impact rating are highlighted. Public authorities with space greater than 1000 square meters (10,764 square feet) must display a valid EPC. As of 2013, listed (or historic) buildings are exempt.

Since 2007, all single-family homes in the UK and Wales require an energy rating before they can be sold.[31] EPCs are included in the Home Information Pack, which rates the home from A to G and lists efficiency measures the homeowner can take.

Linked with EPCs are *DECs*. DECs show up to three years of data on energy used in the building. They must be provided by an accredited assessor (appraiser) and must be displayed on the building.

Increasing awareness, communication strategies, transparency, and labeling are valuable components of an overall strategy to increase investment in high-performance buildings—but they are limited in scope. There also needs to be the means to deploy the improvements that lead to high-performance buildings. Financing is a means to that end.

4 Financial and Policy Mechanisms

4.1 Financing Mechanisms

Certain existing and potential financing and policy mechanisms, individually and in combination, if scaled, will help drive deployment of energy efficiency investment in the real estate sector (Table 11.1).

Beyond traditional government and utility incentives, several financing mechanisms are cropping up across the country. Some of the new and reformulated ideas include on-bill pay or on-bill financing (OBF), energy services companies (ESCOs) and energy services performance contracts (ESPCs), energy and efficiency services agreements (ESA), managed energy service agreements (MESA), energy efficiency power purchase agreements (PPAs), and property-assessed clean energy (PACE), all of which focus on the retrofit of existing buildings or renewables. Policy mechanisms include disclosure requirements, EPCs, minimum energy performance standards, renewable and energy efficiency certificates/credits (RECs), carbon offsets, cap and trade, or a carbon tax. On the market-driven front are carbon trading, emissions trading,[32]

[31] https://www.gov.uk/buy-sell-your-home/energy-performance-certificates

[32] https://icapcarbonaction.com/images/StatusReport2016/ICAP_Status_Report_2016_Online.pdf

Table 11.1 Available financing mechanisms

Type	*Mechanism*
Traditional	Loans • secured loans (mortgage/equipment) • unsecured loans Leases • operating • capital leases (equipment)
Specialized	On-bill financing (OBF) Property-assessed clean energy (PACE) Energy savings performance contracts (ESPCs)/energy services companies (ESCOs) Efficiency or energy services agreements (ESAs), managed energy services agreements (MESAs) Power purchase agreements (PPAs) Revolving loan funds Utility incentives, grants, and rebates
Innovative strategies	Modified lease structures Climate benefit districts Foundation investments Green loans/loan guarantees Tenant incentives
Government and policy supported	Government incentives, tax credits Energy performance labeling Energy performance standards Energy trading schemes (ETS) Energy efficiency trading scheme Voluntary carbon trading White certificates Clean development mechanisms

and even modified lease structures. In November 2016, Lawrence Berkeley National Lab published a comprehensive report detailing different financing mechanisms. The primary objective of their work was to provide state and local government decision-makers with information and tools to support various energy efficiency financing approaches. Though targeted at the public-sector, the information is useful for a wide variety of stakeholders.

Following Lawrence Berkeley National Laboratory's (LBNL's) lead, we'll distinguish here between "'traditional' financing products (e.g., loans and leases) that are commonly used to pay for energy efficiency as well as many other goods and services, and 'specialized' products (e.g., PACE and on-bill financing products) that are specifically designed to support energy efficiency and other clean energy installations and to overcome market barriers."[33] Per the LBNL report, a 2015 study by Opinion Dynamics and Dunsky Energy Consulting suggest that traditional financing products, such as loans and leases, are still more widely used by customers that choose to finance projects.

Both Fannie Mae and the Department of HUD, through the Federal Housing Administration, have offered energy-efficient mortgages. Fannie Mae for example offers a suite of "green" financing products. These include lower pricing and greater proceeds (up to 5%) for multifamily properties that achieve certain green building certifications.

- Both equipment operating and capital leases are common in the private and public-sector. Capital leases are typically long term and for large items such as machinery. The lessee counts the asset on their balance sheet and can depreciate the asset. Similar to an installment sale contract. In an operating lease the lessor retains ownership of the asset and the lease cost is treated as operating expense. In this case, the lessor retains ownership of the leased asset and it does not appear on the lessee's balance sheet. While leases are used extensively in the private-sector for all kinds of equipment; there has not been significant use of leasing among private-sector customers in energy efficiency-focused programs. Leases specifically for funding energy efficiency measures have been targeted at public/institutional sector customers because they allow them to take on projects without exceeding debt limits or requiring difficult approval processes (e.g., public votes, legislative approval)

Several innovative ideas and specialized products have emerged to facilitate the movement of investment capital to the sector. The most promising of these financing structures aim to monetize energy efficiency, identify new types of collateral and means of ensuring repayment, and extend financing terms to address long payback periods.

[33] https://energy.gov/sites/prod/files/2017/05/f34/current-practices-efficiency-financing.pdf

- **PACE**: The PACE structure builds upon the common practice of special land assessment districts used for infrastructure improvements deemed to be in the public interest. PACE allows state and local governments to provide for energy efficiency and renewable energy improvements on private property, repaid through property tax bills. The structure requires each state to approve enabling legislation.

  The local government loans money to owners to make energy-efficient improvements or add renewable power to their property. To secure the loan, a lien is placed on the property in the form of an additional property tax assessment. Liens are repaid via an add-on to the property tax bill at an established rate of interest over a specific period, generally 20 years. The lien remains with the property, even upon sale, until fully repaid. As the PACE assessment attaches to the property, rather than the borrower, the lien sits in priority to the property's first mortgage. Consequently, this has raised concern with regulators and financial institutions, especially in the residential markets, about loan priority and collateral sufficiency. In the commercial markets, mortgage language typically requires lender consent when incurring new debt (which generally includes tax assessments) and they are notified when tax assessments are added to the property.
- **OBF** or On-bill Repayment (OBR): A utility company (or some other entity) finances the energy efficiency improvements. The property owner receives the benefit of the efficiency reduction in the form of a partial reduction in the monthly utility with the balance between the actual savings and the rate payment used to amortize the improvements plus interest. The obligation runs with the property, is attached to the utility bill, and would be passed along to subsequent purchasers. On-bill financing has been around in some form since the 1970s. Presently, at least 45 programs are active offering some sort of OBF to both their residential and commercial customers.[34]

  The benefits of OBF include a one-stop provider, vetted certified professional contractors, long-term financing, ease of repayment (through a regular billing cycle), and a lien that attaches to the property instead of to the borrower. Further, because both the local municipality and/or utility touch all members of the community, the program could be scaled. In the short run, the scalability of the model is hampered by a financial structure for utilities that disincen-

[34] ibid.

tivizes efficiency, the fragmented nature of the utility industry. In addition to federal regulations, each state has its own overarching requirements for utilities and many states have more than one regulated utility. Further, neither the utility nor the municipality has lending (or energy efficiency) as a core business. Consequently, a new core competency and protocol would need to be developed for success.

- **ESAs**: An ESA requires no upfront capital from the commercial property owner; third-party financing cover all project costs. The provider initiates and maintains the contractual relationship with the efficiency retrofit contractor and handles ongoing management of the systems. The client continues to pay the energy bill plus an energy services payment to the provider, who takes a fee for managing the process and repays the debt and equity. The combined net payment is intended to be equal to or less than the pre-retrofit energy cost. In a Managed Energy Services Agreement (MESA), the provider becomes a signer on the customer's utility account and takes over responsibility for paying the customer's utility bill. The client pays a predetermined bill to the MESA provider that incorporates an estimate of the utility expenses plus a provider fee.
- **ESPC**: ESPCs are typically provided by **ESCO**s that provide energy-efficiency–related and other value-added services to building owners and performance contracting is a core part of its business. ESCOs have been around since the late 1970s and early 1980s when energy prices spiked after the Arab oil embargo. Although a relatively young industry in the US, they have been around in Europe for about a century. They typically provide four main services: the development, installation, and arrangement of financing for energy efficiency improvements and then, through an ESPC, ongoing maintenance, operation, and a guarantee of energy savings. The cost of the improvements is paid from the savings generated by the efficiency.

Through an ESPC, the ESCO "guarantees" the project will maintain a stipulated level of energy savings over a certain period—anywhere from 7 to 20 or even 25 years, based upon specific parameters such as load, usage patterns, hours of operation, and maintenance. The ESCO model has worked almost exclusively in the so-called MUSH (municipalities (state/local governments), universities, K-12 schools, and hospitals) market, which along with federal government clients, accounts for about 84% of total revenues for the ESCO industry. In 2014, $4.1 billion in investment were made through ESPCs, with $3.9 billion in the public and institutional market and $171 million in the commercial and industrial market.[35]

Due to the nature of the financing structure, the applicability of the ESCO model is generally limited to an entity with a desire for outside financing, a high credit rating (generally investment grade), and planned continued ownership.

Anecdotally, private commercial property owners report a distrust of the energy savings purported to be achieved by the ESCOs as well as an unwillingness to "give away" excessive economic returns. As noted previously, the inability to maintain persistent energy efficiency over time is common. Most buildings and facilities exhibit the same basic limitations with respect to energy conservation and optimum maintenance.

US government studies show that due to the lack of ongoing commissioning and robust maintenance, building systems routinely fail to meet performance expectations, and these faults often go unnoticed over time. For example, a 2005 report released by the US Government Accountability Office (GAO) validates the concerns raised by private property owners. The study, which looked at federal ESPCs, suggested there might not be sufficient data to prove that the gains delivered by ESCOs were sustainable over time. The report further questions the practice of having ESCOs monitoring and validating the performance of their own projects (GAO, 2005).[36]

A LBNL report (Hopper, Goldman, Gilligan, Singer, & Birr, 2007) shows that residential and public housing markets together account for only 5% of industry revenues and are targeted by only a handful of ESCOs. Due to high transaction costs and institutional barriers in the case of public housing, these remain a niche market for ESCOs. In small-size properties, the energy cost savings are generally not significant enough to offset the transaction costs inherent in implementing performance-based contracts.

[35] Deason, Leventis, Goldman, & Carvallo, 2016

[36] The Office of the Under Secretary of Defense for Technology, Acquisition, and Logistics agreed with the GAO findings, stating "Although these complicated contracts are structured to ensure that savings will exceed costs," and further, "we recognize that our measurement and verification procedures must be improved to confirm estimates with actual data."

The core market in which the ESCO business model has been most successful is in energy efficiency retrofits to large buildings owned primarily by institutional clients. There is increasing interest in energy efficiency and clean energy among municipal governments that are pursuing sustainable energy and/or climate change initiatives. There are untapped opportunities in both the residential and commercial markets that will require some sort of aggregation of small projects to reduce the transaction costs.

In addition to providing financing, an ESCO provides energy audits, recommendations, and performance contracting as a core part of the business. The majority of the market is driven by federal, state, local, university, and educational projects. Barriers in the typical commercial and/or residential real estate markets include the high transaction costs per project, credit-worthy borrowers (single-family residential and/or multifamily, along with single-asset partnerships and an expectation of nonrecourse debt) and an inability to adequately secure the loans (collateral and first mortgage-holder challenges). From the borrower/property owner perspective, ESCOs are not always viewed as being transparent. The ESCO industry is dominated by product manufacturers who combine the energy audit with purchase recommendations and ultimately sell their products to meet the needs identified through the audit—potentially an inherent conflict of interest.

- **PPA:** In simplest terms, a PPA is a legal contract between an electricity generator and a purchaser of energy or capacity (power or ancillary services). Prologis, a large real estate investment trust of warehouse space, has entered into several of these types of contracts in the US (Southern California, Virginia, Oregon), Japan, and the EU (Spain, Germany, France, Italy, UK) through feed-in tariff laws that promote investment in renewable energy. Under the EU feed-in tariff laws, regional or national utilities are obligated to purchase renewable energy at rates set by the government based on the cost of the generating the renewable power. The Prologis properties have incorporated solar panels onto their rooftops (typically flat, industrial properties) and have entered into 20- to 25-year agreements to sell energy back to the utility grid. In the case of the Southern California property, the sales price to the utility is based on the amount of energy produced by the rooftop. The properties are metered and send a bill to the utility on a monthly basis. Prologis reports that between 2007 and 2016, they installed solar on 95 rooftops in 8 countries and generated 140 megawatts of solar energy, enough to power nearly 23,000 homes. The company's goal is to generate 200 megawatts of solar power by 2020.[37]

- **Revolving Loan Funds:** *Revolving loan funds* deploy public-sector capital to meet needs that contribute to the public good. They are applicable to commercial, residential, and neighborhood buildings. Generally speaking, these funds supplement private capital in areas where private capital is less available. A revolving loan program (similar to a community development block grant) lends money and earns a return on their capital. As loan funds are repaid, the principal and interest are added back into the fund and become available for future projects. These funds also can be used in conjunction with private-sector capital to leverage project financing.

  One such municipality currently using this tool to combat climate change and encourage energy efficiency is the Toronto Atmospheric Fund (TAF).[38] Originally endowed by public funds in 1992, TAF, which is run by an agency of the City of Toronto, has innovated a program called the Green Condo Loan and Towerwise (both targeted at high-rise apartments and condominiums) whereby efficiency loans are made to the condo association for the building efficiency measures and repaid by the residents/owners via their energy bill savings. The TAF developed a loan concept, the energy retrofit STEP Loan, which facilitates deep efficiency. The STEP Loan is essentially three loans rolled into one: a short-term loan covering fast payback items (like lighting); a medium term-loan for items with a mid-term payback (e.g., HVAC equipment); and a long-term loan for items with long paybacks (e.g., cladding).

4.2 Barriers

The applicability of each mechanism depends not only on the property type but also on regional context and existing market structures. Currently,

[37] https://americas.uli.org/uli-connect/solar-energy-commercial-real-estate-navigating-opportunities-risks/

[38] http://www.toronto.ca/taf/ and http://www.toronto.ca/taf/pdf/leveraging-leadership.pdf and www.towerwise.ca

the most prevalent are incentives, grants, and rebates, and conventional loans for those who can qualify. These structures limit the amount and depth of efficiency that can be achieved. Beyond federal inducements, regional incentive structures, amounts, and requirements vary across the country, making it difficult for portfolio owners to implement a strategy that scales across their assets. For portfolio owners, transaction costs associated with meeting individual program requirements for a single asset can offset the benefits associated with retrofit rebates.

Hurdles posed on the financial side can be pivotal. They include lack of data, first cost, capital versus operating budgets, risk exposure, the low ratio of energy costs to total operating expenses, high transaction costs, discount factor issues, and the inadequacy of traditional financing mechanisms for energy efficiency projects, as follows:

- Most financial institutions are accustomed to an asset-based lending structure and are not equipped to view cash flow generated from energy efficiency as an asset that can be monetized or used as credit enhancement.
- Identifying the means to collateralize the financing of improvements has been challenging (as illustrated by the current issues with PACE[39] financing). One option is to take the equipment (or efficiency features) as collateral. Difficulties with holding the equipment or improvements as collateral are threefold:
  - First, the property owners (at least in the commercial markets) have a contractual obligation with their tenants to provide a specific level of comfort and safety in the building. Hence, they want to maintain control of systems.
  - Second, any improvements would, by their nature, be affixed to the building (e.g., windows, chillers). As a consequence, they become *real property* as defined by law. This compares to furniture, fixtures, and equipment, which are considered personal property, not integral to the operations of the building, and which

[39] Property-assessed clean energy (PACE) provides for energy investments to be financed and collateralized through a property tax lien, which has, from the mortgage lenders' perspective, raised issues of priority in collecting debt. Updates on PACE are available from http://pacenation.us

can have a Uniform Commercial Code (UCC) filing[40] placed on it. Clearly, in the event of a default, it would be impractical to remove many of the efficiency improvements (e.g., consider windows).
  - Third, mortgage holders take a blanket lien on the real property. They need to ensure the property is able to perform as intended, both while owned by their borrower and in the event of a foreclosure. Consequently, they are not willing to allow anyone else to have a claim on assets that are necessary to keep the building operational.
- In the case of energy per se, there are ordinances related to safety and security that are dictated by local laws.
- Financing periods are generally short (less than ten years), and interest rates can be high.

Financing remains a critical component in deploying the necessary technology and is a significant hurdle, even if in some cases only a psychological one, to seeing substantial investment in high-performance attributes. A concerted approach to facilitating these mechanisms is necessary. Research shows no single response will meet all needs, there are significant barriers and competing interests, public/private partnerships add value, the solutions must be contextual, a value must be put on energy usage, and government has a significant role to play.

5 The Path Forward

To support and encourage investment in and deployment of high-performance measures in all building classes, both quickly and at scale, we need to engage real estate professionals on the basis of financial returns over the holding period of the property and include a wide variety of inputs beyond energy or resource cost. The following criteria must be addressed:

[40] A Uniform Commercial Code (UCC) filing is made under the UCC and is a lien placed upon a business or the assets of a business and registered with the state in which the business is located.

- value proposition that articulates the link between efficiency and returns;
- leadership modeled and best practices publicized;
- clear action steps that set the framework for success;
- transparency and certainty around energy use and efficiency performance;
- persistence of high-performance measures over time;
- education/training tailored for key stakeholders such as occupants, operators, and investors;
- investment/financing which values high-performance and efficiency as a *bankable* asset; and
- ease and simplicity of solutions that make adoption of high-performance measures effortless.

Many of these needs identified (Table 11.2) can be addressed by individual actors alone, or in partnership to promote investments in high-performance buildings. These efforts include:

- Facilitate (and publicize) pilot projects between property owners, utilities, and financing sources.
- Develop a set of consistent, agreed-upon standardized metrics and valuation methodology so that properties can be evaluated across the sector allowing for comparison between assets and enhancing uniform lending and investment strategies.
- Partnerships between industry organizations to present tailored and targeted training for major stakeholder groups, such as the Building Owners and Managers Association (BOMA), Urban Land Institute, Institute of Real Estate Managers, National Association of State Energy Officials, and the American Bankers Association.
- Develop databases to collect and widely disseminate meaningful performance and valuation data on high-performance buildings, allowing real estate professionals to compare properties more effectively and ultimately allowing for data to be standardized, risk analyzed, and financial market mechanisms crafted.
- Evaluate the correlation between the default rate on property mortgages and incremental increases in energy prices, to enable investors, owners, financiers, and tenants to evaluate the potential for risk reduction associated with persistent high-efficiency performance.

6 Conclusion

While we have the technology to achieve increased efficiency, we must tie efficiency and high performance to the real risk, return, and value impact in order to facilitate meaningful action. Deployment must incorporate a multidisciplinary approach and collectively address the issues of finance, investment, and incentives; metrics and verification; O&M; awareness, education, and training; design and construction; and the energy and utility landscape.

- Current technology is capable of delivering substantial efficiency. However, technology alone cannot solve the problem.
  - While there is an increasing level of consciousness around energy efficiency, this does not reflect a concrete commitment to actual investment in, or implementation of, efficiency or high-performance measures.
  - The equipment must be purchased, installed, and properly run for efficiency to be realized.
- Financing remains a critical component in deploying the necessary technology and is a significant hurdle to seeing substantial investment in high-performance attributes. Hurdles can be pivotal and include a lack of data, first cost, capital versus operating budgets, risk exposure, the low ratio of energy costs to total operating expenses, high transaction costs, discount factor issues, and the inadequacy of traditional financing mechanisms for energy efficiency projects.
- Deployment is accelerated with the right mix of financial tools.
  - Direct funding for efficiency retrofits is neither sustainable nor scalable; tactics must leverage a range of options.
  - Deployment must incorporate a multidisciplinary approach and collectively address the issues of finance, investment and incentives; metrics and verification; O&M; awareness, education, and training; design and construction; and the energy and utility landscape.
- For real estate investors, owners, and financiers, traditional bottom-line factors such as revenue, expenses, risk, and return, lead investment analysis and decision-making rather than the narrower life-cycle cost analysis (LCCA).

Table 11.2 Identified needs

Criterion	*Solution*
Value proposition	Tie to risk/return Tie to health and safety (which leads to improved building performance and reduced risk)
Leadership	Publicize successes and failures to generate best-practices summary Model construction and retrofit of high-performance buildings Provide technical assistance
Clear action steps	Step-by-step decision-making tool box, addressing impact of key performance attributes on risk and return • road map that outlines discrete path for the investment decision process—Including short- and long-term outcomes • easily replicable and customizable by property type and specific property Quick wins • facilitate pilot projects—Engage property owners and lenders around a real building, a real project, with real leases and real tenants. • encourage use of model lease language. List available at www.greenleaselibrary.com, BOMA and GSA
Transparency/ certainty	Standardized baseline and metrics Industry benchmarking—For example, EnergyStar, GRESB, GreenPrint, DOE buildings performance database Dashboard Standardized underwriting[(a)] Social networking postings Competitions
Persistence	Measurement and verification—Metering, real-time monitoring Robust O&M—Ongoing commissioning, active and immediate tuning, and correction of identified problems.
Education/ training	Detailed summary of finance/investment options that address key points for each: • description, applicability, availability, maturity, terms and limits, benefits, and hurdles. • capacity building of service providers, municipalities, real estate professionals • partnerships between key stakeholder organizations to provide education and training: – building owners and managers association, urban land institute, National Association of realtors, International Council of Shopping Centers, National Association of state energy officials, American bankers association, and so on. – webinars, presentations to property owners, investors, realtors, energy officials, financiers, rating agencies, and municipalities through industry meetings, conventions, trainings, events, and online presence.

(*continued*)

Table 11.2 (continued)

Criterion	*Solution*
Investment/ financing	On-bill pay Energy-efficiency services agreement Property-assessed clean energy (PACE) —Modified to incorporate greater transparency of performance metrics Incentives/rebates to supplement and leverage internal cash and financing options.
Ease	"One-stop" providers, including financing, approved (and trained) contractors, performance guarantee, real-time monitoring, verification, and maintenance.

- Real estate investment decisions are multi-faceted and complex. Different owner strata have differing motivations. Decisions involve numerous stakeholders with often competing and complimentary objectives. To be successful, solutions and messaging must directly address value and bottom-line results.
- Value considerations are important in framing the message.

Broadly speaking, the industry judges the market risks associated with high-performance attributes to be greater than potential benefits. In part, this is based in reality, and in part due to cultural barriers, business norms, and competing stakeholder interests.

The perception of value depends on the stakeholders, investment objectives, access to and cost of capital, property type, and lease structure.

Reducing the uncertainty around energy savings is critical. The investment community must believe the efficiency is both meaningful and persistent over time in order to finance and invest in improvements. Continued focus on baselines and metrics, as well as encouraging best practices for measurement, verification, and monitoring, will reduce the perceived risk and help provide a means for defining the value of high-performance attributes.

- To monetize energy savings, the savings must be *bankable*. To be bankable, the investment community must believe the efficiency is meaningful and will be persistent over time, or else they will not invest in or finance the improvements.

- Monitoring and verification, ongoing commissioning, and robust maintenance are critical. Through metering and response, they provide transparency and enable persistent efficiency, increasing stability and continuity, and reducing uncertainty over time.

Language and messaging must tie directly to the overall investment analysis, not just life-cycle cost. Traditional bottom-line factors such as revenue, expenses, risk, and return drive the investment analysis and decision-making.

- There is a need to create partnerships between seemingly disparate groups, some with competing agendas and differing financial and regulatory incentives. This includes engaging the regulated utility market and addressing inherent complexities that serve to dampen rather than promote investment in efficiency.
- To forge common understanding and shared objectives, language needs to be broadened to incorporate financial and energy metrics in the same medium; for example, cost per kilowatt-hour needs to be translated easily to cost per square foot.

Real estate investment decisions are multi-faceted and complex. Different owner strata have differing motivations. Decisions involve numerous stakeholders with often competing and complimentary objectives. To be successful, solutions and messaging must directly address value, bottom-line results and the often complex interests of the stakeholders.

References

Allen, J. G., MacNaughton, P., Satish, U., Santanam, S., Vallarino, J., & Spengler, J. D. (2016). Associations of Cognitive Function Scores with Carbon Dioxide, Ventilation, and Volatile Organic Compound Exposures in Office Workers: A Controlled Exposure Study of Green and Conventional Office Environments. *Environmental Health Perspectives, 124*(6). Harvard T.H. Chan School of Public Health, Boston, MA. Retrieved from https://ehp.niehs.nih.gov/wpcontent/uploads/124/6/ehp.1510037.alt.pdf

American Recovery and Reinvestment Act of 2009. (2009). Public Law 111-5, as Amended, 26 USC 1 et seq.

ANSI/ASHRAE/USGBC/IES Standard 189.1-2009. Standard for the Design of High-Performance Green Buildings Except Low-Rise Residential Buildings.

American Society of Heating, Refrigerating and Air-Conditioning Engineers, Inc., Atlanta, Georgia.

Attari S. Z, DeKay, M. L., Davidson, C. I., & Bruin de Bruin, W. (2010). *Public Perceptions of Energy Consumption and Savings*. Proceedings of the National Academy of Sciences. PNAS Direct Submission. Retrieved September, 2010, from The PNAS Open Access Option http://www.pnas.org/cgi/doi/10.1073/pnas.1001509107

Deason, J., Leventis, G., Goldman, C., & Carvallo, J. (2016). *Energy Efficiency Program Financing: Where It Comes From, Where It Goes, and How It Gets There*. Lawrence Berkeley National Laboratory. Retrieved from https://eta.lbl.gov/sites/default/files/publications/lbnl-1005754.pdf

Dembo, R. (2009). *Let's Do For Buildings What We Have Done For Cars*. Toronto, ON: Zerofootprint Foundation. Retrieved September, 2010, from http://www.zerofootprintfoundation.org/images/uploads/Lets_Do_For_Buildings_What_We_Have_Done_For_Cars_US.pdf

Eastern Research Group, InnoVest Group, et al. (2003). *Estimating the Value of Participation in EPA's Energy Star Program*. Presented at the United Nations Environment Programme–Principles for Responsible Investment (UNEP–PRI) Webinar, January 2009.

EIA. (2016). 2012 CBECS Detailed Tables. Building Characteristics Tables for All Buildings (Including Malls), Table A1. Energy Information Administration, U.S. Department of Energy, Washington, DC. Retrieved May, 2017, from https://www.eia.gov/consumption/commercial/data/2012/

Emergency Planning and Community Right-to-Know Act. (1986). Public Law 99-499, as amended, 42 USC 11001 et seq.

GAO. (2005). *Energy Savings – Performance Contracts Offer Benefits, But Vigilance Is Needed to Protect Government Interests*. GAO-05-340. Washington, DC: U.S. Government Accountability Office. Retrieved September, 2010, from http://www.gao.gov/products/GAO-05-340

Gladwell, M. (2002). *The Tipping Point: How Little Things Can Make a Big Difference*. Boston, MA: Back Bay Books, Hachette Book Group.

Global Buildings Performance Network. What Is a Deep Renovation Definition? (2013, February). Technical Report. Paris, France. Retrieved from http://www.gbpn.org/sites/default/files/08.DR_TechRep.low_.pdf

Granade, H. C., Creyts, J., Derkach, A., Farese, P., Nyquist, S., & Ostrowski, K. (2009). *Unlocking Energy Efficiency in the U.S. Economy*. New York: McKinsey & Company.

Hamilton, J. T. (2005). *Regulation Through Revelation: The Origin, Politics, and Impacts of the Toxics Release Inventory Program*. New York: Cambridge University Press.

Hawken, P., Lovins, A., & Lovins, L. H. (2008). *Natural Capitalism: Creating the Next Industrial Revolution* (Chapter 6). Boston, MA: Back Bay Books,

Hachette Book Group. Retrieved February, 2011, from http://www.natcap.org/images/other/NCchapter6.pdf
Hendricks, B., Campbell, B., & Goodale, P. (2010). Efficiency Works—Creating Good Jobs and New Markets Through Energy Efficiency. Energy Resource Management Corporation, Southfield, Michigan. Retrieved September, 2010, from http://www.americanprogress.org/issues/2010/08/pdf/good_jobs_new_markets.pdf
Hopper N., Goldman, C., Gilligan, D., Singer, T. E., & Birr, D. (2007). *A Survey of the U.S. ESCO Industry: Market Growth and Development from 2000 to 2006.* LBNL-62679. Berkeley, CA: Lawrence Berkeley National Laboratory.
ICAP. (2016). *Emissions Trading Worldwide: Status Report 2016.* Berlin: ICAP. Retrieved from https://icapcarbonaction.com/images/StatusReport2016/ICAP_Status_Report_2016_Online.pdf
International Energy Agency. (2016). World Energy Outlook 2016. International Energy Agency, Paris, France. Retrieved from http://www.iea.org/Textbase/npsum/WEO2016SUM.pdf
Kibert, C. J. (2007). *Sustainable Construction: Green Building Design and Delivery* (2nd ed.). Indianapolis, IN: John Wiley & Sons, Inc.
Kok, N., Eichholz, P., & Quigley, J. (2009). *Doing Well by Doing Good? Green Office Buildings.* Berkeley, CA: Center for the Study of Energy Markets, University of California Energy Institute. Retrieved September, 2010, from http://escholarship.org/uc/item/4bf4j0gw
Leventis, G., Fadrhonc, E. M., Kramer, C., & Goldman, C. (2016). Current Practices in Efficiency Financing: An Overview for State and Local Governments. LBNL-1006406. Ernest Orlando Lawrence Berkeley National Laboratory (LBNL). Berkeley, CA. Retrieved November, 2016, from https://energy.gov/sites/prod/files/2017/05/f34/current-practices-efficiency-financing.pdf
Lutzenhiser, L., Biggart, N. W., Kunkle, R., Beamish, T. D., & Burr, T. (2001). *Market Structure and Energy Efficiency: The Case of New Commercial Buildings.* Institute for Energy Efficiency, College of Engineering, UC Santa Barbara, California (Formerly the California Institute for Energy Efficiency).
McKinsey & Co. (2009). *Pathways to a Low-Carbon Economy – Version 2 of the Global Greenhouse Gas Abatement Cost Curve.* New York: McKinsey & Company. Retrieved September, 2010, from www.mckinsey.com/clientservice/ccsi/pathways_low_carbon_economy.asp
McKinsey & Co. (2017). *Pathways and Obstacles to a Low-Carbon Economy—Podcast.* New York: McKinsey & Company. Retrieved from http://www.mckinsey.com/business-functions/sustainability-and-resource-productivity/our-insights/pathways-and-obstacles-to-a-low-carbon-economy
Muldavin, S. R. (2010). *Value Beyond Cost Savings: How to Underwrite Sustainable Properties.* San Rafael, CA: Green Building Finance Consortium, The Muldavin Company, Inc. Retrieved September, 2010, from http://www.greenbuildingfc.com/

NREL. (2009). *Decoupling Policies: Options to Encourage Energy Efficiency Policies for Utilities.* NREL/BR-6A2-46606. Golden, CO: National Renewable Energy Laboratory. Retrieved September, 2010, from http://www.nrel.gov/docs/fy10osti/46606.pdf

Pivo, G., & Fischer, J. (2009). Investment Returns from Responsible Property Investments: Energy Efficient, Transit Oriented and Urban Regeneration Office Properties in the US from 1998–2008.

Real Estate Settlement Procedures Act. (1974). 12 USC 27, Sections 2601–2617.

Risser, R., & Wood, L. (2009). *Making the Business of Energy Efficiency Both Scalable and Sustainable.* Policy Brief 09-01. Washington, DC: The Brookings Institution. Retrieved September, 2010, from http://www.brookings.edu/papers/2009/04_energy_efficiency_wood.aspx

Rogers, E. M. (2003). *Diffusion of Innovations* (5th ed.). New York: Free Press, Simon & Schuster.

Sinek, S. (2009). *Start with Why: How Great Leaders Inspire Everyone to Take Action.* New York: Portfolio Hardcover, Penguin Group (USA).

Thaler, R. H., & Sunstein, C. R. (2008). *Nudge—Improving Decisions About Health, Wealth and Happiness.* New Haven, CT: Yale University Press.

WBCSD. (2009). Energy Efficiency in Buildings—Transforming the Market. World Business Council for Sustainable Development. Retrieved September, 2010, from http://www.wbcsd.org/Plugins/DocSearch/details.asp?DocTypeId=251&ObjectId=Mzc5NDk

CHAPTER 12

Financing Rooftop Solar for Single-Family Rental Properties

Russell Heller

1 Background

The US solar energy industry has grown rapidly over the past decade, largely due to manufacturing and installation cost decreases, federal tax credits, state clean energy mandates, net metering, and innovative financing tools like the power purchase agreement (PPA). Low interest rates following the 2008 financial crisis reduced financing costs for solar investments and assisted in spurring deployment of the renewable energy technology. This chapter focuses on the residential solar industry, where the tenants of more than 15 million single-family rental [SFR] homes are often unable to access rooftop solar, even when installing solar panels would save renters money.

Cost decreases have assisted in the growth of solar energy. As global installations increased exponentially, residential solar costs in the United States decreased by 56%, from \$7.06 to \$3.11 per installed watt, from year-end 2009 through the first quarter 2016 (Fu et al., 2016). Decreases in hard costs, or the combined expense of modules, inverters, and other electrical or mechanical components, have outpaced declines in soft

R. Heller (✉)
Yale University, New Haven, CT, USA
e-mail: Russell.heller@yale.edu

T. Walker et al. (eds.), *Sustainable Real Estate*, Palgrave Studies in Sustainable Business In Association with Future Earth,
https://doi.org/10.1007/978-3-319-94565-1_12

costs—spending on labor, overhead, advertising, and permitting—so that soft costs increased from 50% to 58% of total installation expense for residential solar in the 2009–2016 period (Fu et al., 2016). Soft costs for residential installations make up a much higher percentage of total installation expenditures than for commercial and utility-scale solar, where soft costs made up only 49% and 34% of build costs, respectively. The US solar industry reached a cumulative one million installations in February 2016, and the pace of deployment is largely expected to increase over time, further depressing prices as economies of scale improve (Pyper, 2016).

Tax benefits at the state and federal levels also contributed to the boom in the residential solar industry. The main subsidy for solar installations is a 30% Investment Tax Credit (ITC) that applies to the cost of installation for all solar arrays. Such an incentive allows the owner of a solar project to deduct 30% of a solar system's installation cost from his or her tax burden. Also, Modified Accelerated Cost Recovery System (MACRS) depreciation allows solar system owners to deduct 85% of the cost of a system from their income over a period of five years (*"How to depreciate property," 2016*). Normally the tax deduction for a capital investment is spread over the useful life of the investment—anywhere from 25 to 30 years for a solar system—but the IRS allows the cost of a solar installation to be deducted over a much shorter time frame, reducing the tax obligation of a solar system's owner and increasing the attractiveness of investments in solar energy. Some states, like California, also offer property tax exemptions for solar energy, which means that even though rooftop solar installations increase property values, property tax appraisals do not consider the solar systems' positive impact on a home's market value.

PPAs are financial agreements that enable homeowners to access rooftop solar without upfront costs. The innovative mechanism enables an investor to fund the installation of a residential solar system after a homeowner agrees to purchase the electricity generated by the panels at set prices over a fixed time period, typically at a rate lower than that offered by the local utility. The homeowner enters into an agreement to purchase the electricity produced by the system for a predetermined period of time, typically 15–20 years. The PPA contract guarantees future payments at fixed rates that gradually increase each year and allows the investor to project future cash flows from the solar system so as to ensure a predictable return on investment. With a PPA, a homeowner does not own the solar panels, but does pay for the electricity generated. The panel owner is liable to repair any damages to the system, so the homeowner is able to acquire the less expensive solar energy without risks associated with the solar system's performance. The energy consumed by the home beyond that produced by the panels is drawn from the grid at retail rates and any excess energy produced by the panels is typically sold back to the grid at rates that vary by state and local utility. The current market for solar PPAs is led by a few major players: SolarCity (now Tesla Energy), Sunrun, and Vivint Solar. Since much of the data cited in this chapter is from SolarCity's period as a standalone company prior to its late-2016 acquisition, the company that is now a part of Tesla will be referred to as SolarCity.

Net Energy Metering (NEM) is a system that allows properties with solar installations to export excess solar electricity back into the grid, offsetting energy imported from the grid over the course of a billing cycle so that the utility customer pays for the net amount of electricity consumed. Forty-one states offer net metering, and some utilities in Idaho and Texas, states without mandated net metering, also offer NEM for distributed energy sources like rooftop solar (Cleveland & Durkay, 2016). NEM rates vary based on the state and utility provider, but a vast majority of solar customers receive credits at retail rates, allowing them to export electricity back into the grid and earn bill credits at the local energy price—above the price paid on the PPA. Such a system forces utility companies to purchase excess solar energy at retail rates, which does not allow room for profit when the energy is sold, at the purchase price, to other grid connected customers. In fact, utilities pay large fixed costs associated with maintaining a grid and therefore lose money when selling net-metered solar to other customers. Laws surrounding NEM will inevitably change as more distributed energy is added to grids across the United States and the burden on utilities, and therefore ratepayers, increases as more customers begin to export energy onto the grid at retail rates. A number of states have instituted caps on the total installed capacity of net-metered systems. Other electricity providers, like Austin Energy in Texas, offer Value of Solar rates that take into account the grid costs and benefits of distributed energy, like the value of reduced emissions and avoided new power plant construction, energy production, and transmission costs.

2 The Problem for Renters

Despite the success of the aforementioned policies and the resulting growth in solar deployment in the United States, a number of existing barriers prevent widespread adoption of distributed solar energy. One major obstacle for residential solar growth is found in the single-family home rental market, where a split incentive between renters and landlords hinders rooftop solar adoption.

A split incentive is a situation in which the costs and benefits of an investment accrue to differing parties. In the case of rooftop solar on rental homes, an investment in solar energy might reduce utility bills for the tenant but requires a cash investment that both the renter and the property owner lack the financial incentive to make. Tenants do not want to make long-term investments in properties they do not own because they might not occupy these properties long enough to recoup their costs. Furthermore, tenants rarely have the legal authority to install solar panels on a property they do not own. Since landlords typically do not pay the utility bills of their residents, there is little incentive for a property owner to invest in solar energy if the renter will receive the benefits of the reduced utility bills offered by solar energy—even if the solar system increases property value. Additionally, landlords would not see much benefit if a PPA was signed with a company like SolarCity because tenants would benefit from the electricity cost savings, and property owners would have little incentive to spend the energy to approve an installation or repair a roof in advance of a solar project.

3 The Current "Solution"

Right now the leading "solution" to the split incentive is Community Solar.

Community Solar, also known as Shared Solar or Virtual Net Metering, is a solar ownership structure that allows renters and homeowners whose roofs are unfit for solar to offset their energy use by acquiring stakes in local, ground-mounted solar installations. Customers can collectively pay to build a solar array or subscribe to the electricity produced by a system owned by a utility or solar developer and use pro rata shares of the energy produced to offset home electricity consumption the same way a net-metered rooftop system would.

Though Community Solar could prove a suitable option for some renters seeking to consume solar energy, a number of impediments exist, delaying or preventing widespread adoption. First, many utility companies are opposed to any expansion of net metering and lobby against shared solar legislation. As previously explained, net metering often erodes utility profits, and though Shared Solar has at times been implemented without legislation, Community Solar bills vastly improve the success rates of projects of this type. Additionally, utilization of tax credits on customer-owned systems can be difficult when dividing shares of a project between a number of owners that may not have enough income or the accounting wherewithal to take full advantage of the tax credits and depreciation write-offs. For utility-sponsored installations, customers can choose to have their energy supplied by a solar array but typically must pay above-retail prices for the electricity. As of early 2016, only 102 megawatts of shared solar had been installed in the United States, representing a small fraction of total solar deployment.

Though Community Solar holds long-term potential, its current financial and legislative constraints leave the market for single-family home renters seeking access to solar open to other potential solutions.

4 A Superior Solution

A potentially viable solution to this split incentive could be a Renter's PPA [RPPA].

An **RPPA** is a straightforward concept—property owners install solar panels on their properties and require tenants to purchase the produced energy. Property owners can include electricity PPAs into rental agreements by including a clause requiring renters to purchase solar electricity at fixed, below retail rates. Existing rental agreements would not be altered to include language regarding electricity purchases, but future rental agreements could be designed to incorporate the sale of electricity to captive tenant customers. The RPPA provides a number of benefits over standard PPA contracts by removing the need for tax equity investors and by eliminating a large portion of the soft costs associated with solar installations. These benefits are discussed at length below. Renters would benefit from electricity rates below market levels and enjoy access to clean solar energy, while property owners would be able to create a new, immediately cash flow positive revenue stream if electricity sales exceed borrowing costs. Repayment risks would be low and predictable because landlords would already have access to rental payment histories and could be able to target reliable renters with high credit scores for the RPPA. Landlords without the expertise or infrastructure to add solar to their properties themselves could contract out installation and operations and maintenance (O&M) to third-party experts like SolarCity and Enphase that would build and manage the solar systems. The concept will likely perform best on single-family home rental properties that only have one meter because multifamily rentals contain a number of meters, complicating the process of determining the end users of the energy produced by a solar system. Though this problem likely could be addressed with technology that tracks the consumption of the solar energy on a meter-to-meter basis in a rental building, this chapter focuses exclusively on the potential of the RPPA in the single-family home rental market.

5 Addressable Market: Single-Family Rentals

The **SFR** market has seen tremendous growth since 2005. Currently, 15.1 million SFR homes account for 13% of the entire US housing market and 35% of all occupied rental housing stock (Smith & Koch, 2016). The 2008 financial crisis sparked or accelerated a number of major trends in the American real estate market. Housing prices fell as a result of a wave of subprime mortgage foreclosures and nationwide job losses. Institutional investors began to acquire single-family properties that they correctly identified as undervalued relative to achievable market rental prices. By mid-2017, the seven largest institutional SFR portfolios included approximately 200,000 properties, largely concentrated in "Sun Belt" states like Arizona and Nevada (Dezember & Kusisto, 2017).

Additionally, lending standards for mortgages became more stringent following the financial crisis, preventing individuals from purchasing homes. From 2007–2012, all-cash home sales increased from 23.1% to 39.5% of total home sales, explained by the decrease in mortgage-fueled home purchases and the increase in all-cash institutional investments (Goodman, Zhu, & George, 2014). As average student debt among college graduates rose by 53% from 2004–2014 to nearly $27,000 per borrower, fewer graduates could afford to purchase homes, especially considering tightened mortgage lending standards and a poor job market ("Student debt and the class of 2014," 2015). These factors led to a sea change in the American housing market as the number of single-family rental units increased by 3.8 million from 2005–2014, accounting for 89% of the net increase in single-family units and 62.5% of the growth in total occupied housing over the same period (Smith & Koch, 2016). After peaking at 69.2% in 2004, the American homeownership rate declined to 62.9% in mid-2016, the lowest level in 50 years (Gopal, 2016). The market for SFR homes is large, continues to grow, and is increasingly dominated by a number of institutional investors who could successfully implement the RPPA at scale.

6 Why the Renter's PPA Could Work: The Economics of Rooftop Solar

Three installers comprise a large portion of the rooftop solar market. In the second quarter 2016, SolarCity (now Tesla), Sunrun, and Vivint Solar together commanded 47.5% of the rooftop solar market (Mond, 2016). Despite their dominance, all three of these corporations remain unprofitable for a few reasons. SolarCity will be used as the primary example herein as it is the largest individual company in the industry.

Sales costs, the expenses associated with acquiring new customers, are high in the rooftop solar industry. SolarCity has successfully reduced hard costs, cutting such installation expenses per watt from $2.40 in the first quarter 2014 to $1.98 through the same period in 2016 ("SolarCity Q1 2016 earnings presentation", 2016). Despite the reduction in hard installation expenditures, the company struggles with its soft costs. In Q4 2015, 20% of total costs per watt were associated with sales. In 2016s first quarter, sales expenditures ballooned from $0.54 to $0.97 per watt, representing 38% of total installation expenses of $3.18 per watt. The RPPA would require no advertising because existing tenants are captive customers and would have little choice but to agree to purchase the electricity or to live somewhere else. With the RPPA, there would be limited administrative costs associated with installing the solar systems other than the expenses associated with rewriting rental agreements and billing tenants.

Solar companies do not currently recognize SFR homes as a market for potential sales and therefore likely target none of their marketing toward renters. Sales to single-family rentals would, therefore, involve limited sales costs. Additionally, advertising costs are fixed in the short term for sellers, meaning that they are motivated to spread such expenses over a larger installation base by increasing sales volume. As the number of installed watts increases, the sales expenditure per watt decreases. The cost to a company like SolarCity to install an additional watt is equivalent only to the marginal expense of installing a new watt, which would exclude sunk costs like past advertising spending. As a result, installers might agree to sell solar arrays for less than their total published costs per watt and still earn a profit. For institutional SFR owners that might purchase solar for thousands of roofs at once, the pricing benefits could be more pronounced.

The cost of capital is also high across the industry. In the first quarter 2016, SolarCity claimed it held a blended debt rate of 5.1%, but its more recent debt offerings carried higher rates. In Q2 2016, SolarCity could not sell 18-month bonds paying 6.5% interest before Elon Musk and two other senior executives at the company purchased a combined $100 million of the $124 million offering (Owens, 2016). Though Tesla's merger with SolarCity might reduce borrowing costs for the company, many lenders view direct lending to rooftop solar installers as risky. Additionally, because the PPA originators are all unprofitable, they have no choice but to partner with tax equity investors in order to take advantage of the ITC and MACRS depreciation incentives. Tax equity investments are situations in which a taxable entity invests in a project with a tax incentive attached in order to take advantage of the tax benefit. Since Tesla, and by extension SolarCity, is not yet profitable, it must work with tax equity investors and sacrifice large portions of project cash flows as a result. According to the US Department of Energy SunShot Initiative, tax equity investments typically offer a cost of capital of 9.8% and repayment periods are weighted heavily toward the first seven years following the investment (Feldman, Boff, & Margolis, 2016). In SolarCity's case, approximately 30% of project cash flows are returned to the tax equity investor in each of the first seven years after a project is completed. SolarCity requires about 40% of each project to be funded by tax equity, so the blended cost of capital between both debt and tax equity is likely well above 5.1%. For a stable and profitable firm that owns thousands of properties, tax equity would be unnecessary and borrowing costs would likely be much lower than at SolarCity. As an example, Blackstone was able to raise €300 million in 2015 at an interest rate of 2% ("Blackstone form 10-K 2015," 2016). At the time, the company owned the nation's largest portfolio of SFR homes through its former subsidiary Invitation Homes.

7 Hypothetical Target Company

An institutional investor that owns a large number of single-family rental properties, like Blackstone before it spun off Invitation Homes, would be an ideal target to implement the RPPA at the lowest possible cost. Such a large company would be able to borrow at relatively low rates, take full advantage of subsidies for solar without the need for tax equity, and achieve economies of scale by negotiating installation prices for bulk purchases. Additionally, as an RPPA-generated electricity, it would provide the panel owner with Renewable Energy Certificates (RECs). These companies could gain a public image boost by claiming the greenhouse gas emission reductions associated with the RECs or could sell the certificates in the open market. Even with the high cost of capital and substantial selling, general, and administrative (SG&A) expenses, SolarCity was cash flow positive in Q1 2016 excluding its investment in a solar panel factory, demonstrating the potential for the PPA model to produce a profit even under difficult conditions. SolarCity claimed that its increased SG&A expenses in first quarter 2016 were due to installations failing to meet expectations, resulting in the spread of fixed sales expenses over a smaller number of projects. An institutional investor could partner with a leading installer like SolarCity to utilize its excess installation capacity and take advantage of the company's track record and expertise in building reliable solar systems at low cost.

8 Asset-Backed Securities

Many large institutional SFR investors aggregate and securitize their real estate portfolios. By selling asset-backed securities (ABS), or bonds backed by the rental payments on portfolios of homes, companies like Blackstone are able to raise billions of dollars of new cash at low interest rates to invest in purchasing more homes. Through April 2014, rental-backed securities issued by major institutional investors in SFR real estate totaled $9.45 billion (Layton, 2015). If an institutional investor installs enough solar systems on its properties, it could sell an ABS secured by the solar electricity payments or combine the solar and rental payments for future ABS offerings, allowing the companies to raise more capital while shifting repayment risk to outside investors. SolarCity has already raised hundreds of millions of dollars by securitizing the payments from its distributed solar assets (Maloney, 2016).

9 An Alternative RPPA

Though the SFR market has seen substantial institutional investor engagement since 2008, many property owners are incorporated as real estate investment trusts (REITs). A REIT is a company structured in a way that enables income from real estate assets to avoid taxation if at least 90% of profits are paid to investors as dividends. Large single-family rental REITs like American Homes 4 Rent, Colony American Homes, and Invitation Homes own tens of thousands of properties in markets like California, Texas, and Arizona. These companies are tax-exempt and therefore would be unable to utilize tax credits on rooftop solar installations. In order to overcome such a gap, these institutional investors could utilize more expensive tax equity investments or take on a "Pass-Through PPA."

The Pass-Through PPA would occur if a landlord signed a PPA with a company like SolarCity in which she would purchase and immediately sell the electricity to a tenant at a slight premium. This way, the electricity would "pass-through" the property owner to the tenant. For example, in a market with electricity prices of $0.12 per kWh, a typical SolarCity PPA might cost $0.08 per kWh. A Pass-Through PPA would enable a property owner to sign a PPA with a solar installer and, like in an RPPA, work electricity purchases into a rental agreement with a tenant. The property owner might charge the tenant $0.095 per kWh, offering a below market rate and satisfying tenants with cheap, clean electricity while retaining the profitable "spread" of $0.015 between the two contracts.

Such an arrangement would offer property owners a number of benefits and disadvantages compared to the RPPA. The Pass-Through PPA would allow property owners to avoid upfront investments and any associated increases in borrowing. The model would also allow property owners to bypass other ownership risks such as the obligation to repair any damage to a solar system. The main risk associated with the Pass-Through PPA would be associated with guaranteeing payments to the installer. Companies like SolarCity would not agree to build the rooftop solar systems without a committed, creditworthy buyer for the electricity produced. When tenants cannot afford electricity payments or homes with solar systems sit unoccupied, the cost of the energy produced would be borne by the property owner, who might be only able to monetize the electricity on the grid at a wholesale price below that paid to the installer. As a result, property owners would require a substantial enough spread between rates received from tenants and rates paid to installers to justify the risk of guaranteeing electricity payments to an installer. The necessary spread might limit the use of this model to states with abnormally high electricity prices and favorable policy environments.

10 A Risk to Consider Regarding the Renter's PPA and Rooftop Solar

Changes to NEM laws and regulations might pose the largest long-term threat to the rooftop solar industry. As distributed energy sources increase as a percentage of total electricity generation, NEM will become a burden for utilities and ratepayers, requiring alterations to NEM policy. Technological innovations will ease this transition, as will decreasing energy storage costs, but inevitably the laws are likely to change. Smart inverters, a technology that can help regulate the output of a rooftop solar array based on grid conditions, will likely become ubiquitous as utilities in a number of states, including Arizona and California, are currently testing and implementing the technology. California began requiring smart inverters on all new solar installations beginning in September 2017 (St. John, 2016). Smart inverters can reduce voltage during periods of over-production and direct electricity between a home, the grid, or a battery system in order to maximize panel efficiency and reduce grid strain. They will help prevent grid damage during peak solar production periods and will likely be complemented by cheaper batteries. Though the laws surrounding net metering are set to change, old systems are likely to be grandfathered into new regulatory schemes, meaning that the net-metered rates for solar systems built prior to any regulatory changes will not be affected by future alterations to the NEM scheme.

11 Where This Might Work: California

California is a preferred state for investing in solar. The state has very high levels of solar radiation, especially in Southern California. In 2015, residential electricity prices were $0.169, ranking seventh highest in the country (Annual Electric Power Industry Report, 2016). There are no property taxes applied to solar systems in the state. California recently updated its net-metering laws but grandfathered in old systems, which indicates that future changes will likely include grandfather clauses for old systems. As a result of California's drought, hydroelectric production decreased 67.5% from 2011–2015, making up only 7% of Californian electricity in 2015 compared to over 21% in 2011. Similarly, nuclear energy production declined from 18.2% to 9.4% of electricity generated in California over the same period. Both of these trends leave room for growth in solar generation, which remained at only 7.5% of energy produced in the state in 2015 (Annual Electric Power Industry Report, 2016).

Net Metering 2.0 encourages the implementation of the RPPA in California. The state is one of the first to modernize its net-metering policy. The new regulatory regime, NEM 2.0, will be in effect until 2019, providing ample time to design and implement an RPPA pilot project before the state redesigns regulations. NEM 2.0 allows excess energy fed into the grid to be credited back to utility customers at retail rates and prohibits fixed monthly charges like demand or grid access charges that undermine the economics of rooftop solar. Investment in California also carries some risks. Mandatory time-of-use (TOU) rates will enter into effect with NEM 2.0, but the rates have not yet been decided. TOU rates might diminish the value of solar energy production by lowering energy prices during times of peak oversupply, which correspond with major solar production periods. Orienting solar arrays to face west will limit the impact of the TOU rates by shifting panel production later into the day, matching peak demand hours while shifting panel production peaks away from those of most grid-tied solar. Such a shift would allow excess energy to be sold back to the grid at increased rates. NEM 2.0 requires interconnection fees of $75–150 depending on system size and local utility and removes a prior exemption on non-bypassable charges, which are fees of $0.02–0.03 per kWh applied to all Californian utility bills to fund energy efficiency and low-income bill assistance programs. The non-bypassable charge will have a limited impact on RPPA customers because it only applies to energy consumed from the grid, not from solar panels, and homes without solar already pay the charge.

12 Where This Might Work: Connecticut

Connecticut is a state where RPPA implementation would likely not initially take place, as there has been very little institutional investment in Connecticut's SFR market. The state would serve as an ideal location for RPPA expansion to non-institutional SFR property owners if the concept was proven successful in a more consolidated SFR market like California. In 2015, Connecticut had the highest residential electricity rates in the contiguous 48 states at $0.209 per kWh—almost double the national average (Annual Electric Power Industry Report, 2016). Connecticut has a strong net-metering framework that requires both major utilities, Eversource and United Illuminating, to provide retail rate net metering with no net-metered capacity cap. Due to the lack of SFR ownership consolidation, the rental property owners in the state own smaller portfolios of homes and would face higher borrowing costs, but high electricity prices and a favorable regulatory environment make Connecticut a top state for solar investments. The smaller property owners would still be able to take advantage of tax credits and avoid the need for tax equity investors, so the most valuable benefits of RPPA would still apply. However, the economies of scale, low borrowing costs, and ability to issue ABS would not apply.

13 Potential Social Impacts

The RPPA has the potential to revolutionize both the rooftop solar and SFR housing industries. By installing 6.5kW solar arrays on just 353,850 homes, 2.3% of the SFR market, 2.9 GW would be added to the grid, equivalent to the total US rooftop solar capacity built in 2015. The RPPA could help diversify the US energy supply and reduce electricity bills for renters, who tend to be less wealthy than those who own homes—49% of SFR homes are categorized as "affordable," compared to just 24% of single-family owned properties and 63% of single-family rental occupants are in the bottom two income quartiles (Drew, 2015). Though no southern states were discussed in this chapter, it is worth noting that 42% of the American single-family detached rental market is located in the South, where solar adoption is very low. A Pew Research survey found that only 35% of homeowners in the South had seriously considered installing solar on their homes, compared to 66% of homeowners in the West (Funk & Kennedy, 2016). When photovoltaic systems are installed on roofs, neighbors within a one-mile radius are significantly more likely to consider installing solar on their own roofs (Graziano & Gillingham, 2014). Implementation of the RPPA in the southern United States could help spark a movement toward rooftop solar in a largely untapped yet sunny region, helping increase solar adoption and reduce fossil fuel dependence in often-conservative states that have historically moved more slowly than the rest of the country toward renewable energy adoption.

14 Concluding Thoughts

As a result of cost decreases for solar installations, net metering, favorable government policy, low interest rates, and financing tools like PPAs, the American residential solar industry has grown rapidly in recent years. The single-family home rental market in the United States has steadily grown since the 2008 recession, and its solar energy potential remains untapped due to the split incentive between property owners and tenants. The RPPA model has the potential to create new revenue streams for both institutional and small-scale SFR property owners alike. Unlike major solar installers like SolarCity that struggle to achieve profits, institutional investors have the capability to take direct advantage of government tax incentives, borrow at low interest rates, and limit most sales and administration costs associated with installing solar systems while securitizing solar payments into ABS to fund more investments. In states like California, the RPPA model could be viable under current market conditions and state regulations. If institutional investors can demonstrate the value of the RPPA, small-scale SFR owners might also employ the RPPA on their properties across the country, beginning in states like Connecticut with high electricity prices and favorable net-metering policies. The potential social impacts of the RPPA include decreases in greenhouse gas emissions, a reduction in electricity prices for typically middle or lower class home renters, and the possibility of a public demonstration of the economic viability of rooftop solar so that American homeowners more seriously consider installing solar systems on their properties.

References

Annual Electric Power Industry Report (Vol. Form EIA-861, Rep.). (2016, October). U.S. Energy Information Administration. Retrieved July 19, 2017, from https://www.eia.gov/electricity/data/eia861/

Cleveland, M., & Durkay, J. (2016, November 3). State Net Metering Policies. Retrieved July 4, 2017, from http://www.ncsl.org/research/energy/net-metering-policy-overview-and-state-legislative-updates.aspx

Dezember, R., & Kusisto, L. (2017, July 21). Meet Your New Landlord: Wall Street. *The Wall Street Journal*.

Drew, R. (2015), July. *A New Look at the Characteristics of Single-Family Rentals and Their Residents* (Working paper No. W15-6). Retrieved July 4, 2017, from Joint Center for Housing Studies Harvard University Website: http://www.jchs.harvard.edu/sites/jchs.harvard.edu/files/w15-6_drew.pdf

Feldman, D., Boff, D., & Margolis, R. (2016, October 11). *Q2/Q3 2016 Solar Industry Update* (Rep.). Retrieved July 4, 2017, from U.S. Department of Energy Website: http://www.nrel.gov/docs/fy17osti/67246.pdf

Fu, R., Chung, D., Lowder, T., Feldman, D., Ardani, K., & Margolis, R. (2016, September). *U.S. solar photovoltaic system cost benchmark: Q1 2016* (Rep. No. NREL/TP-6A20-66532). Retrieved http://www.nrel.gov/docs/fy16osti/67142.pdf

Funk, C., & Kennedy, B. (2016, October). *The Politics of Climate*. Pew Research Center.

Goodman, L. S., Zhu, J., & George, T. (2014). *Where Have All the Loans Gone? The Impact of Credit Availability on Mortgage Volume* (Rep.). doi:https://doi.org/10.3905/jsf.2014.20.2.045

Gopal, P. (2016, July 28). Homeownership Rate in the U.S. Drops to Lowest Since 1965. Retrieved July 04, 2017, from https://www.bloomberg.com/news/articles/2016-07-28/homeownership-rate-in-the-u-s-tumbles-to-the-lowest-since-1965

Graziano, M., & Gillingham, K. (2014). Spatial Patterns of Solar Photovoltaic System Adoption: The Influence of Neighbors and the Built Environment. *Journal of Economic Geography, 15*(4), 815–839. https://doi.org/10.1093/jeg/lbu036

Layton, J. (2015). *Single-Family Rental Securitizations* (Rep.). Retrieved July 26, 2017, from Institute for Real Estate Studies, Penn State website: https://www.smeal.psu.edu/ires/documents/single-family-rental-securitizations-spring-2015

Maloney, P. (2016, April 08). SolarCity Closes $150M Securitization for Commercial Solar Storage. Retrieved July 26, 2017, from http://www.utilitydive.com/news/solarcity-closes-150m-securitization-for-commercial-solar-storage/417069/

Mond, A. (2016, June 22). The Rise of the Regional Solar Installer. Retrieved July 25, 2017, from https://www.greentechmedia.com/articles/read/the-rise-of-the-regional-solar-installer

Owens, J. C. (2016, August 24). Elon Musk, SolarCity execs to Buy Most of SolarCity Bond Offering. Retrieved July 04, 2017, from http://www.marketwatch.com/story/elon-musk-solarcity-execs-to-buy-most-of-solarcity-bond-offering-2016-08-23

Pyper, J. (2016, April 21). The US Solar Market Is Now 1 Million Installations Strong. Retrieved July 04, 2017, from https://www.greentechmedia.com/articles/read/The-U.S.-Solar-Market-Now-One-Million-Installations-Strong

Smith, C., & Koch, C. (2016, May 19). *Why the Boom in Single family Rentals? Renters with Kids, But No Cash; Owners with Cash, But No Kids.* (Rep.). Retrieved July 4, 2017, from RCLCO Website: http://www.rclco.com/advisory-single-family

SolarCity Q1 2016 Earnings Presentation (Earnings Release). (2016, May 9). Retrieved July 4, 2017, from SolarCity Website: http://files.shareholder.com/downloads/AMDA-14LQRE/2295608251x0x890865/FDB54665-8531-4F66-B545-4F9D057C8300/SolarCity_1Q16_Earnings_Presentation_FINAL.pdf

St. John, J. (2016, July). PG&E to Plug Enphase Smart Inverters and SolarCity Storage Systems Into Its Grid Control Platform. Retrieved July 19, 2017, from https://www.greentechmedia.com/articles/read/pge-to-plug-enphase-smart-inverters-solarcity-storage-systems-into-new-derm

Student Debt and the Class of 2014 (Rep.). (2015, October). Retrieved July 4, 2017, from The Institute for College Access & Success Website: http://ticas.org/sites/default/files/pub_files/classof2014.pdf

The Blackstone Group L.P. (2016). *Blackstone Form 10-K 2015.* Retrieved from https://www.sec.gov/Archives/edgar/data/1393818/000119312516481948/d129194d10k.htm

PART IV

Sustainable Cities and Communities

CHAPTER 13

A Case for Sustainable Affordable Housing in the United States

Sarah Gomez

A well-paying job, a loving family consisting of 2.5 kids, a car, and a spacious suburban home with a postage-stamp backyard and white picket fence: this is the elusive "American Dream" of history books, advertisements, and national myth. For many, this American Dream is unattainable. What people tend to focus on less is the fact that it is also unsustainable. In the coming decade, as a result of pressure factors like population growth and climate change, the United States will be forced to dramatically alter the way in which it currently thinks about and manages critical resources like water, energy, and land. Housing, as the mechanism by which communities are organized and resources are allocated and expended, lies at the nexus of many of these concerns. In order to tackle many of the nation's sustainability-related problems, U.S. governments, developers, and citizens will soon have to think more creatively about residential development. To adapt to and survive the consequences of global climate change, the country will have to address the urban sprawl that lies at the heart of its national myth, and embrace new imaginative possibilities of what ideal American communities might look like. This chapter describes

S. Gomez (✉)
Yale University, New Haven, CT, USA

T. Walker et al. (eds.), *Sustainable Real Estate*, Palgrave Studies in Sustainable Business In Association with Future Earth,
https://doi.org/10.1007/978-3-319-94565-1_13

current deficiencies of the Unites States housing market to locate a promising solution to these challenges in the field of sustainable affordable housing.

The American Dream sprawled over and colonized the country's natural landscape. Beginning around 1945, encouraged by tax incentives, pop culture, and the G.I. Bill, Americans began to move from cities to suburbs.[1] This new generation of government-sponsored, postwar suburbanites laid claim to formerly unattractive corners of the country. They created communities outside of cities, which were now considered dangerous.[2] They engineered ways to remain connected to the rest of the country, relying on national highways, personal automobiles, shopping malls, supermarkets, and the television to survive on the fringe of urban areas. In doing so, this generation that benefitted from the postwar economic boom, the emergence of consumer culture, and the newfound ability to live pop-art lifestyles significantly increased the amount of resources people consumed and the area that these resources needed to travel in order to reach them.[3] The consumption patterns, homes, communities, and lifestyle habits they created have since become defining features of both the American landscape and the American psyche.

1 Challenges in the Current Housing Market

1.1 Urban Sprawl

Today, the suburbs post-World War II Americans built continue to place a disproportionate burden on national commons and resources like air, land, and water. In 2014, despite the fact that suburban residents accounted for less than half of the U.S. population (37.3% in 2015),[4] suburbs were found to generate half of all household greenhouse gas emissions

[1] Beauregard, Robert A. *When America Became Suburban*. Minneapolis: University of Minnesota Press, 2006.

[2] Chauncey, George. "World War II and the Remaking of American Sexual Culture." Lecture, HIST 127; Lecture, YUAG Auditorium, New Haven, CT, September 29, 2016.

[3] Rhodes, Edwardo Lao. *Environmental Justice in America a New Paradigm*. Bloomington: Indiana University Press, 2005.

[4] @uscensusbureau. "U.S. Cities Home to 62.7% of Population but Comprise 3.5% of Land Area." The United States Census Bureau. 2015. Accessed December 23, 2016. http://www.census.gov/newsroom/press-releases/2015/cb15-33.html.

nationwide.[5] As a result, the average carbon footprint of households located in the center of large, population-dense cities was about 50 percent below the national average, while that of households located in distant suburbs was twice the national average.[6] Additionally, the national highways, parking lots, and long, wide suburban roads that this generation began to pave also increased the area of impervious surfaces covering American land, blocking groundwater recharge.[7] In 2005, around 65% of the total impervious cover in the U.S. came from "habitats for cars" alone, which are concentrated in suburban areas and include paved streets, parking lots, and driveways.[8] These impervious surfaces collect pollutants that get deposited into waterways when it rains, leading to ecological problems like contamination and fish kills.[9] Furthermore, sprawled habitats for people and cars were built at the expense of the species that had originally lived there; sprawl has placed 30% of the nation's plant and animal species at current risk of extinction.[10]

These damages are not limited to plant and animal life. When confronted with the externalities of sprawl, humans assume the high costs of pollution cleanup and daily exposures. Poorly planned development directly harms human health. For example, the construction of contiguous suburban zones contributes to a heat island effect.[11] A given metropolitan area is said to experience the heat island effect when the temperature of that densely populated area is around 20 degrees Fahrenheit hotter

[5] Sanders, Robert. "Suburban sprawl cancels carbon-footprint savings of dense urban cores." Berkeley News. 2015. Accessed December 23, 2016. http://news.berkeley.edu/2014/01/06/suburban-sprawl-cancels-carbon-footprint-savings-of-dense-urban-cores/.

[6] Ibid.

[7] Wilson, Bev, and Arnab Chakraborty. "The Environmental Impacts of Sprawl: Emergent Themes from the Past Decade of Planning Research." *Sustainability*, August 5, 2013. MDPI.

[8] Frazer, Lance. "Paving Paradise: The Peril of Impervious Surfaces." Environmental Health Perspectives. 2005. Accessed December 23, 2016. https://www.ncbi.nlm.nih.gov/pmc/articles/PMC1257665/.

[9] Ibid.

[10] Ewing, R., J. Kostyack, D. Chen, B. Stein, and M. Ernst. Endangered by Sprawl: How Runaway Development Threatens America's Wildlife. National Wildlife Federation, Smart Growth America, and NatureServe. Washington, DC, January 2005.

[11] Neil Debbage, J. Marshall Shepherd, The urban heat island effect and city contiguity, Computers, Environment and Urban Systems, Volume 54, 2015, Pages 181–194, ISSN 0198-9715, https://doi.org/10.1016/j.compenvurbsys.2015.08.002. (http://www.sciencedirect.com/science/article/pii/S0198971515300089)

than the temperature of surrounding, more rural areas.[12] In a metropolitan community experiencing the heat island effect, roof and pavement surface temperatures can climb to be 50–90 degrees Fahrenheit hotter than the air.[13] This works to significantly raise local demand for cooling, creating a surge in electricity usage and leading to an increase in greenhouse gas emissions from nearby power plants used to supply electricity. Heat island effect has been linked to physical discomfort, respiratory difficulties, and heat-related mortality.[14]

As this information has come to light in recent years, it has become clear that the sun has set on the era of sprawl. Such developments can no longer be considered a viable solution to accommodate future population growth and subsequent housing needs.[15]

1.2 Housing Affordability and Accessibility

Despite this suburban development, America still faces a shortage of affordable homes and a housing and homelessness crisis. This issue is so severe that it has received international attention in popular human rights discourse. A letter submitted to the United Nations Universal Periodic Review by the National Law Center and endorsed by 40 separate U.S. organizations and nonprofits provides compelling evidence to express why the current housing system in the United States is not only problematic, but fundamentally unjust. They cited the facts that,

> In no U.S. jurisdiction can a person working full time at the federal minimum wage afford a one-bedroom apartment. Due to lack of funding, only one quarter of renters eligible for federal housing assistance actually receive it, and the federal budget for developing and maintaining public housing and providing for low-income housing subsidies has decreased. No binding requirements exist for jurisdictions to plan for and create incentives for the

[12] Shmaefsky, Brian R. "One Hot Demonstration: The Urban Heat Island Effect." *Journal of College Science Teaching* 35, no. 7 (2006): 52–54. http://www.jstor.org/stable/42992461.

[13] "Heat Island Impacts." EPA. June 20, 2017. Accessed August 09, 2017. https://www.epa.gov/heat-islands/heat-island-impacts.

[14] Ibid.

[15] Freilich, Robert H., and Neil M. Popowitz. "The Umbrella of Sustainability: Smart Growth, New Urbanism, Renewable Energy and Green Development in the 21st Century." *The Urban Lawyer* 42, no. 1 (2010): 1–39. http://www.jstor.org/stable/27895766.

> production of sufficient adequate, affordable housing for low-income persons.[16] (US Human Rights Network UPR Housing Working Group, 2014, 3)

The letter further pointed out and condemned discrimination in the housing market based on race, disability, gender, national origin, and criminal background.[17] Signatories determined that these issues in the US housing market constitute not only a crisis of affordability but also a human rights violation. Matthew Desmond's research on the prevalence and negative consequences of evictions adds further evidence to support these criticisms of the current housing market.[18] Further, the Urban Land Institute finds that due to an increase in rents, decrease in number of units, and increase in the number of low-income families, only 28% of renter households with incomes at or below 30 percent of the area median income can access viable, affordable housing units.[19] It is clear that the United States' status quo housing market is deeply flawed and socially harmful.

2 The Path Forward

2.1 *Sustainable Affordable Housing*

To combat the wide range of problems associated with sprawl and a lack of affordable and equitable access to housing, the nation must navigate a series of obstacles. The country needs to build more homes, but cannot colonize more natural space. Residential developments need to be denser, but not at the expense of providing inhabitants with a decent quality of life. Federal government needs to more equitably allocate resources and ensure that citizens have equal access to valuable goods and services, but

[16] "Housing and Homelessness in the United States of America." National Law Center on Homelessness & Poverty, Chair, US Human Rights Network UPR Housing Working Group to Submission to the United Nations Universal Periodic Review of United States of America. September 15, 2014.

[17] Ibid.

[18] Desmond, Matthew. "Eviction and the Reproduction of Urban Poverty." *American Journal of Sociology* 118, no. 1 (2012): 88–133. doi:10.1086/666082.

[19] Leopold, Josh, Getsinger, Lisa, Blumenthal, Pamela, Abazajian, Katya, Jordan, Reed. Housing Affordability Gap for Extremely Low-Income Renters in 2013. Washington, D.C.: Urban Land Institute, 2015. Accessed December 11, 2016. http://www.urban.org/sites/default/files/alfresco/publication-pdfs/2000260-The-Housing-Affordability-Gap-for-Extremely-Low-Income-Renters-2013.pdf.

needs to do so in a fiscally, environmentally, and socially responsible way. The country needs smart, sustainable planning to address current housing deficiencies and accommodate future population growth. The answer to these many constraints lies in a large-scale effort to increase the availability and attractiveness of green affordable housing developments.

Sustainable affordable housing development provides an opportunity to address issues related to sustainability, affordability, and accessibility in the current housing market. Affordable housing in the United States is defined as housing for which an occupant is not required to pay more than 30 percent of her gross income, taking into consideration gross housing costs and utilities.[20] Based on the philosophy that all citizens should be entitled to a basic standard of living, affordable housing should ideally also be conveniently located next to public transportation, situated within a healthy and safe environment, and work to foster and protect the comfort and pride of occupants.[21]

Green housing comes in many different shapes and sizes, but generally seeks to address these same problems through a set of broadly conceived sustainability measures. These buildings are planned to conserve energy, reduce water usage, reduce reliance on personal motor vehicles, and overall minimize the resource use and ecological impact of the home's occupants. Less resource-intensive lifestyles translate into lower utility and overall costs of living, making sustainability and affordable housing a natural partnership.[22,23]

Sustainable affordable housing provides quantifiable and qualitative benefits to families.[24] First, green affordable housing reduces the energy costs of occupant families.[25] Some general energy-saving green building strategies include the use of energy-efficient appliances and lighting units, passive solar design, energy metering, and the ability to harness renewable

[20] "Glossary of HUD Terms." HUD USER. Accessed December 23, 2016. https://www.huduser.gov/portal/glossary/glossary_a.html.

[21] Boehland, Jessica. "Greening Affordable Housing." *Race, Poverty & the Environment* 13, no. 1 (2006): 59–61. http://www.jstor.org/stable/41495691.

[22] "Top 5 Reasons to be Energy Efficient." Alliance to Save Energy. November 13, 2013. Accessed August 10, 2017. http://www.ase.org/resources/top-5-reasons-be-energy-efficient.

[23] Gorman-Murray, Andrew. Material Geographies of Household Sustainability. Farnham: Taylor and Francis, 2011. Accessed August 10, 2017. ProQuest Ebook Central.

[24] Burlinghouse, Gerald N., ed. Green Affordable Housing. New York: Nova Science Publishers, Inc., 2009. Accessed August 10, 2017. ProQuest Ebook Central.

[25] Ibid.

energy.[26,27] The savings that result from these tactics have significant positive implications for families who qualify for affordable housing and earn annual incomes far lower than the area median income. A case study in a book by Greg Kats outlines these benefits. The Oregon Green Community project Clara Vista Town Homes was able to provide occupants with energy savings of 73% as compared to the energy costs in standard, nearby affordable housing complexes.[28] These gains in efficiency are no small feat. For families forced to devote such massive percentages of their income to housing costs, heads-of-households must frequently make extremely painful financial tradeoffs to pay unaffordable energy bills. When families living in poverty were surveyed about the tradeoffs they made to pay their energy bills, 57% of non-senior owners and 36% of non-senior renters reported that they went without dental care, 25% of non-seniors made a partial rent or mortgage payment or missed a payment, and 20% of non-seniors went without food for at least a day.[29] By dramatically lowering energy bills that disproportionately burden the nation's poor, green affordable housing presents an opportunity to reduce these appalling figures and address a clear-cut crisis.

Further, sustainable affordable housing features lead to improvements in occupants' health. Green building projects ensure sufficient ventilation, mitigate the presence of moisture, mold, pests, and radon within the home,[30] and use non-toxic construction materials.[31] Several studies have shown that such improvements provide significant health benefits to occupants. The EPA cites indoor air pollution as a top environmental risk to

[26] "Buildings: Sustainable Strategies." Sustainable Cities Institute. 2013. Accessed August 10, 2017. http://www.sustainablecitiesinstitute.org/topics/buildings-and-energy/green-building-101/buildings-sustainable-strategies.

[27] "Checklist: LEED v4 for Building Design and Construction." Usgbc.org. April 5, 2016. Accessed August 10, 2017. https://www.usgbc.org/resources/leed-v4-building-design-and-construction-checklist.

[28] Kats, Gregory, Jon Braman, and Michael James. *Greening our Built World: Costs, Benefits, and Strategies*. Washington, DC: Island Press, 2010.

[29] Ibid.

[30] Breysse, Jill, David E. Jacobs, William Weber, Sherry Dixon, Carol Kawecki, Susan Aceti, and Jorge Lopez. "Health Outcomes and Green Renovation of Affordable Housing." *Public Health Reports (1974–)* 126 (2011): 64–75. http://www.jstor.org/stable/41639267.

[31] Vittori, Gail D.A. "Affordable Housing: Greening Affordable Housing." *Journal of Affordable Housing & Community Development Law* 13, no. 4 (2004): 458–62. http://www.jstor.org/stable/25782712.

public health.[32] America's low-income population is particularly vulnerable to this as it experiences the highest rates of asthma nationwide.[33] Asthma is a serious health condition that green housing can effectively combat; when moved from their old homes to breathe-easy homes, asthmatic children's average yearly visits to emergency rooms dropped from 60 to 21.[34] Sustainable affordable housing can therefore benefit both low-income families and the federal government by reducing healthcare costs, limiting the number of school and work absences due to environment-induced illness, and increasing inhabitants' overall productivity and quality of life.

2.2 *Sustainable Community Development*

Thoughtfully planned communities can also provide families with greater access to transportation opportunities. Both sustainable and affordable housing frameworks require that developments be located near abundant, high-density, low-carbon, relatively inexpensive forms of transportation.[35,36,37] The principle of opportunity-based housing argues that equitable housing should provide inhabitants with access to other opportunity structures through deliberate regional connections. These opportunity structures include, "high performing schools, employment, transportation, childcare, and civic and political networks."[38] Mass-transportation structures help low-income residents connect with broader regions that possess these vital services, and enable greater overall mobility and opportunity. Access to

[32] United States. Department of Housing and Urban Development. Federal Healthy Homes Work Group. *Executive Summary Advancing Healthy Housing: A Strategy for Action*. Department of Housing and Urban Development, 2013.

[33] Ibid, Vittori.

[34] Ibid, Kats.

[35] "Checklist: LEED v4 for Building Design and Construction." Usgbc.org. April 5, 2016. Accessed August 10, 2017. https://www.usgbc.org/resources/leed-v4-building-design-and-construction-checklist.

[36] Connected Communities: Linking Affordable Housing and Transportation | HUD USER. Accessed August 10, 2017. https://www.huduser.gov/portal/pdredge/pdr_edge_research_071414.html.

[37] "Location Affordability Index." Location Affordability Portal. Accessed August 10, 2017. http://www.locationaffordability.info/.

[38] Weiss, Jonathan D. "Preface: Smart Growth and Affordable Housing." *Journal of Affordable Housing & Community Development Law* 12, no. 2 (2003): 165–72. http://www.jstor.org/stable/25782595.

affordable mass-transit structures would provide substantial monetary savings to families with incomes between $20–50,000, who typically spend 29% of their income on transportation costs.[39] Additionally, encouraging a national shift from personal vehicles to high-density public transportation systems will reduce greenhouse gas emissions, air pollution, traffic, accidents, and national reliance on fossil fuels.[40] Sustainable affordable housing community development, in promoting mass transit, can improve the quality of life of development occupants, other commuters, and community residents.

2.3 *Public Policy Initiatives*

Investors, legislations, and non-profit organizations have recognized the many benefits sustainable real estate has the potential to provide their communities. The field of green affordable housing is relatively new, but quite vibrant and continuously evolving. Thus far, the major innovations and successes in sustainable building have largely been the product of strong federal, state, and local policy initiatives. The United States Department of Housing and Urban Development (HUD) has been particularly active in this space, recognizing that the department itself devoted more than 10% of its total budget to pay the energy costs of families living in federally-assisted affordable housing in 2008.[41] The federal government could benefit from lowering these costs, and sees green affordable housing as a method of accomplishing this goal. Further, over the past two decades, the federal government has begun to consider sustainable affordable housing as a method of accomplishing other national objectives such as job growth and community investment. Following this logic, it has coordinated policy interventions aimed to flow funds in the direction of sustainable affordable construction and build a financial infrastructure to encourage the movement.

HUD's green affordable housing track record since 2001 reflects this sort of thinking, and demonstrates how it has evolved over time. The federal government has mostly contributed to this field through its strate-

[39] Ibid, Kats.

[40] Gomez, Sarah. "The Case for Bus Rapid Transit (BRT): Successfully Shifting the Status Quo While Managing Risk." *Innovation and Sustainability* (2016).

[41] Shear, William B. *Green Affordable Housing: HUD Has Made Progress in Promoting Green Building, but Expanding Efforts Could Help Reduce Energy Costs and Benefit Tenants.* Washington, D.C.: United States Government Accountability Office, Diane Publishing Co., 2008.

gic allocation of funds and creation of incentive programs. In 2001, HUD established an Energy Taskforce to investigate potential opportunities for federal involvement in green building, and in 2005, the department used its findings to implement the comprehensive Energy Action Plan to promote national energy efficiency.[42] This plan included disseminating educational information, encouraging retrofits, providing stronger rewards and incentives for new green construction and retrofits of existing units, and strengthening energy standards and monitoring processes.[43]

Additionally, the federal government has recently looked to green building as a way to promote job growth. Since 2009, as part of the American Recovery and Reinvestment Act (ARRA), the federal government has issued energy efficiency and conservation block grants that encourage efficient and renewable energy retrofitting.[44] Since 2010, the federal government has also stimulated development in sustainable affordable housing through the Sustainable Communities initiative. Through this program, HUD and The US Department of Transportation (DOT) provide Regional Planning Grants to nonprofits and government entities involved in sustainable planning, and Challenge Grants to states and local municipalities undertaking projects to integrate housing and transportation.[45]

Many nonprofits have investigated the efficacy of these federal grant programs and pointed to some of their shortcomings. Their criticisms typically center around the fact that the federal initiatives encourage voluntary participation in this space, but relying on such measures alone will not have a large enough impact on either affordable housing or sustainable development in the long-term.[46] Regardless, it is clear that the federal

[42] United States. Department of Housing and Urban Development. Office of Policy Development and Research, Office of Community Planning and Development. *HUD'S ENERGY ACTION PLAN*. By Michael Freedberg and Robert Groberg. Washington, D.C.: HUD.

[43] Ibid.

[44] "Energy Efficiency and Conservation Block Grant Program Guidance." Energy.gov. Accessed December 23, 2016. https://energy.gov/eere/wipo/energy-efficiency-and-conservation-block-grant-program-guidance.

[45] "Office of Sustainable Communities_SCI." Office of Sustainable Communities_SCI. Accessed December 23, 2016. https://portal.hud.gov/hudportal/HUD?src=%2Fhudprograms%2Fsci.

[46] "Docket No. FR-5396-N-01: Sustainable Communities Planning Grant Program Advance Notice and Request for Comment." Enterprise Community Partners and Adrienne E. Quinn to Office of Sustainable Housing and Communities; US Department of Housing and Urban Development. March 10, 2010.

government has recognized how it stands to benefit from investing in green affordable housing. In spite of its ample room for improvement and expansion, thus far, the federal government's concerted monetary push has served as one of the primary engines driving the sustainable affordable housing movement.

Federal funds have also fueled a large part of the innovation in sustainable affordable housing at the state and local levels through Low-Income Housing Tax Credits (LIHTCs). States have relied on LIHTCs, which are funded by the federal government but administered at a state level, as a financial leverage encouraging investment in affordable housing.[47] LIHTCs accomplish this as they reward private investors who invest in affordable rental housing with tax credits on their federal income tax returns.[48] This financing structure allows for the financing of projects that would not otherwise be undertaken due to limited resources or split-incentives between owners paying for the renovations and renters benefiting from energy savings. Thus, as LIHTCs attract the attention and capital of a certain class of private investors to the affordable housing market, they have become the most valuable tool employed by the federal government to finance the construction and renovation of projects in this space in the status quo. In fact, LIHTCs account for 90% of all affordable housing created today.[49] Harnessing the potential power of this incentive to promote green affordable housing, states can decide to selectively grant LIHTCs only to developers who follow sustainable building models. Many states have done so quite effectively, ***and 36 agencies have added green policies to LIHTC regulations since 2005.***[50]

Alternatively, some of the most innovative, high-impact work that states and local governments have accomplished in this field has had nothing to do with project finance. A lot of the barriers obstructing sustainable affordable housing stem from legal challenges, like state construction

[47] Ibid, Shear.

[48] United States. Office of the Comptroller of the Currency, Community Affairs Department. *Low-Income Housing Tax Credits: Affordable Housing Investment Opportunities for Banks.* By David Black and Sherrie L.W. Rhine. Washington, DC: Office of the Comptroller of the Currency, 2014.

[49] "About LIHTC." About the Low Income Housing Tax Credit | National Equity Fund, Inc. Accessed December 23, 2016. http://www.nefinc.org/whoweare/aboutlihtc.html.

[50] Ibid.

regulations and zoning bylaws. Many cities, like San Francisco,[51] Los Angeles,[52] New York,[53] Portland,[54] and Seattle,[55] are leading the way with policy measures and targeted initiatives aimed at promoting green growth in affordable housing. For example, the City of Oakland offers complementary green building technical assistance and public promotion to private developers,[56] and Gainesville, Florida and Washington D.C. now expedite permitting processes for green building projects assessed and certified by the USGBC.[57] Many cities have followed the example set by cities like Boston, where since 2007 the zoning code has required that all new private development construction projects comply with at least the minimum level of LEED certification,[58] and Vancouver City, which since 2011 has required that projects on rezoned sites in the city be built to achieve a LEED Gold rating standard.[59] States have also helped to encourage these strategies. North Carolina, for example, allows its cities to charge "reduced building permit fees or provide partial rebates of building permit fees" for buildings that comply with "green" ratings systems including LEED, Green Globes, and similarly systems.[60] Focusing on another important aspect of progress in this space, some states have developed their own energy standards that take into account local climate and regional regulations, and require new construction to adhere to these standards.[61] State

[51] Abair, Jesse W. "Green Buildings: What It Means To Be "Green" and the Evolution of Green Building Laws." *The Urban Lawyer* 40, no. 3 (2008): 623–32. http://www.jstor.org/stable/23801459.

[52] Ibid.

[53] Ibid.

[54] "Planning and Sustainability." The City of Portland Oregon. Accessed December 23, 2016. https://www.portlandoregon.gov/bps/.

[55] United States. Office of Housing. *SeaGreen: Greening Seattle's Affordable Housing*. By Katie Hong and Greg Nickels. Seattle, WA: City of Seattle, 2002.

[56] Ibid.

[57] Ibid, Abair. City of Gainesville, Fla., Code of Ordinances art. 1.5, § 6–12. D.C. Code §6-1451.06(a) (2007).

[58] Ibid, Abair.

[59] Vancouver, City Of. "Sustainable Zoning." City of Vancouver. May 16, 2012. Accessed August 11, 2017. http://vancouver.ca/home-property-development/sustainable-zoning-landing.aspx.

[60] United States. General Assembly of North Carolina. Senate. *An Act to Allow Counties and Cities to Provide Building Permit Fee Reductions or Partial Rebates to Encourage Construction of Buildings Using Sustainable Design Principles to Achieve Energy Efficiency*. Senate Bill 581 ed. Session Law 2007-381. General Assembly of North Carolina, 2007.

[61] Ibid, Shear.

and local governments have also adopted smart growth initiatives, which center on compact developments, transit corridors, and independent mixed-use communities.[62] Through green legislation, zoning reform, and smart growth initiatives, state and local governments have provided increasing amounts of legislative support to the sustainable affordable housing.

2.4 *Non-profit and Public Organization Support*

The green affordable housing movement has also benefitted from the valuable and varied work of committed non-profit and private organizations. Leaders in this realm include Enterprise Community Partners, Energy and Environmental Building Alliance, Green Affordable Housing Coalition, The Home Depot Foundation, and the U.S. Green Building Council (USGBC), among many more.[63] Organizations like these have helped to engage, educate, and assist all participants involved in sustainable affordable housing, from politicians to developers. They lobby on behalf of sustainable affordable housing, help finance projects, offer consulting services to municipalities, and produce research that measures the impact of green housing projects once they are constructed. They have also helped to create various sets of standards for green building that many states have now adopted as the minimum required features for construction projects seeking to receive government bids. Such certification programs include Energy Star, LEED, Green Globes, Living Building Challenge, NZEB, Passive House Institute US, SITES, WELL Building Standard, and Enterprise Green Communities Criteria.[64,65] Non-profit and private organizations have played an important role in providing guidance and support to actors involved in green affordable housing initiatives.

[62] Ibid, Freilich.

[63] Mann, Bonnie, and Tim Davis. *Municipal Action Guide: Creating Green Affordable Housing*. Washington, DC: National League of Cities, 2009.

[64] "Green Building Standards and Certification Systems" Green Building Standards and Certification Systems | WBDG Whole Building Design Guide. Accessed December 23, 2016. https://www.wbdg.org/resources/green-building-standards-and-certification-systems.

[65] "2015 Criteria." Enterprise Community Partners. Accessed December 23, 2016. http://www.enterprisecommunity.org/solutions-and-innovation/green-communities/criteria.

2.5 *Multi-disciplinary Collaboration and Innovation*

It is obvious that another crucial component of these projects is innovative design and development. Via Verde, a mixed-income development in the South Bronx, is one example of a successful sustainable affordable housing project made possible by such creativity.[66] Located on a former brownfield, but only four blocks away from the subway, Via Verde used to be an empty site that New York City wanted to revitalize. The city arrived at the idea of turning the site into an affordable sustainable housing complex as a means of fulfilling a local need for federally-assisted housing, combating asthma rates, which are among the highest in the country, and a municipal interest in sustainable design. In 2006, the city hosted a design competition for sustainable affordable housing. The Via Verde project, designed by the private developers and designers Phipps Houses Group, Jonathan Rose Companies, Dattner Architects, and Grimshaw Architects, won the competition. As a result, they obtained ownership of the lot for a nominal fee and the opportunity to work alongside city planners to transform 1.5 acres of the Bronx.

This public/private partnership provided unique, mutually beneficial collaboration opportunities for all parties involved. Because of this partnership, developers were able to circumvent zoning regulations that could have otherwise blocked the project, secure funding from a variety of sources (NYC bonds, federal grants, tax credits, bank loans) and receive community input throughout the development process. In turn, the city was able to revitalize a brownfield, provide new affordable housing opportunities to its inhabitants, and beautifully transform the landscape of the Bronx. The final plans for Via Verde included 222 units within stepped townhouse, mid-rise, and high-rise buildings. Via Verde, a LEED Gold complex, featured retail and community space, green roofs that could grow produce for occupants, stepped solar panels, a stormwater reclamation system, and design features to encourage healthy living. "Financially feasible, successful in the market, and critically acclaimed,"[67] Via Verde serves as a model for creative work in sustainable affordable housing by developers, designers, and city planners.

The Via Verde case study also invites an interesting discussion about future trends to watch for in green affordable housing. The Via Verde

[66] "Via Verde." ULI Case Studies. 2016. Accessed December 23, 2016. http://casestudies.uli.org/via-verde/.

[67] Ibid.

model, and the success of its mixed townhouse, high-, and mid-rise units track the transition in affordable housing trends from favoring high-rise to mid-rise housing. At the same time, Via Verde suggests that future sustainable affordable housing projects might try to revive high-rises, integrate them within mixed-level design structures, and price these units at rates catered to middle-income families. Via Verde also points to a growing interest in restoring brownfields, and increasing attention to liminal spaces on the outskirts of cities, or between cities and suburbs. Further, Via Verde implies the future of sustainable affordable housing might face financing obstacles. The numerous federal grants and subsidies that funded Via Verde are expected to decrease in quantity in the coming years. LIHTCs, which helped to fund a large portion of the project, may become less attractive if the president follows through with his intentions to reduce taxes on the wealthy. Similarly, Via Verde hints at the potential role banks might play in financing sustainable affordable housing. This will be something particularly interesting to look out for in the future because banks became involved in this space in the late 2000s, but quickly abandoned the idea around 2010. Other financing schemes that could help sustainable affordable housing developments grow might involve project-specific green bonds, which Governor Cuomo released in New York in November of 2016.[68] Furthermore, Via Verde highlights how valuable private/public collaborations might increasingly be used in this realm to help navigate complex zoning and tax codes that can represent significant barriers for such projects. Another future development that might affect green affordable housing is increased interest in sustainable transportation infrastructure and densifying urban and suburban areas. Finally, every day new technologies emerge and affect the design aspect of sustainable housing. Innovations like manufactured housing, shipping container housing, and more effective resource-saving and usage-monitoring devices constitute impressive advancements in sustainable technology, and promise more will follow. Sustainable affordable housing is currently fertile ground for innovation.

[68] "Governor Cuomo Announces Nearly $100 Million in New Green Bonds for Affordable Housing." Governor Andrew M. Cuomo. 2016. Accessed December 23, 2016. https://www.governor.ny.gov/news/governor-cuomo-announces-nearly-100-million-new-green-bonds-affordable-housing.

3 Conclusion

The progress that has been made in the realm of sustainable affordable housing has occurred, more or less, over the past twenty years. It has benefitted families, communities, investors, developers, the environment, and the economy. It has blossomed largely as a result of the federal government's interest in cultivating the field, and it has relied on tax incentives to attract private investors. Green affordable housing has also been made possible by the creativity and legislative ambition of state and local governments, and the talent and support of nonprofits and private organizations. It has benefitted from the expertise and creative and collaborative efforts of developers, urban planners, and designers. Confronted with many obstacles since its birth, the space of sustainable affordable housing has been constantly changing, adapting, and growing.

As history repeatedly reminds us, the world does not follow a single, steady march towards progress.[69] Just because this field has been cleared within the last twenty years does not necessarily ensure this trend will survive the next twenty years, though its incredible projects will almost certainly remain. Environmental issues have never been as politically polarizing nor as high-stakes as they are now. The U.S. Congress is partisan and stagnant while carbon dioxide levels creep ever-upwards from 400 ppm.[70] President Trump is unpredictable, but America's state and municipal governments have grown more powerful, and proven their willingness to both speak out against and separate their policy agendas from that of the President.[71] The country has an affinity for blue-collar jobs, and sustainable affordable housing offers the possibility of new green-collar jobs. It is quite likely that this space will change in the next four years, but it is unclear exactly how. Will the country trade-in its high energy bills for passive solar and renewables, sick buildings for healthy ones, cars for mass-transit, and blue collars for green ones? Perhaps.

[69] Shear, Michael D. "*Trump will Withdraw U.S. From Paris Climate Agreement* (New York, NY), June. 1, 2017.

[70] "Graphic: The relentless rise of carbon dioxide." NASA. Accessed December 23, 2016. http://climate.nasa.gov/climate_resources/24/.

[71] Tachuchi, Hiroko and Fountain, Henry. "*Bucking Trump, These Cities, States and Companies Commit to Paris Accord.*" *New York Times* (New York, NY), June. 1, 2017.

CHAPTER 14

Passive House Standard: A Strategic Mean for Building Affordable Sustainable Housing in Nova Scotia

Ramzi Kawar

This chapter discusses the approach taken by Housing Nova Scotia (HNS) between 2014 and 2016 to address the need to build more energy-efficient housing. Working with Passive House (PH) consultants, HNS has designed and completed the construction of three PH affordable housing pilot projects.

Following a brief background on HNS including the main challenges it faces in managing its existing housing portfolio, the chapter describes HNS's greening strategy adopted in 2008. This contextual information is followed by a description of how the PH standard was adopted and expanded on the experience of working with the multidisciplinary teams involved in the design and construction of these buildings, as well as the lessons learnt through this process.

R. Kawar (✉)
Housing Nova Scotia, Halifax, NS, Canada
e-mail: Ramzi.Kawar@novascotia.ca

T. Walker et al. (eds.), *Sustainable Real Estate*, Palgrave Studies in Sustainable Business In Association with Future Earth,
https://doi.org/10.1007/978-3-319-94565-1_14

1 Housing Nova Scotia

HNS mandate is "To ensure all Nova Scotians can find a home that is right for them, at a price they can afford, in a healthy and vibrant community that offers the services, supports, and opportunities they need" (HNS, 2013, p. 13). Specifically, HNS provides housing solutions for low- to modest-income Nova Scotians, offers programs throughout the housing continuum from homeless shelters to home ownership, and, while HNS does not fund or provide ongoing support services to clients, it works with others who may offer them. Since housing need is a complicated/complex issue, HNS therefore recognizes that cooperation and collaboration with a multitude of other players from government, private, and non-profit sectors is required (HNS, 2017, p. 2).

HNS is the largest residential landlord in Nova Scotia with CAD 13 billion in real estate assets. It owns, maintains, and operates 12,600 social housing units for low-income families and seniors that are managed by 5 regional housing authorities across the province. The HNS portfolio of buildings is built primarily for rental public housing that includes near-single family dwellings (duplex, townhomes, etc.), and low-, mid-, and high-rise Multi-Unit Residential Buildings (MURBs). Seventy five percent of the units are for seniors over the age of 58 and are typically one- to two-bedroom rental units. The rest of the units are for low-income families which are typically three to four bedrooms. Tenants pay rent geared to income, no more than 30% of gross household income, and HNS in most cases pays for energy costs which are included as part of the rent. Housing is often concentrated in a small geographic area and easily identifiable and is concentrated in urban areas where demand is higher, while there is excess supply elsewhere.[1]

Key initiatives that are being undertaken by HNS include:

1. increasing affordable housing opportunities for lower-income families, seniors, and persons with disabilities;
2. preserving existing affordable housing stock;
3. playing a key role in breaking the cycle of homelessness; and
4. reducing our impact on the environment (HNS, 2016, p. 7).

[1] Information in this section is from internal HNS sources.

2 Affordable Public Housing Challenges

The affordable housing challenges facing low-income individuals and families in Nova Scotia include an aging housing stock, an aging population, the rise in the number of people with disabilities, homelessness, low incomes, the lack of affordability for a large segment of the population, rural to urban migration, rising energy costs, changing housing types leading to more complex housing needs, and the lack of long-term federal funding for housing. Since the Province of Nova Scotia has a responsibility for providing safe, affordable housing, these challenges have a direct impact on its finances.

Sixty percent of HNS's aging housing stock was built between 1954 and 1978. This has had a severe impact on building performance since "Building envelope performance is strongly linked to the age of the housing stock. Inferior products and methods (by today's standards) used in the original construction result in excessive air infiltration and heat loss" (NS DCS Greening Strategy, 2008, p. 2).

In addition, several hindrances impact HNS and drive up its operational costs. First, are the rising costs of utilities (electricity, oil, propane, natural gas, water) which range between CAD 20 million and CAD 30 million, amounting to 15–20% of HNS annual budget. Second, energy prices are volatile. Third, tenants who pay for heat and electricity have a limited capacity to absorb utility price increases. Fourth, it is difficult to reduce heating and electrical demand due to the type of tenancy composed of mostly seniors who spend most of their time indoors and, anecdotally, have a tendency to keep higher temperatures in their homes. Fifth, since HNS pays for most of the utilities, tenants do not benefit from any energy savings. Sixth, the increase in operational costs reduces any savings that could go toward capital investments or to increase the supply of affordable housing. Lastly, allocated budgets do not dedicate funding specifically for energy efficiency projects making it a challenge to devote resources for sustainability run initiatives. Given the list of obstacles, focusing on improving energy efficiency and construction quality to reduce the energy costs for the housing units will benefit HNS indirectly through utility cost savings, thus making funds available for other areas of housing.[2]

[2] HNS internal documents.

3 HNS Sustainability Initiatives

Despite these challenges, HNS made a commitment to sustainability and has been improving the energy efficiency of its portfolio for over 30 years. In 2008, HNS authored a greening strategy that set out to reduce costs and increase efficiency by improving five key energy usage drivers:

1. building envelope performance;
2. mechanical and electrical systems;
3. maintenance and operations of the portfolio;
4. raising energy conservation awareness among building occupants; and
5. products and services and information systems

In early 2014, the Building Design Team (BDT) at HNS put forward a proposal (Energy Reduction Initiative [ERI] (HNS, 2014a)) aimed at improving the performance of its buildings. The plan focused on strategies to improve building envelopes and targeted reductions in space heating loads and increased efficiency. In November of 2014, HNS signed a Memorandum of Understanding with Efficiency Nova Scotia (ENS) (HNS, 2014b) to benefit from their expertise and rebate programs. ENS is a franchise operated by EfficiencyOne, an independent, non-profit organization which manages energy saving programs and services for Nova Scotians. Lastly, the ERI explored the possibility of using PH standards as a potential path to achieve sustainability and affordability for HNS and the private-sector.

Since one of the pillars of the HNS's housing strategy is building "healthy vibrant communities," it developed a pilot Neighborhood Revitalization Initiative (HNS, 2013, p. 19) to upgrade the condition of dwellings and, where feasible, build new ones through residential infill construction in targeted neighborhoods across the province. The stated purpose of this pilot program was to vitalize areas in need of stabilization due to adjacent or internal pressures that may include development pressures, high crime rates, or general need to upgrade the visual appearance. The first targeted neighborhood (Alice Street) was designated in collaboration with the Town of Truro and included one or more of the following characteristics: older residential properties in need of exterior building improvements, much of the properties being owner occupied and having predominantly low- to modest-income homeowners and tenants. Accomplishments of this program are documented in HNS's *Annual Accountability Report 2015–2016* (HNS, n.d.).

4 The Passive House Standard

According to the PH Institute, "Passive House is a building standard that is truly energy efficient, comfortable and affordable at the same time" (Passive House Institute, n.d.). The focus of the design standard is to conserve energy by reducing heat loss through the building envelope and maximizing solar heat gains. A building constructed using PH principles is very well-insulated, airtight, and primarily heated by passive solar gains and internal gains from people, electrical equipment, and so on. Energy losses are minimized, and any remaining heat demand is provided by a source that is smaller than what would otherwise be required for a conventional home. Cooling loads are limited by minimizing heat gains through shading and window orientation. An energy recovery ventilator (ERV) provides a constant, balanced fresh air supply and excellent indoor air quality.

The key principles of PH are:

1. Superinsulation: Installing a continuous layer of thick insulation below the foundation, on the walls, and in the attic.
2. Airtightness: 0.6 Air Changes per Hour (ACH) which is at least two times tighter than the R2000 standard which is "no greater than 1.5 air changes per hour" (Natural Resources Canada, 2012).
3. Minimize thermal bridging: Avoiding "cold spots" by designing thermal breaks in the building assemblies.
4. High-performance windows and doors: Triple-glazed, argon-filled, custom low-e coatings, airtight. This insures more solar heat and reduces transmission losses.
5. Use very high-efficiency heat recovery ventilator (HRV): Installed with best practices, the HRV will provide adequate fresh air while reducing heat losses.

The benefits of building to PH standards are as follows. First, it helps cut energy costs since "Passive Houses allow for space heating and cooling related energy savings of up to 90% compared with typical building stock and over 75% compared to average new builds" (Passive House Institute, n.d.). Second, a PH does not require a conventional heating system as it relies on passive heat sources of solar and internal heat gains. Third, having an airtight envelope minimizes outside noise. Fourth, the quality of indoor space is improved with careful ventilation and natural daylighting.

Fifth, according to the "majority of costing studies and construction estimates report that the cost increment of building to Passive House standards is less than 10%, with the average value being around 6%" (Pembina Institute, 2016, p. 52). Sixth, even though there is a significant increase in the embodied energy of added insulation layers in the envelope and other building elements, the operational cost of the building is reduced and "the measured energy use reductions in passive buildings compared to typical construction ranges from 40% to over 80% when considering total energy use intensity" (Pembina Institute, 2016, p. 34).

According to a recently published research by the Pembina Institute, there are "several reasons to prioritize an enclosure-focused approach to energy efficiency:

- Building enclosures are long lasting and costly to refurbish, unlike other systems that can be more easily replaced as better technologies become available.
- Enclosures are simple systems; their performance does not depend on complex energy management systems and they are more tolerant to delayed maintenance.
- Reducing heating and cooling demand early in the design process allows for reduction of the size of space conditioning systems, reducing construction cost and ongoing energy demand.
- High-performance enclosures also offer significant non-energy benefits, such as thermal comfort, acoustic isolation, durability, and increased resiliency to power outages and extreme temperature events" (Pembina Institute, 2016, p. 1).

In providing affordable housing, HNS strives to identify efficient and cost-effective solutions. Therefore, the focus of PH on simple conservation aligns with HNS's corporate philosophy. There are two standards commonly used: The PH Institute Standard and the PH Institute US (PHIUS). These two standards are the basis for acquiring certification or a PH building. The advantages of certification are quality assurance and guarantee that the building has met the defined criteria set out in the standards. For HNS, this was doubly important because it was building pilot projects using PH standards for the first time using public money.

Table 14.1 summarizes these requirements.

Table 14.1 Passive House certification standards

	PH institute standard	*PHIUS climate adjusted standard*
Thermal performance of envelope	≤15 kWh/SM	Varies by climate (≤7.1 KBTU/SF/yr. in NS)
Total energy consumption	≤120 kWh/SM	≤6000 kWh/person/yr
Airtightness	≤0.6 ACH @ 50 Pa	+ ≤0.05 cfm/SF @ 50 Pa

5 Passive House Case Studies: Passive House Pilot #1: 74 Alice Street, Truro

5.1 Project Context

In mid-2013, the first area chosen for revitalization under the Neighbourhood Improvement Initiative pilot program was the Alice Street neighborhood. This area is located near the Town of Truro's Eastern boundary. In addition to upgrading existing buildings, HNS planned the demolition of a provincially owned two-story single family dwelling at 74 Alice Street that was deemed structurally unsafe. The plan was to redevelop the property into two new affordable family dwellings that were to become part of the first subsidized affordable pilot housing project built and certified to PH standards in Nova Scotia.

In early 2014, a feasibility study was conducted to verify the viability of applying these standards to the Alice Street project. This was particularly important since HNS's BDT had already designed a three-bedroom duplex for the site and had obtained a development agreement (DA) from the Town of Truro's planning department. An immediate challenge facing the project was the fact that the south-facing windows were shaded and solar incidence, one of the PH principles, was minimized, making them energy neutral. While this meant that the building could not achieve certification under the PH International (PHI) standard, it was still deemed possible to move ahead to achieve certification using the climate adjusted PH standard developed by PHIUS.

5.2 Project Design

Shortly following the decision to pursue certification through PHIUS, a tender was issued for consulting services to apply these design principles to the new units. A certified local PH consultant who had completed 14 projects brought extensive PH knowledge and construction experience in the Nova Scotia climate to this project. Next, the PH consultant conducted the energy modeling required using the proprietary PH Planning Package (PHPP) (Passive House Institute, n.d.). Based on the results of the modeling, the PH consultant worked closely with the BDT to incorporate PH design principles and provided recommendations to execute the requirements to achieve certification as set out by the PHIUS. The consultant also specified assemblies and mechanical systems that have been successfully installed in projects built in Nova Scotia. Finally, the consultant was engaged to provide construction administration technical services, support, and training to the contractor and quality assurance from the tendering, through construction, till the end of the contractor's warranty period.

The first step in designing the Alice Street redevelopment project was to leverage the site's natural solar gains by strategically orienting its windows and doors, while at the same time maintaining an aesthetic that compliments the neighborhood and creates a pleasing space for the occupants to live in. the building's orientation facing the street is north-south. The existing street had a specific building pattern which the new design respected and made sure that it fit within. The proposed building was close to maximum buildable area with each housing unit of 2030 Square Foot (SF). Thicker walls required redesign and filled remaining space in the allowable footprint. There was a need to shift some rooms and walls for more usable space but it still followed the original design.

5.3 *Project Construction*

In mid-2015, through a public tender that specified tested and reliable assemblies, a construction contract was awarded to a local construction firm with a cost of approximately CAD 125/SF. As part of the project, the consultant was contracted to provide hands-on training and construction support to the contractor on the project. At appropriate times during the construction schedule, the consultant worked hands-on to demonstrate the techniques necessary to build the PH assemblies correctly. The site training was scheduled for specific crucial tasks for the project.

As part of the support that this project received from ENS, there was an instructional video made with a professional crew that captured the major milestone steps in the construction process (Picture 14.1). The purpose of the video was to raise awareness among HNS staff and the construction community about PH. The video covered the following six key steps:

Picture 14.1 Truro Passive House video documenting air-sealing walls and penetrations

1. laying sub-slab insulation and vapor barrier installation;
2. installation of exterior walls and air-sealing exterior walls and penetrations;
3. installation and air sealing of windows and doors;
4. electrical rough in, plumbing rough in, heat pump rough in, ventilation rough in;
5. blower door pre-drywall, final blower door, and ventilation commissioning; and
6. summary of completed home—review of costs and savings.

The following sections describe the building process documented in the video which applies to any PH construction project.

Vapor Barrier and Slab Foundation Insulation: The Alice Street house had a full basement built using insulated concrete forms (ICF) walls. A significant amount of foam insulation was added below the foundation.

ICF walls just meet National Building Code (NBC) requirements for thermal performance, but additional foam inserts were introduced to increase the R-value of the wall. PH principles can be applied to a full basement like this project as well as with slab-on-grade construction. Careful attention was given where penetrations were made in the foundation; for example, sealing toilet penetrations.

Wall construction: Two walls were constructed: an interior, 2x6 load-bearing wall and an exterior wall built from Truss I-Joists (TJI) to provide a significant amount of additional insulation. Conventional construction only calls for the single interior 2x6 wall. The exterior wall was taped as it is the airtight layer. To ensure the building is airtight, transitions to other building components and assemblies required careful detailing. For example, where the window was mounted, where the wall meets the foundation and where the wall meets the roof. Windows used were triple-pane, argon-filled, insulated fiberglass frames, with custom coatings to maximize solar gains (Picture 14.2).

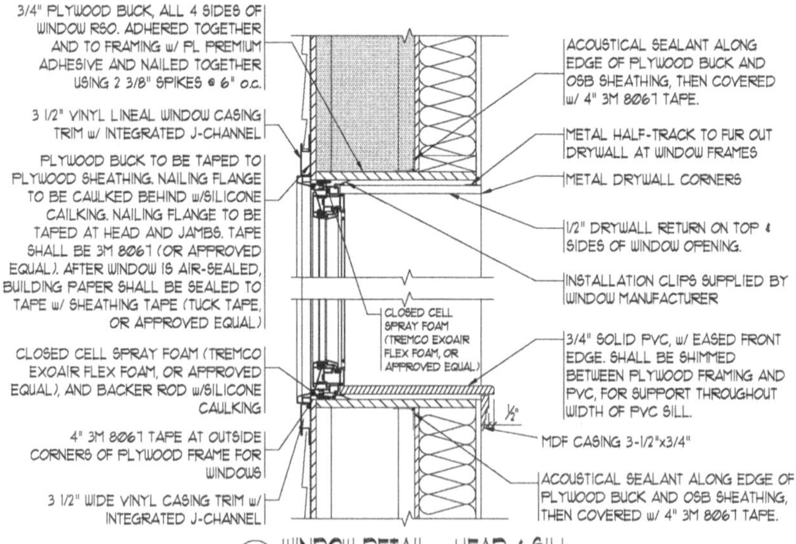

Picture 14.2 Truro Passive House window detail

Penetrations: It was crucial to take extra care around mechanical and electrical rough in work. The contractors were asked to run everything they can inside the plywood box and once they leave the box, they had to use a controlled penetration. Even if the project does not plan to install a security system, it is good to rough in the wiring for the system so that if a system is installed in the future, no additional penetrations are needed.

Blower door testing: Two tests are done: one "pre-drywall" test and one final test when the home was complete. The purpose of the pre-drywall test is to evaluate the airtightness of the building while there is still an opportunity to identify the location of the leaks and seal them before finishes are applied.

Ventilation: Once the building enclosure was addressed and a very airtight home was achieved, the crucial next step was to provide proper ventilation to insure good indoor air quality for the occupants and, at the same time, minimize heat loss to ventilation. All new construction requires mechanical ventilation; this is especially important in a PH as the home achieves very high levels of airtightness. For comparison, the airtightness target for a PH is almost three times higher than an R2000 home. A very efficient HRV is installed in a PH, with careful attention paid to the penetrations and system balancing.

Mechanical Equipment: The next biggest source of energy use in the home was domestic hot water. To address this, a heat pump water heater was installed, which is much more efficient than any conventional water heating appliance. Since the home was super-insulated and airtight, much of the heating demand was met by solar gains and internal loads such as appliances, lighting, and the heat generated by the occupants themselves. As such, only a simple, inexpensive heating system was needed, and electric baseboards were installed. This led to substantial savings over a central heating system, for example, a fully ducted air source heat pump, boiler, or furnace.

Table 14.2 is a fact sheet for Alice Street.

The Alice Street project was completed in May 2016 and achieved PHIUS certification in September of the same year (Picture 14.3). The final cost of the project was CAD 519,498 and when compared with a code-built building, using the 2015 NBC of Canada, with the same specifications, the increase in costs was 16%. The calculations were based on the actual financial information obtained from the contractor who built the project.

One of the unforeseen factors that caused a cost increase was the need to raise the foundation by one foot to take into a water stream, which was encountered after excavations. On the other hand, there was no significant

Table 14.2 Truro Passive House project fact sheet

Truro Passive House Project fact sheet	
Location	Truro, Nova Scotia
Construction	New
Type	Duplex
Size	2030 SF/Unit
Treated floor area	1685 SF/Unit (156.5 SM/Unit)
Bedroom	3
Bathroom	1.5
Architect	Building Design Team, Housing Nova Scotia
Energy consultant	Passive House E-Design
Builder	Global Construction
Construction costs	CAD 519,498
Date completed	May 2016
Construction	
Foundation slab	4 in. slab over 8 in. EPS Type 2 rigid insulation
Basement wall	8″ ICF block wall with additional 2″ rigid insulation on exterior and interior 2x4 Roxul service wall
Walls	Vertical 9–1/2″ Trus Joist I-Joist (TJI) w/cellulose insulation; 7/16″ Oriented Strand Board (OSB) sheathing caulked and taped at all joints and 2x6 Roxul structural stud wall
Roof	Insulation 28″ loose fill cellulose, 7/16″ OSB sheathing caulked and taped at all joints on open-web wood trusses
Windows	Triple-pane, argon-filled, low-e, fiberglass frames
Key energy efficiency measures	
HVAC	
Heating	Electric baseboard backup
Ventilation	High-efficiency heat recovery ventilator. All bathroom and kitchen exhaust ventilation is run through switches on the HRV system

Envelope

- Wall R-Value = 53.2*
- Basement Wall R-Value: 42.2*
- Slab-on-grade R-value = 33.3*
- Ceiling R-value = 101.9*
- Windows U-value = 0.15 to 0.20
- Air sealing, ACH50 = 0.4 (tested)

*R-values come from the energy model and considers all bridging, layers and air films.

Lighting, appliances, and water heating

- A domestic hot water: heat-pump electric hot water heater, with a seasonal COP of 2.5.
- A 100% compact fluorescent lamps and light-emitting diodes.

Picture 14.3 Truro Passive House front view

reduction in useable space due to the increased insulation thickness in the walls since the building was extended in length to the back of the lot to make up for the loss in the building width (Table 14.3).

Preliminary energy data acquired from Nova Scotia Power (NSP)[3] bills showed actual average monthly electrical consumption for Unit-1 was 990 kWh, while actual monthly electrical consumption for Unit-2 was 715 kWh. The differences are attributed to tenant usage. Compared to the average household energy use by a code-built dwelling with three household members in Nova Scotia 2570 kWh/month[4] (Statistics Canada, 2015) there appears to be reduction in the range of 62–72% reduction over code-built dwelling (Table 14.4).

[3] We do not have accurate readings from the energy monitoring system and instead NSP bills were used from June 13, 2016, to June 12, 2017.

[4] This figure is from Statistics Canada (http://www.statcan.gc.ca/pub/11-526-s/11-526-s2013002-eng.pdf) Table 4–1 Average household energy use, by household and dwelling characteristics, 2011—gigajoules per m 2 of heated area (0.71GJ*156.5 SM = 111GJ per unit). This is equivalent to 2570 ekWh/month per unit.

Table 14.3 Truro Passive House cost comparison with code compliant construction cost

Truro Comparison Cost Report
December 20, 2016

Description	Passive house standard Amount ($)	Code compliant Amount ($)	Premium ($)
Exterior			
Concrete foundation	49,413	25,900	23,513
Windows	18,682	12,500	6182
Doors	6505	3580	2925
Framed wall insulation	3095	3895	(800)
TJI wall insulation	2750	0	2750
Slab insulation	4100	1300	2800
Roof insulation	2100	850	1250
Taped OSB	1500	0	1500
Vertical TJIs	8300	0	8300
Attic hatch	800	90	710
Vinyl cladding, fascia, soffit	3500	3800	(300)
Decks and porches	0	0	0
Roofing	0	0	0
Excavation	0	0	0
Interior & systems			
Sheetrock	0	0	0
Doors	0	0	0
Paint	0	0	0
Floor finish	0	0	0
Elect baseboard	5800	4800	1000
Subfloor	0	0	0
HRV & ductwork	12,200	7900	4300
Plumbing fixtures	4800	1900	2900
Stairs & railing	0	0	0
Cabinetry	0	0	0
Devices, switches	0	0	0
Wiring	2200	0	2200
Plumbing	2400	0	2400
Light fixtures	0	0	0
Total Building Costs (including taxes)	497,498	435,868	61,630
PASSIVE HOUSE CONSULTANT & CERTIFICATION (including taxes)	22,000	0	22,000
Total project costs including passive components	519,498		

(*continued*)

Table 14.3 (continued)

Truro Comparison Cost Report *December 20, 2016*		
Total project costs excluding passive components	435,868	
PREMIUM FOR PASSIVE DESIGN—VALUE		**83,630**
PREMIUM FOR PASSIVE DESIGN—PERCENTAGE		**16%**

Source: Global Construction.

Table 14.4 Truro Passive House project analysis

Truro Passive House project analysis

Total cost

1. Total, project cost for Truro = CAD 519,498
2. Additional cost related to PH cost @ 16% of total project costs = CAD 83,630 (CAD 41,815/unit)

Total actual energy consumption (per the Truro NSP bills,)

1. Actual Average Total Monthly Electrical Cost of both units CAD 277
2. Actual Average Total Annual Electrical Cost of both units CAD 3324
3. Actual Average Total Annual Electrical Cost of each unit CAD 1662

Equivalent energy consumption

1. Monthly equivalent energy consumption for code-built dwelling is 2570 ekWh.
2. Estimated, monthly, cost of energy is CAD 463 @CAD 0.18/kWh.
3. Estimated, total, annual, energy consumption cost per unit = CAD 5551/yr.

Return-on-investment (ROI) based on actual energy consumption

1. Return-on-Investment
   At 10 yrs. would require estimated, annual, savings of CAD 8363 (CAD 4181/unit)
   At 20 yrs. would require estimated, annual, savings of CAD 4181 (CAD 2090/unit)
2. Estimated, annual, electrical consumption savings due to Passive House Design = CAD 5551 − CAD 1662 = CAD 3889/yr.
3. ROI for PH costs @ 16% of total project costs = CAD 41,815/CAD 3889 = 10 Years

5.4 *Communication, Education, and Marketing*

HNS learnt tremendously from this project and made every effort to share these lessons. HNS invited interested stakeholders to visit the newly constructed duplex during an open house with BDT and the PH consultant available to answer questions. One open house was specifically dedicated to

HNS and regional Housing Authorities staff, a second for provincial government employees, and a third for the public. Specific invitations were sent to relevant groups such as the Nova Scotia Association of Architects, the Nova Scotia Home Builders Association, and Dalhousie School of Architecture and Planning, among others. There were media reports on the radio as well as interviews with HNS's chief executive officer. Finally, the video produced by ENS was shared on the internet on Vimeo (https://vimeo.com/user24834665/review/173926323/48370de629).

The Alice Street project won several awards including the 2016 ENS Bright Business Award jointly with the PH consultant and the 2017 Department of Community Services Minister's Ideal Innovation Team Award, and the 2017 Nova Scotia Premier's Excellence Award. It was also the finalist in the 2016 Smart Energy Communities Award under the real estate sector.

6 Passive House Pilot #2: 831 Highway 1, Hebron Heights

6.1 *Project Context*

This project involved the retrofit of an existing vacant building that was formerly used as an institutional residential care center. The property located at 831 Highway 1 in Hebron, Yarmouth County in southwest Nova Scotia, formerly known as the Hebron Resource Centre, was operated under the umbrella of the Department of Community Services who no longer used the facility and it sat vacant for many years. Since the property was owned by HNS, an evaluation study in late 2015 established the viability and suitability of converting it to a multi-residential senior complex of approximately eight units with at least 50% of the units to be fully accessible. In addition, the study confirmed that the property could also be renovated to meet PH design requirements.

The Western Regional Housing Authority (WRHA) director and staff met with the Municipality of the District of Yarmouth Planning Department who were very excited about the opportunity to see the property developed into a senior apartment complex. ADA was submitted, and due to the urgency, the process only took two months instead of the usual four to six months. During that time, work continued on tender documents, design, revenue models, and any renovations not dependent on the DA, such as demolition, windows, roof, and siding replacements.

The existing building orientation has excellent southwest exposure overlooking Doctors Lake and is situated on a large parcel of land providing an opportunity for outdoor garden spaces and offering the possibility of expansion or subdividing the land to provide additional housing units. The project is composed of two levels with a total combined area of approximately 8000 square feet and consists of 8 one-bedroom plus den units and 1 one-bedroom unit aimed at low-income seniors, singles, or families and will be operated by the WRHA. This project was realized as part of HNS's efforts to increase the supply of affordable rental housing in response to market demand for seniors' independent living, which is consistent with the provincial housing strategy.

6.2 *Project Design*

This project was the first affordable multi-unit apartment PH complex in Nova Scotia seeking certification. The initial conditions had several design challenges. First, the design team had to work with an existing building footprint and structural system. Second, as per the latest NBC requirement, the bedroom had to have an egress door to the outside on each level which meant that the layout of the apartment had the bedroom located on the exterior of the building. Third, there was the potential for overheating during summer months from existing large south- and west-facing windows. Fourth, there needed to be a central heating system while, at the same time, providing residents in each unit the ability to control temperature. Finally, using a central HRV in a multi-family building required fire separations between apartment units which, in a multi-family PH pose a challenge in terms of maintaining airtightness and avoiding thermal bridges.

For the design approach, the BDT at HNS worked with the PH consultant to apply PHIUS's Climate Adjusted Standard (PHCAS). Using Wärme Und Feuchte Instationär (WUFI) Passive (Passive House Institute US, n.d.) as the modeling software, the goal was to seek certification based on PHIUS+ 2015 Standard. This required an integrated design approach with WRHA, HNS BDT, external consultants, and equipment suppliers.

An initial WUFI model was created regarding the existing and schematic architectural documents provided. Several iterations of the model were created as mechanical systems and envelope components were refined in accordance with inputs from the PH consultant, equipment suppliers, and the BDT architects and engineers. The final iteration considered the best way to achieve the PHCAS on the original schematic design provided.

The design response for heating was to use an air-to-water heat pump unit that uses a hot water system for hydronic heating and domestic hot water with a propane boiler used as backup heat source. The unit was chosen with a high coefficient of performance. Low-heat baseboard hydronic units in each unit with individual thermostats were installed. Hot water is recirculated and hot water tanks are used to maintain the necessary hot water demand. The air-to-water heat pump provides the needed flexibility for controls in each unit. It also supplies space heating and cooling as well as water heating and it reduces energy and cost by producing 2–5 kW of heat energy for each kW it consumes.

Regarding ventilation, a central ERV was used, which provided ventilation, humidity control, and return air heat recovery. The ERV delivers continuous low volume supply and exhaust ventilation for the whole building and supplies ventilation based on demand per apartment with an independent high booster control. The installed unit provides 1000 Cubic Feet per Minute (CFM) supply air and 1000 CFM exhaust air, has a dual core air handling unit with a regenerative cyclic dual core heat exchanger with supply and exhaust fans, and two cores acting as heat accumulators. Heat recovery is automatically activated on request. Using a central ERV that provides heating and cooling with up to 90% efficiency offsets the cost of fire dampers.

The electrical design response included a backup generator which is typical for seniors' buildings. Each unit has its own "emergency" circuits on a generator in case utility power goes out. The boiler is on the generator for heating in case of power outage. The building was also designed to be photovoltaic solar-ready for installation of a 15 kW, 60-panel, 3-phase, grid-tied, micro-inverter-based PV system.

The project was cost shared between HNS and Canada Mortgage Housing Corporation (CMHC) with a funding of CAD 1.6 million. These funds were made available under the Investment in Affordable Housing (IAH) Agreement and were approved as part of the 2015–2016 fiscal budget. By using energy-efficient PH design, WRHA could potentially save on heating costs which would be verified once data from the energy monitoring devices is compiled.

6.3 *Project Construction*

The project had a very tight timeline to be completed by March 2016, the end of the 2015–2016 fiscal year. At first, this seemed to necessitate a fast track approach, whereby construction could start before the design was completed to shorten the time to completion. This would have required that the BDT issue separate construction packages. When reviewing the fast track option, it was decided that it is better to design and build instead, since the risks associated with pricing outweighed any time savings.

The construction tender was awarded to a local construction firm that had built the original building. This made the construction process easier since the builder was familiar with the elements of the existing building. Due to the reconfiguration of the original spaces, it was not possible to reuse the existing interior partitions to match the new layouts. Furthermore, the roof did not meet the new building code structural requirements and had to be replaced completely, which added to the construction costs (Table 14.5).

A detailed cost comparison for the Hebron study was commissioned to Hanscomb Limited, a quantity surveying and cost analysis firm in Halifax. The results, summarized in Table 14.6, show a 7% increase for construction built to PH standard compared to code-compliant construction. Since the Hebron pilot was a retrofit project, there were some cost savings owing to the reuse of some of the existing building elements which is not the case in the new construction (Picture 14.4 and 14.5).

At the time of this writing, no data were available to compare the modeled and actual energy use since the Hebron energy management systems has not been providing any reports (Table 14.7).

7 Passive House Pilot #3: 7–9 Brownell Avenue, Amherst

7.1 Project Context

The project in Amherst was a replacement of an existing duplex on Brownell Avenue that was damaged by fire. An assessment of the building was conducted and it was decided that a complete reconstruction would be a better solution than repairs. This was another opportunity to construct to the PH standard and to leverage the experience gained from the Alice Street project. For contractual and budgetary reasons, it was not possible to engage a PH consultant upfront and the BDT developed the design in-house based on the Truro experience. Although the project footprint was smaller (2-bedroom unit of 1000 SF each), it had similar design and specification features as Alice Street (Pictures 14.6 and 14.7).

Table 14.5 Hebron Passive House project fact sheet

Hebron Passive House project fact sheet	
Location	Hebron, Nova Scotia
Construction	Retrofit
Type	Multi-Unit Residential Building (MURB)
Units	9
Estimated occupants	18
Total building size	15,154 SF
Total treated area	7842 SF
Unit treated area	855 SF
Bedrooms	1/Unit
Bathrooms	1/Unit
Architect	Building Design Team, Housing Nova Scotia
Energy consultant	Passive House E-Design
Builder	Graham Construction LTD.
Construction costs	CAD 1,553,749
Date completed	March, 2017
Construction	
Foundation slab	2½" EPS Type 2 rigid insulation over existing 4″ concrete slab and existing, 2″ rigid insulation.
Below grade walls	Existing 8″ concreate foundation with existing 4″ insulation below grade on exterior and new 4" EPS rigid insulation above-grade on exterior.
Exterior walls	3½" Roxul Batt Insulation in 2 × 4 studs, 7/16" OSB sheathing c/w all joints caulked with acoustical sealant and taped, 5½" Roxul Batt Insulation in existing, 2 × 6 studs.
Roof	Insulation 28″ loose fill cellulose, R-3.8/in thermocell procell, 7/16" OSB sheathing c/w all joints caulked with acoustical sealant and taped.
Windows	Triple-pane, argon-filled, low-e, fiberglass frames
Key energy efficiency measures	
HVAC	
Primary heating	Hydronic, air-to-water heat pump, COPmin.3.5.
Secondary heating	High-efficiency, propane-fired, condensing boiler.
Ventilation	High Efficiency Energy Recovery Ventilator (ERV), continuous exhaust from kitchen and bathrooms in units with switch boost.

(*continued*)

Table 14.5 (continued)

Hebron Passive House project fact sheet

Envelope

- Wall R-Value = 63*
- Basement Wall R-Value: 46*
- Slab-on-grade R-value = 27*
- Ceiling R-value = 103*
- Windows U-value = 0.13
- Air sealing, ACH50 = 0.66 (tested)

*R-values come from the energy model and take into account all bridging, layers and air films.

Lighting, appliances, and water heating

Domestic hot water	Indirect hot water tanks.
Appliances	Energy Star rated, energy efficient appliances (Fridge, Dishwasher, Washer, Dryer, Oven, and Range).
Lighting	LED lamps and LED light fixtures.

Table 14.6 Hebron Passive House cost comparison with code compliant construction cost (Hanscomb, 2017, p. 10)

Comparison cost report Hebron
April 19, 2017

Description	Passive house standard Amount ($)	Code compliant Amount ($)	Premium ($)
1. Substructure	594	0	594
2. Structure	18,318	0	18,318
3. Exterior enclosure	93,585	32,369	61,216
4. Mechanical	110,475	126,100	−15,625
5. Electrical	0	0	0
6. Site	0	0	0
Subtotal (excluding taxes)	222,973	158,469	64,504
Taxes	33,446	23,770	9676
Total passive costs (including taxes)	256,419	182,239	74,179
Total building costs (including taxes)	1,527,134	1,452,955	74,179
Passive House consultant & certification (including taxes)	26,615	0	26,615
Total project costs including passive components	1,553,749		
Total project costs excluding passive components		1,452,955	
PREMIUM FOR PASSIVE DESIGN – VALUE			**100,794**
PREMIUM FOR PASSIVE DESIGN – PERCENTAGE			7%

Picture 14.4 Amherst Passive House front view

At around the same time, ENS initiated a PH Pilot project under its New Home Construction program, which "provides increased incentive levels for home builders who wish to build to the PH standard. The program eligibility allowed for the homes to be semi-detached, be registered in the pilot before construction begins, and have a site inspection performed within one year of registering. Furthermore, energy modeling services were to be performed by a certified PH consultant. Projects that meet minimum performance requirements would receive a rebate of CAD 10,000 if they achieve a modeled annual heating energy intensity of 22.4 k Wh/m^2/year. This could be realized using PHI or PHIUS certifications or using either PHPP or WUFI modeling software.

HNS registered the Brownell project with ENS and it became clear that engaging a PH consultant during the construction phase was crucial to provide quality assurance and ensure that the project was built to the minimum performance requirements to receive the ENS rebates. The tender for the construction of the project was issued in February 2016 and awarded in March with an anticipated six months' period for completion.

Picture 14.5 Amherst Passive House interior view

A change order was issued shortly after the tender was awarded to engage the services of the PH consultant as part of the contractor's responsibility.

7.2 Project Design

Even though the BDT used the same approach as in Alice Street, there were differences in the two projects requiring detailing that the PH consultant provided and had to be adjusted during the construction phase. These differences included an entrance detail which had a cantilever, the wall separating the two units, and detailing of the existing basement wall.

7.3 Project Construction

As with all provincial construction contracts, a public tender was issued for Brownell and was to be awarded to the lowest bid price. One of the construction firms submitted a bid price that was close to the BDT's cost estimate to construct the project. The same firm submitted a new price

Table 14.7 Hebron Passive House project analysis

Hebron Passive house project analysis
Total cost 1. Total, project cost for Hebron = CAD 1,527,134 2. Additional cost related to PH cost @ 7% of total project costs = CAD 100,794 3. Return-on-Investment: At 10 yrs. would require estimated, annual, savings of CAD 10,08 At 20 yrs. would require estimated, annual, savings of CAD 5004
Energy Consumption (per the Hebron WUFI model) 1. Total, floor area = 7824 SF 2. Total, annual, space heating and DHW demand for the facility = 31,350 kWh/yr. 3. Estimated, total, annual, electrical consumption cost to meet the space heating and DHW demand = CAD 3240/yr. (@CAD 0.18/kWh)
Equivalent Energy Consumption (per the Canada Mortgage and Housing Corporation (CMHC). (n.d.)) 1. Annual, equivalent energy consumption (ekWh/SM) of MURBS built between 1980 and present is 212 ekWh/SM which is equivalent to 19.7 ekWh/SF 2. Estimated, annual, equivalent energy consumption = 19.7 ekWh/SF × 7824 SF = 154,133 ekWh/yr. 3. Estimated, total, annual, equivalent energy consumption cost = CAD 27,744/yr. (@CAD 0.18/kWh)
Return-on-investment (ROI) 1. Estimated, annual, electrical consumption savings due to Passive House Design = CAD 27,744 –CAD 3240 = CAD 24,504/yr. 2. ROI for PH costs @ 7% of total project costs = CAD 100,794/CAD 24,504 =4 years

about one hour before the tender closing time with an amount of half of its original bidding price. Since it was the lowest bidder, the bid had to be accepted and the tender was awarded to this construction firm.

Once the project started, it became clear that the contractor did not realize that this was a PH project which required a higher level of care, coordination, and quality control compared to a code-built project. During the project, some of the contractor's staff took the PH Builder's Course, which added to their knowledge and appreciation of PH construction methods.

Other difficulties the project faced were due to: the construction crew having to commute back and forth to Amherst from PEI; the low bid price; a lack of consistent work on site that caused delays; as well as a long wait for the delivery of windows and doors. There were also issues with the quality of construction which did not meet the PH standard in terms of air leakage and had to be addressed on several occasions. Finally, all these delays affected the morale of everyone working on the project (Table 14.8).

Picture 14.6 Hebron Passive House south east view

Picture 14.7 Hebron Passive House south west view

Table 14.8 Amherst Passive House project fact sheet

Amherst passive house project fact sheet	
Location	Amherst, Nova Scotia
Construction	New Construction
Type	Duplex, Split-entry
Units	2
Total building size	15,154 SF
Unit treated area	965 SF/Unit
Bedrooms	3/Unit
Bathrooms	1/Unit
Architect	Building Design Team, Housing Nova Scotia
Energy consultant	Passive House E-Design
Builder	Sperra Construction
Construction costs	CAD 303,262
Date completed	April, 2017
Construction	
Foundation slab	3″ EPS Type 2 rigid insulation over existing concrete slab
Basement walls	Blueskin self-adhesive waterproofing membrane and 2″ EPS Type 2 Rigid insulation on the exterior of existing, concrete wall. 1″ EPS Type 2 Rigid Insulation and 3 ½″ Roxul Batt Insulation on interior side of the existing, concrete foundation wall
Walls	Vertical 9 ½″ TJI w/cellulose insulation. 7/16″ OSB sheathing caulked and taped at all joints and 2x6 Roxul structural stud wall
Roof	Insulation 28″ loose fill cellulose, R-3.8/in Thermo-Cell ProCell, 7/16″ OSB sheathing c/w all joints caulked with acoustical sealant and taped at all joints on open-web wood trusses
Windows	Triple-pane, argon-filled, low-e, vinyl frames
Key energy efficiency measures	
HVAC	
Primary heating	Electric baseboard
Ventilation	High-efficiency heat recovery ventilator (HRV). All bathroom and kitchen exhaust ventilation is run via switches on the HRV system
Envelope	
• Wall R-value = 54*	
• Basement wall R-value: 28*	
• Slab-on-grade R-value = 19*	

(*continued*)

Table 14.8 (continued)

Amherst passive house project fact sheet	
• Ceiling R-value = 105*	
• Windows U-value = 0.17 (average)	
• Air sealing, ACH50 = 0.83 (7 Brownell Ave.) and 0.75 (9 Brownell Ave.) tested	
*R-values come from the energy model and take into account all bridging, layers and air films	
Lighting, Appliances, And Water Heating	
Domestic hot water	Electric hot water tanks
Lighting	LED lamps and LED light fixtures

At the time of this writing, the Brownell project at Amherst had some remaining deficiencies including the energy monitoring systems not being hooked up, which means no energy data could be acquired. Furthermore, the cost analysis for PH construction would have required the contractor to share costs which was unlikely given the difficulties faced and the ongoing contractual deficiencies.

8 HNS PH Pilot Projects: Lessons Learnt

The focus of the PH standard is conserving energy by reducing heat loss through the building envelope and maximizing solar heat gains. Some of the conclusions were that PH is economically viable because it uses simple conservation techniques that are not complicated or expensive. By using PH standards, HNS can adapt conventional construction materials and techniques in its tenders to reduce energy needs. PH is a viable approach for housing in Nova Scotia, given the wealth of consultants' expertise which could be leveraged to create a new standard of construction. While HNS's main role is about creating affordable housing opportunities for low-to modest-income Nova Scotians, it is aware of its unique position to foster innovation and promote energy efficiency in the construction industry. Making PH more common in the province could have a positive impact by reducing overall energy costs and, over the long run, making homes more sustainable. It would also certainly contribute to consultant and contractor capacity building, which in turn could drive down the costs of PH construction and reduce delays caused by having to redo design or construction work to meet the standard.

The lessons learnt from these three pilot projects are summarized below. However, these conclusions are specific to Nova Scotia. Case studies and technical references must be used to apply these results to other Canadian or international locations.

Pre-qualification: Pre-qualify contractors to ensure that they have the minimum capability of delivering PH project requirements. HNS experienced some challenges by not pre-qualifying contractors in its Amherst PH project, which suffered in terms of quality and schedule. It is also worthwhile to research the availability of qualified products and equipment such as windows and doors to confirm availability in the market, preferably by local manufacturers. This should be done in advance of specifying materials and assemblies in tender documents for PH construction.

Predesign: Adopt the highly collaborative integrated design process which "requires that whole project team to think of the entire building and all of its systems together, emphasizing connections and improving communication among professionals and stakeholders throughout the life of the project" (US Green Building Council, 2014). This is especially effective for PH design. In addition, it is best to establish a project budget that includes PH design and construction administration fees to ensure clear cost expectations. The PH consultant should have the contract directly with the client since there are financial decisions that might affect the outcome and should include a contingency for increased PH expertise during construction.

Design: First, establish design parameters that meet the NBC of Canada and the Provincial Building Code. Second, confirm that the project meets either PHI standards or PHIUS Climate Adjusted Standard; the latter proved to be much more cost effective and achievable in Nova Scotia's climate. Third, ensure that specific client requirements, which may require special attention, are met (e.g., seniors housing has a higher heat demand throughout the year than non-senior residences). Fourth, include in the design documents a summary about PH and expectations for meeting PH targets.

Modeling: To achieve major decreases in heating energy consumption required by the PH standard, a building modeling tool such as PHPP or WUFI Passive is used to simulate the performance of the building, using such variables as solar exposure, shading, envelope assembly, window and door types, and electrical and mechanical systems. The tools allow for the PH designer to change any of the variables to optimize the building performance for best results.

Tendering: Require that contractors provide full price breakout of labor and material for all work that is considered above and beyond current NBC and Nova Scotia Building Code (NSBC) regulations; highlight PH requirements in the tender to avoid any misconceptions on what is requested; review expectations and requirements with all potential bidders ahead of tender submittals; and include time to meet with the PH consultant during construction as part of the tender package.

Construction: Provide PH supervision including field reviews at critical milestones built into the project schedule; hands-on training to the contractors as needed; reports with photos on issues and proposed solutions; and blower door testing at critical intervals. Having PH expertise on the Design Team will help save costs during construction.

8.1 Commissioning and Post-Occupancy

Ensure that commissioning is conducted by PH consultant as well as by a third party if you are seeking certification or government subsidies in the form of rebates; there is an easily understood user manual for tenants that includes a project summary and tips for optimal energy consumption in everyday living; and monitoring equipment is installed to measure total energy consumption as well as energy consumed to provide space heating separately.

9 Concluding Remarks

HNS approached these pilot projects as an opportunity to generally showcase its commitment to environmental sustainability and energy efficiency. More specifically, the aim was to evaluate the PH design and construction approach and process outcomes; document energy performance of the building and compare it to a code-built building; and track energy costs of each unit and determine obstacles toward adopting PH as a cost-effective method for HNS. In each of the three buildings, energy monitoring systems will keep track of energy uses and compare the information across projects. Early results from Alice Street were positive and showed a reduction in energy use. However, data from the other two projects was still not available at the time of this writing.

Cost increases over code-built houses averaged about 11% when weighted by total cost. PH design and oversight is one of the cost factors that should always be considered. Despite being important, they were not quantified by HNS as part of the pilot projects. As more builders adopt PH standard for construction projects, costs related to PH consultants during construction will start falling. Furthermore, certification fees increase the overall costs, which in the case of the Alice Street project was significant. ENS support had at first been tied to achieving PHI certification which was not achievable due to the location of trees to the south that reduced solar incidence. Instead, HNS achieved certification through PHIUS while ENS support was used to produce the instructional video. It is hoped that further awareness of PH may lead to supporting performance criteria, instead of specific certifications, being tied to funding. This would also lead to a higher rate of success in cases where contractors are less familiar with PH construction, as in the case of Amherst, and hopefully save on time and costs.

Scale of a project is another important cost factor. When moving from a semi-detached building to a multi-unit one, there are some advantages in the modeling due to the increased volume to area ratio, the increased number of occupants that generate internal heat, and the larger facades that provide the ability to have more solar gains. In addition, it should be noted that certification to PH standard is more economically feasible in larger projects since the costs incurred are distributed over more units. On the other hand, there are challenges related to the centralized mechanical systems that also allow for tenants to control their units through localized thermostats. This is especially true when modeling since a certain temperature is assumed for all units to simulate the energy consumption of the building, which may be different for each unit because occupants control ventilation, space heating, and domestic hot water (DHW) consumption.

The HNS PH initiative, as it was specifically implemented in Nova Scotia, was a success in demonstrating that affordable sustainable housing can be built using local materials and techniques with conventional and small building contractors within a reasonable margin of increased cost. HNS plays a role in promoting innovation in the overall housing sector. Making PH construction more common could have a significant impact on long-term sustainability, from both an economic and environmental perspective. The importance of energy efficiency and reducing the carbon footprint of buildings is increasing as the effects of climate change are being felt more rapidly on a global scale.

These PH projects have generated a lot of interest in Nova Scotia. HNS has been contacted by several local companies and service providers who expressed an interest in cooperating with HNS on demonstrating existing alternative energy technologies or piloting new innovative ones in existing buildings. HNS will continue to pursue its sustainability initiative through exploring potential energy savings in its buildings independently or through partnerships with other organizations that share the same goals.

References

Canada Mortgage and Housing Corporation (CMHC). (n.d.). *Analysis of Annual Energy and Water Consumption of Apartment Buildings in CMHC HiStar Database*. Retrieved from https://www.cmhc-schl.gc.ca/publications/en/rh-pr/tech/tech01-142.htm

Hanscomb Limited. (2017, April 19). *Hebron Centre Passive/Non-Passive Comparison Hebron, Nova Scotia*. Halifax.

Housing Nova Scotia. (2013). *A Housing Strategy for Nova Scotia Building (2013) Community and Affordability for Nova Scotia Families*. Retrieved from https://housing.novascotia.ca/Publications

Housing Nova Scotia. (2014a, May 1). *Energy Reduction Initiative*. Unpublished internal memo.

Housing Nova Scotia. (2014b, November 14). *Memorandum of Understanding Between Housing Nova Scotia and Efficiency Nova Scotia*. Unpublished Document, signed.

Housing Nova Scotia. (2016, April 17). *Housing Nova Scotia: Role & Mandate*. Webinar presented by CEO.

Housing Nova Scotia. (2017, May 1). *Helping Nova Scotians Access Safe, Affordable Housing*. PowerPoint presentation delivered at Housing Partnership Canada meeting in Halifax.

Housing Nova Scotia. (n.d.). *Annual Accountability Report 2015–2016*. Retrieved July 20, 2017, from https://housing.novascotia.ca/Publications

Natural Resources Canada. (2012, July 1). Retrieved July 20, 2017, from https://www.nrcan.gc.ca/node/5089/

Nova Scotia Department of Community Services Housing Authorities and Property Operations. (2008, July 18). *Greening strategy for public housing*. Unpublished internal document.

Passive House Institute (n.d.). *About Passive House—What is a Passive House?* Retrieved July 20, 2017, from http://passivehouse.com/02_informations/01_whatisapassivehouse/01_whatisapassivehouse.htm

Passive House Institute US (PHIUS). (n.d.). WUFI Passive 3.0. Retrieved July 20, 2017, from http://www.phius.org/software-resources/wufi-passive-and-other-modeling-tools/wufi-passive-3-0

Pembina Institute. (2016). *Accelerating market transformation for high-performance building enclosures.* Retrieved from http://www.pembina.org/pub/passive-house-report

Statistics Canada. (2015, November 27). Retrieved July 20, 2017 from http://www.statcan.gc.ca/pub/11-526-s/2013002/part-partie1-eng.htm

US Green Building Council. (2014, May 7). *Green Building 101: What is an integrated process?* Retrieved July 20, 2017, from https://www.usgbc.org/articles/green-building-101-what-integrated-process

CHAPTER 15

Sustainable Investing in Community Sporting Facilities

Gordon Noble

1 Introduction

Sporting facilities are the backbone of community participation in sport. While most media and political attention focuses on professional sports, sporting facilities at the local level are heavily used on a day-to-day basis and are, in many cases, in need of renewal. Data on sporting facilities indicates that installations are, overall, of poor quality despite clear evidence of the universality of sport participation. Approximately 60% of European citizens participate in sporting activities on a regular basis within or outside some 700,000 clubs (European Commission, 2007). In Australia, 2.3 million people, or 14% of the population, volunteer for sporting and recreational associations (Australia Bureau of Statistics, 2013).

Despite the universality of interest in sport, the story of sporting facilities is a story of "haves and have nots", with Yankee Stadium, valued at USD 2.5 billion (Gayer, Drucker, & Gold, 2016, p. 12) comparing to the

G. Noble (✉)
John Grill Centre for Project Leadership, Sydney, NSW, Australia

Network of Sustainable Financial Markets, Sydney, NSW, Australia
e-mail: noble@gnbk.com.au

T. Walker et al. (eds.), *Sustainable Real Estate*, Palgrave Studies in Sustainable Business In Association with Future Earth,
https://doi.org/10.1007/978-3-319-94565-1_15

aging and often inadequate sporting facilities in many communities. The core premise of this chapter is that the integration of sustainability into sporting facilities requires new funding and finance models. Without these, the capacity of communities to find the capital to make investments that reduce energy consumption and improve the quality of services offered to promote community health and reduce inequalities is limited. This chapter examines the funding models that currently exist in Australia, Europe and the United States and identifies flaws that undermine the ability of communities to build the facilities that they desire and deserve. This discussion is followed by the description of Community Futures Investment Model, a new model based on the modern adaptation of debentures, a financing mechanism historically used to develop community assets. Australia is used as a case study to outline how community bonds can be structured to unlock institutional investment and deliver the sought after social and environmental benefits.

In Australia, sporting facilities are principally owned by local governments that are under financial pressure, which impacts their ability to make new capital investments. The lack of a local municipal bond market has meant that Australian local authorities have limited access to capital. Government grant funding is one source of funding; however, this is irregular and supports a variety of different policy goals, including national success at Olympic Games.

Though the ownership structure of sporting facilities varies throughout Europe, there is still a strong involvement of local authorities. In many European countries, funding of sport and sporting facilities is linked to taxation of national lotteries and betting. The emergence of online betting disrupting markets and changing betting behaviors raises the question as to whether this is a sustainable funding model.

The United States benefits from the deepest and most liquid municipal bond market in the world. Sporting facilities are a component of market issuances, but taxation incentives have also incited many local authorities to issue bonds to help develop new sporting stadiums. The economic benefits of sporting stadiums have been challenged and there are examples of projects that have not met their ambitious targets (McKenna, 2015; Povich, 2016). But perhaps the greatest impact of public financing of private stadiums is to crowd out investment in community-based sporting facilities.

The funding and financing models for sporting facilities are also influenced by competing national sporting priorities including the desire for Olympic success. National sporting organization, such as SportsEngland, are used to fund sports through national sporting associations. While this may result in success for elite athletes, it creates an environment, at a local level, where it is difficult for amateur sports to thrive or benefit from synergies between all levels of sporting activities.

To unlock new investment in community sporting facilities, it is argued that there is a need for a change in the way facilities are run. Addressing the latency of assets outside of sports use may open up new sources of funding. Focusing on developing shared facilities requires a new approach to the way assets are managed with increased utilization of professional managers that work with local volunteers. An example in Australia is Beaumaris Sports Club where three sports, cricket, football and tennis, have come together to develop a new sports facility which the three clubs will share with the local community. Capital markets offer a source of financing at a lower cost than unsecured bank loans. However, the small size of individual projects makes it difficult, if not impossible, to attract institutional capital. It is proposed that established financial service techniques, such as securitization and credit enhancement, can be adapted to provide a mechanism for sporting facilities to be financed through wholesale markets. Community bonds that securitize a group of projects with credit enhancement to support credit ratings represent a new kind of bond offering that focuses on delivering investment returns while at the same time delivering clear environmental, social and economic benefits.

The use of community bonds would integrate sustainability into community sporting facility projects including the potential to incorporate green building practices and renewable energy installations into their design. There are also strong links between sporting facilities and health outcomes. In particular, community bonds can support addressing obesity. To ensure that there is accountability around the environmental and social outcomes from community bonds, it is proposed that standards should be established based on the successful model of the Climate Bonds Initiative[1].

[1] https://www.climatebonds.net/.

2 Brief History of Sport

The history of sport dates back to ancient times where it may have played a role in military training, but it was the emergence of leisure time in the 1800s, as a result of the Industrial Revolution and the passage of labor laws that allowed sport to become an active communal pastime. The development and popularity of Australian Rules Football in 1859 in Melbourne, Australia, owed much to the success of trade union campaigns for shorter working hours in the 1850s which resulted in factory workers only working three and a half hours on Saturdays. With Saturday afternoons off, attending sporting events became popular and by the 1880s crowds of up to 15,000 would attend matches (Herriman, 2013). In the United Kingdom, Sheffield Football Club was established in 1857, codifying the original rules of football with a focus on social values of integrity, respect and community (Sheffield Football Club, 2017). Not long after the establishment of the rules of the game of Australian Rules Football and Football, followed the payment of players. In the United States, the first baseball game with paid admission was between New York City and Brooklyn which was held at Fashion Race Course on Long Island in July 1858 (Fried, Kindle Location 520, 2015), heralding in the era of enclosed stadiums and paid tickets.

As sports developed, the focus turned to establishing facilities to support games. The first task for outdoor sports was to establish a playing field which involved converting open space used for agriculture. As games attracted larger crowds, grandstands were built in order to support them. The first public grandstand was built in 1854 at the Melbourne Cricket Ground, the "G", which is now one the world's largest stadiums. Today, every community has a range of sporting facilities that relates to their unique interests. What is extraordinary about sport is that no single sport is dominant everywhere in the world. Sporting facilities reflect this variety of community interests.

The role of sport in supporting communities has been recognized globally, with the Sustainable Development Goals (SDGs) passed by resolution adopted by the United Nations General Assembly on 25 September 2015 (RES/70/1) specifically recognizing the importance of sport. The SDGs include a number of direct references to sport with the UN General Assembly stating "we recognize the growing contribution of sport to the realization of development and peace in its promotion of tolerance and respect and the contributions it makes to the empowerment of women and of young people, individuals and communities as well as to health, education and social inclusion objectives" (http://www.un.org/ga/search/view_doc.asp?symbol=A/RES/70/1&Lang=E).

Robert Putnam, the author of Bowling Alone, argued in his recent book that for children, involvement in extracurricular activities such as sport is strongly associated with a variety of positive outcomes, stating "these positive outcomes include higher grade-point averages, lower dropout rates, lower truancy, better work habits, higher educational aspirations, lower delinquency rates, greater self-esteem, more psychological resilience, less risky behavior, more civic engagement (like voting and volunteering), and higher future wages and occupational attainment" (Putnam, Kindle location 160–161, 2016).

2.1 Dominance of Professional Sport

Since the early days of crowds gathering to watch teams play in the late 1800s, sports has professionalized and the management of sporting teams has become a significant business in its own right. According to Forbes, the average net worth of the world's 50 most valuable sports teams is USD 1.75 billion (Badenhausen, 2015) while Deloitte estimates that the aggregate revenue of the top 20 football clubs was €7.4 billion in 2015–2016 (Deloitte, 2017).

The dominance of professional sport has resulted in an increased demand to build stadiums that can cater to large crowds. Though these stadiums can accommodate large numbers of spectators, their involvement in sport is predominantly passive while in community sporting facilities individuals play an active role, either through direct participation or through volunteering. Because of this fundamental distinction, community sporting facilities can play a greater role in social policy to encourage healthy lifestyles and reduce inequalities. According to the European Commission's White Paper "A Strategy for Europe on Nutrition, Overweight and Obesity", as a tool for health-enhancing physical activity, the sports movement has a greater influence than any other social movement (European Commission, 2007). McKinsey Global Institute estimates that more than 2.1 billion people, or nearly 30% of the global population, are overweight or obese with obesity responsible for around 5% of all deaths worldwide. The economic cost of obesity alone is estimated by McKinsey to be roughly USD 2.0 trillion, or 2.8% of global gross domestic product (GDP) (McKinsey Global Institute, 2014). This statistic alone warrants examination into how community sports facilities can contribute to addressing this global epidemic.

Research demonstrates that the provision of public sports facilities and fields/courts is associated with increased sport participation. In turn, participation in organized sport is associated with better physical and mental health. These benefits include outcomes such as lower prevalence of obesity, lower rate of Type 2 diabetes and improved social, emotional and psychosocial well-being for children, adolescents and adults (McKinsey Global Institute, 2014). When it comes to considering where valuable public subsidies are placed, the social benefits of sport participation needs to be recognized.

In contrast to the potential positive social impacts of investing in community sporting facilities, there are significant environmental costs associated with the construction and operation of stadiums dedicated to professional sport. Stadiums and professional sporting events are energy and resource intensive. It is estimated that an average Super Bowl can generate approximately 70 tons of trash (Fried Kindle Locations 6667–6668, 2015). There has been a wide range of green-led innovations over the last decade including installation of solar panels, enhanced recycling practices and donation of surplus food to food charities being some examples. One example is MetLife Stadium, which houses the New York Jets and New York Giants. This stadium was designed to reduce annual water usage by 25%, energy usage by 35% and increase in-event recycling by 25%, saving the equivalent of 1.68 million metric tons of CO_2 annually (Fried, Kindle Locations 6787–6789, 2015). Unfortunately, the incorporation of sustainability into the design and operation of stadiums is not standard practice and the differing ownership models of stadiums means that there is less publicly available information on their operational performance than would be desirable. This lack of transparency with respect to energy, water consumption and waste generation prevents researchers from conducting meaningful comparisons between public and private sporting facilities based on these and other important environmental metrics.

3 Community Sporting Facility Funding and Financing Models

One of the major reasons why community sporting facilities, despite the high level of community participation, are not reaching their potential to deliver positive social and environmental outcomes relates to flaws in funding and financing models. Funding and financing models for community sporting facilities vary globally. The United States, for example, utilizes its municipal bond market as a major means to finance redevelopment of community sporting facilities while, among European Union countries, funding from lotteries is commonly used. The main features of these financing methods are briefly summarized later. The case of Australia is covered in greater detail in the following sections.

3.1 US Municipal Bond Market

The US municipal bond market is a major source of financing for sporting facilities. The market consists of over one million individual municipal bonds with USD 3.14 trillion traded in 2016 (Municipal Securities Rulemaking Board, Annual Fact Book, 2016). The US municipal bond market is dominated by retail investors, who make up 75% of the market and are able to access income tax concessions from investing in municipal bonds. The market is notable for the small average size of transaction. In 2016, the average size of a municipal securities transaction was USD 335,017, up 28% from a year earlier (Press Release, MSRB PUBLISHES ANNUAL FACT BOOK OF MUNICIPAL SECURITIES MARKET DATA, 6 March 2017 Municipal Securities Rulemaking Board, Annual Fact Book, 2016 http://www.msrb.org/News-and-Events/Press-Releases/2017/MSRB-Publishes-Annual-Fact-Book-of-Municipal-Securities-Market-Data.aspx).

The federal government effectively incentivizes investment in stadiums through rules which provide tax concessions for certain municipal bonds. The Tax Reform Act (TRA86) effectively requires that in order for a municipal authority to receive a federal subsidy, they must rely on tax revenue unrelated to the stadium for the financing, such as general sales taxes, property taxes, income taxes, lotteries or taxes on alcohol and cigarettes. The most popular taxes are tourism taxes, which are placed on hotel rooms and rental cars. According to the Brookings Institute, while in the first half of the twentieth century the majority of stadiums were financed by the private-sector, since 1953, the public has effectively subsidized their development and "absent the subsidies from all levels of government, there would be little incentive for the teams or private investors to finance so many new (and increasingly luxurious) stadiums" (Gayer et al., 2016, p. 8). This report argues that leagues and teams are able to exercise significant monopoly power and "therefore have a strategic incentive to expand the number of teams fast enough to deter the formation of rival leagues, yet slow enough to ensure that threats by existing franchises to relocate are taken seriously" (Gayer et al., 2016, p. 8).

While the US municipal bond market gives local authorities the ability to access cost-effective financing, TRA86 has the impact of incentivizing a flow of capital to the benefit of professional sports and not to community sporting facilities. More broadly the ability of a city to issue new municipal bonds to finance community infrastructure is dependent on the financial capacity of the city. As demonstrated through a series of downgrades, including the City of Ferguson, fiscal budget pressures can lead to higher borrowing costs and can dissuade cities from seeking to access markets for new projects (https://www.moodys.com/research/Moodys-downgrades-Ferguson-MOs-GO-rating-to-Ba1-from-Aa3-PR_334856). The limitation of the US municipal bond market is that it entrenches local government to rely principally on debt for projects. Because the ability to access debt is in itself reliant on a city's financial capacity, struggling cities that could benefit the most from the social outcomes generated by new investment are limited in their scope to initiate new community infrastructure.

3.2 European Lottery Funding

The major source of funding of sport and sporting facilities among European Union countries are taxes on national lotteries and betting. The following information on the funding of grassroots sports in Denmark, France, Germany and the United Kingdom is based on the comprehensive study published by Eurostrategies in 2011.

Denmark has an estimated 14,000 sport clubs and the promotion of grassroots sport is a public policy priority with a focus on getting children enrolled in sport and supporting volunteers. The Danish Foundation for Culture and Sport Facilities supports the development and construction of sport facilities. Funding for sport comes from the taxation of lotteries and horse and dog racing. However, only 6.94% of funds are distributed to the Danish Foundation for Culture and Sport Facilities with the remaining 73% of funds being distributed to support Denmark's Olympic team and the Sport Confederation of Denmark, both devoted to elite athletes. (Eurostrategies, Amnyos, CDES, Deutsche Sporthochschule Köln, Study on the funding of grassroots sports in the EU, With a focus on the internal market aspects concerning legislative frameworks and systems of financing, Final report, Volume II—Country Reports, 27 June 2011, page 60).

In France, 168,045 sport associations and grassroot sport clubs are supported by household contributions with the public-sector contributing around 40% of total revenues. Local authorities are the main contributors to sport associations' revenues, especially for sport equipment and facilities (Eurostrategies, p. 89).

In Germany, approximately 90,000 sport clubs are supported principally by households who contribute around 75% of revenues. Taxation from lotteries and sport betting are estimated to contribute around € 450 million per annum. Contributions from Germany's central government account for less than 1% of the total with local authorities contributing 15.3% (Eurostrategies, p. 100).

In the United Kingdom, there are around 6.9 million members of 150,000 clubs (Eurostrategies, p. 251). Local authorities collectively invest around £1.5 billion a year in sport. Sport is one of many areas supported by the National Lottery established in 1994. Sport betting is liberalized in the UK and the various different private operators are not bound to contribute to supporting sport. Sport England receives on average £108 million from lottery funding (Eurostrategies, 2011). In England 326 local authorities are responsible for funding and delivering sporting facilities (Jaekel, 2017, p. 6).

4 Australia's Community Infrastructure

Approximately 6.5 million Australians participate in organized sport and 2.3 million people volunteer time for sport each year, representing the largest volunteer group in the country (Australian Government, 2015). Sport and recreation industries generated AUD 12.8 billion in income and employed around 134,000 Australians in 2011–2012 (Australian Bureau of Statistics, 2013). In Australia, community sporting facilities are generally owned by local governments and funding for clubs comes from a variety of sources including grants. These facilities are principally the responsibility of local governments and, in many cases, clubs operate out of local government owned land. Though various funding programs have been put in place by federal and state governments and grassroots clubs may be the beneficiaries of grants, grant funding has not been sufficient to meet the overall needs. This government ownership and funding structure has, in many forums, been deemed responsible for a growing deficit in investment in these community assets despite their recognized social and economic value.

According to the Australian Local Government Association, there is currently AUD 47 billion worth of community infrastructure that is in poor condition (Jeff Roorda and Associates, 2015). One example is the country's aquatic centers. According to a review by the Victorian Auditor General, there are 153 aquatic centers in Victoria that are over 26 years old, with 41 that are over 51 years of age. More than half of Victoria's aquatic centers are likely to be in need of repair or upgrading and responses to the Auditor General's survey indicate that over a quarter of councils will conduct significant upgrades at a cost of more than AUD 1 million over the next four years (Victorian Auditor-General's Office, 2016).

4.1 *Ad hoc Funding Creates Inequitable Distribution*

Funding of community sporting facilities in Australia is provided from a mix of local government funding and ad hoc state and federal government grants with national sporting bodies providing grants depending on identification of need. Sporting clubs are experiencing a surge in demand for team sports with a significant increase in participation by girls and women. Growth in demand for women's Australian Rules Football teams has been particularly significant, with growth of 162% in the last 6 years (VAFA Women's Football Club n.d.). Female participation in Australian football soared by 46% in 2016 alone and there were 163 new female football teams that began in 2015, with the number of women taking part in the Australian Football League (AFL) reaching 284,501 participants in 2016. In the state of Victoria, a further 250 new women's teams were established in 2017 (Women's game kicks off boom, 2017). Current facilities have mostly been designed without appropriate changing facilities for women and girls, potentially impacting on the future participation of women. The ad hoc grant model demand results in some communities being delivered with new facilities, while their neighbors miss out. The existing funding model is not well equipped to address current community infrastructure deficits, let alone respond to changing demand in the community and in fact has the potential to lead to inequity as some communities are able to attract funding and others do not.

4.2 *Elite Athlete Focused Sports Policy*

A further challenge for community sports clubs is the way in which sports policy is run at a national level, often focusing on delivering medals at Olympics games. Jaekel argues that public funding for sport often goes through sport governing bodies that distribute funds to regional and local sport clubs. However, sport governing bodies often keep a share of public funding for their own administrative purposes and face "multiple ambiguous, complex, and sometimes contradictory agency goals" (Jaekel, 2017, p. 4).

Another issue identified by Jaekel, with respect to Sport England in particular but that exists elsewhere, is the level of collaboration between national and local sporting organizations. The problem with delivering sports funding through national sports bodies that focus on achieving elite sporting success is that the interests of communities and their clubs are not the number one priority. Public financial support for sport, whether it be subsidies to build stadiums in the United States, reliance on lottery and gaming revenues or the focus on funding sport governing bodies, has a tendency to support elite athletes, professional or Olympic. It is arguable that if the focus was placed principally on communities and their sporting facility needs that the facilities that would be delivered and the models of finance and funding utilized would be very different. The next section develops an alternative financing model for community sporting facilities using Australia as a case study.

5 Community Asset Financing Challenges

The first stage in developing a model for financing community sporting facilities is to understand the challenges faced by local sporting clubs. The reasons that community sporting clubs find it hard to finance the development of their own facilities were identified by the Australian Government's Productivity Commission which considered impediments to financing Australia's 600,000 not-for-profits. The Commission found that while the sector contributed around AUD 43 billion to the national economy, there were significant impediments to accessing capital including:

- the lack of collateral to guarantee loans
- the lack of a reliable revenue streams to service debt
- the large transaction costs relative to the amount of capital required
- the lack of experience in developing sustainable business plans
- the lack of a suitable organizational structure which would allow organizations to raise equity capital. (Kumic & Noble, 2017)

These impediments, which are likely to be common across other jurisdictions, are examined in further detail.

5.1 *Lack of Collateral*

In many environments, local sporting clubs do not own the land that they operate from. Depending on the jurisdiction, there are a range of agreements that exist between local authorities (which are often the landowners) and clubs. In the Australian context, it is common for sporting clubs to operate on the basis of peppercorn rents. In the case of older clubs, there may not be formal contractual agreements in place. The lack of ownership rights and uncertainty around leases means that sporting clubs may only be able to access financing on terms given to unsecured lenders. Finding a way to provide sporting clubs with access to long-term financing is important but the objective is not to overload clubs with debt but to empower sporting clubs to pursue their own interests, whatever they may be.

One option that could support sporting clubs to access more cost-effective longer-term financing is securitization. Securitization was born in 1970 with the establishment of the Government National Mortgage Association or "Ginnie Mae", which provided the ability to pool mortgage assets into Mortgage Backed Securities. The technique has been used to parcel up many different kinds of illiquid assets in order to make them investable. The recent appetite for Green and Climate Bonds is demonstrating the opportunity to issue bonds that deliver clear impacts. According to the Climate Bonds Initiative "Bonds & Climate Change: State of the Market 2016" report, it is estimated that there are currently USD 694 billion of climate-aligned bonds outstanding, an increase of USD 96 billion in 2015 (Climate Bonds Initiative, 2016).

5.2 *Lack of Reliable Revenue*

A key issue for not-for-profit community sporting clubs is the volatility of revenues. In their study on New Zealand grassroots community sporting clubs, Cordery and Baskerville argue that reliance on grant funding is detrimental to the long-term sustainability of clubs. They cite research on not-for-profit community sporting clubs that suggest that increasing the number of revenue sources has a positive effect on revenue stability and is important in addressing the growing costs of maintaining community assets. Not-for-profit organizations with few revenue sources have been demonstrated to be more financially vulnerable than those with many sources (Cordery & Baskerville, 2011). For long-term viability, generating sufficient funding from a diversity of revenue streams is a critical issue.

Community sporting facilities have often been built with a single focus, often with no changing facilities for women and girls, particularly where sports were originally seen as for males only. As social norms change, and women and girls increasingly seek to play new sports, there is a need to adapt the supporting infrastructure to tap into this new source of revenue. Sporting facilities are also often only heavily used at peak times such as weekends and may lie dormant during the week. As communities grow in population, there is a need to develop new models that can open up facilities to be used by communities seven days a week and year-round. Through shared use of facilities, it is possible to develop new revenue models which in turn support the development and renewal of facilities while providing greater access to quality facilities to more members of the community.

The model of single purpose community infrastructure, popularized in the 1950s when land was relatively plentiful particularly in developing outer suburbs, is now being replaced. In Australia, Hornsby Council located in the north of Greater Sydney region has, in its Community and Cultural Facilities Strategic Plan, identified the need to share facilities that are capable of responding and adapting to the changing needs and preferences of the community. Hornsby Council is focusing on developing community infrastructure assets that include movable furniture, changeable wall partitions and building designs with expansion in mind (Elton Consulting, 2015). Hornsby's intention is to design, build and fit out facilities that maximize flexibility of use and, when upgrading facilities, are capable of delivering a range of services, rather than designated single uses.

Through shared facilities, sporting clubs can build diversified revenues that are essential for long-term financial viability. Examples of additional revenue streams that can diversify sporting club revenues include bars, cafes, function centers providing large event and meeting spaces, co-working and innovation working spaces, gyms, child play centers and education programs.

5.3 *Small Investments, Large Transaction Costs*

A challenge for sporting clubs is that the distributed nature and small size of projects means that they have been unable to access larger pools of capital such as pension funds, who invest through capital markets. A challenge in developing products that are suitable for pension funds to invest in is the size of investment and associated transaction costs. In order to create the incentives for pension funds to invest in community sporting clubs, there is a need to offer investments that match their appetite in terms of size, liquidity, costs and returns.

Aggregating multiple projects can create larger, longer-term investments with a lower overall risk profile. This reduces the overall cost of the investments, by gaining access to preferential finance rates only available to large institutional investors. Low cost is an important element in delivering returns to superannuation and pension fund members.

5.4 *Lack of Business Development Expertise*

In the Australian context, one of the strengths of sporting clubs is the large number of volunteers. The reliance on volunteers however limits the ability of sporting clubs to build and implement sustainable business plans. For unpaid club executives that are responsible for all the logistics of getting a sporting team onto a field, there is little time or incentive to dedicate to long-term business planning. With sport becoming more sophisticated, with increased requirements even at junior levels to monitor and report conduct of players, ensure the safety and oversee drug-testing regimes, there is a need to support the professionalization of clubs at a community level. Professionalization would allow clubs to pay individuals to manage business activities including long-term facilities planning, as well as potentially outsourcing some functions such as food and beverage functions in order to deliver increased revenues to the club. Professionalization is not about reducing the importance of volunteers. It is about providing volunteers with the support to focus on what they love doing best—which is helping their teams prosper.

5.5 *Lack of Suitable Organizational Structure for Raising Capital*

Sporting clubs are generally incorporated bodies and have all the powers of businesses to contract with parties. The challenge that sporting clubs face is that they are owned by their members and are therefore not able to issue share equity. This deprives sporting clubs of one of the main avenues that corporations use to expand their activities. What this means is that the sources of funds that clubs can use to develop their assets are limited to grants and debt financing. Because sporting clubs have mainly accessed debt through costly unsecured bank financing, when developing and renewing facilities, grants have become the major source of funds.

In Australia, sources of grants have included federal, state and local governments, as well as sporting organizations themselves that have been able to use broadcast revenues from elite competitions to support local community sporting facilities.

Unfortunately, grant funding, whether state, federal or from sporting bodies, is proving to be insufficient in terms of delivering to communities what they need, when they need it. Grant funding is suited to an environment where change is incremental and predicable but is not able to respond flexibly to rapid societal changes. As an example, Cricket Australia recently conducted a nationwide audit of 5500 cricket facilities and 7100 ovals, finding that 80% are not female-friendly. Bringing facilities up to modern standards, which would support the increased female participation in cricket, would according to Cricket Australia cost AUD 10 billion (http://www.theaustralian.com.au/sport/cricket/grassroots-cricket-makes-its-pitch-amid-elite-pay-row/news-story/4ee0c05df04d9208efe9b757bfba8ed6).

6 Community Futures Investment Model

The Community Futures Investment Model has been developed by Gordon Noble and Dr. Ingo Kumic as a multi-stakeholder approach that aims to create an environment that enables institutional investors to invest in communities at scale through community bonds.

The Community Futures Investment Model aims to align the various objectives of local and national authorities, institutional investors and citizens in order to deliver environmental and social outcomes for communities. This approach, which allows institutional investors to invest in community assets, decreases the dependency on grants and high interest unsecured bank financing thus generating more social, environmental, economic and financial wealth in a way that distributes financial and political risk. Furthermore, this model allows for investments to be made across a broad range of communities, thereby reducing the impact of income and social inequity as factors that influence where investments may be made.

7 Community Bonds

A community bond is a modern equivalent of the debenture, which allowed not-for-profit sports organizations to raise debt from investors. By using established capital market techniques, such as securitization and credit enhancement, community bonds can be established that would be of sufficient size and liquidity and would deliver investment returns that would be attractive to institutional investors. Through securitization, community bonds could enable smaller shorter-term projects to be offered to the bond markets as part of an aggregated package with a better risk profile and longer borrowing period.

7.1 Debentures and the Funding of Community Assets

Debentures are unsecured loans that are backed by general credit rather than by specific assets. There are many examples of the use of debentures to finance community assets. Perhaps the best known debenture is the Wimbledon tennis tournament, which has used the vehicle to fund capital investment, with debenture holders entitled to seats at Centre Court over the period of the investment. Wimbledon Debentures are traded on the London Stock Exchange and hold definite value for those who have invested (White, 2016).

In Australia, many community assets have been built by communities pooling resources and issuing debentures. The reasons that communities came together depended on their individual interests and needs. The Mounties Club, which was originally established by a group of locals from the Mt Pritchard community in the 1920s, simply wanted to have a place to have a beer without having to travel to the nearest pubs in Cabramatta, on the outskirts of Sydney. Another example is the Mulgrave Country Club. In 1960, 18 people in the outskirts of Melbourne's growing suburbs got together and committed to a debenture to purchase 5 acres of land on which they progressively established installations for tennis, squash, golf, snooker, darts and cricket.

In an era before sophisticated financial services laws, it was a relatively simple thing for a club to issue debentures. There were no legal requirements on how debentures could be issued with early examples of debentures being little more than documenting who had provided funds in a log book. One of the challenges in developing a modern debenture is the introduction of financial services regulations which require sophisticated legal documents for capital raising. Another factor is the rising cost of land, which in the post-war era was plentiful and relatively cheap.

A modern example in Australia of a community driving the development of its own facilities through issuing a debenture to its members is Beaumaris Sport Club in Melbourne where three clubs—cricket, tennis and football—merged to form a single entity. Members of the club invested in a debenture with returns of 5% per annum with the objective that the funds would be repaid in ten years. While the approach by Beaumaris Sports Club of tapping club members to support the redevelopment of club facilities was successful, it is nevertheless difficult to roll out community debentures at scale. One of the challenges is that not all communities have the luxury of having disposable cash to invest directly.

7.2 How Would Community Bonds Work?

As a hypothetical example, a community bond would bring together 10–20 separate projects that would range from USD 5 to 20 million. A total bond of $100 million would be of sufficient size to attract institutional investors.

A community bond would need to be issued by a special purpose investment vehicle, called the Community Investment Funding Vehicle (CIFV). Specifically the features of a CIFV would include:

- Community Investment Program Trust would be established as the structure through which an aggregated portfolio of community loans was issued to institutional investors.
- Security for community bonds would consist of credit enhancement that could be provided by local authorities and other stakeholders. In the event that a community group defaulted on a bond, then credit enhancement would ensure that institutional investors did not bare first losses. This would support a higher credit rating for the bond.

- A governance board (known as the Community Investment Governance Board) would be established under the terms of the Community Investment Program Trust Deed. The governance board would be responsible for working with local community groups to develop enhanced accounting and governance practices.

Capital market innovations, such as credit enhancement, which have been used in the financial services industry to mitigate project risks and enable financing of a project, would be an important element of a community bond. In its simplest form, credit enhancement seeks to increase the credit rating/credit worthiness of the financeable aspects of an infrastructure project. The main objective of a credit-enhancement mechanism is to ameliorate the credit quality of infrastructure projects that have already achieved a certain minimum threshold, in order to attract more private financing for the project.

There is the potential for credit enhancement to come from stakeholders, including sports organizations and sporting leagues, which have deep balance sheets and income from television broadcast of elite sports but who are also incentivized to support the ongoing development of sports in the community.

7.3 Setting Standards

A securitized community bond would be offered to capital markets on commercial terms. In addition to the risk and return equation, community bonds would be attractive as impact investments since they would be able to demonstrate very clear social, environmental and economic benefits. In order to attract investors that have a focus on financial returns and social and environmental impacts, there is a need for a community bond to establish a clear set of standards which would enable investors to understand the impacts of the bond.

An example of the importance of standard setting in unlocking new investment is the Climate Bonds Initiative[2], which initially started as a project of the Network for Sustainable Financial Markets (NSFM)[3], an international network of finance sector professionals, academics and oth-

[2] https://www.climatebonds.net/.

[3] http://www.sustainablefinancialmarkets.net/.

ers dedicated to improving financial market integrity and efficiency. Climate Bonds aim to provide greater certainty for investors about the climate benefits of investments. The Climate Bonds Initiative certifies assets and projects that meet the requirements of the Climate Bond Standards. In order to receive the "Climate Bond Certified" stamp of approval, a prospective issuer of a Green or Climate Bond must appoint an approved third party verifier, who will provide a verification statement that the bond meets the Climate Bond Standard. The Climate Bond Standard allows Certification of a bond prior to its issuance, enabling the issuer to use the Climate Bond Certification Mark in marketing efforts and investor roadshows. The Climate Bonds Standards Board, comprised of members representing USD 34 trillion of assets under management, confirms Climate Bond Certification once the bond has been issued and the proceeds have been allocated to projects and assets.

Community Bonds would require a similar framework that would ensure that the interests of communities are aligned with those of investors. In particular, community bonds would need to ensure that the community is integral to decisions the decision-making process. A culture of patronage and responsibility must be ensured and representation is at the heart of the co-creation process with the community.

There is the capacity for Community Bonds to deliver significant social and environmental impacts. As impacts will vary by project, there exists a need to establish standardized reporting at an individual project level, in order to enable aggregation at the bond level. There are a number of areas where social impacts can be delivered, including through the benefits of participation in sports as a mechanism to address obesity. The environmental standards of a community bonds could include linking to established green building ratings, which would provide information on design features including energy efficiency. There is also the opportunity for projects to work with partners to either directly install renewable energy or to buy from established renewable energy providers. Community Bonds therefore have the opportunity to directly contribute to lowering the emissions of a community and the measurement of this contribution will be of growing importance going forward.

Social and environmental impacts from community bonds would be captured and reported as part of a Community Partnership Agreement that would form a foundation for managing community investments.

8 Community Partnership Agreements

A critical component of the Community Futures Investment Model is the establishment of Community Partnership Agreements (CPAs) between clubs, local government and stakeholders. They are the means by which differing interests are managed. CPAs are necessary in order to clearly define the responsibilities of all the parties that must come together to unlock investment and ensure debt repayment under any number of defined scenarios.

A CPA would set out the terms by which community clubs are able to access debt and outline the mechanism by which stakeholders will support community bond repayment through interest payments or involvement in club revenue generating activities.

CPAs would set out:

- length and terms of lease
- insurance obligations of clubs
- allocation of responsibilities for use of facility
- allocation of responsibilities for repairs, maintenance of facilities and grounds
- strategic long-term development plans of the facility
- details of grants and financial commitments made by local council and stakeholders to support the development of facilities
- mechanisms by which the impact of environmental, social and economic benefits from investment will be measured and reported
- terms by which Clubs can reduce their annual interest obligations by making principal reductions to local government
- governance and dispute resolution processes (Kumic & Noble, 2017).

9 Conclusion

With hundreds of thousands of community sporting clubs operating around the world, the carbon footprint and social impact from local sports are significant. Sport is funded in many different ways which has an impact on the ability for communities to make the capital investments that are necessary to reduce the energy intensity of facilities and make available the high-quality facilities to the greatest number of community members. The key to reducing the energy intensity of sporting facilities and maximizing their social impact lies in the development of new funding and financing models. One of the challenges that community sporting clubs face is that their size, variable revenues and lack of ownership of the land on which they operate, means that they have been, in many cases, unable to finance the renewal of their sporting facilities. An approach that combines revenue diversification and a new model of investment—the Community Futures Investment Model—would provide community sporting clubs with the opportunity to build the facilities that they need and deserve.

The key elements of the Community Futures Investment Model are:

1. Long-term investment: Community bonds are structured to enable institutional investors to invest in community projects by aggregating projects to create investments that meet the needs of institutional investors in terms of size, liquidity and cost. Communities are able to access finance at rates normally only available to governments, delivering long-term savings and opening up opportunities for capital investments to renew and develop community assets.

2. Sharing the load: Reflecting that sporting codes and governments benefit in different ways from community facilities, it is fair that the costs renewing and developing community assets are shared by transitioning from ad hoc capital grants to supporting a portion of interest payments on community bonds.

3. Connecting communities: Community facilities play a major role in connecting communities which can be enhanced by addressing the latency of community facilities at certain times of the week and using community assets more intensively. New activities can provide additional revenues that support the capital costs for renewal and development of community assets.

A critical component of the Community Futures Investment Model is the establishment of CPAs between clubs, local government and stakeholders. CPAs are necessary in order to define the responsibilities of all the parties that must come together to unlock investment. Under the proposed model, a CPA can be used to enshrine many different partnerships and therefore "debt repayment" scenarios.

The aim in the long term is for the Community Futures Investment Model to innovate local government's pathway dependencies on grants and the rate-base. In so doing, local government can simultaneously generate more social, environmental, economic and financial wealth in a way that distributes financial and political risk.

The Community Futures Investment Model represents a multi-stakeholder approach that seeks to address not only the need for investment in facilities so as to optimize their utility but also the importance of these types of facilities in connecting communities.

By changing the way that club facilities are managed, and bringing in new activities such as co-working/innovation hubs, community gyms, learning and child activities at times when assets were previously latent, there is the potential for sporting facilities to serve a larger role in their community. Community bonds can support economic development, job creation and play a role in supporting a range of social issues.

References

Australia Bureau of Statistics. (2013). *Value of Sport, Australia (cat no 4165.0.55.002)*. Canberra. Retrieved August 15, 2017, from http://www.ausstats.abs.gov.au/ausstats/subscriber.nsf/0/A48910CF5F68EE18CA257C0D000F95F2/$File/4156055002_2013.pdf

Australian Bureau of Statistics. (2013, October 24). *Sport Scores Goals for Aussie Economy*. Australian Bureau of Statistics. Retrieved August 16, 2017, from http://www.abs.gov.au/ausstats/abs@.nsf/latestProducts/4156.0.55.002Media%20Release12013

Australian Government. (2015). *The Australian Sports Commission's Participation Game PLan*. Retrieved August 16, 2017, from http://www.ausport.gov.au/__data/assets/pdf_file/0006/625902/PlaySportAustralia_brochure_MARCH_15_web.pdf

Badenhausen, K. (2015, July 15). *The World's 50 Most Valuable Sports Teams 2015*. Forbes. Retrieved May 29, 2017, from https://www.forbes.com/sites/kurtbadenhausen/2015/07/15/the-worlds-50-most-valuable-sports-teams-2015/#3a1eac1227cb

Climate Bonds Initiative. (2016). *Bonds and Climate Change: The State of the Market in 2016*. Climate Bonds Initiative & HSBC Climate Change Center of Excellent. Retrieved May 29, 2017, from https://www.climatebonds.net/files/files/reports/cbi-hsbc-state-of-the-market-2016.pdf

Cordery, C. J., & Baskerville, R. F. (2011, 11). *Understanding the Significance of Revenue Diversification in Nonprofit Sports Clubs*. Victoria University, School of Accounting and Commercial Law. Retrieved May 29, 2017, from https://papers.ssrn.com/sol3/papers.cfm?abstract_id=1634476

Deloitte. (2017, 01). *Deloitte Football Money League 2017*. Deloitte. Retrieved May 29, 2017, from https://www2.deloitte.com/uk/en/pages/sports-business-group/articles/deloitte-football-money-league.html

Elton Consulting. (2015). *Community and Cultural Facilities Strategic Plan.* Hornsby Shire Council. Retrieved May 29, 2017, from http://www.hornsby.nsw.gov.au/__data/assets/pdf_file/0005/58937/Community-and-Cultural-Facilities-Strategic-Plan-August-2015.pdf

European Commission. (2007). *White Paper on Sport.* Luxembourg: Office for Official Publications of the European Communities. Retrieved August 15, 2017, from http://www.aop.pt/upload/tb_content/320160419151552/35716314642829/whitepaperfullen.pdf

Eurostrategies. (2011). *Study of the Funding of Grassroots Sports in the EU.* Retrieved May 29, 2017, from http://www.bloso-kics.be/Sporteneu/Documents/110601_EU_study_funding_grassroots_sports_finalreport_vol2.pdf

Fried, G. (2015). *Managing Sport Facilities* (3rd ed.). Champaign, IL: Human Kinetics.

Gayer, T., Drucker, A. J., & Gold, A. K. (2016). *Tax-Exempt Municipal Bonds and the Financing of Professional Sports Stadiums.* Brookings Economic Studies. Retrieved August 16, 2017, from https://www.brookings.edu/wp-content/uploads/2016/09/gayerdrukkergold_stadiumsubsidies_090816.pdf

Herriman, N. (2013, March 22). *The Conversation.* Australian Rules: How a Nation Fell in Love with Footy. Retrieved May 29, 2017, from http://theconversation.com/australian-rules-how-a-nation-fell-in-love-with-footy-12888

Jaekel, T. (2017). *Modern Sports-for-All Policy: An International Comparison of Policy Goals and Models of Service Delivery—Working Paper no. WP BRP 04/PSP/2017.* National Research University Higher School of Economics. Retrieved August 16, 2017, from https://wp.hse.ru/data/2017/03/06/1166665949/04PSP2017.pdf

Jeff Roorda and Associates. (2015). *National State of the Assets.* Australian Local Government Association. Retrieved August 16, 2017, from http://alga.asn.au/site/misc/alga/downloads/publications/ALGA_State_Of_The_Assets_Report_2015.pdf

Kumic, I., & Noble, G. (2017). *Investing in Community Futures: A New Model to Invest in Communities.*

McKenna, B. (2015, July 17). *The Losing Game of Publicly Financed Sports Venues.* The Globe and Mail. Retrieved August 15, 2017, from https://www.theglobeandmail.com/report-on-business/the-losing-game-of-publicly-financed-sports-venues/article25563294/

McKinsey Global Institute. (2014). *Overcoming Obesity: An Initial Economic Analysis.* McKinsey & Company. Retrieved July 31 2018, from https://www.mckinsey.com/~/media/mckinsey/business%20functions/economic%20studies%20temp/our%20insights/how%20the%20world%20could%20better%20fight%20obesity/mgi_overcoming_obesity_executive_summary.ashx

Povich, E. S. (2016, July 13). *Why Should Public Money be Used to Build Sports Stadiums.* PBS Newshour. Retrieved August 15, 2017, from http://www.pbs.org/newshour/rundown/public-money-used-build-sports-stadiums/

Putnam, R. D. (2016). *Our Kids, The American Dream in Crisis.* New York: Simon & Schuster.

Sheffield Football Club. (2017). *Protect the Heritage of Football.* Retrieved 08 15, 2017, from Sheffield Football Club: http://www.sheffieldfc.com/foundation

VAFA Women's Football Club. (n.d.). VAFA Women's Football Club Guide. Australia. Retrieved August 16, 2017, from http://www.vafa.com.au/wp-content/uploads/2015/02/VAFA-Womens-Football-Guide_v7a.pdf

Victorian Auditor-General's Office. (2016). *Local Government Service Delivery: Recreational Facilities.* Retrieved August 16, 2017, from https://www.parliament.vic.gov.au/file_uploads/20160323-Rec-Facilities_8Lpv18Cc.pdf

White, D. (2016, May 9). *The Guardian.* Net Gains: Why Wimbledon Debentures Could Be Worth Their 31,000 Price Tag. Retrieved August 17, 2017, from https://www.theguardian.com/money/2016/may/09/wimbledon-debentures-31000-price-pros-cons

Women's Game Kicks Off Boom. (2017, May 14). *Herald Sun.*

CHAPTER 16

Sustainable Real Estate in the Middle East: Challenges and Future Trends

Amir Rahdari, Asma Mehan, and Behzad Malekpourasl

1 Introduction

During the past four decades, the Middle East has been experiencing drastic droughts, intense warming, and numerous economic, social and environmental challenges due, in part, to these climatic conditions. With

A. Rahdari (✉)
Tarbiat Modares University, Tehran, Iran

Sustainability Research Group (SRG), Universal Scientific Education and Research Network (USERN), Tehran, Iran
e-mail: ah.rahdari@modares.ac.ir

A. Mehan
Postdoctoral Research Fellow at the Iran University of Science and Technology (IUST), Tehran, Iran

Iran's National Elites Foundation (INEF), Tehran, Iran

Adjunct Research Fellow with the Politecnico di Torino, Turin, Italy

B. Malekpourasl
Shahid Beheshti University, Tehran, Iran

T. Walker et al. (eds.), *Sustainable Real Estate*, Palgrave Studies in Sustainable Business In Association with Future Earth,
https://doi.org/10.1007/978-3-319-94565-1_16

growing urbanization, increased consumption and a drastic upsurge in energy use, there is a considerable demand for infrastructure development, affordable housing and building projects in the region. Such demands need to take account of economic viability, social inclusiveness and environmental sustainability; the construction and real estate industries have a crucial role to play in this process.

Some scholars define "sustainable construction" as a method of creating and managing the built environment based on resource efficiency and ecological principles (Manoliadis, Tsolas, & Nakou, 2006; Shi, Ye, Lu, & Hu, 2014). However, recent definitions are more wide-ranging. For example, Mehan (2016a, 2016b) suggests that the construction industry should be viewed both as a means to resolve urban challenges and environmental crises ***and*** as a means to create balance between the fundamental components ("pillars") of sustainable urban development, that is, economic, environmental and social sustainability. Viewed in these terms, the real estate industry has the potential to make a significant impact on quality of life. That said, it is widely acknowledged that developing countries have experienced great difficulty in forging a holistic approach to sustainability within their construction industries (Plessis, 2007; Ye & Zuo, 2013). In part, this may be due to the fact that contemporary climate-related crises, such as a shortage of (and inadequate access to) potable water, global warming and increased carbon dioxide emissions are currently seen as the greatest priority, meaning that the focus has been on the ecological footprint of buildings.[1] Nevertheless, ecological improvements can still affect the other pillars of sustainability. For example, the economic value of a building can be linked to its environmental sustainability and ecological footprint (Repellino, Martini, & Mehan, 2016).

Bosteels and Sweatman (2016) argued that the real estate industry has a fiduciary duty to implement the Paris Agreement. They stated (p. 4) that "every real estate asset owner, investor and stakeholder must now recognize they have a clear fiduciary duty to understand and actively manage environmental, social, governance (ESG) and climate-related risks as a routine component of their business thinking, practices and management processes". In line with such thinking, there has been a surge of interest in

[1] The World Green Building Council, founded in 1998, is composed of national councils from 12 countries. Based on the 2015/2016 annual report by the WorldGBC, buildings account for over 30% of carbon dioxide emissions and use about 14% of the world's drinking water.

voluntary certification systems and an increasing demand for rating systems that assess buildings on key measures of sustainability as identified by the global sustainability agenda (Rahdari & Anvary Rostamy, 2015). These rating systems and certification programs reduce information asymmetries between buyers and sellers, and between landlords and tenants, regarding important sustainability features of the properties being traded.

While sustainable real estate practices have been widely discussed in the context of developed countries, many emerging economies have been left out of the debate. The Middle East is an interesting case in point. Its history is steeped in examples of long-term sustainable practices in construction that were attuned to local conditions—from the windmills of Nashtifan and the windcatcher and natural air-conditioning of Yazd in Iran to the Egyptian pyramids made of so-called geopolymer concrete. However, despite this early history of ecologically friendly practices, current approaches to construction are mostly predicated upon a myopic mindset inherited from globalized neo-classical economics; accordingly, until recently, there have been only a few notable instances of sustainable practices of a more holistic kind. This chapter provides an overview of recent developments in sustainable real estate and construction in the Middle East as well as a discussion of the challenges and likely future trends.

2 Sustainable Real Estate in the Middle East: The Current Status

In developing countries, it is increasingly the case that rapidly growing urban areas are competing for resources. In the Middle East, Dubai is a prime example of this phenomenon. As a result of the construction boom, and fueled by increasing oil prices, Dubai has become one of the fastest growing cities in the world. Additionally, as a major tourist destination, it has become a magnet for the development of outstanding modern real estate projects to satisfy its occupants' appetite for luxury. The growing real estate industry in Dubai has thus imposed a heavy demand on natural resources, such as potable water, mineral-based materials and energy resources (Almarashi & Bhinder, 2008, p. 4). The consequence of 15 years of heedless expansion and reckless design decisions is that Dubai's real estate has generally been developed without taking account of fundamental environmental factors such as climate or geography. Only recently, in an effort to better integrate this fast growth with the vision of a more sustainable future, has the United Arab Emirates' (UAE's) government begun to regulate the construction industry, applying local benchmarks to ensure sustainable construction.

For very different reasons to Dubai, old Cairo is also densely populated and has become one of the most congested cities on earth (Kingsley, 2015). In 2015, the Egyptian government announced plans to address this overpopulation problem by building a new capital from scratch to the east of Cairo. The Emirati businessman *Mohamed Alabbar*, Chairman of the Dubai Developer *Emaar*, leads a key part of the "New Capital" development. The 700 sq.km new city will become a home to at least five million residents.

The Kingdom of Bahrain provides a further example of a policy shift designed to reverse or avert historical deficiencies which threaten sustainable growth. In this case, the perceived problems arose from the view that the country had become over-dependent on government-funded development and that it was at risk of being unable to sustain competitiveness and innovation. Bahrain's Vision 2030 and its National Economic Strategy aim to redefine how a contemporary Arab city should look by encouraging sustainable growth, protecting the natural environment of the sensitive coastal and desert ecology, and preserving the local values and culture of the community (Mouzughi, Bryde, & Al-Shaer, 2014). It is clear that these policy developments can be used to leverage more sustainable approaches to real estate projects.

A generic element of the problems outlined above is the information asymmetry between producers and users of buildings. This is a longstanding feature of the way that real estate markets operate, especially in relation to information about the sustainability of buildings. It is an important issue because transparency is the basis of trust between those who produce buildings and the stakeholders who use, trade or otherwise interact with them (Rahdari, 2016b); it is also the linchpin of long-term organizational success. However, an examination of sustainability reporting in the real estate industry reveals that only 1168 companies in the world have issued a sustainability report since 2000—and of this total, only 19 are from the Middle East.[2] Nonetheless, sustainability reporting is improving and there has been a substantial increase in such reporting within the industry since 2010.

[2] Data retrieved from the Global Reporting Initiative (GRI) database on 1 May 2017.

2.1 *Evaluation, Rating and Green Building Codes*

Measurement is clearly fundamental to the process of change since it is the only reliable means of setting targets and charting progress toward them. Many developed countries have already introduced new evaluation systems to measure levels of sustainability in their own real estate industries. Depending upon geographical region, there are four predominant ranking systems in use: Australia and New Zealand follow Green Star; the UK uses the Building Research Establishment Environmental Assessment Method (BREEAM); Japan uses the Comprehensive Assessment System for Building Environmental Efficiency (CASBEE); and the US, Brazil, Canada and India make use of the Leadership in Energy and Environmental Design (LEED) metric, with slight variations (Say & Wood, 2008, p. 18). In addition, many countries have established Green Building Councils[3] (GBCs) whose mission is to improve the sustainability of the built environment. Globally, as of June 2017, there were 75 such councils of which 35 were considered established, 11 emerging and 29 prospective. Focusing on the Middle East regional networks, at the time of writing only a few countries have been listed as members of the World Green Building Council (WGBC), such as Bahrain, Qatar, UAE, Palestine, Lebanon, Kuwait and Jordan. However, of these, only the UAE and Jordan are recognized as having established GBCs while all the others are classified as merely prospective candidates with the exception of Lebanon and Qatar which are identified as having emerging GBCs. Hence, the level of organizational support for sustainable building practices in the Middle East is not as strong as elsewhere. However, as the region continues to experience rapid population increases and urbanization, the role of the construction industry will become more critical as will the need for the industry to embrace environmental sustainability.

Since sustainability is a key determinant of the long-term value and short-term profitability of any construction project, there is every reason to expect the real estate industry to start to deliver buildings with reduced energy consumption and increased operational efficiency. There is evidence that this is happening in the Middle East, with the recent development of green building codes in the UAE, Qatar, Iran and Lebanon. In addition, Middle Eastern governments have started to develop their own standards to reflect local conditions, needs and challenges. For example, in

[3] See footnote 2.

2009 the Gulf Organization for Research and Development designed a Global Sustainability Assessment System (GSAS) part of which has already been made mandatory in Qatar. This was one of the first green building rating systems in the Middle East, developed in response to a review of green building codes in use around the world. GSAS is based on eight criteria: water, energy, indoor environment, cultural and economic value, site, urban connectivity, material, management and operations. Of these, the most heavily weighted categories are water and energy, reflecting the region's most challenging environmental issues.

In a similar vein, the Abu Dhabi Urban Planning Council has developed an initiative known as "Estidama". Originally announced in 2008, Estidama (the Arabic word for sustainability) incorporates the Pearl Building Rating System (PBRS) which aims to promote the development of sustainable buildings and improve the quality of life of their residents. The PBRS encourages water, energy and waste minimization and local material use. It also aims to improve supply chains for sustainable and recycled materials and products (Council, 2010). Like the LEED and BREEAM systems, the Pearl Rating System is a points-based, environmental assessment tool which awards points to projects that meet specific sustainability criteria. The points are weighted in accordance with the judged importance of each criterion and are aggregated to produce a total score expressed in Pearls; levels of achieved sustainability are thus represented on a scale from 1 to 5 Pearls. When it was first introduced in September 2010, all privately developed new buildings in Abu Dhabi were required to achieve at least one Pearl, whereas all government-funded buildings had to achieve a minimum of two Pearls.

Around the same time, the Dubai Municipality introduced its Green Building Regulations which applied to all new buildings constructed from 2009. It has been suggested that this, and other policy initiatives in Dubai, may have been motivated by a desire to cultivate a more environmentally progressive image than its neighbor Abu Dhabi (Reiche, 2010, p. 381). A fourth example is the Lebanese Green Building Council's in-house "ARZ" rating system. This is also a points-based environmental sustainability assessment scheme introduced in 2012.

The situation in Iran is somewhat more fluid. In principle, issues like sustainable construction, the ecological footprints of buildings and reduced fossil-fuel energy consumption should be at the top of construction company agendas (Mehan, Alavi, & Behraveh, 2015; Mehan, 2017), particularly as the industry accounts for around 9% of Gross Domestic

Product (GDP). Noting that the UN, the EU and the US lifted their ten-year economic and political sanctions on Iran in January 2016, it has been argued that "[in] post-sanctions Iran, there already exists a high demand for international leading environmental assessment methodologies like BREEAM and LEED" (Pourmatin, 2016). However, whether and how this will translate into concrete changes in the building sector remains to be seen.

2.2 Design, Construction and Post-Occupancy Evaluation

An integrated approach to the design process is generally recognized as the optimal way to implement sustainable construction projects. Agencies that adopt the most progressive building policies, such as the CASCADIA Green Building Council in the US, have played a major role in encouraging the use of integrated design processes (IDPs) in green building projects. In the Middle Eastern context, the Estidama Integrative Design Process (EIDP) seeks to promote integrated design among design professionals by encouraging coordination at the early stages of the project. In fact, the EIDP requires the implementation of a number of analyses before the main design process is permitted to begin, such as passive solar design analyses, energy modeling, water efficiency calculations and low-carbon material analyses.

The Estidama process, developed by the Abu Dhabi Urban Planning Committee (UPC) was described more fully in Sect. 2.1. We note here that the UPC required its use in the development of Abu Dhabi's low-carbon "City of Tomorrow" project, thereby ensuring that all its buildings would incorporate carbon-efficient, sustainable principles at the design and construction stage and would be subject to a post-occupancy evaluation (POE) (Kansara & Ridley, 2012, p. 23). This makes Abu Dhabi the first government in the Middle East to introduce a mandatory sustainability initiative incorporating a POE (in this case to be carried out two years after occupation).

The emphasis of Estidama (which incorporates the Pearl Rating System) on integrated design and POE reflects the important lessons learned from other rating and design systems. While performance assessment systems exist in the US and in the UK (Energy Performance Certificates), their scope is limited to energy and they are independent of the Green Buildings Rating systems. In contrast, Estidama adopts a holistic approach and seeks to assess results rather than intentions.

2.3 Urbanization and the Role of Resilience

Folke emphasized the need to focus on resilience, adaptability, transformability and sustainability in order to address the dynamics and development of complex socio-ecological systems (Folke et al., 2010). This echoes the frequent claim that the sustainable cities of the future will be resilient, smart cities (Harrison et al., 2010; Redman, 2014). Resilience is the ability to withstand, adapt to and embrace change by employing appropriate mechanisms to deal with its undesirable effects. The key challenges to the resilience and sustainability of urban areas arise from the increasingly damaging outcomes of human action.

In the Middle East, the shortage of resources to meet human demands, together with environmental and political crises, has led to increased vulnerabilities of major metropolises. Rapid population growth has been occasioned by an influx of skilled foreign workers who require central residential and commercial accommodation. One example, as noted in the introduction to Sect. 2, is oil-rich Dubai which enjoys one of the most active real estate industries of all global cities. The consequence is that it relies heavily on fossil fuels and places huge demands on natural resources.

A further example is Tehran; with a population of around 9 million[4] in the city and 16 million in the wider metropolitan area, it is the third largest metropolitan area in the Middle East. Figure 16.1 demonstrates the structural, social and physical distance vulnerability of 22 areas of the capital city of Tehran (Rezaie & Panahi, 2015). According to one source, "there are about fourteen thousand hectares of very vulnerable buildings against earthquakes, and out of the whole population of Tehran, 2.9 million settle in these areas" (Habibipourzare, 2015, p. 79).

In contrast to these examples, Masdar City, located near Abu Dhabi's international airport, was launched in 2006 to generate the human and intellectual capital necessary to position Abu Dhabi, and the UAE, as world leaders in industries based on low-carbon technologies. Apart from Dubai, Abu Dhabi is the most important emirate in the UAE. It has now started a process of "transforming oil wealth into renewable energy leadership" and has set the long-term goal of a "transition from a 20th Century, carbon-based economy into a 21st Century sustainable economy" (Reiche, 2010, p. 378). Masdar City's large-scale, integrated application of

[4] Based on the official statistical information provided by *World Population Review* in 2017, Tehran city has a population around 8,604,000. Retrieved 11 May 2017, from http://worldpopulationreview.com/world-cities/tehran-population/.

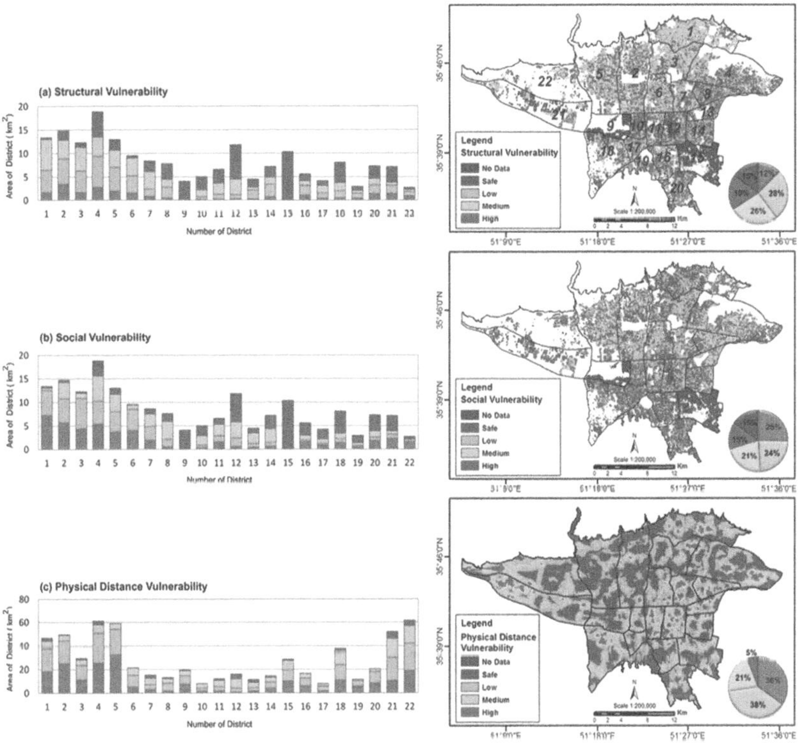

Fig. 16.1 Structural, social and physical distance vulnerability of 22 areas of the capital city of Tehran (adapted from Rezaie and Panahi, 2015)

renewable energy technologies and sustainable living principles is a pilot project like no other. The original aim was to create the world's first carbon neutral, zero-waste, sustainable city based on a revolutionary futuristic approach. This would have positioned Abu Dhabi as a world leader in renewable energy and sustainability. However, in 2008, "plans withered in the global economic recession that soon followed when investors put their green dreams on hold" (Goldenberg, 2016). The recession occasioned a series of delays in the project and it is now estimated to be completed by 2030, with a more modest set of environmental goals. Nonetheless, if we are to understand the radical approach to a sustainable future that was embodied in the Masdar initiative, we need to do so through the lens of resilience theory in combination with sustainability. Such an approach can provide a framework for understanding "the full range of the complex social and ecological interactions that underpin sustainable cities" (Seeliger & Turok, 2013, p. 2108). For further discussion of urban resilience, see Sect. 3.3.

3 Future of the Sustainable Real Estate Industry in the Middle East

The future of the sustainable real estate industry in the Middle East has been limited by various contributory factors, many of which were discussed in previous sections. These factors include limited availability of renewable resources and materials; land use issues; difficulty in achieving waste, water and energy efficiency; limited public awareness of environmental issues; a lack of transparency and communication among stakeholders; and the absence of regulatory enforcement to set standards. Although some Middle Eastern countries have introduced green building assessment tools (see 2.1), a holistic approach to sustainability (including economic, social and environmental components) needs to be widely implemented if a truly sustainable outcome is to be achieved. Thus, green rating tools are only a small part of the total sustainability process and in any case, they have been applied only to new construction and renovation projects and not to existing buildings. What is needed to establish a platform for sustainable construction is careful consideration of the complex and dynamic issues involved and close engagement with the wide array of stakeholders, market leaders and public-sector actors. In this respect, local Middle Eastern governments must accept responsibility for creating national, integrated regulatory frameworks for the transition to low-carbon, environmentally friendly and sustainable real estate. Along with government and the private-sector, local communities have a very significant role to play in encouraging sustainability.

The following sections describe the most important trends with regard to the future of sustainable real estate in the Middle East, where we use "trends" to refer to both the challenges and their putative solutions. These trends can be considered to operate at the macro-, meso- and micro-levels (Rahdari, Sepasi, & Moradi, 2016).

3.1 Macro Trends: Climate, Population and Global Warming

Macro-level trends have a long-term, often indirect, yet considerable impact on the state of sustainable real estate. These trends include, but are not limited to, global and local changes in the climate, urban population growth and changes in regulatory policy. The three macro-level problems considered in this section are climate change, overpopulation and global warming. Responses to these problems can occur at many different levels, but those that involve national and international strategies are classified as macro-level responses.

3.1.1 Climate Change

Global real estate is a $50 trillion industry and is highly exposed to extreme weather events. Therefore, it is increasingly important to consider the impact of local conditions and climate circumstances on the design of buildings. The Köppen climate classification provides useful insights into the Middle East's current climate conditions and is a good starting point. Figure 16.2 demonstrates the Köppen climate classification for the Middle East.

Humans have a high tolerance for dry bulb temperature but can only tolerate a threshold "wet bulb temperature" (combined measure of temperature and humidity) of 35°C (Sherwood & Huber, 2010). A recent study has shown that, under a high emission scenario (i.e., RCP8.5[5]), by 2100 the weather in the Middle East could become so hot and humid that staying outside for more than six hours would become intolerable (Pal & Eltahir, 2015). If the current level of global emissions continues, by 2100 it would produce the projected extreme temperatures shown in Fig. 16.3.

This study also found that these climate conditions in the Persian Gulf could limit development of the coastal region, as outdoor working conditions would become intolerable, impacting all economic activities including those of the construction industry.

The predominantly arid climate of the Middle East demands a more delicate design process than that required in more easily tolerated environments. New research has shown that the anticipated drastic temperature rises in parts of the Middle East and Africa—together home to around

[5] The Representative Concentration Pathway 8.5 presupposes high population growth and relatively slow income growth with modest rates of energy intensity improvements and technological change, leading to high-energy demand and emissions in the long term if no climate change policies are put forth.

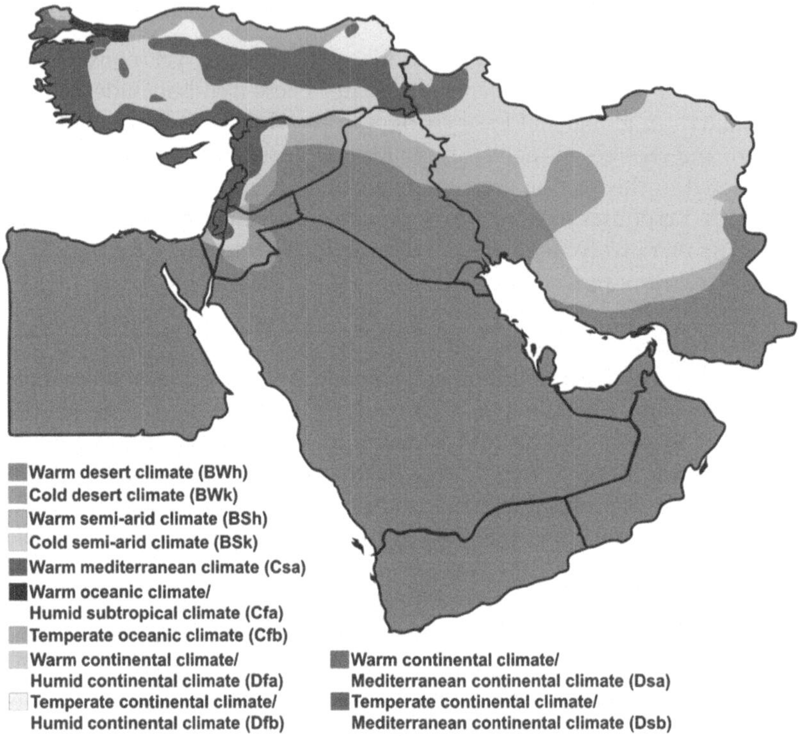

Fig. 16.2 The Köppen climate classification map for the Middle East (as climate change intensifies, this map should be updated accordingly)

500 million people—could trigger a climate-exodus of epic proportions, referred to as "apocalyptic Mad Max scary" (Lelieveld et al., 2016). Therefore, it is essential that the real estate industry strives to provide buildings and services that are fully adapted to the environmental character of the region and the needs of its inhabitants. The construction industry will need to integrate these demanding climatic conditions into future construction planning as well as current retrofitting practices.

3.1.2 Urban Population Growth

Another important macro-level trend is urban population growth, the dynamics of which will also be affected by climatic conditions. The Middle East and North Africa region (MENA) accounts for 6% of the world's

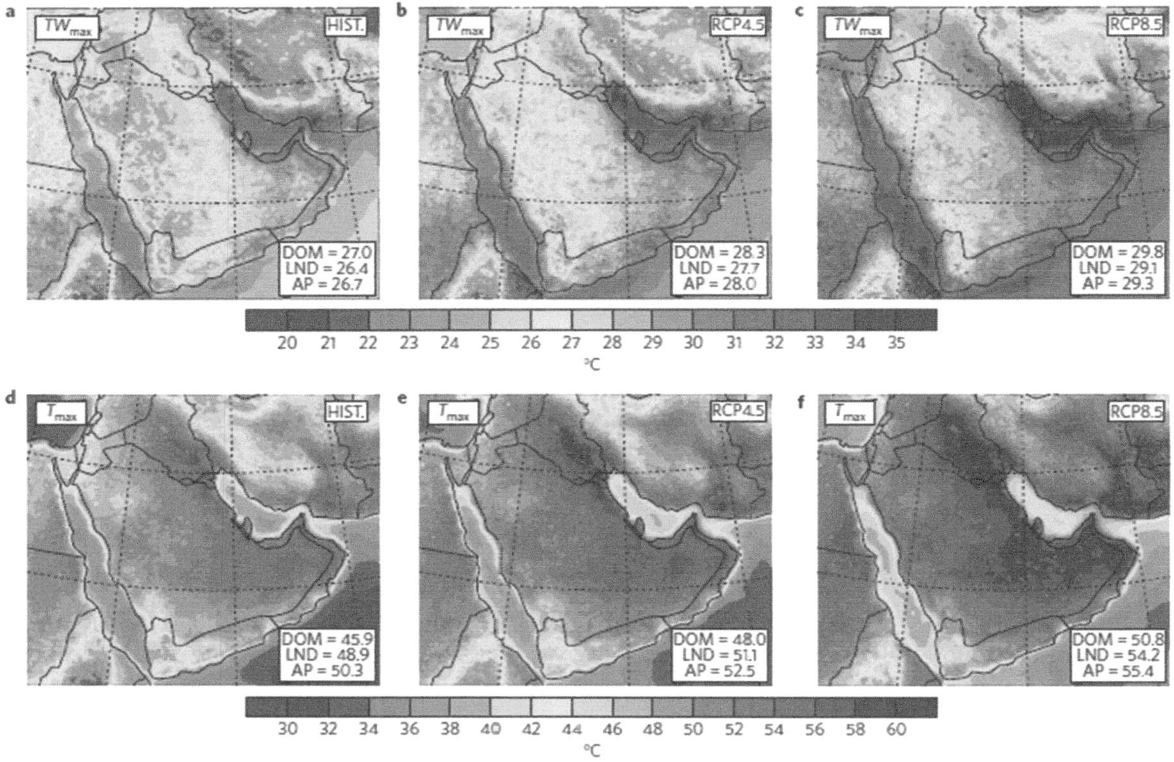

Fig. 16.3 Extreme temperatures in the Middle East by 2100 (adapted from Pal and Eltahir, 2015)

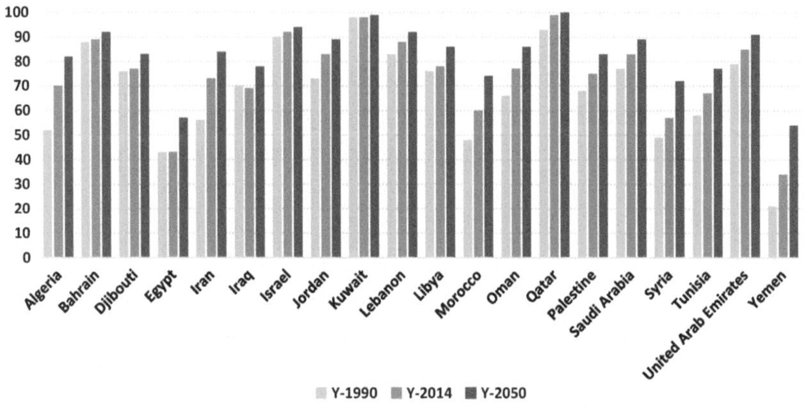

Fig. 16.4 Urban Population in the MENA region for 1990-2014-2050

population. Figure 16.4 shows how the ratio of the urban population to total population in MENA varies through the period 1990–2014–2050 (Department of Economic and Social Affairs of the Population Division of the United Nations, 2014).

The highest urban population growth rates (above 10%) for 1990–2014 were experienced by Algeria (18%), Iran (17%), Yemen (13%), Morocco (12%) and Oman (11%). For the period 2014–2050, the highest predicted growth rates are for Yemen (20%), Syria (15%)[6], Morocco (14%), Egypt (14%), Algeria (12%) and Iran (11%). Thus, all of these countries are expected to experience above 10% urban population growth. This population burden creates excessive demand and presents a fresh set of problems for sustainable real estate and the construction industry. The population growth factor, in tandem with political issues, social movements and environmental changes, has already created several humanitarian crises across the Middle East and has raised considerable challenges for the economy of the region including the real estate industry. As with climate changes, it will be necessary for the real estate industry to integrate and respond to population growth predictions in its planning and construction processes.

[6]The effects of forced immigration and the ongoing conflict in Syria have not been factored into the urban population growth estimate for the country.

3.1.3 Global Warming

Global warming is a particularly critical macro-level trend. To achieve the generally accepted goal of a maximum increase of 2°C, carbon dioxide emissions per dollar of GDP would need to be reduced by a factor of six. This is based on the historical observation that every 1% increase in GDP has led to a 1% increase in carbon dioxide (The World Bank, 2006). The drastic reduction of carbon dioxide emissions per dollar of GDP is called decarbonization and can take several forms. These strategies are described in detail in Sect. 3.3.

3.2 Macro-Level Responses to Macro-Level Trends: Rating Systems

Existing certification schemes and rating systems generally focus on a particular aspect of sustainability ranging from energy efficiency to sustainable materials and processes. Energy Star, for instance, focuses on energy efficiency. By way of an exception, LEED has a broader focus (incorporating, e.g., socio-ecological factors and water efficiency as well as energy), but it is fair to say that the majority of green building rating systems were developed with one dominant issue in mind—usually energy efficiency. In the language of McDonough and Braungart (2002), "efficiency" seeks to make things "less bad" whereas the pursuit of "effectiveness" would be a more imaginative strategy, as it seeks to achieve what is intrinsically "good". They argue that efficiency does not have any intrinsic value but is a useful tool as a part of a larger system that strives to be *effective*. They further claim that this shift in mindset will encourage the development of practices consistent with a circular economy, that is, an economy in which waste is seen as a technical nutrient for new products rather than disposable matter. This kind of thinking needs to be reflected in real estate rating systems which must evolve to take account of new sustainability practices and technologies (Rahdari, 2016a). Thus, the next generation of such systems should include consideration of zero-impact/waste technology, synergy/positive-energy buildings and the use of natural elements in the building based on real-time and big data integration (known as the "biosphere-technosphere interaction").

3.3 Meso-Level Responses to Macro-Level Trends: Resilience

In our view, significant progress toward a sustainable real estate industry will hinge on responses to macro-level problems that are implemented at the meso- and micro-levels. Meso-level actions require cities (not nations or governments) to develop agendas that will shape the response to harmful environmental and socio-economic trends. A recent Guardian article concerning the need to mitigate the effects of climate change put cities, not countries in charge (Barber, 2017). It cited Oslo as one of the leading sustainable cities with a zero-emission goal to be achieved by 2025. Cities, particularly big ones, are better placed to enforce regulations and lay down policies to further sustainability in general and in the real estate industry in particular. Cities can integrate sustainable practices into their policy framework more effectively and more efficiently than governments.

By 2070 it is predicted that globally, large coastal cities will host 150 million people and that they will incorporate $35 trillion worth of property, representing around 10% of the world's GDP (Bosteels & Sweatman, 2016). These cities, their inhabitants and the property will be at risk of coastal flooding accentuated by sea level rises due to climate change. It can be argued that these challenges, although due to macro-level climatic and population trends, are best addressed by actions taken at city-state level. Resilience should be the key focus of these strategies.

Sustainable cities are economically productive, socially inclusive and, by definition, environmentally sustainable. They invest in smart infrastructure and implement resilient policies that could not be achieved without the support of the real estate industry. Two sets of measures can be taken to promote resilience: adaptation and mitigation. The concept of adaptation is derived from biology and refers to the capacity of an organism to vary its form or function so as to better survive in a changing environment. In relation to buildings, adaptation entails physical and technological innovations that prepare for changing environmental conditions (such as a rise in sea level) so as to withstand natural disasters and human-induced predicaments. However, there is a limit to what can be achieved by means of adaptation alone because some changes might be so profound that their consequences may turn out to be out of control. Thus, the second measure, mitigation, comprises actions to *avoid or reduce* the occurrence of harmful environmental changes, for example, by reducing the ecological footprint of a development or its level of greenhouse gas (GHG) emissions. As most carbon dioxide emissions come from the burning of fossil fuels, mitigation of energy-related carbon dioxide emissions should be at the top of the agenda.

Mitigation and decarbonization measures can take several forms. The three main energy system transformations required to reduce GHG emissions are generation decarbonization, electrification and energy efficiency (Williams et al., 2012). All three have direct or indirect applications in the construction industry.

Generation decarbonization consists of reducing emissions of carbon dioxide per unit of electricity produced. Efficient distributed generation (or onsite renewable energy) has proven to be one of the most popular and effective approaches to generation decarbonization. The Mapdwell Solar System is an example of a system to achieve this by the 3D mapping of solar potential in the US. The extension of projects like this to the Middle East is essential to help with top-down and bottom-up generation decarbonization and it is beginning to happen at the level of economies, cities and organizations. Recent strategic restructuring of the Saudi oil giant, Aramco, demonstrates the growing recognition of the importance of decoupling economic growth from environmental degradation and, in so doing, of weaning the region off fossil-fuel dependency. By way of illustration, in a recent memorandum of understanding, Abu Dhabi's Masdar City and Aramco agreed to collaborate on sustainable development and renewable energy to yield advances in carbon capture and clean electricity generation (Sen, 2017).

Electrification entails changing the infrastructure and design of products so that they require clean energy (renewably generated electricity) rather than fossil fuels. Electrification potential in the real estate industry in the Middle East is quite substantial. For example, according to the International Energy Agency (2016), the residential sector could experience an annual 1.9% growth in energy consumption and the share of that energy that is provided by electricity could increase to 53% (from 36% in 2012), replacing the natural gas share. By 2040, electricity could become the main source of energy in residential buildings in the Middle East (International Energy Agency, 2016). However, the International Energy Agency also predicts that this target is unlikely to be met and in fact only a small fraction of residential sector electricity in the Middle East is likely to come from renewable sources by 2040. This projection is based on the IEO2016 scenario, which assumes that current laws and regulations are maintained throughout the period of the projections. Considering the substantial scale of global problems such as climate change, together with the environmental challenges specific to the Middle East, the region needs to move beyond these projections and craft effective and timely policies that are in tune with the low-carbon agenda. This is essential if the grave consequences of drastic climate change are to be avoided.

Over one-third of total GHG emissions come from the real estate industry. Less than 10% of the real estate share comes from (1) construction and materials (particularly cement) or from (2) *onsite* energy generation (e.g., the burning of wood for heating or cooking in homes). The remaining 90% (of the real estate share) comes from the burning of coal, natural gas and oil for the generation of electricity that is to be used in buildings (IPCC, 2014). This highlights the key role of energy efficiency in buildings. Higher energy efficiency requires achieving higher output per unit of energy. Energy efficiency has been at the core of sustainable real estate and green building discussions for decades. This includes residential, commercial and other types of real estate. Between 30% and 50% of energy in buildings is wasted, constituting a notable factor in climate change (Reichardt, 2016). Turner and Frankel (2008) found that savings of up to 30% in energy use and GHG emissions are achievable in commercial buildings. Sustainably designed buildings not only save energy but also provide a healthier and more conducive environment for living and working that results in higher productivity (Glicksman, 2006). Higher energy efficiency can be achieved by (1) developing new technologies (e.g., IoT-based sensors in smart homes), (2) using renewable sources of energy (e.g., onsite wind turbines and solar panels), (3) using multiplicity in design (e.g., onsite thermal energy generation which also provides hot water), (4) replacing energy-wasting equipment with more efficient devices, (5) instituting timely and effective repair schedules, (6) reducing energy use through consumer behavior and (7) using design thinking and biomimicry.

Efficiency is better achieved if it is embedded in the design process from the beginning and not just as a retrofitting exercise or a post-occupancy quick fix. The pursuit of integrated sustainable design in the Middle East is globally significant because most Middle Eastern countries are currently developing countries. Their design infrastructure is flexible and in a state of flux and so there is the potential for sustainable approaches to be implemented rapidly, producing substantial local and global ecological benefits. Designing a building for 2020 in the Middle East can have locked-in economic and environmental costs and benefits for decades to come.

3.4 Micro-Level Responses to Macro-Level Trends: Materials Revolution

Micro-level trends refer to bottom-up technological developments that can feed into or influence the actions of cities, governments and global organizations. Given that the global middle class is projected to grow from two to five billion by 2030, there is likely to be a surge in demand for construction materials (Raworth, 2017). Many innovative and sustainable solutions have surfaced in the past decade running the gamut from the development of easily recyclable materials to the use of new materials with lower energy intensity. These innovations are mostly driven by the greater tendency for businesses to favor what has become known as a circular economy. This approach manifests itself in the form of sustainable construction using local, durable and totally recyclable materials—materials that are naturally inspired, ergonomically designed and have self-sustaining properties. Such materials not only reduce the long-term demand for construction materials, but they can also be used to produce positive-energy buildings, that is, buildings that produce more energy than they consume.

One of the key enablers of sustainable construction is innovation in materials science. A significant case in point is the development of greener methods of concrete and cement production. Cement is the most commonly used material in the construction industry (WBCSD, 2009) and has a major environmental impact in terms of the consumption of water and energy and the generation of emissions and waste. The production of each ton of cement results in the emission of approximately 0.89 tons of carbon dioxide (WWF, 2008). Recent innovations in the field mean that cement and concrete production can be achieved with less water and energy as well as lower emissions and waste. As they become more readily available, these new techniques will significantly reduce the carbon footprint of the real estate industry. A second example is the process developed by BioMASON to use microorganisms to naturally harden bricks in lieu of firing them in a kiln. These microorganisms bond the sand and aggregate particles organically, in a similar way to the growth of coral reefs, providing an interesting example of sustainability through biomimicry. It takes three to four days to harden clay for traditional bricks through an energy intensive and highly pollutant firing process; these naturally hardened bricks can be made using local materials on site, therefore eliminating transportation cost and its environmental impacts. As 1.5 trillion bricks are produced globally, accounting for 800 million tons of global carbon dioxide emissions per annum, such innovations can make a sizeable dent in the environmental impact of the construction industry and pave the way for sustainable real estate practices.

Sustainable construction innovations are particularly relevant to the Middle East for several reasons. Firstly, the Middle East is a fast-growing region and home to emerging economies with a huge appetite for real estate development. It has, for example, one of the highest growth rates in the construction of skyscrapers in the world having accumulated some 289 skyscrapers and tall buildings (above 150 meters) by 2015, virtually all of which were constructed in the past 20 years (Council on Tall Buildings and Urban Habitat (2013)). The industry has the potential to use innovative materials and sustainable design practices to good effect, and has already done so. For example, the Bahrain World Trade Centre was the world's first skyscraper to incorporate wind turbines in its design. Secondly, the region is highly vulnerable to changes in climate, as discussed previously. This has fueled an interest in, and a need for, the introduction of the latest green technologies and sustainable design practices. Thirdly, the region has been lagging behind other economies in achieving Millennium Development Goals (2000–2015). Sustainable business practices have been impeded by the Middle East's high dependence on fossil fuels and by the prevalence of cultural and political conflicts. If the region is to achieve Sustainable Development Goals (SDGs), it is imperative to pursue sustainable design practices and to put forth stricter environmental legislation with regard to the use of materials.

4 Concluding Remarks

To date, the introduction of sustainable construction initiatives in the Middle East can be characterized as ad hoc rather than systematic. As a result, its sustainable real estate industry has remained in an incipient state. We argue that the Middle East could become a pioneer/pilot for some of the progressive ideas and trends outlined in this chapter, notwithstanding the fact that it currently lags behind Europe, East Asia and the US. There are many individual projects, some of which have been referred to earlier, that could herald an impressive advance in the sustainable real estate industry in the Middle East. To extend and develop this potential, Middle Eastern countries need to adopt Next Practices and global standards while keeping local conditions in mind. They must integrate sustainable and smart technologies, demand improved sustainable practices from international developers and implement policies to curb energy consumption and emissions across the whole industry.

References

Almarashi, H., & Bhinder, J. (2008). From the Tallest to the Greenest: Paradigm Shift in Dubai. *CTBUH 2008 8th World Congress, Dubai*, (pp. 1–8).

Barber, B. (2017). How to Fix Climate Change: Put Cities, Not Countries, in Charge, May 7-2017, The Guardian.

Bosteels, T., & Sweatman, P. (2016). Sustainable Real Estate Investment Implementing the Paris Climate Agreement: An Action Framework, February 2016, Climate and Strategy Partners.

Council, A. D. (2010). *Estidama*. Retrieved March 24, 2017, from http://estidama.upc.gov.ae/pearl-rating-system-v10/pearl-building-rating-system.aspx

Council on Tall Buildings and Urban Habitat. 2013. The Middle East: 20 Years of Building Skyscrapers, CTBUH Journal, Issue IV, pp. 44–45.

Department of Economic and Social Affairs of the Population Division of the United Nations. (2014). World Urbanization Prospects: The 2014 Revision, Highlights (ST/ESA/SER.A/352).

Folke, C., Carpenter, S., Walker, B., Marten, S., Chapin, T., & Rockstrom, J. (2010). Resilience Thinking: Integrating Resilience, Adaptability and Transformability. *Ecology and Society, 15*(4), 20.

Glicksman, L. 2006. Sustainability and the Building Sector, in L. Glicksman, & J. Lin (Eds), Sustainable Urban Housing in China, pp. 2–7.

Goldenberg, S. (2016). Masdar's Zero-carbon Dream Could Become World's First Green Ghost Town, *The Guardian*. https://www.theguardian.com/environment/2016/feb/16/masdars-zero-carbon-dream-could-become-worlds-first-green-ghost-town#img-1

Habibipourzare, A. (2015). Pushing Tehran Across a Threshold: Applying the Social-ecological Resilience Approach to a Vulnerable City. *Spaces and Flows: An International Journal of Urban and ExtraUrban Studies, 6*(2), 75–87.

Harrison, C., Eckman, B., Hamilton, P., Hartswick, P., Kalagnanam, J., Paraszczack, J., et al. (2010). Foundations for smarter cities. *IBM Journal of Research and Development, 54*(4), 1–16.

International Energy Agency. 2016, Industrial Sector Energy consumption-International Energy Outlook, *U.S. Energy Information Administration*, Washington.

IPCC. (2014). Climate Change 2014: Mitigation of Climate Change, The Intergovernmental Panel on Climate Change.

Kansara, T., & Ridley, I. (2012). Post Occupancy Evaluation of buildings in a Zero Carbon City. *Sustainable Cities and Society, 5*, 23–25.

Kingsley, P. (2015). A New New Cairo: Egypt Plans £30bn Purpose-built Capital in Desert. *The Guardians.* https://www.theguardian.com/cities/2015/mar/16/new-cairo-egypt-plans-capital-city-desert

Lelieveld, J., et al. (2016). Strongly Increasing Heat Extremes in the Middle East and North Africa (MENA) in the 21st Century. *Climatic Change, 137*(1–2), 245–260.

Manoliadis, O., Tsolas, I., & Nakou, A. (2006). Sustainable Construction and Drivers of Change in Greece: A Delphi Study. *Construction Management and Economics, 24*, 113–120.

McDonough, W., & Braungart, M. (2002). *Cradle to Cradle: Remaking the Way We Make Things.* New York: North Point Press.

Mehan, A. (2016a). Investigating the Role of Historical Public Squares on Promotion of Citizens' Quality of Life. *Procedia Engineering, 161*, 1768–1773. https://doi.org/10.1016/j.proeng.2016.08.774

Mehan, A. (2016b). Urban Regeneration: A Comprehensive Strategy For Achieving Social Sustainability in Historical Squares. *3rd International Multidisciplinary Scientific Conference on Social Sciences and Arts SGEM2016, www.sgemsocial.org.* (Vol. 2, No. ISBN 978-619-7105-54-4/ISSN 2367-5659, pp. 861–868). SGEM2016 Conference Proceedings, Book 4.

Mehan, A. (2017). In Razing Its Modernist Buildings, Iran Is Erasing Its Past Western Influence. *The Conversation*, 1–7. http://porto.polito.it/2673027/1/In_razing_its_modernist_buildings_Iran_is_erasing_its_past_Western_influence.pdf

Mehan, A., Alavi, H., & Behraveh, H. (2015). Analysis and Investigation of Lasting Architectural Projects and Plans in Housing in Post Era of Ghajar, Tehran. *Journal UMP Social Sciences and Technology Management, 3*(2), 561–571.

Mouzughi, Y., Bryde, D., & Al-Shaer, M. (2014). The Role of Real Estate in Sustainable Development in Developing Countries: The Case of Kingdom of Bahrain. *Sustainability, 6*(4), 1709–1728.

Pal, S. J., & Eltahir, E. A. B.. (2015). Future Temperature in Southwest Asia Projected to Exceed a Threshold for Human Adaptability, *Nature Climate Change*, doi: https://doi.org/10.1038/nclimate2833

Plessis, C. D. (2007). A Strategic Framework for Sustainable Construction in Developing Countries. *Construction Management and Economics, 25*, 67–76.

Pourmatin, R. (2016, June 15). *Embracing New Markets-BREEAM in Iran.* Retrieved April 17, 2017, from BRE BUZZ: http://brebuzz.net/2016/06/15/embracing-new-markets/

Rahdari, A., Sepasi, S., & Moradi, M. (2016). Achieving Sustainability Through Schumpeterian Social Entrepreneurship: The Role of Social Enterprises. *Journal of Cleaner Production, 137*, 347–360.

Rahdari, A. H. (2016a). Developing a Fuzzy Corporate Performance Rating System: A Petrochemical Industry Case Study. *Journal of Cleaner Production, 131*, 421–434.

Rahdari, A. H. (2016b). Hyper-Transparency: The Stakeholders Uprising. In D. Crowther & S. Seifi (Eds.), *Corporate Responsibility and Stakeholding (Developments in Corporate Governance and Responsibility)* (Vol. 10, pp. 3–30). London: Emerald Group Publishing Limited.

Rahdari, A. H., & Anvary Rostamy, A. A. (2015). Designing a General Set of Sustainability Indicators at the Corporate Level. *Journal of Cleaner Production, 108*, 757–771.

Raworth, K. (2017). Doughnut Economics: Seven Ways to Think Like a 21st-Century Economist. *Chelsea Green Publishing.*

Redman, C. L. (2014). Should Sustainability and Resilience Be Combined or Remain Distinct Pursuits? *Ecology and Society, 19*(2), 37.

Reichardt, A. (2016). Sustainability in Commercial Real Estate Markets, Gabler Verlag.

Reiche, D. (2010). Renewable Energy Policies in the Gulf Countries: A Case Study of the Carbon-neutral "Masdar City" in Abu Dhabi. *Energy Policy, 38*, 378–382.

Repellino, M. P., Martini, L., & Mehan, A. (2016). Growing Environment Culture Through Urban Design Processes 城市设计促进环境文化. *NANFANG JIANZHU, 2*(2), 67–73.

Rezaie, F., & Panahi, M. (2015). GIS Modeling of Seismic Vulnerability of Residential Fabrics Considering Geotechnical, Structural, Social and Physical Distance Indicators in Tehran Using Multi-Criteria Decision-Making Techniques. *Natural Hazards Earth System Science, 15*, 461–474.

Say, C., & Wood, A. (2008). Sustainable Rating Systems Around the World. *Council on Tall Buildings and Urban Habitat (CTBUH) Journal* (II), 18–29.

Seeliger, L., & Turok, I. (2013). Towards Sustainable Cities: Extending Resilience with Insights from Vulnerability and Transition Theory. *Sustainability, 5*, 2108–2128.

Sen, I. (2017). Saudi Energy Sector at Forefront of IKTVA, *Oil and Gas Middle East*, Vol. 13, Issue 05, May 2017.

Sherwood, S. C., & Huber, M. (2010). An Adaptability Limit to Climate Change Due to Heat Stress. *Proceedings of the National Academy of Sciences, 107*(21), 9552–9555.

Shi, L., Ye, K., Lu, W., & Hu, X. (2014). Improving the Competence of Construction Management Consultants to Underpin Sustainable Construction in China. *Habitat International, 41*, 236–242.

The World Bank. (2006). *The Road to 2050: Sustainable Development for the 21st Century, The International Bank for Reconstruction and Development.* Washington, DC: The World Bank.

Turner, C., & Frankel, M. (2008). *Energy Performance of LEED for New Construction Buildings. Research Report.* Vancouver: New Buildings Institute.
WBCSD. (2009). Recycling Concrete, The Cement Sustainability Initiative, Switzerland.
Williams, J. H., et al. (2012). The Technology Path to Deep Greenhouse Gas Emissions Cuts by 2050: The Pivotal Role of Electricity. *Science, 335*(6064), 53–59. https://doi.org/10.1126/science.1208365
WWF. (2008). A Blueprint for a Climate Friendly Cement Industry, WWF International, Switzerland.
Ye, K. S., & Zuo, J. (2013). Utilizing the Linkage Between Domestic Demand and the Ability to Export to Achieve Sustainable Growth of Construction Industry in Developing Countries. *Habitat International, 38*, 135–142.

CHAPTER 17

Sustainable Community Development in Nigeria: The Role of Real Estate Development

Saheed Matemilola, Isa Olalekan Elegbede, and Muhammad Umar Bello

1 Introduction

Sustainable development is the bedrock of community development. All efforts targeted at community development can be rendered futile or short-lived without sustainability. Thus, achieving sustainable community development is rested, to a great extent, on the sustainability of the various projects embarked on in the community. In Nigeria, successive regimes of government have inaugurated numerous development commissions, agencies and departments to foster development at local, regional and national levels. But more often than not, these governmental strategies have failed on the premise of poor integration of important variables such as culture and/or poorly coordinated community development activities.

S. Matemilola (✉) • I. O. Elegbede
Brandenburg University of Technology, Cottbus, Germany

M. U. Bello
Abubakar Tafawa Balewa University, Bauchi, Nigeria

T. Walker et al. (eds.), *Sustainable Real Estate*, Palgrave Studies in Sustainable Business In Association with Future Earth,
https://doi.org/10.1007/978-3-319-94565-1_17

To ensure sustainable development of a community, public participation, development of human capacity and environmental considerations must be duly integrated (Oloyede, 2009; Uche, Okoye, & Uche, 2014).

The concept of sustainability has now become the fulcrum of discussion for every community development project. It is regarded a 'new planning agenda' (Chan & Huang, 2004). However, sustainability planning has been found to be inefficient when integrated at a vast regional scale. Therefore, experts have proposed that sustainability be integrated at the local community levels. This local approach will engender an adequate consideration of the sociopolitical and cultural challenges peculiar to the various communities, through understanding the local opportunities and challenges that may vary in terms of the environmental, natural and human resources, socioeconomic and physical development as well as climatic conditions, in an attempt to achieve national sustainable development (Oloyede, 2009).

Usually, to stimulate community development, one of the most important sectors targeted for development is the real estate development sector in the bid to provide affordable housing to the local population. Housing is one of the most important basic needs for human survival (Ugonabo & Emoh, 2013). Thus, housing has become an important discourse in many international summits and conventions such as (1) the United Nations Conference on Environment and Development (UNCED), otherwise referred to as the United Nations Conference on Human Settlements (UN-Habitat) I, II, III which respectively took place in Vancouver, 1976, Istanbul, 1996 and Quito, 2016; (2) the United Nations Millennium Summit in New York, 2000; and (3) the World Summit on Sustainable Development also known as the Earth Summit in Johannesburg, 2002 (Keating, 1992; Shah, 2002; Ugonabo & Emoh, 2013; UN-Habitat, 2010). Housing and community development are inseparable. Hence, sustainable community development will remain a mirage if a corresponding sustainable practice in real estate development is not in place. To achieve this, Graaskamp (1989) identifies three key stakeholders in the real estate development process, namely consumers, production teams and public infrastructure groups. Each of these stakeholder groups need to cooperate to develop meaningful development objectives and benefit from the immediate and future outcomes of the development. In this regard, it makes sense to argue from Apanavičienė, Daugėlienė, Baltramonaitis, and Maliene (2015) analysis that, while sustainable real estate development is critical to sustainable community development, it relies heavily on the cooperation of the real estate development participants on the subject of sustainable practice (Apanavičienė et al., 2015; Graaskamp, 1989).

Nigeria is the most populous nation in Africa with an annual growth rate of over 2% and annual urbanization rate of 4%. As the populations of urban centers, towns and cities continue to soar, it is natural that the demand for all types of real estate grows accordingly. This situation has created a favorable context for the continued growth and maturation of a viable real estate industry in Nigeria (Emiedafe, 2015). Nigeria's real estate industry has greatly evolved over the last few decades, even in the face of economic recession (Olofinji, 2016). A study by PricewaterhouseCoopers estimated that the value of Nigeria's real estate industry would reach US $13.65 billion by 2016 (PwC, 2015). Unfortunately, inefficacy in the government's housing policies and strategies has left the growing housing demand grossly unmet, a situation that has led to overcrowding and over-usage of the inadequate housing facilities (Ugonabo & Emoh, 2013; Ya'u-Kumo, 2014). Also, illegal dwellings constructed and finished with substandard or inappropriate materials have begun to spring up without official permits and in locations where development is unapproved such as the floating slum in Makoko area of Lagos which spread out underneath the third mainland bridge. Such dwellings are characteristically highly populated and poorly ventilated while also devoid of basic housing amenities such as electricity and basic sanitary facilities. These types of real estate developments will evidently face acute sanitary and municipal solid waste problems, creating air, noise and surface water pollution (Ugonabo & Emoh, 2013).

Scenarios such as the foregoing cannot exist if a community is to develop in a sustainable manner. Against this backdrop, this study examines the critical importance of environmental responsibility in real estate practice and sustainable community development in Nigeria. The study also explored the prospects and challenges of sustainable real estate practice in achieving community development.

2 Sustainability in Community and Real Estate Development

Stemming from the understanding of the need for developments to be executed sustainably, the calls for sustainable forward-looking community development are growing louder. The argument for sustainable communities is formed against the backdrop of globalization, urbanization, economic development and climate change issues (Smith, 2008). However, when it comes to the implementation of sustainability, the very concept has always generated division (Jacobs, 1995; Oloyede, 2009). The contestation of the concept of sustainable development in terms of implementation became so profound that the UN Agenda 21 program, that encourages the localization of concept, was relaunched in 2002 as Local Action 21 (Winston, 2014). In fact, this situation has led to the conceptualization of the phenomenon of strong and weak sustainability (CEECEC Glossary, 2010). Weak sustainability considers that natural capital and manufactured capital can essentially be substitutes and no major differences exist between the well-being derived from them (Pelenc, Ballet, & Dedeurwaerdere, 2015). On the contrary, strong sustainability, which is favored by many ecologists, assumes that natural and man-made capital are complementary than substitutes and their separate capital stocks should be maintained (Antunes, 2012). Thus, it can be argued that there is no consensus on the definition of sustainable community.

It has been suggested that a sustainable community is made up of *"an aggregate of characteristics including among others economic security and growth, environmental quality and integrity, social cohesion and quality of life, empowerment and governance"* (Winston, 2014). Nevertheless, the following definition of sustainable communities, posited in the Bristol Accord, has gained prominence: Sustainable communities are

> places where people want to live and work, now and in the future. They meet the diverse needs of existing and future residents, are sensitive to their environment, and contribute to a high quality of life. They are safe and inclusive, well planned, built and run, and offer equality of opportunity and good services for all. (Winston, 2014)

Cavaye (2004) identified five capitals of a community; physical landscape, human and environmental resources, social and financial capital and suggested that community development is the process of bringing about improvements to the capital to improve the people's well-being (Cavaye, 2004). Sustainable community development, in simple terms, can be summed as the way a community's resources are used to responsibly develop its capital without depriving the future generations. The social and economic development of a sustainable community must thus be planned, designed, built, managed and promoted to support the sustainable development goals (Cam, 2003).

Cam (2003) further suggested, based on recent experiences around the world, that in planning the development of a sustainable community, focus should be on:

1. provision or improvement of physical infrastructures and services while making the most of local renewable resources;
2. improving the economy through non-conventional environmentally responsible means; and
3. strengthening community ties and the social well-being through inclusiveness and consultation in community projects as well as enlightenment programs

These areas of priority are particularly suitable for sustainable development of communities with low economic resources or low-income communities (Cam, 2003).

As can be figured from Cam's focus areas and Cavaye's community capitals, sustainability in physical infrastructure, social and economic development as well as resource use are core components upon which sustainable community development is built. In this regard, it is these components that must be attended to if we are to meet the target of developing a sustainable community.

The real estate industry is a cornerstone in achieving the development need and improving the quality of life of all communities (Razali & Adnan, 2015). Today, the quality of a community development is not only judged by the size, shape and edification of the buildings but also by the degree of sustainability of such structures and their interrelations with the social, economic and environmental contexts in which they are built. Over the different phases of the building life-cycle, varying degrees of environmental and social problems are faced. Since the impact of development activities on the environmental, health and economic status of a community can be significant, these problems need to be factored in from the conception stage of the building. This realization has led to the prioritization and growing attention to the implementation of sustainable real estate development in the last two decades. Conversely, despite the enormous interest, there is till today no universally accepted definition of the concept of sustainable real estate (DeLisle, Grissom, & Hogberg, 2009; Kariuki, NziokiI, & Murigu, 2014).

As in the case of green technologies, the global interest in sustainable or green built environment has grown recently significantly (Zhang, Wu, Feng, & Xu, 2014). Sustainability in the real estate sector has moved on from being a luxury to a necessity, because it can play a major role in reducing the carbon footprint in urban communities (Seng, 2017). It portends therefore that, in mitigating climate change, if the objective of limiting the volume of greenhouse gas (GHG) emissions is to be achieved, controlling the contribution from the real estate is fundamental, hence the critical need for sustainable real estate development (Kariuki et al., 2014).

In the real estate sense, sustainability will therefore mean the provision of products and services in the real estate business with due consideration of the long-term economic, social and environmental impacts (Razali & Adnan, 2015). This will involve efforts to limit energy usage and waste generation from the real estate from the design through development, occupancy and demolition phases of the buildings' life-cycle (Keeping & Shiers, 2004). To realize this objective, Keeping and Shiers (2004) and Kariuki et al. (2014) identified key targets (reflected in Fig. 17.1) that form the baseline for the designers, engineers and other stakeholders in the real estate industry:

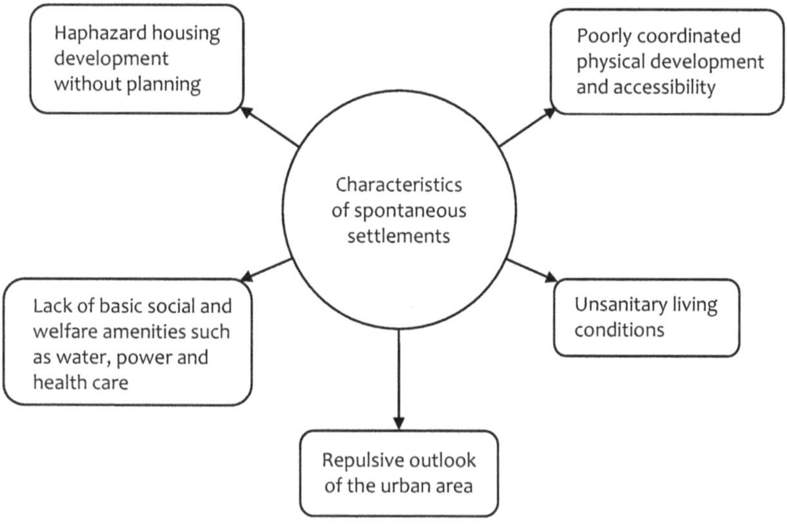

Fig. 17.1 Sustainable real estate objectives and strategies—Adapted from Kadiri, Chinyio, and Olomolaiye (2012)

1. Strategically selecting the site will reduce urban sprawl, destruction of the ecosystem and green areas
2. Reducing energy consumption as far as possible without compromising user's ability to enjoy the property
3. Limiting the impacts of the building on its immediate environment
4. Limiting excesses in resource exploitation
5. Reducing impacts on the environment that could emanate from building materials
6. General waste reduction throughout building life-cycle
7. Provision of facilities and initiatives that encourages environment-friendly use of the property or Indoor Environmental Quality (IEQ)
8. Providing facilities and initiatives that encourage the best and environment-friendly use of the transport system

Therefore, the environmental, economic as well as social characteristics of the community must be equally factored into the planning of sustainable development of real estate. The common practice of lack of responsibility in the usage of resources can be best described as 'unsustainable' (Raslanas & Stasiukynas, 2015). While some efforts have been made in the developed countries, more need to be done, particularly in countries in transition, to encourage stakeholders in the real estate industry to shift toward greener approach without the industry losing its commercial competitiveness. Voluntary standard, rating and green certification schemes along with the introduction of new legislations have been effectively employed with minimal cost effects, in some developed nations and are now being patronized in some developing nations such as Brazil, Mexico (Soebarto & Ness, 2010), South Africa (Ding, 2007), Kenya (Kariuki et al., 2014), Singapore (Seng, 2017), China, India, Vietnam, Malaysia, Indonesia and Philippines (Keeping & Shiers, 2004; Soebarto & Ness, 2010). Table 17.1 below shows some commonly applied assessment tools and their respective origin.

3 Community and Real Estate Development in Nigeria

The Nigerian real estate industry has undergone tremendous evolution in the last few decades (Ekpenyong, 2015). During this period, urbanization in the country has been phenomenal due to rapid population growth. With an overall population of 170 million, Nigeria's urban population is

Table 17.1 Overview of common tools for the assessment of environmental performance of buildings

Assessment tool	*origin*	*Year*	*Reference*
Australian building greenhouse rating (ABGR)	Australia	2005	Ding (2007)
BEAT	Denmark	1999	Cheng, Sodagar, and Sun (2017)
Building sustainability index (BASIX)	New South Wales (NSW)	2004	EDO NSW (2014), Ding (2007)
Building research establishment environmental assessment method (BREEAM)	UK	1990	BRE (2011), Chehrzad, Pooshideh, Hosseini, and Sardroud (2016)
Building environmental performance assessment criteria (BEPAC)	Canada	1993	Ding (2007)
Comprehensive assessment system for building environmental efficiency (CASBEE)	Japan	2004	Ding (2007)
Comprehensive environmental performance assessment scheme (CEPAS)	Hong Kong	2001	Ding (2007)
Deutsche Gesellschaft für nachhaltiges Bauen (DGNB)	Germany	2007	Chehrzad et al. (2016)
Eco-quantum (EQ)	Netherlands	1999	Cheng et al. (2017), Ding (2007)
Evaluation manual for green buildings (EMGB)	Taiwan	1998	Ding (2007)
Green building challenge (GBTool)	International	1995	Ding (2007)
Green home evaluation manual (GHEM)	China	2001	Ding (2007)
GreenMark	Singapore	2005	Chehrzad et al. (2016)
Haute Qualité Environnementale (HQE)	France	1994	Chehrzad et al. (2016)
Leadership in energy and environmental design (LEED)	USA	1998	DeLisle et al. (2009), Chehrzad et al. (2016)
Sustainable building assessment tool (SBAT)	South Africa	2001	Ding (2007), Hill (2002)

estimated to be around 50% in the year 2010 and expected to double in 30 years' time or even sooner. Lagos is the largest urban center in Nigeria and one of the most populous in the world with over 14 million estimated inhabitants. The result of this urban population explosion is the expansion of the existing built environment and the creation of new settlements (Bloch, Monroy, Fox, & Ojo, 2015; Odusote, 2008).

National Bureau of Statistics (2015) estimated that, as of August 2012, housing shortage in Nigeria is at 17 million units. Thus, the real estate development business in Nigeria has been very viable in recent years owing to the excessive demand created by the fast-growing population (National Bureau of Statistics, 2015). However due to economic inequalities, the vast majority of the population can hardly afford the rising prices of accommodation. This situation has also given rise to many illegal settlements and slums in many Nigerian urban centers particularly in Lagos, Kano, Ibadan, Benin and Onitsha among others (Ajayi, Oviasogie, Azuh, & Duruji, 2014; National Bureau of Statistics, 2015). Two types of slum settlements have been identified in Nigeria: the traditional and the spontaneous slum settlements. The traditional slum settlement is stimulated by the continuous dilapidation of existing structures while spontaneous slum settlements are occasioned by erection of illegal squatters in unapproved locations (Ajayi et al., 2014). Figure 17.2 shows the common features of a typical spontaneous settlement in Nigeria.

Although the Nigerian government realizes the urgency of the need for intervention to forestall the shortage in real estate supply, it is faced with many bureaucratic and administrative challenges. The Land Use Act of 1978 is the main tool used by the government which vested all the

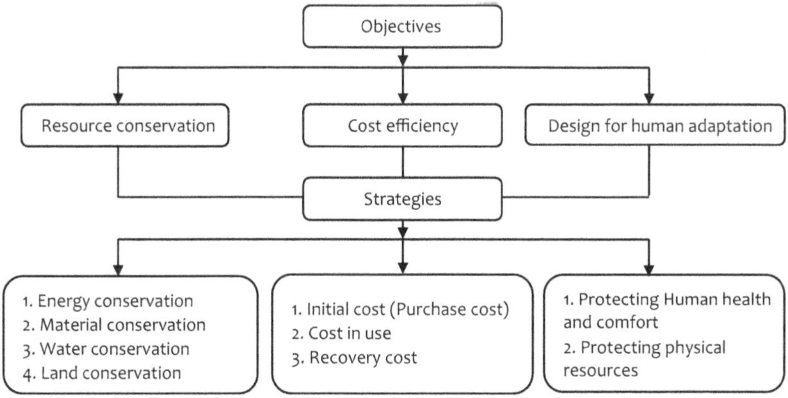

Fig. 17.2 Characteristics of spontaneous settlements in Nigeria. Source: Adapted from Ekandem, Daudu, Lamidi, Ayegba, and Adekunle (2014)

Nigerian lands in the government. With this act giving so much power to the government in real estate-related services, many residential and office buildings, industrial plants as well as other real estate products were developed. This effort led to the development of such edifices as the Cocoa house, FESTAC town, Liberty Stadium and the Premier and Lafia hotels (Odusote, 2008). But lack of willpower of the government to pursue land use development through controlled urban planning and management has subsequently facilitated uncontrolled illegal use of land and development that gave birth to the chaotic and blighted urbanization (Ajayi et al., 2014).

Sadly, as though the problem of short supply of real estate is not enough, recently, there has been a growing number of reports of building collapse particularly in the most populated urban centers in Nigeria such as Lagos, Abuja, Port Harcourt, Ibadan and Enugu. For instance, there were more than 112 reported cases of building collapse in the period between 1978 and 2008 in Lagos metropolis alone (Windapo & Rotimi, 2012). Generally, the rate of collapse of buildings in Nigeria in the last two decades has been trending upward. Unfortunately, despite the number of casualties recorded yearly from the alarming rate of building collapse, it is not enough to draw the attention of the stakeholders in the real estate development sector (public and private). There is only one destination that this negligence can lead Nigeria to—unsustainable development of communities (Babalola, 2015; Windapo & Rotimi, 2012).

The primary causes of this building collapse menace have been a major concern for experts in the real estate industry and scholars alike. Thus, many authors such as Oloyede, Omoogun, and Akinjare (2010), Chendo and Obi (2015), Akinyemi, Dare, Anthony, and Dabara (2016), Babalola (2015), Windapo and Rotimi (2012), Ayininuola and Olalusi (2004) and Fakere and Fadairo (2012) have attempted to study the causes in a bid to find a lasting solution to the scourge. In their study, Ayininuola and Olalusi (2004) suggested that 50% of collapsed buildings in Nigeria result from design problems, 40% from construction faults and 10% from product failure. All the aforementioned factors are related to developers seeking substandard services or products in order to reduce costs in the delivery of real estate services. Table 17.2 shows that the vast majority of building failures are caused by faulty designs, structural failures, unapproved conversion of property or usage, employment of unqualified personnel, low-quality materials or non-compliance with building regulations, all of which

Table 17.2 Selected investigated incidences of building collapse (2000–2015)

S/n	*Building type*	*Location*	*Year*	*Investigated cause(s)*
1	Residential story building	Mushin, Lagos	2000	Faulty design
2	Estate building	Lekki rd., Lagos	2000	Structural failure
3	Two-story mosque building	Mushin Lagos	2001	Unauthorized conversion of former bungalow to a two-story building
4	One-story residential building (under construction)	Iwoye-Ijesha Oshun state	2001	Structural failure/poor supervision
5	Not available	Ikare	2002	Fire disaster
6	Onyearugbule market, Akure	Akure, Ondo	2003	Poor workmanship & under reinforcement of the cantilevering end
7	Multistory commercial residential building	Ebute-meta, Lagos	2007	Unauthorized conversion/ poor supervision/use of quality materials
8	Multistory building	Kano	2007	Faulty design/structural failure
9	Nursery/primary school property	Olomi area, Ibadan	2008	Use of low-quality building materials
10	Five story shopping complex building under construction	Wuse area, Abuja	2008	Structural failure incompetent/bad workmanship
11	Two-story residential building under construction	Asero, Abeokuta	2008	Contravening the given planning Approval, use of substandard materials incompetency
12	Two-story university teaching hospital complex under construction	Ogbomosho	2009	Use of substandard materials, poor workmanship/ supervision
13	Uncompleted building	Ita-morin, Abeokuta	2009	Use of substandard building materials
14	Building under construction	Osodi, Lagos	2010	Use of substandard building materials
15	Uncompleted four-story building	Abuja	2010	Substandard materials and non-compliance to building regulations
16	Four-story building	Victoria Island, Lagos	2010	Structural defect/overloading

(*continued*)

Table 17.2 (continued)

S/n	*Building type*	*Location*	*Year*	*Investigated cause(s)*
17	Modern five-story office complex	Maryland, Lagos	2011	Indications of an imminent failure of the structure
18	An uncompleted one-story building	Akwa, Anambra	2012	Defective material
19	Three-story building	Enugu	2012	Structural failure
20	Four-story building	Onitsha	2013	Weak sub-structure, flooding
21	Six-story guest house building	Ikotun, Lagos	2014	Structural failure/faulty foundation
22	Three-story building	Ebute-meta Lagos	2015	Weak structure
23	Residential building	Ikoyi, Lagos	2015	Gas explosion

Source: Fakere and Fadairo (2012); Babalola (2015); Akinyemi et al. (2016); Chendo and Obi (2015)

are problems related to the predevelopment and development stages of the building life-cycle.

It is estimated that at least 800,000 residential properties must be developed yearly to meet the demand for shelter in Nigeria while housing production is presently put at about 100,000 units yearly (Ohajuruka, 2015). To achieve this, private investors must participate in the real estate sector. Since the Land Use Act has vested all lands in the government, for private investors or individuals to participate in real estate development, they must first procure land from the government. But the delivery of real estate involves a lot of resources including land, labor, funds and building materials (Agbola & Olatubara, 2003). The National Bureau of Statistics (2015) identified three main bottle-necks faced by private investors in real estate development which have remained the bane of the Nigerian real estate sector:

I. Inadequate mortgage financing for development

Despite the viability of the real estate industry in Nigeria, the standards and quality of products and services in the industry has been very poor due to poor funding. Corporate real estate developers lack adequate access to finance and although the Nigerian government has over time attempted to finance the housing subsector with the establishment of the National Housing Policy in 1980 and Housing Fund Act and the Federal Mortgage Bank of Nigeria (FMBN) in 1992 which was even expanded to include estate development loan for real estate developers with the National Policy on Housing and Urban Development in 2002, the fund released was still inadequate to finance the sector (National Bureau of Statistics, 2015).

II. Complicated bureaucracy in the procurement of land

A community cannot be developed on nothing; every development requires a significant amount of land. While land seems to be generally available for individuals and investors in real estate businesses in Nigeria, excessive hike in land prices still limit access to land particularly in the urban communities (Butler, 2012). Inadequate access to land has constituted a major stumbling block to development in Nigeria and, in 2002, the Presidential Committee on Urban Development and Housing highlighted access to land in urban centers among the 15 areas requiring urgent and critical government attention (Aluko, Olaleye, & Amidu, 2004). Unfortunately, the Land Use Act, which is the primary basis for land governance, has major loopholes in content and implementation leaving room for informal transactions in land to thrive (Birner & Okumo, 2012). The degree of informality in the land market has become a big challenge for the land registration system and good land use practices causing poor land documentation and irregular subdivision of land since landholders will normally transfer their land to any buyer regardless of the planned development.

III. Inaccessibility of good quality and affordable building materials

Good quality building material is inevitably linked to the process of building a sustainable real estate industry (Ihuah, 2015). Building materials are the major inputs in real estate development. In Nigeria, it consumes more than half of the total expenditure for developing real estate. The use of substandard building materials has been heavily blamed for many collapsed buildings in Nigeria and most developing nations (Njoku, 2012). However, the swelling costs of building materials constitute a major challenge for real estate delivery in Nigeria (Iwuagwu & Iwuagwu, 2015). Overdependence on imported building materials due to low quality of locally made ones, poor infrastructure to improve accessibility, unfavorable government policies, and overpricing and depreciation of local currency among other factors have synergized to a devastating effect on the building material costs (Ihuah, 2015).

4 Achieving Sustainable Community Development through Sustainable Real Estate

In the previous sections, relevant literature has been analyzed relating to the state of community development in Nigeria and the impact of unsustainable real estate practices. It was established that besides homelessness, lack of environmental awareness and poor financing, complicated government bureaucracy and ineffective community initiatives have hindered any meaningful sustainable development in traditional Nigerian communities. Overall, the successes of some countries from the Global North with respect to sustainable community development was built upon the pillars of efficiency in the urban space usage, optimum use of essential natural resources, multiplying social capital and reorientation of the government and public in the direction of sustainability. The last pillar is perhaps the most important in ensuring a balance in the system (Roseland, 2000).

From the foregoing therefore, the public can do little on their own to achieve a sustainable community development with the local trend in real estate practice, so the different levels of government in Nigeria with supports from international agencies must lead this drive. Efficient tools must be fashioned. To achieve this, Zuo and Zhao (2014) identify three critical factors; technological, managerial and cultural.

4.1 Technological Factor

Technological inventions leading to sustainable use of essential natural resources and providing alternatives to environment depleting technologies is critical to the drive for sustainable community development (Zuo & Zhao, 2014). Human survival is rested on the natural environment. Therefore, the government must create conditions that encourage the healthy coexistence of the public with the environment in achieving its economic and social goals. The government must develop policies that, while considering the social, economic and environmental context, support technologies for renewable energy development and optimum use (Kalua, 2015). In the case of real estate, such policies will focus on strategies and technologies for:

1. Public awareness
2. Affordable costs of green technologies and services
3. Sustainable building design

4. Minimum construction and demolition wastes
5. Minimum household waste generation
6. Minimum energy consumption
7. Optimum use of essential resources

4.2 *Managerial Factor*

Sustainable development involves adequate comprehension and management of complex multilevel and interrelated issues (Rekola, Mäkeläinen, & Häkkinen, 2012). Other than poor technological innovations to achieve sustainable built environment, complex bureaucracy in government procedures, administration and organization has been identified as a major bottleneck of governance in Nigeria. Bureaucracy has its sociocultural aspects. Epko (1979) and Udoji (1974) agreed that Nigerian bureaucracy is characterized by corruption, nepotism and lack of result orientation (Aluko & Adesopo, 2014), though this problem is not peculiar to Nigeria as has been substantiated in Zuo and Zhao (2014). The government must work more with experts and technocrats to improve administrative and organizational efficiency for sustainable development of communities through adequate public participation and related environmental administration. In relation to real estate development, three administrative categories can be identified at project, company and market levels.

Management at the project level requires professionals with distinguished sets of skill in the field of sustainable real estate. Such a manager will possess requisite knowhow that will enable him to make decisions on which green building consultants, evaluation methods (e.g. leadership in energy and environmental design [LEED]), capacity building for officers and extent of stakeholder involvement are needed for the project (Robichaud & Anantatmula, 2011; Zuo & Zhao, 2014). At the company level, dedication of top management officials will determine how successful the planning of sustainable real estate will be. For instance, commitment organization management to the implementation of Environmental Management System (EMS) can reduce consumption of energy by up to 90%, construction and demolition wastes by up to 63%, industrial rate of accidents up to 20% and water usage by up to 70% (Zuo & Zhao, 2014). Market-level management focuses on the general health and competitiveness of the sustainable real estate market through relevant government policies. For instance, government policy requiring commercial property to publish property performance data such as energy performance and CO2 emission makes buildings with certificates of good performances more attractive to buyers or tenants. This will encourage investors to develop high performance real estates and retrofit existing low performing ones (Zuo & Zhao, 2014).

4.3 Cultural Factor

No community can be developed in a sustainable manner without adequate consideration of the local culture. That is why the United Nations Educational, Scientific and Cultural Organization (UNESCO) ensures the reflection of culture in its sustainable development goals through a dedicated attention to pattern and quality of education, consumption and production patterns, gender equality and food security. Culture represents a major facilitator of the environmental, economic and social attributes of sustainable development (UNESCO, 2017). The way of life of a people is a crucial factor in achieving sustainable community development through green real estate practices. In Nigeria, cultural values are used as yardsticks for what is right and acceptable or wrong and unacceptable (Ibietan, 2017). In the Southwestern region of Nigeria, for instance, the Yoruba culture give so much regards to the monarch's authority, and till date the royal families have influence on the acceptability of any developmental projects within their provinces (Akanle, 2012). It is therefore essential to create awareness of sustainability among real estate stakeholders from the planner to designers, clients, contractors and the users (Zuo & Zhao, 2014).

5 Conclusion

This study explores the strategic importance of the real estate sector in achieving a sustainable community development with particular focus on residential real estate in Nigeria. In a bid to achieve this objective, this study was classified into three sections. The first section introduced the concept of sustainability in community development and real estate development. A review of various scholarly works showed that there is no consensus on the concept of sustainability, especially when it comes to implementation. However, in planning sustainable real estate for community development, strategies should be formed around resource conservation, cost efficiency and design for human adaptation. Building Research Establishment Environmental Assessment Method (BREEAM), LEED and Sustainable Building Assessment Tool (SBAT) are some of the common tools developed for assessment of environmental performance of buildings. The second section established the state of residential real estate practice in Nigeria and how it has contributed in defining the pattern of community development in the country. Here it was established that the revolution in the real estate industry within the last three decades has been phenomenal due to unprecedented housing demand. Reports from the National Bureau of Statistics showed that housing deficit reached 17 million in 2012, a situation that resulted in the development of slum communities in the major urban centers in Nigeria. This situation has worsened with the rise in the rate of building collapse particularly in densely populated communities, mostly due to faulty designs, structural failure, unauthorized conversion of property use, low-quality building materials and unqualified workmanship among others. Finally, this study discusses strategies for achieving a sustainable community development through sustainable real estate in Nigeria. Alternative technologies that support drive for sustainability, green experts with requisite management skills and consideration of cultural patter were identified as three factors that are critical to achieving any meaningful success.

References

Agbola, T., & Olatubara, C. (2003). Private Sector Driven Housing Delivery (in Nigeria): Issues, Constraints, Challenges and Prospects, A lead paper presented at the 2nd Annual National Workshop Organised by the Department of Estate Management. Lagos: University of Lagos, Lagos in collaboration with Real Estate Developers Association of Nigeria (REDAN).

Ajayi, O. O., Oviasogie, F. O., Azuh, D. E., & Duruji, M. M. (2014). Urban Design and Sustainable Development: A Case of Makoko Area of Lagos State, Nigeria. *European Scientific Journal, 2*, 90–98.

Akanle, O. (2012). The Ligaments of Culture and Development in Nigeria. *International Journal of Applied Sociology, 2*(3), 16–21.

Akinyemi, A. P., Dare, G. M., Anthony, A. I., & Dabara, D. I. (2016). Building Collapse in Nigeria: Issues: Issues and Challenges. *Conference of the International Journal of Arts & Sciences, 9*(1), 99–108.

Aluko, B. T., Olaleye, A., & Amidu, A.-R. (2004). Problems of Land Delivery for Housing Development in Lagos State, Nigeria. *Globalization and construction* (pp. 601–610). Rotterdam: In-house publishing. Retrieved from http://www.baufachinformation.de/kostenlos.jsp?sid=0D074781D54FCD63EC896C4E8FE6EDE8&id=2008011000753&link=http%3A%2F%2Fwww.irbnet.de%2Fdaten%2Ficonda%2FCIB6038.pdf

Aluko, M. A., & Adesopo, A. (2014). An Appraisal of the Two Faces of Bureaucracy in Relation to the Nigerian Society. *Journal of Social Science, 8*(1), 13–21.
Antunes, P. (2012). *Weak vs. Strong Sustainability.* Environmental Justice Organisation, Liabilities and Trade. Retrieved from http://www.ejolt.org/2012/11/weak-vs-strong-sustainability/
Apanavičienė, R., Daugėlienė, A., Baltramonaitis, T., & Maliene, V. (2015). Sustainability Aspects of Real Estate Development: Lithuanian Case Study of Sports and Entertainment Arenas. *Sustainability, 7*, 6497–6522.
Ayininuola, G., & Olalusi, O. (2004). Assessment of Building Failures in Nigeria: Lagos and Ibadan Case Study. *African Journal of Science and Technology (AJST), 5*(1), 73–78.
Babalola, H. I. (2015). Building Collapse: Causes and Policy Direction in Nigeria. *International Journal of Scientific Research and Innovative Technology, 2*(8), 1–8.
Birner, R., & Okumo, A. (2012). *Challenges of Land Governance in Nigeria: Insight from a Case Study in Ondo State.* Stuttgart: International Food Policy Research Institute.
Bloch, R., Monroy, J., Fox, S., & Ojo, A. (2015). *Urbanization and Urban Expansion in Nigeria.* London: Urban Research Nigeria (URN) Research report.
BRE. (2011). *The World's Foremost Environmental Assessment Method and Rating System for Buildings.* Watford: BRE Global.
Butler, S. (2012, October). Nigerian Land Markets and the Land Use Law of 1978. *Focus on land in Africa brief.*
Cam, W. C.-N. (2003). *Sustainable Community Design and Practices.* Retrieved May 15, 2017, from ClimateTechWik: http://www.climatetechwiki.org/technology/sustainable-community-design-and-practices
Cavaye, J. (2004). *Understanding Community Development.* Toowoomba: Cavaye Community Development. Retrieved May 18, 2017, from http://vibrantcanada.ca/files/understanding_community_development.pdf
CEECEC Glossary. (2010). *Weak vs. Strong Sustainability | The Forest of Brocéliande.* Module:ECOLECON. Retrieved from https://proxy.eplanete.net/galleries/broceliande7/weak-vs-strong-sustainability
Chan, S.-L., & Huang, S.-L. (2004). A Systems Approach for the Development of a Sustainable. *Journal of Environmental Management, 72*, 133–147.
Chehrzad, M., Pooshideh, S. M., Hosseini, A., & Sardroud, J. M. (2016). A Review on Green Building Assessment Tools: Rating, Calculation and Decision-making. *WIT Transactions on Ecology and The Environment.* Tehran: WIT press. doi:https://doi.org/10.2495/SC160341
Chendo, I., & Obi, A. N. (2015). Building collapse in Nigeria: The Causes, Effects and Consequences. *International Journal of Civil Engineering, Construction and Estate Management, 3*(4), 41–49.

Cheng, W., Sodagar, B., & Sun, F. (2017). Comparative Analysis of Environmental Performance of an Office Building Using BREEAM and GBL. In C. Brebbia & A. Galiano-Garrigos (Eds.), *Urban Regeneration and Sustainability* (pp. 172–184). Southampton: WIT Press.

DeLisle, J., Grissom, T., & Hogberg, L. (2009). Sustainable Real Estate: An Empirical Study of the Behavioral Response of Developers and Investors to the LEED Rating System. *Part of a paper titled, A Holistic Approach to Sustainable Real Estate: A Market-Based Perspective, Presented at the 25th ARES National Conference.* Monterey CA.

Ding, G. K. (2007). Sustainable Construction—The Role of Environmental Assessment Tools. *Journal of Environmental Management, 86*(2008), 451–464.

EDO NSW. (2014). *Submission on the Building Sustainability Index (BASIX) Target Review*. Sydney: EDO NSW.

Ekandem, E., Daudu, P., Lamidi, R., Ayegba, M., & Adekunle, A. (2014). Spontaneous Settlements: Roles and Challenges to Urban Planning. *Journal of Sustainable Development Studies, 6*(2), 361–390.

Ekpenyong, E. (2015, January 22). *An analysis of the challenges and prospects in real estate development in Nigeria*. Retrieved May 10, 2017, from http://www.mondaq.com/Nigeria/x/366364/agriculture+land+law/An+Appraisal+Of+Copyright+Infringements+And+Remedies+Under+Nigerian+Law

Emiedafe, W. (2015, October 10). *Top 10 Issues Affecting Nigeria Real Estate Industry*. Retrieved May 4, 2017, from http://sapientvendors.com.ng/10-issues-affecting-nigeria-real-estate-industry/

Fakere, A. A., Fadairo, G., & F. R. (2012). Assessment of Building Collapse in Nigeria: A Case of Naval Building, Abuja, Nigeria. *International Journal of Engineering and Technology, 2*(4), 584–591.

Graaskamp, J. A. (1989). *Fundamentals of Real Estate Development* (3rd ed.). Washington, DC: The Urban Land Institute (ULI).

Hill, R. (2002). Sustainable Building Assessment Methods in South Africa: An Agenda for Research. *Paper Presented at the International Conference on Sustainable Building*. Oslo, Norway. Retrieved from http://www.irbnet.de/daten/iconda/CIB2333.pdf

Ibietan, O. (2017, January 10). Deepening Nigeria's Development: The Role of Culture and Communication. *Premium Times*. Retrieved July 14, 2017, from http://opinion.premiumtimesng.com/2017/01/10/deepening-nigerias-development-role-culture-communication-omoniyi-ibietan/

Ihuah, P. W. (2015). Building Materials Costs Increases and Sustainability in Real Estate Development in Nigeria. *African J. Economic and Sustainable Development, 4*(3), 218–233.

Iwuagwu, B. U., & Iwuagwu, B. C. (2015). Local Building Materials: Affordable Strategy for Housing the Urban Poor in Nigeria. *International Conference on Sustainable Design, Engineering and Construction* (pp. 42–49). Procedia Engineering.

Jacobs, M. (1995). Sustainable Development, Capital Substitution and Economic Humility: A Response to Beckerman. *Environmental Values, 4*(1), 57–68.

Kadiri, P. O., Chinyio, E. A., & Olomolaiye, P. O. (2012). Design of a Sustainable Building: A Conceptual Framework for Implementing Sustainability in the Building Sector. *Buildings, 2*, 126–152.

Kalua, A. (2015). Economic Sustainability of Green Building Practices in Least Developed Countries. *Journal of Civil Engineering and Construction Technology, 6*(5), 71–79.

Kariuki, C., NziokiI, N., & Murigu, J. (2014). Sustainable Real Estate Development in Kenya: An Empirical Investigation. *Engaging the Challenges—Enhancing the Relevance*. Kuala Lumpur: FIG Congress 2014.

Keating, M. (1992, September). The Earth Summit's Agenda for Change. *Earth Summit Times*.

Keeping, M., & Shiers, D. E. (2004). Green Property: The Design of Buildings That Have Lower Environmental Impact. In B. S. Ltd (Ed.), *Sustainable Property Development: A guide to Real Estate and the Environment* (1st ed., pp. 84–133). Oxford: Blackwell Publishing Company.

National Bureau of Statistics. (2015). *Nigerian Real Estate Sector: 2015 Real Estate Outlook in Nigeria*. National Bureau of Statistics.

Njoku, J. (2012, July 31). Dearth of Affordable Building Materials: Experts Proffer Solutions. *Vanguard*. Retrieved July 13, 2017, from http://www.vanguardngr.com/2012/07/dearth-of-affordable-building-materials-experts-proffer-solutions/

Odusote, O. (2008). *Stimulating Nigeria's Emerging Real Estate Markets: Investment Opportunities Through the Public Sector*. Cambridge, MA: Massachusetts Institute of Technology.

Ohajuruka, C. (2015, March 3). *Affordable Green Housing for Nigeria*. HEINRICH-BÖLL-STIFTUNG-Nigeria. Retrieved August 13, 2017, from https://ng.boell.org/2015/03/03/affordable-green-housing-nigeria

Olofinji, L. (2016, August 9). *Top 10 Challenges Facing Nigeria's Real Estate Sector*. Retrieved May 4, 2017, from http://nigeriarealestatehub.com/challenges-facing-nigerias-real-estate-sector.html/

Oloyede, O. (2009). Developing Sustainable Communities in Africa: Components for a Framework. *Identity, Culture and Politics: An Afro-Asian Dialogue*, pp. 56–64.

Oloyede, S., Omoogun, C., & Akinjare, O. (2010). Tackling Causes of Frequent Building Collapse in Nigeria. *Journal of Sustainable Development, 3*(*3*), 127–132.

Pelenc, J., Ballet, J., & Dedeurwaerdere, T. (2015). *Weak Sustainability Versus Strong Sustainability: Brief for GSDR 2015*. United Nations. Retrieved from https://sustainabledevelopment.un.org/content/documents/6569122-Pelenc-Weak%20Sustainability%20versus%20Strong%20Sustainability.pdf

PwC. (2015). *Real Estate: Building the Future of Africa*. PricewaterhouseCoopers. Retrieved July 11, 2017, from http://www.arbinternational.es/ARCHIVO/documentos/sectorial/1473665957_real-building-the-future-of-africa-brochure-2-mar-2015.pdf

Raslanas, S., & Stasiukynas, A. (2015). Sustainable Real Estate Development and Assessment. In A. Kaklauskas, E. K. Zavadskas, R. Dargis, & D. Bardauskienė (Eds.), *Sustainable Development of Real Estate: Monograph* (pp. 309–358). Vilnius: VGTU Press TECHNIKA id.

Razali, M. N., & Adnan, Y. M. (2015). Sustainable Property Development by Malaysian Property Companies. *Property Management, 32*(5), 451–477. https://doi.org/10.1108/PM-02-2014-0008

Rekola, M., Mäkeläinen, T., & Häkkinen, T. (2012). The Role of Design Management in the Sustainable Building Process. *Architectural Engineering and Design Management, 8*(2), 78–89.

Robichaud, L. B., & Anantatmula, V. S. (2011). Greening Project Management Practices for Sustainable Construction. *Journal of Management in Engineering, 27*(1), 48–57. https://doi.org/10.1061/(ASCE)ME.1943-5479.0000030

Roseland, M. (2000). Sustainable Community Development: Integrating Environmental, Economic, and Social Objectives. *Progress in Planning, 54*, 73–132.

Seng, A. K. (2017, January 5). *Why Green Real Estate Is the Way Forward*. Retrieved May 16, 2017, from JLL Real views: http://www.jllrealviews.com/viewpoint/whygreenrealestateisthewayforward/

Shah, A. (2002, September 7). *World Summit on Sustainable Development*. Retrieved May 4, 2017, from http://www.globalissues.org/article/366/world-summit-on-sustainable-development

Smith, M. K. (2008). *Sustainable Communities and Neighbourhoods: Theory, Policy and Practice*. The Encyclopaedia of Informal Education. Retrieved from www.infed.org/communities/sustainable_communities.htm

Soebarto, V., & Ness, D. (2010). Rethinking the Adoption of Green Building Rating Systems in Developing Countries. *11th International Conference on Sustainable Environmental Architecture (SENVAR), October 14th–16th, 2010. Innovation, technology and design of architecture in changing environment*. Surabaya, Indonesia: Institut Teknologi Sepuluh Nopember (ITS).

Uche, O. A., Okoye, U. O., & Uche, I. B. (2014). Sustainable Community Development: An Insight into the Niger Delta Development Commission (NDDC) Community Development Projects in Abia State. *Global Advanced Research Journal of Management and Business Studies, 3*(12), 529–536.

Ugonabo, C. U., & Emoh, F. I. (2013). The Major Challenges to Housing Development and Delivery in Anambra State of Nigeria. *Civil and Environmental Research, 3*(4), 1–20.

UNESCO. (2017). *Culture for Sustainable Development.* Retrieved May 24, 2017, from http://en.unesco.org/themes/culture-sustainable-development

UN-Habitat. (2010). *Planning Sustainable Cities: UN-Habitat Practices and Perspectives.* Nairobi: United Nations Human Settlements Programme (UN-HABITAT).

Windapo, A. O., & Rotimi, J. O. (2012). Contemporary Issues in Building Collapse and Its Implications for Sustainable Development. *Buildings, 2,* 283–299.

Winston, N. (2014). Sustainable Communities: A Comparative Perspective on Urban Housing in the European Union. *European Planning Studies, 22*(7), 1384–1406. https://doi.org/10.1080/09654313.2013.788612

Ya'u-Kumo, G. (2014). Real Estate Development as a Platform for the Transformation of the Nigerian Economy. Real Estate Developers Association of Nigeria (REDAN)/World Bank.

Zhang, X., Wu, Z., Feng, Y., & Xu, P. (2014). "Turning green into Gold": A Framework for Energy Performance Contracting (EPC) in China's Real Estate Industry. *Journal of Cleaner Production, 109*(2015), 166–173.

Zuo, J., & Zhao, Z.-Y. (2014). Green Building Research–Current Status and Future Agenda: A Review. *Renewable and Sustainable Energy Reviews, 30,* 271–281.

Index[1]

[1] Note: Page numbers followed by 'n' refer to notes.

T. Walker et al. (eds.), *Sustainable Real Estate*, Palgrave Studies in Sustainable Business In Association with Future Earth,
https://doi.org/10.1007/978-3-319-94565-1

The manufacturer's authorised representative in the EU is Springer Nature Customer Service Centre GmbH, Europaplatz 3, 69115 Heidelberg, Germany. If you have any concerns regarding our products, please contact ProductSafety@springernature.com

Printed and bound by CPI Group (UK) Ltd, Croydon, CR0 4YY
30/09/2026
02225660-0014